Introducing GCSE Psychology

Introducing
GCSE Psychology

G.C. Davenport

Collins Educational
An imprint of HarperCollins*Publishers*

Published by Collins Educational
An imprint of HarperCollins*Publishers*
77–85 Fulham Palace Road
Hammersmith, London W6 8JB

First published in 1995
Reprinted 1995

ISBN 0–00–322367–1

Edited by Patricia Briggs
Design by Derek Lee
Illustrations by Anna Hancock and Patricia Briggs
Cover artwork by Ruth Cox
Cover typography by David Jones
Printed and bound by Scotprint Ltd, Musselburgh

Contents

Acknowledgements

To Jane, for her help and support during the writing of this book and to my parents, Rosa and Dennis for their continuing love and support.

To Alison Wadeley and Phil Banyard for their patience and diligence in reading this book and for their countless suggestions and improvements.

To Patricia Briggs at Collins Educational for her attention to detail in editing and her flair for design and desk-top publishing that has contributed so much to this book.

And to countless students who continue to inspire, and sometimes to frustrate, in so many ways.

The author and publisher would like to thank the following for their kind permission to reproduce photographs: Colorific Photo Library, page 196 (Jean Piaget); Mary Evans Picture Library, page 6 (Sigmund Freud) and page 8 (Ivan Pavlov).

Ways of explaining human behaviour

Psychology is about 120 years old as an academic subject. The word psychology literally means the study of the mind, although most modern psychology has little to do with what people think of as the mind, and there isn't a single definition of psychology that all psychologists would accept. Even the *Penguin Dictionary of Psychology* avoids defining it. It says that 'Psychology simply cannot be defined ... psychology is what scientists and philosophers ... have created to try to ... understand the minds and behaviours of various organisms.' Although we can't easily define psychology, however, we can at least say what some of its main interests are, and these are what we shall be looking at in this first chapter.

Activity
When you tell other people that you are studying psychology, they might ask you what it is all about. Although we seem not to have a definition, we can nevertheless give a description. As you read the rest of this chapter make some notes on what sorts of things psychologists do. These notes should be a reasonable starting point for answering the question.

In this first chapter we will discuss some of psychology's main areas of concern. One concern of early psychologists was the influence of biological forces on behaviour. Another concern was how behaviour was learned. For instance, in the 1960s many psychologists became interested in how an individual's behaviour was shaped by the influence of other people. More recently, attention has turned to understanding human mental events such as thinking, perception, and memory. We will summarize each of these concerns here, as they will apply to many of the topics that we talk about in later chapters.

Some effects of genes and biology

▷
Finding food, safety, and a mate are essential if any species is to survive.

▷
The study of heredity is called genetics. Heredity is also referred to as biological transmission, or genetic inheritance, and involves inborn or innate characteristics.

▷
A gene is a unit of heredity and determines a biological characteristic of an individual.

▷
Consciousness is the sense of awareness that we have. You are aware of yourself and the impression that you make on others.

Many early ideas in psychology were influenced by the revolutionary research of the biologist, **Charles Darwin** (1809–1882). Darwin argued that any species of animal could only survive if it solved three main sets of problems. First, it must find food enough to maintain sufficient energy to live. If too many members of the species died of starvation there would be too few members left to mate and to rear successful offspring. Second, it must guard against predators. Many species have evolved amazing tactics to avoid being seen or caught. Third, it must breed, or it will become extinct.

Darwin called these responses **biological adaptations**, and claimed that it is these biological adaptations which have helped species to survive. Our biological characteristics – such as our sex, colouring, size or even the likelihood of our suffering certain diseases – are determined at birth by the pattern of our genes. The process by which genes are passed from one generation to another, i.e. from parent to offspring, is called **heredity**.

At conception in humans a male sperm fertilizes a female ovum. (An unfertilized egg is called an ovum and more than one are called ova.) The resulting egg contains twenty-three chromosomes from the sperm, and twenty-three chromosomes from the ovum. Each chromosome carries thousands of genes, and each gene contains some information about how part of the body will be formed. For Darwin, every biological structure, such as gills on a fish, markings on a butterfly, and the thickness of a polar bear's coat, has some purpose. It has evolved to help the animal species to survive at some point in its evolution.

If there are genes for determining the organs in our body, and the brain is one of those organs, then much of what the brain does might also be influenced or determined by our genetic inheritance. Many biologists and psychologists have claimed that some aspects of how humans function are determined genetically. For example, one of the major interests within psychology has been the origin of human intelligence. Some early psychologists claimed that intelligence is genetically inherited, and a few present-day psychologists support this view.

Other psychologists reject this approach. They claim that because human beings possess **consciousness** and self-awareness, because they can think, learn, and predict, then their social experiences are far more important than their biological origin.

The argument between these two views is called the **nature–nurture debate**. The belief that some characteristics are fixed by genetic transmission has become known as the **nature approach**. This promotes the view that many human skills and actions are the result of genetically inherited urges. Intelligence, personality, maternal instinct and aggression, for example, have all been explained by genetic inheritance. On the other hand is the view that our main skills and characteristics are socially learned and developed through experience. This is known as the **nurture approach**. Most psychologists today recognize that both biology and environment are important in shaping development. They are said to take an **interactionist approach**.

Jean Piaget spent most of his life studying the ways in which children think and reason. Thinking and reasoning are both part of our **cognition**. Cognition is the process by which knowledge is gained, and Piaget concluded that reasoning skills mature during childhood and adolescence. He believed that we are genetically prepared to respond to stimuli in certain ways, depending on our state of maturation. However, how far our thinking and reasoning mature is the result of our own particular social experiences.

Exercise on genes

1 What is heredity?
2 Name three human biological structures.
3 Outline briefly what genes are and what their function is.
4 How would supporters of the nature approach explain human personality?
5 How would supporters of the nurture approach explain human personality?
6 How would interactionist psychologists explain the development of aggression?

Exercise on consciousness

According to Wilhelm Wundt, a founding father of psychology, an organism (any living animal) has consciousness if it is capable of:

(a) having sensations and perceptions,
(b) reacting to stimuli,
(c) having feelings and emotions,
(d) having thoughts, ideas, plans and images, and,
(e) being aware of each of the above.

Which of these do the following have?

		a	b	c	d	e
1	Your parents					
2	A pet dog					
3	Dolphins					
4	A 12-month-old human					
5	A large hairy spider					
6	An old and senile person					
7	You now					
8	You when the alarm clock first rings					
9	Someone who is drunk					

The study of twins is one area where the influence of nature and nurture on intelligence has been investigated. There are two types of twins.

Fraternal twins

Dizygotic twins (also known as fraternal twins) are formed when two female eggs are fertilized by two sperms at conception. Ova are produced by the female and will be abandoned if not fertilized. A fertilized egg is called a zygote so here two zygotes are created. These twins, therefore, are called **dizygotic (DZ) twins**. They have the same parents, are almost exactly the same age, and they are usually reared in the same **environment**. Their genetic inheritance will be similar, but no more so than that of ordinary brothers and sisters, as the mix of genes and chromosomes in each zygote is not identical. The twins could be of different sex, different size, have different hair and eye colour, and different **temperaments**. If the environment is important in determining an individual's maturation, then the twins should have similar levels of intelligence, as they share a similar environment in the same way as other people.

▷
A zygote is a fertilized egg.

▷
Your temperament is your basic nature, especially as it is shown in the way that you react to situations or to other people.

Activity
Ask your parents what your temperament was like, and compare it to the temperaments of any brothers or sisters you have.

Identical twins

The second type of twins is **Monozygotic (MZ) twins**, more commonly known as identical twins. Monozygotic twins are formed when an ovum is fertilized by a sperm to become a zygote. This zygote then divides into two. MZ twins have an identical genetic inheritance, and so will be the same sex and very similar in appearance. If intelligence is largely determined by genetic factors they will have very similar intellectual abilities too. We will investigate this in Chapter 7.

▷
Monozygotic twins have identical genes, although there can be tiny differences, however, even between identical twins.

Maturation

The activity of development – in zygotes, in the foetus, at birth, throughout infancy, childhood, puberty, adolescence and into adulthood – is called **maturation**. There are many ways in which we mature. When we are sexually mature we are able to reproduce successfully. When we are physically mature we stop growing. Both of these stages of maturation can be measured, and the age at which they are achieved can be found. Psychological maturity is rather more tricky. When will someone be intellectually mature? Are you emotionally mature? Is your personality as mature as it will ever be? Do you know any middle-aged people, or people older than you, whom you would describe as not fully mature? Also, different societies expect different behaviour from people, so what might be regarded as a sign of emotional maturity in one country might be thought of as being immature elsewhere. For example, do you think boys or men should cry if they are upset? People from another culture might regard

▷
Maturation is the process of development towards an ultimate state called maturity. Although it seems a fairly simple concept to understand, in fact, it is very difficult to measure.

crying as a sign of immaturity in men, or as a sign of maturity, or as something which has nothing to do with either.

According to **Konrad Lorenz**, there is a particular time, usually very early in the development of many skills or abilities, when an animal is especially sensitive to stimulation involving that skill. This is called a **sensitive period**. For example, humans are said to be especially sensitive to language between a few months of age and puberty. If we hear and are encouraged to use language during this time, then our language skills should develop efficiently towards maturity. The language skills of people who are not stimulated in this way during their sensitive period may not develop so efficiently. Once past the sensitive period, people who haven't used language before can still acquire it, but it will be much more difficult for them to do so.

The duration of this sensitive period is different for different areas of development. The sensitive period for language, for instance, continues to puberty. **John Bowlby**, who studied and wrote about emotional development in children, believed that there was a sensitive period of between six months and five years for developing emotional bonds. **Wayne and Marsena Dennis** thought there was a sensitive period of the first two years for intellectual development.

▷
A sensitive period for developing a particular skill exists usually near the beginning of the maturation process for that skill, and is thought to exist for many different human abilities. The abilities might still develop outside that period, but they may take longer to do so, or they may never reach maturity.

Comment on whether or not intelligence is genetically inherited

The problem with claiming that intelligence (or any other skill) is genetically inherited in humans is that we can only refer to where the intelligent behaviour comes from – our genes. We can't explain what the behaviour actually is. What exactly is intelligence? Is having a good sense of direction so that you are never lost an example of intelligence? Are you displaying intelligence if you have a memory good enough to help you remember facts just long enough to pass a psychology test? It's much easier to understand the role of genetic inheritance on aspects of human behaviour when we know exactly what the behaviour is.

Exercise on environment and inheritance

1 What is temperament?
2 What is the difference between DZ and MZ twins?
3 What might we assume about the role of the environment in developing intelligence if DZ twins were found to have similar levels of intelligence?
4 What might we assume about the role of biological inheritance in intelligence if MZ twins were found to have similar levels of intelligence?
5 Outline the relationship between sensitive periods and the process of maturation.

So far we have talked about the influence of genes and maturation on human behaviour. **Instincts** are another possible influence. **Konrad**

▷

An experiment is a method scientists use to find whether one thing is involved in causing some change in another (see Chapter 15). Ethology is the study of animal behaviour in its natural environment (although ethologists can conduct laboratory-based experiments as well).

▷

Instincts automatically trigger certain responses. We can see that an animal always behaves in the same way under the same circumstances so we claim that its behaviour results from an instinct. However, we can't know that instincts really do exist, but from watching animals' behaviour, we assume they do.

Sigmund Freud

Lorenz studied animals both in the wild and by using animal **experiments**. The study of animal behaviour in its natural setting is called **ethology**. Lorenz claimed that most ducks and geese, among other animals, behave in similar ways under the same circumstances. For example, when their time for breeding is approaching male ducks begin raising and lowering their heads and moving their tails when they are near a female of their species. This is courtship behaviour in these ducks. The male is trying to attract the female. Similar species of duck behave in the same way. This behaviour could not have been learned and so must be the result of instinct.

A great deal of animal behaviour is controlled by **instincts**. When an animal experiences hunger it will be driven to seek food. When it is time for mating, it will seek a mate. If it becomes aware of an enemy, it will try to avoid being spotted or it will try to escape. The behaviour is the result of an instinctive urge to survive. Instincts in animals are said to be genetically inherited and do not need to be learned. Different species have different instincts which trigger different types of behaviour. For example, if a ground-nesting bird detects a predator it will fly away. Rabbits can't fly so their instinct might be to escape down an underground burrow. Even some well-fed domestic cats kill small birds. They are instinctively driven by their nature to kill. However, it is unlikely that any useful comparisons can be made with human beings. Humans are able to behave as they do for many different reasons, and can take so many different things into account.

Sigmund Freud (1856–1939) was an Austrian doctor who claimed that instincts do control some aspects of human behaviour. He noticed that some of his patients complained of symptoms such as paralysis, severe headaches, temporary loss of memory, and blindness, for which he could find no physical causes. He spent many years listening to and interpreting his patients' symptoms. He tried hypnotizing them, asking them questions, letting them talk freely about their memories and experiences, identifying their sense of humour, and interpreting their dreams. Freud's clinical method is called **psychoanalysis.** This led him to advance several theories about the nature of the **unconscious mind.**

One theory was that we are born with two opposing groups of instinctive forms of mental energy. First, there is the **libido** which contains instincts for achieving fulfilment in life. Second, there are the **death instincts,** which we are supposed to possess for self destruction. The death instincts encourage us to take chances and to risk our own safety. Destructive acts such as fights, war, arson, and murder were all said to be expressions of the death instincts. Freud thought that the libido is in constant battle with the death instincts (a battle which it finally loses at the moment of our death). There is no evidence for the existence of libido or death instincts. They are useful ways of imagining what something is like.

Exercise on instincts

1 What are instincts?
2 How could we discover all of the instincts that a cat possesses?
3 What does Freud mean by the libido?
4 What are the death instincts?
5 How could we discover all of the instincts that a human being possesses? (Look at your answer to question 2.)
6 How did Sigmund Freud gather his data?

Summary of biological influences on behaviour

Humans have evolved the ability to use their mental capacities more than any other animal. We inherit biological influences through our genes, and may be instinctively driven to behave in certain ways. However, our mental abilities also allow us to think and plan, and even to overcome our biological urges. Biology influences human behaviour: it does not control it.

The role of learning influencing behaviour

▷
Humans have much greater cognitive capacities (abilities to understand, think, reason and learn) than any other animal on Earth. This is why we are able to dominate this planet and all its other species.

One of the most obvious features about human beings is the vast range of human behaviour. Unlike the influence of genes on human functioning, we can observe, test, measure and analyse human behaviour. We can suggest explanations for why people behave on the basis of these observations. (Everyone observes and most people offer explanations for other people's behaviour – everyone is an amateur psychologist.) We can apply many techniques used by the natural and physical sciences of biology, chemistry and physics to studying human behaviour.

People who concentrate on the study of behaviour are called **behaviourists**. Behaviourists wish to apply the methods of the natural or physical sciences in investigating human behaviour. They do not believe that much human behaviour is simply genetically inherited in the way that much animal behaviour is probably genetically inherited. Instead, behaviourists argue that most human behaviour is learned, and they have studied ways in which we learn. Behaviourists reject the nature approach and support the nurture approach. They argue that there are certain fundamental rules or principles which underlie all human learning, and that these rules or principles can be discovered by applying scientific techniques to the study of human and animal behaviour.

▷
Nurture is the word which describes the combined effect that the various factors in our environment have on our growth and behaviour. For instance, what is the effect on us of how our parents brought us up, or how people treated us at school.

Behaviourists claim that most human behaviour has been learned. Learning is the name given to describe any change in our knowledge that allows us to do something that we couldn't do very well before. The problem here is: how can we know whether there has been a change in our learning? We can't see learning. The answer is through testing our performance. If we are better at doing something after learning than we were before, then we must have learned how to do it. There are three main ways in which we learn:

- we make associations with something we can already do;
- we repeat an action;
- we watch and copy others.

Exercise on learning

1 Define the term learning.
2 What is the relationship between learning and performance?
3 List the three main ways in which people learn.
4 Give an example of the use of each one (i.e. something you have learned using each method).

Classical conditioning

▷
Pavlov was an award-winning physiologist who carried out some research into the learning of associations between an event and a reflexive response in dogs.

▷
A stimulus is simply anything which triggers a response. It can be reflexive or it may be learned. A bright light suddenly being turned on elicits the reflexive blinking response. Seeing someone you like elicits the learned response of being happy.

Ivan Pavlov

During the last decades of the 19th century, **Ivan Pavlov** (1849–1936), the Russian physiologist, investigated the digestive system in dogs. Pavlov was not a psychologist and had no interest in psychology. However, one aspect of his work has great significance for psychology and it came about almost by accident.

Pavlov noticed that some of his older laboratory dogs were salivating when the laboratory assistants approached with the animals' food. The dogs must have learned to associate a **stimulus** (the assistants), which wouldn't normally lead to a salivation **response**, with food, which would. This simple type of learning is called **association learning**. Pavlov decided to investigate. The stimulus which naturally elicits the response he called an **unconditional stimulus (US),** and the response it triggers he called an **unconditional response (UR)**, also known as a reflex. So, the US (food) triggers the reflexive UR (salivation).

Pavlov wanted to see if he could teach the dogs to give their reflexive response to a stimulus they had learned. Just before he gave the dogs their food, he sounded a buzzer. The process of placing two events together is called a **pairing**. The dogs may learn to associate one event with the other. This is an experimental procedure called **paired-association learning**. Each time a subject in an experiment is exposed to the experimenter's manipulation, this is called a **trial**. The buzzer is a **conditional stimulus (CS)**, which means that any salivation response to it will only occur if the animal has learned an association between it and food. So US and CS together elicit UR.

After just a few trials the animals did start to salivate to the sound of the buzzer. By the tenth trial the animals had been classically conditioned to salivate to the sound of the buzzer. So CS elicited CR.

Pavlov conditioned a number of dogs to salivate to the sound of buzzers, bells and metronomes. On average, the responses were fully conditioned in ten trials. He altered the original stimulus in a number of ways and measured the responses. From these experiments he derived several principles of learning. These included:

Stages in classical conditioning

Stage 1	US (food) ⟶	UR (salivation)
Stage 2	CS (bell) and US (food) ⟶	UR (salivation)
Stage 3	CS (bell) ⟶	CR (salivation)

▷ NB: the response stays the same – salivation. It is what elicits the response, however, that determines whether it is conditioned or not.

Higher-order conditioning

If an animal is fully conditioned to salivate to a first CS (for example, the sound of a bell tuned to the musical note middle C), and a second CS is then associated with the bell (for example, a buzzer), then the animal would learn to salivate to some extent when it hears the buzzer.

Stimulus generalization

If an animal is conditioned to salivate to a bell of middle C, then ringing a bell tuned to a different note, such as A, will still trigger some salivation. The animal may expect some food reward, even though some aspect of the stimulus was different from the original stimulus.

Stimulus discrimination

Discrimination means being able to tell the difference between two or more things. When the bell tuned to A was not followed by food, the animals soon learned not to salivate when they heard it. The animals learned to discriminate between those stimuli which preceded food (middle-C bells) and those that did not (bells tuned to A).

Response extinction

Pavlov conditioned some animals to salivate to a particular CS, such as a bell tuned to C, but then stopped presenting the food after ringing the bell. The animals soon learned that the particular CS no longer meant the arrival of food. This new learning replaced the previous learning. They stopped salivating when they heard the bell. The salivation response was extinguished.

Spontaneous recovery

Pavlov extinguished the salivation response to a particular stimulus by continuing to ring the original bell without providing food afterwards. After a period of time, ringing the original bell caused the animals to give the salivation response. This spontaneous recovery occurred probably because the response was not, in fact, completely extinguished.

Exercise on the principles of learning

Here are the five principles of classical conditioning, as outlined above.

A higher-order conditioning
B stimulus generalization
C stimulus discrimination
D response extinction
E spontaneous recovery.

Match the right principle to each of the following descriptions, by entering the letter in the corresponding box.

1 A response that the animal has learned not to give suddenly appears. ☐

2 A response to a stimulus which is similar to the original conditional stimulus. ☐

3 To unlearn a response. ☐

4 Learning only to respond to a known stimulus. ☐

5 Responding to a stimulus that has been associated with a conditional stimulus. ☐

▷
Watson and Rayner's research was revolutionary at its time, and certainly would not be allowed now! This experiment investigated whether the child could be taught to give a fear response when he saw something that he had previously appeared to like. We will examine the extremely important issue of what should and should not be allowed in research in the section on ethics in Chapter 15.

Classical conditioning has been used on humans too, even quite young ones. The first experiment was probably conducted early this century by **J.B. Watson** (1879–1958) and his close friend and assistant **Rosalie Rayner**. They used an infant known as 'Little Albert', whom they found had no fear of white furry objects (such as stuffed toys or Santa Claus masks). He appeared to like a white laboratory rat. They conditioned a fear response into the child by showing him a white furry rat, and immediately striking a steel bar with a hammer just behind the child's head. There were 7 pairings, and by the last one the sight of the rat was enough to elicit the fear response (the child screamed). The child also screamed (i.e. he generalized the fear response) at the sight of a fur coat, Santa Claus masks, and even Watson's hair.

Exercise on classical conditioning

Some psychologists wanted to see whether very young babies could be conditioned. They knew that after just a few days infants would make sucking motions when they saw a nipple close to them. With their mothers' permission they sounded a tone just before the infants were breast fed. After a few trials the infants started to make sucking motions when they heard the tone.

1 What is meant by a trial in this passage?
2 What is an experiment?
3 Does this experiment suggest that very young babies can be conditioned? Explain your answer.

●●● **Summary of classical conditioning**

Pavlov's research on the reflexive salivation response in dogs led him to investigate their ability to learn. He found that animals could associate their salivation response to a particular stimulus, or one very much like it. As reflexive responses could be conditioned, this led the way for others to see if voluntary behaviour could also be conditioned.

Operant conditioning

Classical conditioning is concerned with the learning of associations between conditional stimuli and conditioned responses. Operant conditioning is concerned with all other learning (i.e. voluntary, non reflexive learning). Because behaviourists argue that the same principles underlie both human and animal behaviour, they have conducted countless experiments to test how animals learn. This type of learning is called **instrumental conditioning** (an animal has to use some part, or instrument, of the experimental apparatus in order to gain some reward). **Operant conditioning** includes this, but also refers to any other behaviour that we learn to perform in a particular way.

▷
Early laboratory-based experiments required animals to perform various tasks, such as pulling strings or pushing levers. These demonstrated instrumental conditioning. Operant conditioning, on the other hand, refers to all learned, non reflexive behaviour.

Probably the best known writer on operant conditioning during the middle decades of the twentieth century was **Burrhus F. Skinner** (1904–1990). Skinner was a biologist who wanted to apply strict scientific procedures to studying learning and behaviour. In fact he claimed that behaviourism is the only useful approach in psychology, as it is the only one to use strict scientific procedures.

Skinner claimed that it is possible to explain most behaviour as a result of what he calls **ABC**. These initials stand for **Antecedents, Behaviour,** and **Consequences**. Antecedents are conditions which exist and are appropriate for something to happen. It is probably helpful to think of antecedents as being like stimuli. Sitting in class at 9am is an antecedent for the lesson to begin. It doesn't exactly trigger the lesson to begin as a stimulus would (for instance if the teacher was late!). Hearing the fire alarm is an antecedent for leaving the building. In this case the antecedent is (or should be) a stimulus which triggers the response leaving the building.

▷
Three stages need to be identified in understanding why people do what they do, as follows:

1 antecedents (the conditions that the people are in);
2 behaviour (the action they actually take);
3 consequences (the results of those actions).

Behaviour is that which we can be seen to do. Think of behaviour as what we called responses earlier. For instance, paying attention, taking notes, reading pages or copying illustrations are elements of behaviour associated with a lesson.

Consequences are the results of the behaviour. Getting a good mark, an encouraging response, a positive report, a good reference are all consequences of good behaviour in the classroom.

According to Skinner, an association between behaviour and its consequences is something that we learn. For example, Shelley, a first-year secondary-school pupil, is asked a question in class. She thinks and gives the correct answer. The teacher is pleased and says 'well done, Shelley'. The antecedent is being asked a question, the behaviour is Shelley's answer, and the consequence is praise. Skinner claimed that the consequences of our behaviour determine how likely we are to repeat that particular behaviour in the future. If Shelley benefits in some way from the teacher's response, then she is likely to repeat the behaviour if the antecedents recur (i.e. she might answer again when asked another question). If the consequences do not benefit Shelley, then she is unlikely to attempt answering again.

The most important feature in operant conditioning is **reinforcement**. In the first few years of this century **Edward Thorndike** (1874–1949) stated his **Law of Effect,** which claimed that a response will follow a stimulus if it is associated in the organism's mind with a 'satisfying state of affairs'. Thorndike had shown how quickly cats which were kept in cages (called **puzzle boxes**) would learn to pull a string which released them to both freedom and food. Rats also soon learned to press levers which provided them with food pellets. Skinner disagreed and rejected the unscientific concept of 'a satisfying state of affairs'. He claimed that satisfaction is a mental event, and that we cannot know what a cat or rat finds satisfying.

Instead Skinner uses the term **reinforcement**. There are several categories of reinforcer. A **positive reinforcer** is anything which increases the chances that the behaviour will be repeated. So, if you enjoyed eating your first Burgundy-and-Bordeaux-cherry ice cream, then that enjoyment will remind you to eat another if you have the chance. However, if you didn't find Mole-and-Hedgehog flavour ice cream very pleasant then you will not repeat your Mole-and-Hedgehog flavour ice cream eating behaviour when next you have the chance.

▷
Skinner concentrated on the effects of the behaviour rather than on its causes, because it is impossible to observe or measure causes. We can never know why you chose to do one thing rather than another. You may not even know yourself. Skinner maintained that the consequences of behaviour are at least as important as its antecedents.

▷
Reinforcement is a central idea in behaviourist explanations for all aspects of human learning. Reinforcers determine whether any behaviour is repeated or not.

Activity
List some things that you would find positively reinforcing. Try to put them in order of importance to you. Then compare your list to a friend's list.

We can discover what an organism finds positively reinforcing by deliberately creating an antecedent condition, and then giving the organism the potential reinforcer. For example, we give a pigeon some wood with a spot of green paint for the pigeon to peck at. We then put the wood into the pigeon's cage and wait until the bird pecks it. When it does we give it, say, a blob of strawberry jam (i.e. the potential reinforcer). If the bird keeps pecking at the green spot we could say that it finds the jam positively reinforcing.

Apart from positive reinforcers, Skinner identified several other types of reinforcement. There are **primary** and **secondary reinforcers**. A primary reinforcer is anything which satisfies a direct need, such as the need for food or sleep. A secondary reinforcer is anything which can be exchanged for a primary one. Money is probably the most obvious secondary reinforcer.

▷
Humans learn a great deal through avoidance and escape learning. Both these forms of learning help us to be free from consequences that would be unpleasant or even harmful.

Then there are **negative reinforcers**. The result of negative reinforcement is that people acquire **escape learning** and **avoidance learning**. For instance, if a bully in your primary school twists your arm behind your back until it hurts, you might want to give him your crisps and Mars bar so that he will let you go. You are learning what to do in order to escape from an unpleasant experience. Ideally you would go to a teacher and explain what had happened. If he ever grabs you again you will know what to do to escape from the pain. You will learn to avoid the bully in future by arriving from a different direction, arriving with your big brother, or arriving late. Escape and avoidance learning are pretty important to all of us, especially as we are growing up. Having escaped from danger a few times, we learn to spot the signs and avoid that particular danger in future.

●●●
Summary

A   An experimental demonstration of escape learning

1   A loud noise is played continuously near a caged rat. The rat shows signs of distress at the loudness of the noise.
2   The noise can be turned off by pressing a lever in the cage.
3   The rat hits the lever by accident, while trying to escape from the noise. The noise is turned off.
4   After a time the noise is turned on again.
5   After a few trials the animal learns to press the lever as soon as the noise is switched on.

B   An experimental demonstration of avoidance learning

1   A light is turned on just before the noise starts.
2   The rat learns to associate the light and the noise.
3   The rat presses the lever when it sees the light.

The problem with Skinner's use of the term reinforcement, however, is that it can't really be defined satisfactorily. It seems to be saying that anything that increases the chances of some behaviour recurring is a positive reinforcer, and that if some behaviour is repeated then it must have been positively reinforced. So positive reinforcers are those things which positively reinforce. Of course, this isn't a very helpful definition. I could just as well say that transmogrifiers are those things which transmogrify. You aren't any wiser after the definition than you were before, so what's the use of the definition?

Types of reinforcement

	Primary necessary for survival	Secondary associated with primary
Positive	food, sleep, warmth	money
Negative	need to escape from pain	signals the opportunity to avoid having to escape

One other feature of the learning process is **punishment**. Punishment is not a reinforcer because it does not teach someone to do something. In most cases it is supposed to teach them not to do something. Skinner believes that punishment is largely irrelevant. We should be able to predict and control people's behaviour by giving reinforcements when people behave appropriately, so that punishment should never be necessary. He argues that we would all behave in unacceptable ways if we were not reinforced.

Exercise on reinforcement

1 Give three examples of things you would find positively reinforcing.
2 Give three examples of things you would find negatively reinforcing.
3 Explain the difference between positive and negative reinforcement.
4 Give three examples of things that children might learn through escape learning.
5 Give three examples of things that children might learn through avoidance learning.
6 Explain the difference between escape and avoidance learning.

Reinforcement can be used to teach quite complex behaviour in both animals and humans. Skinner taught two pigeons to play a version of ping-pong using the technique called **behaviour-shaping by successive approximations**. In this procedure the task is broken down into its smallest steps. For a pigeon playing ping-pong, for instance, these steps include approaching the ball, hitting the ball, hitting the ball hard enough to make it travel some distance, hitting the ball towards another pigeon, etc. These steps are then arranged in a logical order. The first step may be to prepare the pigeon to allow itself to be struck by a ball. Table-tennis balls are strange, and the pigeon's instinctive response may be to avoid them. Eventually the pigeon will be hit by the ball. It will be reinforced immediately. Repeat this trial several times.

When this particular pattern of behaviour is fully conditioned, the reinforcement stops. The pigeon must now do more to gain its reinforcement, for example, it must approach while the ball is bouncing. Reinforcement is withdrawn again when this behaviour is fully conditioned. The pigeon must now hit the ball with its beak in order to have its reinforcer. Eventually, the pigeon will only be reinforced when it strikes the moving ball with its beak towards another pigeon. If the other pigeon has been similarly conditioned it will, in turn, hit the ball back.

Exercise on successive approximation

How would you begin to train a young horse to be a showjumper using behaviour-shaping by successive approximation?

 Summary of operant conditioning
The term behaviourism applies to the approach of those people – notably

Watson and Skinner – who argue that only those things which can be observed and measured are worthy of study. (Watson and Skinner didn't quite agree with each other, however. Skinner was more concerned with the effects of our behaviour on the environment than Watson was). Skinner argued that much of our behaviour, whether good, normal, bad or disturbed, is learned by reinforcement. Reinforcement has occurred, he said, when some behaviour is more likely to occur to a given stimulus than any other. Reinforcement can be positive or negative, and quite complex behaviours can be shaped by systematically and selectively applying reinforcers.

Social learning theory

Earlier we mentioned Freud's psychoanalytic theory, which attempted to explain the development of personality. One of Freud's ideas has been developed by social learning theorists. It is common knowledge that children imitate their parents' behaviour, including that they may say things they've heard their parents say, or they may apply, as best they can, their parents ideas. Freud believed that the reason for this was that children were **identifying** with their parents. The concept of identification is important.

▷ Identification is the process of discovering some of the qualities of another person (or group of people) and becoming as much like them as possible. We may think of ourselves as one of them. Identification can be seen in the ways children form their friendship groups.

According to Freud, boys of three or four years of age experience their first sexual feelings towards their opposite-sex parents. Boys are unconsciously drawn towards their mothers because mothers are warm, tender, caring and protective towards their sons. Mothers also show affection and are caring towards fathers. This can lead a son to develop unconscious aggressive instincts towards his father. His father is a rival for his mother's love towards him. However, the boy feels anxiety and conflict at finding himself both aggressive and loving towards his father at the same time. In order to resolve these anxieties and conflicts, the child identifies with his father, and becomes as much like his father as he can.

Albert Bandura (b. 1925) used some of the laboratory methods pioneered by other psychologists and combined some of the ideas about identification to develop **social learning theory** during the 1960's and 1970's. Social learning theorists do not deny the value of reinforcement, especially as people are socially reinforcing one another all the time, but they do not believe that reinforcement alone can explain all learning. Children (and adults too) often learn by observing and then imitating someone whom they consider to be a powerful, attractive or important person. (This is known as **observational learning**.) For children, the most important and influential people are parents. Parents need not deliberately try either to influence a child, or to apply a reinforcer, for observational learning to occur.

▷ Albert Bandura uses the term observational learning to describe learning which relies not on reinforcement or shaping, but instead merely on some behaviour being observed.

Summary of the major features in observational learning
For observational learning to be carried out, it is necessary to:
- **pay attention** to those parts of the model's behaviour which are important to the observer, and not to misinterpret, or become distracted by, other environmental events;

- **remember accurately** what has been observed. Older children can model events from some time ago, younger children do not have such cognitive skills;
- **reproduce accurately** the observed behaviour. Younger children may need several observations and trials before successfully modelling some observed behaviour;
- have the **motivation** and desire to imitate one model rather than another.

Modelling is one of the fundamental processes in socialization. Models are seen as very influential people, whom children may feel they need to imitate.

Observational learning is a most efficient form of learning, when it is used appropriately. We can all learn a great deal by watching someone who is experienced doing something, then having a go at the same task ourselves. Young children learn to use language largely by observing others talking then trying to imitate them. However, not everything can be learned by observation alone. You could not, for instance, learn to play the guitar simply by observing someone else playing the guitar. Later we will see how observational learning has been used to explain aggression.

Activity

How do you think observational learning might explain aggression? Make a list of the major influences psychologists have suggested so far for aggressive behaviour in children. Put the list in order of importance for you. Would the order be the same for you as for a member of the opposite sex who is the same age as you? (If not, try to make a list for someone of the opposite sex who is the same age as you.) Would the list be the same for your parents? (You could always ask them.)

Exercise on observational learning

Imagine that some psychologists had arranged for four groups of 5- to 7-year-olds to hear and see videos of an adult model. The first group heard and saw the adult being charitable and saying that it was good to give money to help poor children. This adult was then seen to give some money to a children's charity. A second group heard the adult talking about behaving generously, but then saw him give nothing away when asked. The third group heard the adult saying it was all right to be greedy, and refusing to donate any money. The fourth group heard the adult encouraging greediness, but then saw him being generous.

Later the children were given some tokens which could be exchanged for sweets, and were asked if they would like to donate some of them to needy children instead. Here is a bar chart displaying the results.

Children's behaviour after being exposed to different models

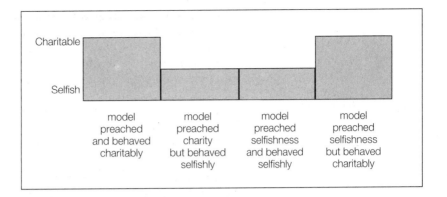

1. How did the model seen by the children who behaved most generously behave?
2. How did the model seen by the children who behaved most selfishly behave?
3. What factor seems to be the most influential in determining the level of charity in these children?
4. Do the findings in this study support the claims of social learning theorists? Explain your answer.
5. Children of parents who smoke are more likely to smoke themselves. True or false?
6. What kind of people are most likely to be modelled, according to Bandura?

Summary of social learning theory

Social learning theorists combine aspects of several theories including the ideas of imitation and identification (from psychoanalysis), and reward and reinforcement (from behaviourism). To these they add the idea of observational learning and modelling to make social learning theory.

Society's and culture's influences on behaviour

Because humans have consciousness they are aware of other people. Most people are also fairly sociable and most of us live in groups. Smaller groups include families, colleagues, friends, team members, workgroups, etc. Larger groups include societies. A society is a larger community of people who usually live in similar ways, mostly sharing similar habits and attitudes. They often develop organizations such as an education system to teach and train, an economic system for producing and distributing goods, a political system for deciding who governs, military organizations for defence, a system of health care, etc. Members of societies usually evolve a language and customs. Celebrating anniversaries, religious festivals and people's birthdays are familiar customs. These customs and habits are called **culture**. Culture refers to the behaviour that members of a society or group learn so as to fit in with the group. The group's customs

▷
Put very simply, society is a group of people who live in a particular place, and culture is the collection of its behaviour that each new generation will have to learn.

and habits, ideas and beliefs, its civilization are that group's culture. One of the first things we learn is our culture's language. Later we will learn its usual style of dress, eating habits, educational systems, etc.

Activity

Consider your own society and one other. Make a list of some of the main features of your society, such as its language, dress, eating habits, family and marriage arrangements, etc. Find what similarities and differences there are between your society and the other one in these areas.

Psychologists are interested in the ways in which human behaviour is influenced by membership of various groups. One of the first steps towards becoming a member of any group is to form a relationship with someone who is already a member of that group. The very first relationships babies will make will be with their caregivers. After a few months of age, infants can recognize their caregivers, and interact with them. By one year of age they definitely prefer the presence of people who are familiar to them, while they may show some fear of other adults. A close emotional relationship that develops between a baby and its caregiver, is called an **attachment bond**. It seems likely that people inherit genes that direct them towards making these bonds. Older children form friendships from among their equals. Adolescents often develop special relationships with members of the opposite sex. People who love each other might live together or marry. Friendship means different things at different ages. The positive need for friendship, cooperation, companionship, and love is called **affiliation**.

During the 1930's, **Henry Murray**, who was influenced by Freud's view of personality development, described twenty basic human motives. Among them was the need to form affiliations (attachments). Because most people do form affiliations, it seems logical that there is some need for us to do so. To investigate this further we need to look at people in other societies. Do they form similar affiliations and similar groups to the ones we form? How does behaviour and culture differ in different societies. To research this we conduct **cross-cultural** research.

Mary Ainsworth found that many children of the Ganda people in Uganda formed their first affiliations several months earlier than children in the West. We need cross-cultural studies here to show how the behaviour of people in different societies is influenced by their different cultures. **Urie Bronfenbrenner** found that American educational systems reflected the individual competitiveness in American society. Individuality is encouraged there, and groups are encouraged always to compete. In Russian education the emphasis was on cooperation and mutual support. If our only knowledge of the role of education was based on American or Russian culture, then we would not understand as much as we need to.

▷
Affiliation refers to the positive relationships that people form which bring them into close contact with each other.

▷
Cross-cultural research involves observing and testing any particular aspects of the behaviour of people who have evolved different cultures. So we might compare attitudes towards punishment or rewards for children in Britain and China, or teaching methods in America and Japan.

Exercise on affiliation

1 What is consciousness?
2 Read the first paragraph in this section and summarize the difference between society and culture.
3 Why do you think babies might form attachment bonds with their caregivers?
4 What do psychologists mean by affiliations?
5 Can you think of some problems that psychologists could face in conducting cross-cultural research?

Earlier in this chapter we mentioned the nature–nurture debate. This is the term given to the debate about the extent to which some human abilities are influenced by either genetic or environmental factors, or both. Were you born intelligent, or has your intelligence developed as a result of the experiences you have had? Are a baby's abilities to judge depth and distance present at birth, or are they learned through experience? Are we genetically programmed to behave aggressively under certain circumstances, or do the things we have seen and been taught make us more or less aggressive? Are our genes more influential than our environment?

▷
Although we usually think our environment influences our thoughts and actions, it also works the other way round. You may have been dumped by your boyfriend or girlfriend recently. This can make you feel miserable, and what you think and feel can shape how you respond to your environment. You decide that there are plenty more fish in the sea and begin to cheer up. In turn, this can change the environment. You go out open to the idea that someone might find you interesting and want a relationship with you.

One way of investigating the nature–nurture debate is by conducting cross-cultural research. If we find that all babies do form emotional attachment bonds, then it is reasonable to conclude that there is probably a biological, genetically transmitted need for these bonds to form. If babies in some societies only – and not in others – form bonds, then the reason is probably social or environmental. If males in all societies are generally more aggressive than females in all societies, then aggression could be, at least partly, explained by biology. If there are a large number of societies where females are more aggressive than males, then genetics alone could not explain aggression.

Moving on from the nature–nurture debate on where human abilities originate, there are other influences on our behaviour that are definitely socially acquired. These are the **social norms** of our society and the roles we learn to play within society. When people live together they develop some behaviour that most of them share. It might start with a few people and others copy it. For example, some people may once have given others presents to celebrate their birthdays. Over the years the habit grew until many of us now give each other birthday gifts. Celebrating a birthday is now a part of our culture. It has become a social norm, and is typical or representative of people in our society. Social norms are useful, because they give us a guide for what we should do under certain circumstances by informing us about what most people would do under those circumstances. For instance, I have never met the Queen, but I know that I would be expected to bow if I were to meet her.

▷
Social norms are expected patterns of behaviour that develop in any social group over time. They become a major part of our culture.

Social norms are the kinds of behaviour that are appropriate in different circumstances. Some of these social norms, and the circumstances under which they should and should not appear, are listed in the table on the following page.

Norm of behaviour	Social circumstances	When not appropriate
Removing clothing down to underwear	Trying on clothes in a shop	In class
Picking up food with your fingers	Eating chips or burgers	Eating in a posh restaurant
Screaming with excitement	On a fairground ride	During a discussion with your parents
Getting up when you want	On holiday	When working
Going to sleep in bed	At bedtime	In a furniture store

Social norms may become fixed in law. For example, you must drive your car on the left hand side of the road in this country. You must stop at a red traffic light and go at a green one. Some social norms change with time. Bald men used to wear wigs (judges still do). Gentlemen used to walk on the side of the pavement nearer the road when escorting a lady, and would stand up when a lady entered the room. In these politically correct times such social norms have largely disappeared.

As any society developed certain people began to be expected to do certain things. Parents were usually expected to look after their children, in Britain the Church minister was expected to pray for our souls and ask God to forgive our sins. The Lord of the region would let the villagers take shelter in his castle and his archers and swordsmen would fight to protect themselves, as well as their master, from attackers. Some people were expected to become fighters, others to become blacksmiths. Wealthy people began to pay others to perform certain roles such as servants and guards. As industry and commerce developed these social roles have expanded to include paid jobs such as teachers and policemen. A social role is simply any pattern of behaviour that we can expect of anyone playing that role. We expect nurses to care for the sick, footballers to play football, policemen to keep order, and park keepers to make sure we stay off the grass.

▷
The roles we play affect our behaviour, too, as we shall see in Chapter 14.

 Activity
How many social roles have you played today?

Exercise on environmental influences

1 Summarize why psychologists might use cross-cultural research.
2 What is an environment?
3 Think of one way in which your behaviour might be affected by your environment.
4 What are social norms?
5 What are social roles?

Summary of social and cultural influences on behaviour
We often modify our behaviour according to how we interpret and understand what we see around us. Some of our behaviour is genetically driven and some is socially learned. Conducting cross-cultural research is one way to investigate the contributions of both to our understanding of social behaviour.

Thinking and Perception

▷
Watson's views would be regarded as rather extreme, even by most behaviourists today.

Thinking involves all cognitive activity, including words, ideas, memories, beliefs, intentions, etc. Early behaviourists such as **J.B. Watson** were rather doubtful about the whole idea of thinking. Watson argued that all behaviour could be explained as being a consequence of learned associations between things. So, if I have experienced pain during a visit to the dentist, then I don't need to think in order to want to avoid a second visit. It's a simple learned association. Watson claimed that the idea of mental activity directing or even influencing human behaviour was simply unnecessary. He once claimed that thinking was merely sub-vocal speech, and that, as speech is observable behaviour, so too is thinking. This view was challenged from several branches of knowledge both from outside and within psychology.

Donald Broadbent was one of many psychologists who had been researching human concentration and attention during the Second World War. How could help be given to those people who stared at radar screens for long periods of time to organize the flow of aircraft in and out of areas of the sky? Experiments in how attention can be divided and applied selectively introduced a new area into psychology. This was **cognitive psychology**. It regards the human brain as an information-processing device. Computers are also information-processing devices, although they differ from the brain both in terms of the way they process information, and in the kinds of information they process.

▷
The information-processing approach challenged the traditional behaviourist explanation for human thinking.

Cognition is generally the process by which we detect and respond to information around us. It involves our senses, our attention, our memory, our reasoning, etc. The first stage in cognition is **perception**. We live in a world where countless things are going on around us all the time. We are vaguely aware of some of them, and more aware of those to which we pay some attention. These sources of stimulation are the perceptions which your senses have detected and you have become aware of, either very slightly or more so.

▷
Thinking is an extremely broad term, covering many forms of processing information within human cognition. Not all mental processing is thinking. Your visual system picks up patterns of light in your eyes and interprets them as objects in your brain. This is mental processing, but it isn't thinking.

Having detected some perceptions we now need the cognitive process of **thinking**. Thinking is the name of those mental activities that humans possess for processing perceptions and other features of mental life, such as memories, language, ideas, hopes, plans, problem-solving skills, and many others. Thinking cannot be observed, as it does not directly involve any behaviour (although it could trigger quite a lot of behaviour!). It is an extremely broad term that covers many activities. We will try to identify some of the main ones here in order to see how they influence human behaviour.

At birth, humans have very few ideas and are not capable of thinking in the ways described above. As we mature and have more experiences so we begin to learn to associate one thing with another. For instance, we begin to associate a parent's face, with all its shape and patterns of movement, with some form of stimulation, such as food or comfort. **Genevieve Carpenter** found that a baby also learns to associate its mother's voice with her face. The learning of this association becomes a memory. The baby has converted one form of physical energy (light or sound) into another (electrical activity in the brain that is the memory). Converting one form of energy into another is called **transduction**.

There are different kinds of thought and different reasons for thinking about one thing rather than another. What we think about depends on what is going on around us (situation factors) or what is going on in our brains (personal factors). If you are selectively paying attention to what you are reading, I hope it is making some sense to you. If you are paying only slight attention and half thinking about something else, don't blame me entirely if you aren't following this. Even if you are deliberately concentrating on this and something happens to distract you, such as a loud noise outside or someone calling your name, then your thinking will switch from what all these words mean to whatever else is attracting your attention.

Selection of what to think about is important. If you are reading this because you have to, rather than because you choose to, then you might well need to go through it a couple of times for it to make much sense. It may be hard work. If you are not interested you will find it difficult to apply your attention. If, on the other hand, you are interested in the subject of psychology, you will find this makes sense more quickly and you will understand it better.

Daniel Kahneman suggests that at any one time your thinking – and therefore your attention – will be tuned to one specific mentally demanding task (or a couple of less demanding ones, depending on how awake you are and how alert your senses are). Imagine that you are concentrating on playing a pinball machine. By choosing to attend to one type of stimulation rather than another (the pinball rather than the music being played in the arcade) you will be more alert to that stimulation (you will keep the ball scoring for longer). However, another stimulation can distract you if it is distracting enough (the fire bell goes off right next to you, for instance!).

An important consideration of how we see each other is the selection of which features to attend to and which to ignore. The features you select will depend on what you think about those features and perhaps on which people possess them. What features do you find attractive in people? Is height important? Or weight? Is hair colour of any importance? What about personality? Must they be generous? Do they need to be truthful? Could you find someone who is disloyal attractive? Whatever features you think are attractive will form the basis on which you select your friends. People who do not possess many of the features you find attractive are

▷
Transduction is the name given to the process in which light, sound waves, the smell or taste of things, etc., are transformed into electrical energy in the nervous system. This activity in the brain is one of the sources of information for what we interpret as thought.

▷
Psychologists list several kinds of thinking. These include creative thought, where perceptions, memories, ideas, etc., are associated in original ways, and autistic thought, where the thoughts are dominated by the thinker's own ideas and ignore the outside world. These two show the extent to which different kinds of thinking can vary.

▷
Some of our perceptions are vast and complicated. We cannot attend to every feature. We pay more attention to some features than others, depending on how we think and feel about them. Our mental concepts and images influence our cognition, as we shall see shortly.

unlikely to become your closest friends.

Organization of the material we think about is also important. Thinking is most effective if the material you are trying to make sense of in your brain is organized in some way. Look at the following activity. Try to do it now.

Activity
Here are 16 words for you to remember. Read them through once, close your eyes, and try to recall them:

And are aspects biologists claimed determined function genetically have how humans many of psychologists some that

It's a bit tricky, but with some effort you could do it. I have organized the list by putting the words in alphabetical order. Unfortunately, the human brain is used to sorting words by meaning rather than by their first letter. It would be easier if we rearranged these words into a sentence from earlier in this chapter: 'Many biologists and psychologists have claimed that some aspects of how humans function are determined genetically.'

Much of our thinking is organized, although we don't consciously try to organize it. For example, we put people into categories such as students, workers, sailors, mothers, business people, and so on. We develop ideas about what members of these groups are like from what we know of them, or from what other people have told us they are like. When we find someone who fits our group label we assume that they will be like our image of the other members of the group. This is called **inference**.

One consequence of organizing our perceptions and drawing inferences from them is that we develop **stereotypes**. A stereotype is a fairly fixed idea about what someone will be like, and encourages us to treat them in a certain way as a result of that fixed idea. If I know what young drivers are like, then I will know whom to blame if I witness a car accident involving a young driver. After all, everyone knows that young drivers drive too quickly and are rather reckless!

We also build up ideas, called **scripts**, about the events and behaviour that happen in familiar situations. For example, if I said that I had filled my car with petrol, could you describe what exactly had happened in order that my car was filled with petrol?

▷
Inference is the name given to the thought processes that lead us to assume that we know what someone or something will be like. This knowledge will influence the way we behave towards that person or in that situation.

Exercise on scripts

Here are the main events of a very familiar experience. Arrange them in a logical sequence.

- hang the nozzle on the pump
- press the trigger on the nozzle
- pay for the petrol
- remove the petrol cap
- drive out of the petrol station
- release the trigger on the nozzle when the pump shows the appropriate

amount of petrol has been pumped
- pick up the nozzle and insert it into the petrol tank
- drive into the petrol station
- notice the petrol gauge is low

Exercise on processing information

1 What is cognition?
2 What term is being defined in the following sentence? 'The name of those mental activities that humans possess for processing perceptions and other features of mental life such as memories, language, ideas, hopes, plans, problem solving skills, and many others.'
3 Give some examples of how our selection of certain features can affect our behaviour towards them.
4 What is the relationship between inferences and stereotypes?
5 Give an example of the major stages in one of the scripts that you know.

The way we think changes as we grow. According to **Jerome Bruner** young children can think only in terms of what they themselves can do, or what specifically happens to them. After a year or so, children begin to be able to handle mental images of what things look like. When they have gained more experience, particularly in using and understanding language, they will also be able to think in ideas. Bruner calls each of these styles of thinking 'a mode of representing the world'.

An alternative view of the way thinking develops during childhood is offered by **Jean Piaget**. Piaget suggested the importance of **schemas**. A schema is an idea of what something is like or a plan of what something does. Schemas can act as guides to help us to explore something new based on something we already know about. If you have a schema for playing the piano, you might soon learn to play an electronic keyboard. Schemas help us to interpret new things too. Having learned that I am a little girl might help me to understand that something else is a little boy. They can also act as outline principles for solving problems. If I have a rough idea about how to perform a simple addition in arithmetic, I might be able to use this as the principle for mastering subtraction.

Piaget's biological background led him to conclude that mental processing involved maintaining a balance between taking perceptions into our brains through our senses, and understanding those perceptions. If we take in more than we can process, we simply won't reach an understanding of what we have taken in. We may be confused or misled. Understanding is achieved by fitting our perception in with schemas we already have. Our schemas may be modified by the new information. If this is the case, then in future we will have more extensive schemas to work with and they should help us to understand even more. The benefit of this isn't just improved knowledge and understanding, but also better adapted behaviour.

▷
Schemas are ideas, plans, strategies or other mental structures that can help us deal with new experiences. Some of our schemas are images and concepts, as we shall see.

▷
Mental images are a type of schema. They are parts of our imagination for they are abstract ideas which allow us to think what something or someone might be like.

We carry imaginary pictures in our heads of what people, objects, and events are like. We may never have actually experienced them, but we can infer what they are like. Such **mental images** influence our perception of people and events. I've never won the National Lottery. I wonder what it would be like to win. Can you imagine what it would feel like to have a great deal of money? These images might affect how I regard someone who has won a large prize. How would you feel if you learned that someone you know quite well had won a million pounds? How might this change your feelings or behaviour towards him or her? What mental image do you have of bullfights where people tease the bulls and stick spears into them when they charge? How might your image of foxhunting affect whether you would give permission for a hunt to cross your farm?

A related term is **mental concept**. Some objects have sufficient things in common to be classed into groups. Most cars have four wheels, an engine, seats, a steering wheel, and need drivers. Most chairs have four legs, a seat, and a backrest. Most houses have windows and doors. Our knowledge about these similarities form a mental concept of what they are like. If you know that most holiday trains are overcrowded and leave on time, then you may make a point of arriving at the station early to ensure you have a seat. If you know that most students are helpful and cooperative, then you may well ask a student to assist you in a project. Our mental images and mental concepts help us to understand our world and make life more predictable for us.

Exercise on mental representation

1 What are schemas?

2 Give two examples of the very first schemas that babies acquire.

3 A girl turns on a tap and some water comes out which is so hot that it hurts when she puts her hand into it. Identify the main schemas here:
(a) What new perception is the girl making?
(b) How might one of her existing schemas be changed?
(c) How could this help her behave more appropriately in the future?

4 What are mental images and mental concepts?

5 Give an example of how each of them can contribute to thinking.

Summary of cognition

Thinking is a part of cognition. It affects how people behave towards things generally, towards other people, and towards themselves. Thinking involves perceptions which are interpreted by existing schemas. Mental images and concepts are types of schemas. They help us to understand and deal with people and events in our world. Most importantly thinking and perception help us to adapt ourselves to the situations we are in.

Affiliation and attachments

Social affiliation refers to the way that people relate to each other, usually in a positive way. It includes the ways we get on together, cooperating, forming friendships, and even falling in love. In this chapter we will be looking at the very first experiences humans have of affiliation. Then, in Chapter 3, we will go on to discuss some of these ways of relating to one another. We form emotional bonds with some of our **caregivers** within the first year of our lives. These emotional bonds are usually called **attachments** or **attachment bonds**. An attachment isn't an absolute thing that a baby either has or doesn't have. Different babies will form different strength attachments with different caregivers. In this chapter we will discuss what these attachments are and why we have them. We will also examine the evidence for what happens when the bonds are never allowed to form or are disrupted by divorce.

▷ A caregiver is the person who generally looks after the child. It is usually a parent, but could be any other helper. Note that, in much early writing, the caregiver is often referred to as the mother. This can cause some confusion.

John Bowlby

Over a century ago **Charles Darwin** had argued that most animal behaviour resulted from genetically inherited instincts. These instincts included, chiefly, the need to survive in order to reproduce. It is essential that animals survive to maturity, find a mate, and produce offspring. Making successful attachments would have such important **survival value**. From the 1940s, **John Bowlby** had been investigating how and why babies make attachments.

Bowlby (and many others) believed that women have **maternal instincts** which drive them to have babies and care for them. This idea might have emerged from the way that many cultures divide up the roles that need to be filled in their society. Men often do the economic work, and obtain the family's food and shelter. Women, in many cultures, look after the young. That doesn't mean that the roles are genetically inherited or the result of instinct. Many mothers look after their children well and some claim they develop a 'sixth sense' which tells them when the baby needs attention, and which works even when the mother is asleep! This kind of claim gives support to the idea that childcare is the natural responsibility of women. As you can imagine, many other women dismiss the idea that they should be totally responsible for childcare.

What is attachment bonding?

▷
You will have noticed the emphasis on mothers rather than parents here. According to Bowlby, nature had given the role of bonding primarily to mothers. He did come to accept that people other than children's natural mothers could provide satisfactory bonding, but in his early writing the emphasis is very much on mothers.

Human babies are defenceless and need a great deal of care. It is important that someone provides this care. Bowlby thought that babies have an instinct to form an attachment. They need to be near their mothers, or to encourage their mothers to come to them, particularly when they are unhappy or unsure about something, Babies use such genetically inherited skills as, for example, smiling, crying, gazing, grasping, clinging, babbling or crawling in order to keep their mothers close to them. Bowlby believed that this would be a two-way relationship, and that mothers also have a biological need to be near, and to protect, their young.

The Penguin Dictionary of Psychology tells us that attachment is 'an emotional bond that is formed between an infant and one or more adults'. A colleague of Bowlby's, Mary Ainsworth, defines it as 'an affectional tie or bond that an individual ... forms between himself and another specific individual'.

The term bonding has been used with reference to two periods in a child's life. First, it can refer to a bond that is said to develop between a baby and its main caregiver in the hours immediately following birth. Second, it can refer to the attachment bond that occurs a few months after birth. In the next section we will review bonding in terms of the first of these two definitions.

How important are very early experiences?

▷
A sample is the group of participants chosen to be studied.

▷
The situation experienced by members of a control group isn't manipulated in any way. Whatever happens to them, and whatever they do is what normally happens and what people in their situation normally do. Any changes in the behaviour of the experimental group may well have been caused by the conditions they went through in the experiment.

Marshall Klaus and **John Kennel** conducted an experiment on early contact between mothers and babies in the mid-1970s. They claimed that the strength of the mother–baby bond is influenced by the amount of contact the mother had with the infant immediately after birth. They brought together twenty-eight expectant mothers, who were to be their **sample**. These twenty-eight mothers were divided into two groups. One was the **experimental group**, and the other was the **control group**. An experimental group is the part of the sample who will undergo some experimental procedures. This means that the conditions in which members of the experimental group find themselves will be manipulated in some way. In this study, the experimental group had sixteen hours more contact with their babies during their stay in hospital than the amount of contact in normal hospital routines. The control group, in contrast, underwent the normal post-natal hospital routine: seeing their babies for a few minutes just after they were born, then seeing them six to twelve hours later, after the babies had had the usual tests and the mothers had rested.

One month later, Klaus and Kennel interviewed the twenty-eight mothers and filmed them with their babies, including during a feeding

▷
A follow-up study is one where a group of people who had some similar experiences in the past are studied to see if any effects of their earlier experiences can be seen.

session. They claimed that the extended-contact group seemed generally to be emotionally closer to their babies, and held them much closer during feeding. Eleven months later, Klaus and Kennel conducted a **follow-up study**. The extended-contact mothers still cuddled and soothed their babies more than the mothers in the control group did, and were also more likely to say they had missed their babies after having been out. Their babies seemed more mature and sociable than those of the normal–routine group. They were also physically bigger and stronger. Five of the pairs in each group were studied again after two years, this time focusing on the language they used. The differences were still there. The mothers in the extended contact group used longer sentences, more adjectives, and needed to give fewer instructions.

Klaus and Kennel's evidence was quite revolutionary. However, while it is an attractive thought that human infants have the ability to take in and benefit from such early experiences, unfortunately, it does not seem highly likely that they really do. Although **neonates** have some (largely reflexive) skills, it is unlikely that they are very aware of much that is going on around them. Other researchers who have replicated Klaus and Kennel's procedures have not reached the same conclusion. Perhaps the original investigators chose to interpret what they saw as differences in the behaviour of the two groups, but what they saw may not have been quite so apparent to others.

▷
A neonate is a new-born baby.

Exercise on early experiences

1 What do Klaus and Kennel mean by:
(a) an extended-contact group, and;
(b) a normal-contact group?

2 What is an experimental group?

3 Why did Klaus and Kennel use a control group?

4 What is survival value?

5 What would Klaus and Kennel's results have contributed – if found to be true – to the study of survival value?

6 Explain your last answer.

Activity
On a sheet of paper, draw a table like the one on the following page, and label it 'Research on attachments'. For each research study quoted in this section, fill in a line of your table. Keep this in a safe place, as it will be very helpful at revision time.

Researcher	Subjects	Claimed	However
Klaus and Kennel			

●●● **Summary of very early experiences**
Klaus and Kennel's research into the effects of early contact between babies and their mothers in the hours following birth was intended to show that those who had most contact developed the strongest bonds. Although the researchers claimed to have found support for their idea, others who have conducted similar studies have not found that extra contact at such a young age makes any difference to the strength of the bond which develops.

How do we know if children have formed attachments?

By about eight months of age, babies could have become firmly attached to their primary caregiver. There are two ways of telling if a baby has formed a firm attachment. First, the baby does not show fear of the primary caregiver, but is afraid of strangers. Second, the baby is said to be attached if it becomes upset when the person to whom it is attached is away. These two conditions are called **stranger fear** and **separation distress**.

Stranger fear

For the first three months of their lives, most babies will respond in much the same way towards strangers as they will towards anyone else. By around four months of age they are likely to stare at people they don't know. By six months of age they often freeze if approached by a stranger. This fear gradually disappears as the child becomes more independent. Whether or not babies show stranger fear depends on several factors.

First, it depends on who the baby is with. If the baby is near to someone to whom it is attached, then it is less likely to be afraid. If the baby is being held by someone to whom it is attached, it will show little fear if a stranger approaches.

Second, it depends on where the baby is. If it is on its own in a familiar place it will show fear. If it is in a strange place but with someone whom it is attached to, it will show fear. If it is alone in a strange place (particularly in the open air) it will show less stranger fear, and may even allow itself to be picked up by a stranger.

Third, it depends on how the stranger behaves. If the stranger approaches slowly, talks quietly, and acts gently, then the baby will show less fear. If the stranger approaches more quickly and gets too close, tries to pick the baby up, or talks too loudly, the baby will show fear.

Exercise on the pattern of stranger fear

1 Under what conditions is a baby least likely to show stranger fear?
2 Under what conditions is a baby most likely to show stranger fear?
3 If you want to speak to someone who is carrying a 12-month-old baby, what might be the best approach to take?

The most obvious explanation for why a baby shows fear of strangers is that it is afraid that either it, or its caregiver, is going to be taken away by the stranger. Babies only show fear of adults they do not know. For some reason they do not show fear of unknown children. Perhaps this is because the baby hasn't much idea of what a child is until it is older. Babies develop stranger fear towards other children during their second year.

Separation distress

Children who are firmly attached to their caregivers, will become distressed when they become separated from them. **Mary Ainsworth** conducted a series of experiments, which have been repeated many times, called the **strange situation experiments**. In these, a child who had formed a strong bond was brought into a room by his or her attached caregiver. The room was wired for sound and vision. The caregiver put the child down, and left the room. The child, once aware that the caregiver had gone, became upset and cried. The caregiver waited and did not return for a while, to see if the child would settle (although the caregiver was able to return if the child's suffering increased unduly). Another person then entered the room, and the child's behaviour was recorded. Would the child ignore the stranger or would he or she not resist when picked up? Typically, Ainsworth found that children do not seek comfort from strangers, although they might accept it. If the caregiver re-enters the room the child will struggle desperately to return to the caregiver.

 Summary of attachment formation
As babies learn to recognize their caregivers, they learn associations between them and being comforted, fed, etc. They grow to be wary or even afraid of strangers who might separate them from their caregivers. As their attachments develop, so babies will show distress if they are separated from their caregivers.

The neonate's role in forming attachments

Although many psychologists do not believe that new-born babies (neonates) are born with the cognitive skills that are suggested by Klaus and Kennel's research, many do believe that neonates are born with some skills which allow them to attract and keep a caregiver's attention. These skills include smiling, gazing, looking, reaching, waving, and grasping. If babies fail to attract attention they may grizzle or cry. Babies will slowly learn whom they enjoy being with, and whom they feel safe with. To do this they must be capable of being **sociable**. A great deal of research has been conducted in the last 30 years – including some ingenious experiments and some detailed observations – on how babies appear to enjoy interacting with other people. Some of the conclusions of this research are summarized here.

Human babies seem to enjoy company. They will give social smiles within a few days of birth, and will start to imitate their caregivers' facial expressions after just a week or so. Babies also have reasonably good hearing and will turn their heads in the direction of a sound. (Our senses of sight and hearing are closely linked, right from birth.) Babies seem to have an **innate** preference for looking at round-shaped things (such as the human face), and for hearing the human voice too.

▷
Innate means inherited and present at birth.

Over thirty years ago **Ahrens** found that one-month old babies will smile at a picture which shows human eyes in an otherwise blank space. Over the next few months more details, such as a nose and a mouth are required to make a baby smile, and by five months the picture has to be three dimensional. Smiling babies are most likely to encourage their caregivers to smile and talk to them.

▷
How might there be some survival value in having a preference for face-shaped objects? (There is a note in the margin earlier which says what survival value is if you aren't sure.)

Ahrens' face shapes

Over twenty years ago **Robert Fantz** designed a set of apparatus called a **looking chamber** which allowed babies to be shown particular things, while their reactions were recorded. Fantz showed various pictures to babies aged a few days, and measured the amount of time they looked at each picture. He found that they preferred to look at round objects, especially those which were most like a face (see page 216).

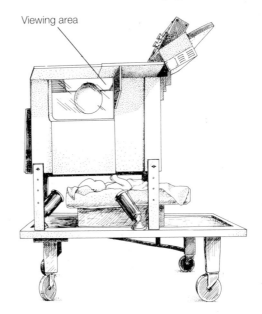

Viewing area

Fantz's looking chamber

Although both of these investigations have their critics, what they do suggest is that babies prefer looking at simple, symmetrical, pleasant objects. Whether this is because these objects are also characteristics of human faces is far from certain. It might be that having a preference for face-shaped objects has some survival value.

Genevieve Carpenter took a sample of babies aged between one week and eight weeks, and put them in some apparatus that had a viewing window at the top, and a small loudspeaker next to it. Through the window, the babies saw either their mother's face or a stranger's face. In both cases the babies could hear their mother's voice. By two weeks of age many of the babies seemed to be able to tell the difference between their mother and a stranger, and preferred to see their mother. When the mother's face was presented with the stranger's voice the babies looked away and became distressed.

In another experiment, Genevieve Carpenter showed the babies their mother's face, keeping perfectly still, and then showed them a face-shaped object (a flesh-coloured kitchen colander with three knobs on it which resembled two eyes and a nose). Finally, they saw a shop-dummy face. The babies were vaguely interested in the colander and the shop dummy. When they saw their mother's unmoving face they looked away. Carpenter's experiment suggests, therefore, that by just a few weeks of age, many babies:

(a) can recognize their mother's face;
(b) can recognize their mother's voice;
(c) expect the face and voice to go together, and;
(d) expect that the face should have movement.

The research so far has investigated the neonate's visual skills and preferences. Vision isn't the only sense that may be ready from very soon after birth to respond differently to human characteristics. **William Condon** and **Lewis Sander** played tape recordings of various sounds, including human speech, to babies who were just a few hours old. The neonates – who were all American – heard a recording of someone speaking with an American accent, another speaking Chinese, someone making vowel sounds, and then a regular tapping sound. The babies reactions as they heard the sounds were filmed. By two-days old, these babies started to move their arms and bodies in time with the American and Chinese speech, while not appearing very interested in the tapping or vowel sounds. This research suggests that humans may be genetically programmed for responding to human speech. (How might this ability have survival value?)

▷
All the research which suggests that babies have an innate preference for looking at or hearing certain sounds support the nature side of the nature–nurture debate.ʳ

Activity
Do biological structures or behaviour patterns which have survival value support the nature or the nurture view? Explain your answer.

Exercise on early skills

1 Define the following terms:
   (a) innate;
   (b) neonate;
   (c) survival value;
   (d) sociability.

2 Summarize the evidence so far on the visual and auditory (hearing) skills of a neonate. Include references to Klaus and Kennel, Ahrens, Fantz, Carpenter, and Condon and Sander.

3 What might the effects be on caregivers of a baby's abilities and willingness to be sociable?

4 What advice would you offer a new mother and father on communicating with their new baby?

▷ Picture two men having a conversation. One will speak at a time, often moving his hands and arms to illustrate his point, while also looking at the person he is talking to. The silent one remains quiet and still until it's his turn to talk. Babies appear to do something similar.

▷ Interactional synchrony describes the way in which people who are talking to each other take it in turns to move their bodies, which shows whether they are listening or talking.

So far in this chapter, we have been discussing communication skills in neonates. Babies develop other social skills during their first few months. **Colwyn Trevarthen** and **Martin Richards** filmed a sample of five babies for an hour each week throughout the first six months of their lives. Sometimes the babies were in their cots with toys hanging in front of them, and sometimes they were with their parents. Their behaviour was quite different in each situation. They explored and played with the toys when in their cots, but when they were with their parents they held a sort of **conversation**.

From around two months of age babies would open their mouths when their parent spoke to them, but remain silent, as though they were only preparing to reply. A few months later the babies and their parents took turns in their conversations. When a parent stopped speaking, the baby would make little sounds. This encouraged the parent to speak again, and again the baby would wait before answering. This highly elaborate activity seems to show that even very young babies are ready, willing, and able to communicate with their caregivers. The babies weren't communicating in order to make their parents do anything, such as feed or change them. They appeared to be communicating because both of them enjoyed it. Trevarthen and Richards gave the name **interactional synchrony** to the act of moving our face and body in time with what is going on around us. Condon and Sander's sample of babies who were just a few hours old showed interactional synchrony with the human speech they heard.

Daniel Stern has spent many years studying parent–child interaction. Although he agrees that there is an instinctive basis for attachment formation, he thinks too much is sometimes made of it. He believes that children develop an idea fairly soon after birth of who they are and what they can do, and that they do this through social interaction. He found that by three months old babies use the same face-to-face behaviour as two adults use. For instance, a baby boy looks for his mother. As his mother approaches, he looks away for a moment. Then he looks again and they hold eye contact. Then he breaks it. He will smile and move his head

Babies are said to be quite skilled at regulating the amount of contact they have. How might we observe this?

in time to what is being said. If he wants to 'butt in' while his mother is talking, he will do the same thing that adults do – he will raise his hands and his head (and his voice!).

Stern argues that babies are extremely good at regulating the amount of contact they have. They will let their caregivers know when they want company, which one of them they want to be talking, and when they want to rest. Stern maintains that all this behaviour is purely for fun, for mutual enjoyment, and for sharing each other's experiences.

Not everyone agrees with those researchers who believe that infants are able to begin, and to contribute to, conversations with their caregivers. Some researchers believe that babies are born with a few primitive reflexes, and that maturation and learning will be necessary before children are capable of any of the communication skills described by Trevarthen, Stern and others. For example, **Kenneth Kaye** argues that whenever infants behave in a way that appears to have some social meaning, such as by smiling, adults interpret the behaviour as though it actually did have this meaning, and treat the infants accordingly. Crying may be a reflexive response to pain or hunger. A parent will interpret a cry, and respond as though the child were actually asking for food. Kaye does not believe that tiny babies are capable of many of the social exchanges described earlier.

Not everyone agrees that babies are so sociable. We may misinterpret their sounds and movements as signs of sociability.

Exercise on early experience

1 What is interactional synchrony?
2 Give some examples of the ways in which – according to Stern – babies regulate the contact they have with their caregivers.
3 Explain Kenneth Kaye's objection to the claims of those who believe that babies have social skills.

▶▶▶ *Activity*
Construct a table like this and fill in the gaps:

Researcher	Claims	Kaye's reply
Trevarthen and Richards		
Dan Stern		

●●● **Summary of the neonate's role in early experiences**
Many psychological studies during the last thirty years have cast doubt on the idea that babies are helpless, passive creatures who have little awareness, less understanding, and no control over their situation. Evidence from Ahrens, Fantz, Carpenter, and Condon and Sander suggests that human babies may be biologically predisposed to interact with humans. Trevarthen and Richards, and Stern think that babies soon learn that social interaction with adults can be fun.

Comment on the neonate's role.

Whether neonates are capable of sociable responses of one kind or another at a given age is not really of great importance. What is important, however, is that caregivers and children establish firm attachment bonds. If these bonds are strengthened by communicating with each other, having cuddles and comfort, responding to the babies' needs, being loving, having fun, and so on, then the infants' awareness and abilities to respond are comparatively unimportant.

The caregiver's role in forming attachments

We have discussed the infant's role in forming attachments. We looked at how infants appear to be genetically prepared to interact with humans and able to form emotional relationships with them. We are less sure that caregivers have instincts to form bonds with their babies because, if they did, there would be few cases of child abuse or neglect. However, caregivers do develop attachment bonds. Developmental psychologists have asked why this is so. One reason may be that the infants attract the caregivers.

Most infants begin to use language at around the time of their first birthday. Until then they must use other signals for communicating their needs, for example, smiling, eye contact, gazing, reaching, grasping, and – at about six months – babbling. All these abilities are genetically inherited. Adults who are sensitive to these signals may become closely involved with their children. Any parent will tell you that one of the most powerful signals an infant has is that of crying.

No parents enjoy hearing their baby cry, so what can they do to reduce the baby's need to cry? **Silvia Bell** and **Mary Ainsworth** conducted a nat-uralistic-observation study of twenty-six mothers and babies in their own homes. Some of the mothers tended to their babies as soon as they began to cry. Others waited to see if they would settle on their own. Some mothers left their babies for several minutes, believing that otherwise they would learn that crying is the way to get whatever they want.

Bell and Ainsworth wanted to see whether there was any relationship between how quickly the mothers responded to their babies' crying, and the amount of crying the babies did. They found that babies cried if every-thing else failed to attract their mothers' attention. The mothers who responded quickest, and who were most attentive to their babies' needs, had babies who cried least. Babies were most likely to cry when they were left alone.

As they grow, infants learn ways other than crying to attract attention and so don't need to use crying so much, particularly if their caregivers have responded sensitively to them when they were younger. As Mary Ainsworth says, 'An infant whose mother has responded to his cries promptly in the past should develop both trust in her responsiveness and confidence in his increased ability to control what happens to him.'

Ainsworth uses the term **the sensitive mother** to refer to one who is

▷
Naturalistic observation is observation conducted in the subject's own natural environment. Its aim is that the subject's behaviour will, as a result, be more natural.

▷
Notice that again here it is only the role of the mother that is being identified. Are fathers and others not supposed to have any involvement in their infant's upbringing?

quick to respond to her baby's needs. A baby whose needs are met quickly should feel secure, and find it easier to become more independent later. The opposite of this may also be true: babies who are not sensitively dealt with may go on to become more demanding and insecure.

Exercise on crying

A young father flops on the settee in the lounge. He picks up the phone and rings his best friend.

'Hi Tom, its George'. His friend asks how he is, and he admits that he's worn out. Tom asks, 'How's the baby?' 'She's the reason I'm so tired', George sighs. 'She's lovely really and we both think the world of her. It's just that she seems to cry all the time. I can't understand it. Mum says that babies have to cry. She says its good for their lungs and I mustn't go to her as soon as she starts or she'll have me running around after her all the time. I put her down for four hours between feeds like Mum says. Her screaming is really wearing us out.'

1 What possible explanation can you give for the baby's constant crying?
2 What advice would you give George if you were Tom?
3 Describe one piece of research on young babies crying. What was its sample size, what method was used, and what are its conclusions?

 Summary of the caregiver's role
According to Bell and Ainsworth, sensitive caregivers realize that babies try to gain their attention in order to have some contact. Sensitive caregivers will respond quickly and enthusiastically to their babies' needs. Babies learn that their needs will be met, and are said to become more content and cry less.

▶▶▶ *Activity*
Ask some parents you know what their attitude is to their children's crying. Draw together your answers and work out what percentage of parents could be described as sensitive as opposed to less sensitive.

How many attachments can children make?

In 1964, **Rudi Schaffer** and **Peggy Emerson** reported the findings of their study of attachment behaviour in sixty Glasgow children. The children were studied from birth to eighteen-months of age. At monthly intervals the investigators asked the parents some questions about their children's social relationships, such as whom did they smile at, whom were they content to be left with, whom did they appear to be happy with, and so on. It seemed that the babies passed through four distinct stages.

1 The parents reported that, for the first six weeks, most of the babies didn't favour anyone, responding equally to all those who handled them.

2 Over the next twenty-four weeks, they became increasingly sociable, responding well to several caregivers.

3 By about seven months of age, they had begun to show preferences for the company of their main caregivers, and started to become wary of strangers. By this time, they were forming their first attachments.

4 Over the next few months, the infants were attaching to other caregivers too.

Schaffer and Emerson claimed that each attachment was equal in quality, and that the infants seemed to prefer some adults for some activities and other adults for others. For example, they appeared to want their mothers when they wanted comfort, and their fathers when they wanted rough-and-tumble play. As Schaffer says: '... being attached to several people does not imply a shallower feeling towards each one, for an infant's capacity for attachment is not like a cake that has to be shared out. Love, even in infancy, has no limits.'

Schaffer and Emerson's findings do not entirely support Bowlby's early predictions. Bowlby claimed that babies made one main attachment, whereas Schaffer and Emerson say they can make several attachments of equal quality. Bowlby said the mother was the first and main attachment object, whereas one-third of the Glasgow sample were found not to be attached to their mothers at all. Several were attached to their siblings. Older siblings were often used as baby-sitters, and siblings often spent more time together than the parents did with their babies. Babies formed attachments with those siblings who enjoyed their company. Children with brothers and sisters are more likely than single children to have to learn to compete and to share. They imitate each other and protect each other. They learn a great deal from these early relationships about love and rivalry, trust and aggression, and many other emotions.

By seven months of age, seventeen of the sixty children had formed two attachments. By ten months, thirty-six of the babies had formed two, and some had more. By eighteen months, fifty had two, and twenty-five of them had formed attachments with up to five caregivers.

▷
Siblings are brothers and sisters.

Exercise on multiple attachments

1 Define the term attachment.

2 Are attachments in infants:
   (a) genetically inherited;
   (b) socially learned in infants; or
   (c) both?

3 Explain your last answer.

4 What are multiple attachments?

5 Summarize the evidence from Schaffer and Emerson's study which suggests that children are capable of forming more than one attachment.

Summary of multiple attachments

Schaffer and Emerson's Glasgow study was a major challenge to Bowlby's claims that babies need their mothers. All the children formed successful attachments, and one-third of them didn't form them with their mothers at all. By their first birthday, over half the sample had formed two attachments of equal quality. Six months later, over three-quarters of them had more than one attachment.

▶▶▶ *Activity*

Find out from your parents how many people you attached to before you were a year old. Find out, also, how many people your brothers or sisters were attached to. Get everyone in your class to do the same. Add up the number of people to whom the males in your class were attached, and find the average. Do the same for the females in your class. Are there any differences between the two averages?

Comment on multiple attachments

Most developmental psychologists today probably agree that babies are capable of forming several attachments and that different attachment objects provide different kinds of stimulation for a baby. The benefits of multiple attaching include the babies' having several people to interact with and learn from, while the parents can share the childminding.

When and how do attachments occur?

From several studies of attachment behaviour we know that for the first three or four months babies do not mind whom they are with, as long as that person can look after them. By five months, most babies have learned whom they feel secure with, and by six to seven months they are expressing their preferences by trying to be close to their chosen caregivers. By around six to eighteen months, they are forming attachments with these chosen caregivers, if the caregivers, in turn, are willing and able to form attachments with them.

If we aren't certain about the importance of very early contact, we do know rather more about how attachment bonds develop later. First, we know that, in order to develop a relationship, the caregivers and infants concerned must spend some quality time together. That is to say that they must have fun together, enjoy one another's company, and interact reasonably often. We also know that young babies need to feel secure and confident that they will be both safe and, when they are upset, cared for.

Babies are willing to be sociable with just about anyone who pays them enough attention. After a few months a closer bond will emerge.

Exercise on the factors in bonding

Identify and explain the factors which each of the following researchers have found to be important in forming attachment bonds:

- Klaus and Kennel;
- Mary Ainsworth;
- Trevarthen and Richards;
- Daniel Stern;
- Schaffer and Emerson.

Is attachment bonding the same everywhere?

Most of the research reported in the West is from Europe or America. However, different patterns of bonding may occur in different parts of the world. Mary Ainsworth conducted a cross-cultural study of some parents and children of the Ganda people in Uganda, central Africa. She found that the children showed separation distress by five to six months of age – two or three months earlier than in the West.

Ganda children spend much of their time physically close to their parents, right from birth. They have more skin-to-skin contact. Ganda children sleep with their mothers, and are breast fed until they are about two years old. They go everywhere with their mothers, carried in a cotton sling. Being separated from their mothers would be very unusual, so they show more anxiety when it happens. Ainsworth concluded that Ganda children have formed attachments with their mothers by the ages of five or six months, which is two or three months earlier than attachments are formed in the West.

In Israel, a considerable number of families live in large agricultural communes called **kibbutzim**. These are made up of farms, some light industry, and some shops and offices in each kibbutz. The families try to be self-sufficient, growing and making enough to keep everyone fully employed. Everyone works, and should be regarded as equal in all respects. This has important implications for child-minding. In order to return to work and start contributing again, the mothers of new-born babies only stay with them for a few weeks. During this time they have lots of quality time together (much cuddling, talking, playing, etc.). The mother then goes back to work for a few hours a day, while a trained children's nurse (called a metapelet) looks after her baby. Gradually, the mother increases the number of hours she works, while the metapelet increases her time with the baby.

By the end of the first year the mother has returned to full-time work and the child is living in the Children's House with all the other youngsters. The children form strong attachments with their parents, and

▷ A cross-cultural study compares some aspect of people's living (such as child-rearing styles, attitude toward aggression or gender, etc.) in one culture with another.

▷ A danger in only studying people from one culture is that we may think that what we find about them would be true for everyone. This clearly is not true in this case.

▷ Kibbutzim are Israeli agricultural communes where all the people share in the work and the benefits of communal living.

usually with the nurse too. The reason why the kibbutz system works for many children is because children can make multiple attachments.

Exercise on cross-cultural data

1 Does the bonding behaviour observed in the kibbutzim confirm or reject John Bowlby's explanations? Explain your answer.
2 Does the behaviour confirm or reject Schaffer and Emerson's findings? Give reasons for your answer.
3 What are the advantages to psychologists of using findings from cross-cultural research? What does it allow them to show which they may not otherwise be able to show?
4 Outline one cross-cultural study of parenting.

●●● Summary of the origin of attachments

Studies in America and Britain suggest that babies begin to form attachments some time after they are six-months old. Mary Ainsworth found that it occurred earlier if there was a great amount of skin-to-skin and verbal contact between the infants and the caregiver. The attachment does not necessarily need to be with the parents. In a kibbutz, children attach with their parents and with their other caregivers.

What are the benefits of having secure attachment bonds?

Children who are firmly attached to one caregiver are likely to develop an awareness that they are safe and secure. They can use this caregiver as a safe base from which to explore their world. They may become more independent and adventurous, knowing that someone will take care of them if they are in trouble. You often see young children reaching out for their caregivers to pick them up, cuddle them, or protect them from something that appears to be frightening.

If a child is attached to several people, then the benefits are increased. For example, from the child's point of view there are several models to learn from. Young children can often choose one caregiver for comfort and another for rough-and-tumble play. From the caregiver's point of view, the children can be left to do other things without suffering separation distress, as they are being cared for by someone else.

Exercise on secure attachments

Secure attachments are good for both children and caregivers. Give as many reasons as you can think of for:

(a) why they are good for children, and
(b) why they are good for caregivers.

Summary of the benefits of secure attachments
There can be benefits both to the child and to the caregiver of having secure attachments. The child will feel safe and will be encouraged to explore. The caregiver will feel happy that the child is developing independence while still knowing that his or her caregiver is there to return to if the need arises.

What happens if attachments are insecure?

John Bowlby thought that instincts, which are a part of our genetic makeup, must not be frustrated, because normal, healthy mental development could be disrupted. (Bowlby's early training had included Freudian explanations of the role of instincts.) He thought that a useful way to discover the effects of forming attachments was to study children (and animals) who either had not formed them, or whose attachments had been disrupted. There are two ways to perform this study. One way is to find some older children or adults who are disturbed in some way, and look back at their early relationships to see whether or not they had formed good attachments. He did this by studying forty-four juvenile thieves who attended his clinic for disturbed children in London. The other way is to find young children who don't have the opportunity to form good attachments, and to see what they are like later. This was Goldfarb's, and Spitz and Wolf's approach.

It may be useful to bear in mind that most of the early researchers referred to here believed that babies and children need their mothers and that, if their mothering is disturbed, their future mental health may suffer.

Bowlby's forty-four juvenile thieves study

During the 1930s and 1940s, Bowlby worked at a clinic in North London for emotionally disturbed adolescents. Between 1936 and 1939 he studied the case histories of forty-four of his patients, all of whom had been thieves, and a few of whom had been convicted of theft. Their case notes revealed that seventeen of them (39 per cent) had been separated from their mothers for six months or more before they were five years old. Bowlby claimed that this maternal separation would have disrupted the children's attachment bonds. He found another forty-four adolescents who also had emotional problems, but who were not known to be thieves. Only two of this second group had been separated from their mothers. Bowlby concluded that **maternal deprivation** contributes to delinquency. Bowlby said: 'there is a very strong case indeed for believing that prolonged separation of a child from his mother (or mother substitute) during the first five years of life stands foremost among the causes of delinquent character development.'

Bowlby is saying that separating children from their mothers for some time during the first five years of its life makes it more likely that the children will behave like delinquents. Notice how the references are to

▷

Maternal deprivation literally means losing one's mother, but it is a term which extends to meaning losing the love, care, and attention that the mother provides. (Notice again the emphasis on the mother. Fathers today, of course, have much more involvement in their children's upbringing than Bowlby might have witnessed.)

mothers, and not caregivers. Bowlby thought that nature dictated the job of childcare and attachment bonding to be mainly for mothers. His evidence in this study comes from finding that almost 40 per cent of a sample of forty-four juvenile thieves had spent some time apart from their mothers during their early childhood.

Bowlby's analysis of his case studies revealed that fourteen of the seventeen juvenile thieves who had been maternally deprived were particularly cold and uncaring about their crimes, their victims, or even themselves. They seemed to feel no shame and had no feelings of guilt for their behaviour. They admitted that they almost certainly would continue to steal. They seemed quite detached from normal standards of decency and appeared to be incapable of normal emotions. Bowlby described their psychological condition as **affectionless psychopathy**. Bowlby believed that these cold and uncaring youngsters had suffered greatly from losing their mothers' love.

Comment on Bowlby's claims

There are several reasons to be cautious about Bowlby's claims. He appears to have overlooked some other factors. Were all the juvenile thieves well attached to their mothers before the separation? If not, then separating them probably would not have had much effect. He also dismisses the reasons for the separation. If the mother is removed because she is unfit, then it would not be the separation itself that caused the emotional disturbance. Many parents separate or divorce, but their children do not necessarily become delinquent.

Furthermore, he ignores all the other influences there are on children to behave in anti-social ways. They may have been influenced by the other children in their neighbourhood, they may have stolen for food or to escape from poverty and squalor, or simply for excitement. None of these reasons has anything to do with being separated from their mothers for six months before the age of five. Scientifically, Bowlby's sample of forty-four thieves isn't acceptable anyway because it is representative not of people generally, but of juvenile thieves only. It isn't acceptable to apply the findings from studies of people in one social group to people in quite different groups.

Exercise on Bowlby's juvenile thieves study

1 Outline the main scientific objections to Bowlby's study of juvenile thieves.
2 Name another study which shows that children who make early attachments are better adjusted than those who do not.
3 Name as many as you can of the types of stimulation that infants might benefit from.
4 Who could provide each of the types of stimulation you have identified?

Rene Spitz's orphanage studies

During the 1930s, **Rene Spitz** studied some children who were being raised in poor orphanages in South America. The orphanages were under-staffed, so the staff were overworked. They only had time to look after the children physically and had little opportunity to play with or stimulate the children. The children had very little appetite and were undersize and underweight for their age. They appeared unnaturally depressed and passive. They mostly ignored anything going on around them, because almost nothing ever did. Spitz claimed that children who were deprived of adults with whom to form attachment bonds for just three months would be highly unlikely ever to recover.

Spitz and Bowlby claimed that it was the frustration of their needs to form attachment bonds which would have caused these orphans' symptoms. However, the orphanages also failed to provide any other stimulation, such as play, games, nature walks, visits, etc. It may be that this lack of cognitive stimulation – as much as the lack of emotional stimulation – contributed to their depression.

Spitz and Wolf's penal institution study

In the 1940s **Rene Spitz** and **Katharine Wolf** had observed 123 babies in the first year of their lives. They were being cared for by their unmarried mothers in a penal institution in America. When the infants were aged between six months and eight months, their mothers were temporarily moved to another block and the infants were looked after by the mother of another child, or by a girl in the later stages of pregnancy. Throughout the three-month separation each child either did not see his or her mother at all, or at best, saw her once a week. Spitz and Wolf noted that the babies cried more, they lost their appetites, and they failed to gain weight during the separation from their mothers. The researchers concluded that these reactions were the result of being separated from their mothers. When their mothers returned the symptoms slowly disappeared.

Comment on Spitz and Wolf's study

What this study showed is that there are short-term physical effects of maternal deprivation, which occurred despite the alternative nursing that they received. However, would these effects have continued if other adults had gone on to provide high quality loving care? If fathers had been available, would we see the same effects? We don't know what these babies were like as adults, so we don't know if their separation had any permanent effects. This study doesn't show that babies must be cared for constantly by their mothers, but it does show that they become distressed when their routines are disturbed.

William Goldfarb's longitudinal study

William Goldfarb published the results of his longitudinal study of the effects of early and late adoption on children. Those children who were adopted early would have more opportunity to form effective attachment bonds with their new parents than would those adopted later.

Goldfarb followed up two groups of children from an understaffed and poorly equipped orphanage. The members of each group had been matched for age, sex, and the social background of their parents. One group consisted of babies who were adopted before they were nine-months old. They were brought up as members of normal families. The other group had all spent at least the first three years in the orphanage before they were adopted. Goldfarb visited each child on four occasions, when the children were 3, 6, 8, and then 12 years old. On each occasion he measured their intelligence, language, skills, and level of social maturity. He also investigated their ability to form relationships. In each case the children in the early-adopted group performed better than those from the late-adopted group. To put it another way, those children who had been looked after by a mother from a very young age, and who could form early attachment bonds did better than those who weren't placed with a family until later.

A longitudinal study is carried out on the same people over a period of months or years. Such a study can show the effects of changing environments and of age and maturation on behaviour.

Comment on Goldfarb's research

Although the evidence here looks quite convincing, even this study does not take account of other possible explanations for why the early-adopted group were more socially, emotionally and intellectually mature. First, the assumption is made that the early-adopted children would have made effective attachments and that the late-adopted children would not. Yet we know that much older children than 3-year-olds can make successful attachments. Second, the early-adopted children may have been brighter to begin with, which could explain why they were chosen by their adoptive parents.

As in Spitz's study, the late-adopted group lacked all sorts of stimulation in the orphanage, not just maternal comfort. For their first nine months they had been isolated in cubicles to prevent the spread of any infectious diseases, and so had had little human contact. The next two years weren't much better, as their nurses had little time to spend with them. This lack of human contact and stimulation may well have had an effect on their future development, but has nothing to do with separation from their mothers.

Summary of Bowlby's evidence

John Bowlby collected evidence to support his view that children need the continued presence of a mother figure for healthy emotional development. His own study found that many children who were emotionally disturbed had been separated from their mothers during their early years. He quoted studies by Goldfarb, and Spitz and Wolf which pointed to the benefits of being reared in a more normal family unit (with a mother). However, each of the studies has its limitations.

James and Joyce Robertson's studies

James and Joyce Robertson conducted some observational studies of children who were between about seventeen months and three years, between 1948 and 1952, and followed these up later, during the 1960s. The children went into hospital or were placed in residential nurseries, separating them from their caregivers for periods from a few days up to several weeks. The Robertsons were convinced that separating babies from their mothers was harmful. The medical profession disagreed. The Robertson's obtained a cine camera and made eight films of children during their separation which could be shown to people involved in caring for children.

Here is a summary of the observations on one separated child.

> John (aged seventeen months) was put into a fairly typical residential nursery for nine days while his mother had a second child in hospital. His father was at work all day, and there were no relatives nearby to look after him. Four of the five other children at the nursery had been there almost all of their lives. They were noisy, demanding, and aggressive. John was a quiet, loving child. He seemed troubled by the noise and fighting going on around him, and tried to approach the nurses for some attention. They had to spend most of their time with the more demanding children, and John was left out. Even when he managed to obtain their attention they soon had to put him down to tend to one of the others. John's protests and anger were ignored. After some days his distress worsened. He started to cry pitifully, for long periods of time.

> This distress lasted for several days. The nurses gave John all the attention they could, but it was nowhere near enough. He began to refuse food, and he wouldn't sleep. With each day that passed John's condition worsened. His cries of distress became huge sobs of despair.

> As the separation neared its end, John's behaviour changed again. He stopped trying to be near to the nurses. Instead he would play with whatever toys he could, particularly a large cuddly toy. He began to ignore his father on his nightly visits. John slowly became emotionally detached. When his mother finally came he didn't seem to want to know her. He wouldn't go to her, wouldn't look at her, and resisted her attempts to comfort him.

> John had started by being loving, and seeking companionship. Over the nine-day separation he had changed to being distressed, despairing, and finally to appearing emotionally detached.

▷ Emotional detachment can be a very serious condition. Children reject comfort, stimulation or guidance. They become removed from normal life and cannot join in with family or school activities. They lack love and have little fear of the consequences of their behaviour. If they continue in this vein, it could lead to affectionless psychopathy.

The Robertsons suggest that children who are separated from their mothers for several days will pass through the same sequence of behaviour as John. They call it the **syndrome of distress**. The child becomes distressed, then despairing, and then, if not attended to, the child will become emotionally detached. However, the Robertsons are not saying that babies or children must always be near their mothers. What children do need is fairly continuous, high-quality care. They should have this from their caregivers. If they have to be separated from their main caregivers, then continued high-quality care provided by someone else can help them through the separation.

Exercise on the Robertson's research

1 What is meant by maternal deprivation?
2 What name did John Bowlby give to the condition which described someone who appeared to have no emotions and no guilt feelings?
3 Bowlby claimed that we develop a need to be near our mothers through evolution because it has some survival value. What does survival value mean?
4 Outline the syndrome of distress.
5 Why did John become emotionally detached?
6 What advice would you give to the nurses in the residential nursery if such a situation were to happen again?

●●● Summary of the Robertson's research

James and Joyce Robertson made some challenging films of young children in periods of brief separation from their normal routines, and especially away from their parents' care. They wanted to make health-care professionals realize that it is potentially damaging to separate children from their parents. Despite fierce resistance and criticism their message eventually won through and routines began to change.

▶▶▶ Activity

Imagine that you have been consulted by a director of social services who wants you to write a brief summary of the effects of having secure or insecure attachments. What recommendations would you make?

Do children really need mothers?

In the early days of the kibbutz system, when it was thought that children could be brought up with little family assistance, many of the children suffered emotional problems (see page 39). The critics claimed that this showed that children need mothers. Automatic assumptions were again being made: that caregiver necessarily meant mother, and that children's early experiences with their mother were fundamentally important to their later emotional, social, and personal development. Both these views have since been re-examined. For example, we know that in the modern kibbutz children can make relationships with several others and do not suffer ill effects from not being reared exclusively by their mother.

Michael Rutter's correlational studies

Michael Rutter and his colleagues did not believe the claim that early experiences automatically would have a disturbing effect on later behaviour. They studied a group of 9- to 12-year-old boys on the Isle of Wight. They also conducted a study of a group of children in London whose parents had suffered some mental problems. Rutter was seeking to understand, in particular, the causes of anti-social behaviour, such as juvenile delinquency and theft, rather than the role of the mother in childrearing. However, he looked for any correlations between separation from either parent and increasing levels of anti-social behaviour. He found no positive **correlation** between juvenile delinquency and separation from either mother or father.

▷ Correlation is a statistical technique for measuring whether two variables seem to change together. It looks at whether a change in one variable matches a change in another.

Rutter did find a positive correlation between the amount of stress which children felt, and the likelihood of their becoming involved in anti-social behaviour. He asked a large number of questions about their early family lives and felt able to divide his sample of adolescents into those coming from good families, from fair families, and from poor families. Good families were those which provided warm, loving, and secure relationships, free from high levels of stress. Rutter found no increase in anti-social behaviour in the children from these homes, or in children from homes described as fair. However, he did find a positive correlation between coming from a poor, stressful home and being involved in anti-social behaviour. In other words, children whose parents argue and fight constantly were more likely to behave in anti-social ways.

▷ It is not the loss of a parent which correlates with the anti-social behaviour, it is the atmosphere in which the family members live. Conflict in the home produces anxiety in the children, which correlates with anti-social behaviour when they grow up.

Ann and Alan Clarke have consistently challenged the idea that the early years are so important and have such great influences on future mental health. They quote several studies of baby animals and humans who have been separated from their parents yet who are not emotionally scarred for life. We will discuss some of them here.

The Bulldogs Bank study

In 1946 **Anna Freud** (Sigmund Freud's daughter) and **Sophie Dann** began a case study of six war orphans who, with their mothers, had been placed in concentration camps by the Nazis during the second World War. Their parents had been killed not long after their imprisonment and the infants were looked after as well as possible by some of the other prisoners. Conditions were very hard, food was scarce, and there were no toys. It would have been impossible to form any strong bonds with adults, as none would have been around for long enough. After the war the infants were moved to several camps, until they eventually arrived at the Bulldogs Bank reception centre in the Lake District in England. At the time of their arrival, the youngest was approximately three years old, and the oldest was about three years and ten months.

> The six children had several things in common. They had probably never known their mothers. They had no opportunities to form attachments with caregivers. They had endured awful living conditions and received virtually no stimulation of any kind. They had

been moved around a lot, and so were not pleased at being moved again. They couldn't talk very much, and they knew only a few German and Czechoslovakian swear words. They didn't know what to do with normal toys, and they destroyed all of the toys they could find – and most of the furniture too! They did each adopt one special toy, usually a cuddly toy, which they kept near them and always took to bed with them.

They were also fairly hostile and aggressive towards adults. They would only turn to an adult if they actually needed something which they couldn't have in any other way. Two other things they had in common were that they had been together for all their lives and they were totally devoted to each other. They did everything together and refused to be separated for any reason. For example, if one couldn't go out, none would want to go out. If one woke up at night, the others would soon be awake. When one stopped eating, they would all stop eating. They did everything as a group. There wasn't any single child who was always the leader, each would take the lead in different activities. To put it simply, they appeared to be totally attached to each other.

▷

These children had had no opportunities to form attachments with adult caregivers but had formed attachments with each other.

Although they each had different needs it was impossible to treat any one of them as an individual, as they were always together as a group. No one child was dominant all the time: they cooperated over nearly everything. Eventually they learned to speak and play like normal children. Gradually they formed emotional relationships with some of the adult members of staff. They slowly recovered from their early deprivation, but remained attached to each other.

What this study shows is that children can survive without mothers, although we do not know if any of these children suffered emotional problems in their later lives.

Exercise on six war orphans at Bulldogs Bank

1 What kind of mothering do you think the children received throughout their first few years?
2 How would you describe and explain their behaviour towards each other?
3 What does John Bowlby mean by affectionless psychopathy, and what might cause it?
4 Bowlby said that children who hadn't made attachments to their mothers would suffer later on in their lives. What alternative explanation might the Bulldogs Bank study suggest?

Orphanage studies

Barbara Tizard, Judith Rees, and Jill Hodges conducted a follow-up study of sixty-five children from deprived families who had been placed in residential nurseries before they were six months old. They hadn't formed strong attachments, and they didn't have the opportunity to form any in the nursery either. There were plenty of toys and games and other stimulating materials. The nurses rarely stayed long before going to find other jobs and, while they were there, they were discouraged from becoming too involved with the children. Apart from being fairly noisy, rather afraid of strange adults, and very clinging, the children seemed to be coping fairly well in their nursery.

Some children were adopted when they were between two to three years of age. Some were returned to their natural mothers who were better able to cope than before, and some stayed in the nursery (because their mothers couldn't be found and so couldn't sign the forms for the babies to be adopted). Barbara Tizard and her colleagues followed up these three groups, as well as a control group of babies (who were being brought up in a 'normal' family). The four groups were all studied at the age of two, then at four-and-a-half, and then at eight years.

At two years of age the nursery children were all fairly similar. They were largely unattached. They were quite different from the controls, who were more secure and independent.

By four-and-a-half years of age, some differences between the nursery groups were emerging. Those who had been adopted formed attachments with their new parents, but made great demands on them. They had almost caught up with the controls intellectually, but their emotional behaviour was not as advanced. They were still rather shy and weren't very adventurous. They would cling to their parents, and still showed stranger fear. The next most mature group, at four-and-a-half years, comprised those infants who had stayed in the orphanage. They received some stimulation, both from toys and from humans. They were often noisy and boisterous. Some had made weak attachments. The least well-developed intellectually were those who had been returned to their mothers. Their families still lived in rather deprived conditions and the children lacked two of the main things they seem to need for healthy psychological development: people who enjoy interacting with them, and things to play with and manipulate.

By eight years of age those in the adopted group were still the most advanced group, (after the controls). They had developed strong attachments but were still rather restless and timid. They didn't make friends as easily as the controls, and they were still rather clinging towards their new parents. The lack of early stimulation was still being felt. They weren't able to concentrate on schoolwork for very long either. Those who returned to their mothers, and those who had stayed in the orphanage were not as well developed in their social relationships, or intellectual abilities.

Evidence from this and other studies suggests that children can overcome even the most deprived early experiences. Adoption into a family that desperately wants a child, and which is capable of providing the kind of care the child needs, is the best solution for a child from a deprived background. John Bowlby claimed that children need their mothers, and

▷
Children who have to be separated from their caregivers used to be placed in residential nurseries. Temporary fostering is much more usual today.

▷
Having continuous care and attention will help babies and young children feel secure and confident. It may not be a mother, necessarily, who provides that care and attention.

▷
Children need care, comfort, love and stimulation. Families are in an ideal position to provide these things. However, families and caregivers do not have to be mothers. Others can meet children's needs just as well.

that even a bad home is likely to be better than a good institution. Tizard's study does not support this claim. The children who were returned to their mothers did not develop as well as many of the others who were adopted. An American study by **Alfred Kadushin** found that children up to the age of twelve have been adopted satisfactorily, and have developed good, loving relationships.

Severe deprivation and isolation

In 1972 **Jarmila Koluchova** began reporting the case of identical twin boys in Czechoslovakia who had suffered the most severe deprivations.

The mother died soon after the twins were born (in 1960) and their father had to place the children in care. Their father remarried a few months later and the twins returned home when they were eighteen months old. Their stepmother had no interest in bringing up young children (despite having had four of her own) and was selfish and uncaring. The father was of below average intelligence, and his job on the railways took him away from home quite a lot. The family had recently moved to a city suburb where nobody knew them, or knew that the family should have contained six children.

Their stepmother treated the twins terribly. They were kept in a small unheated room with a sheet of polythene for a bed and with very little furniture. They were poorly fed. Sometimes the mother would lock them in the cellar and beat them with a wooden kitchen spoon, covering their heads with a mattress in case anyone heard their screams. The twins suffered these conditions for five-and-a-half years. When they were finally examined, at the age of seven, they were severely physically and mentally retarded. Their bodies were covered in scar tissue from the beatings. They had severe rickets (a disease of the bones caused by lack of vitamin D). They couldn't stand up straight, walk or run, and their coordination was poor. They hadn't been taught to speak, had no knowledge of eating habits and were very frightened of people, and of the dark. It was impossible to give them a standard intelligence test as they couldn't understand the instructions, and they weren't familiar with things like pictures, which were included in some of the tests. It was estimated that their IQ would have been in the 40s. (The average IQ is 100.) Their stage of development was equivalent to that of a child aged three years.

The twins were put in hospital until they were well enough to go to a special school for mentally disadvantaged children. There they made good progress. When they were more sociable they were fostered by a particularly kind and loving woman who lived with her sister, who had already fostered children. By the age of eleven the twins' speech was normal for their age. They enjoyed reading and playing the piano, and they were both fairly active. By the age of fifteen, the twins' IQ scores were normal, and their emotional state had improved greatly. The atmosphere at home was warm and friendly and, although the boys still remembered their early experiences, they rarely talked about them, even to their foster mother.

It appears that even these terrible early experiences could be overcome with the right kind of care. Koluchova's latest report on the twins (in 1991) showed that they had continued to make progress and they have made a full recovery from their earlier mistreatment. **Ann and Alan Clarke** claim that if early experiences were so important then these children would be emotionally disturbed for the rest of their lives. At the very least they would suffer severe affectionless psychopathy, they claimed – but they didn't.

Another study by the Robertsons

Earlier we mentioned the Robertson's study of a seventeen-month-old infant called John, in a residential nursery (see page 45). The Robertsons studied several such children, and noticed the same sequence of behaviour in each of them. The sequence started with protest or distress, this gave way to despair, and finally turned into detachment. One reason why John had suffered was because no one would offer to be a substitute caregiver for him.

Thomas was one of four children to whom the Robertsons offered temporary fostering in their own home. He was twenty-eight months old (a year older than John) when his mother went into hospital to have another baby. The Robertsons visited Thomas in his own home before his mother went away and he visited their home to become familiar with it.

Thomas settled in with the Robertsons well, although he obviously missed his mother. Every day during the separation Thomas received constant, patient, high-quality care from Joyce Robertson, supported by her husband and teenage daughter, Jean. Thomas had brought some favourite things from home, including a photograph of his mother and him together. Thomas was pleased when his father visited each night, but became understandably upset when his father had to leave. Thomas also had a few problems with food and sleep, and as the separation went into the second week he did cry more for his mother. Nevertheless Joyce Robertsons' patience and reassurance always quietened him.

When Thomas's mother finally came to take him home he was happily and successfully reunited with her. He had changed a little. He was rather more aggressive and harder to control than he had been before. Separating him from his usual routines may have had some unfortunate effects, despite the care he had received. However, there was a new baby in the family and Thomas wouldn't be quite the centre of attention that he had been. This may have been enough, anyway, to affect some of his behaviour following his return.

Exercise on the Robertson's study of Thomas

1 Outline briefly the main differences between the ways in which John and Thomas were treated. Mention in your answer the main differences in the ways the two boys responded.
2 What do you think was the point of Thomas's bringing some toys and a photograph from home?
3 What is meant by the 'syndrome of distress'?
4 Why didn't Thomas suffer the worse symptoms of the syndrome of distress?

 Summary of the evidence against Bowlby

Bowlby said that growing up at home – even in a poor home – would be preferable to growing up in even the best institution, as the mother–child attachment bond could develop at home. However, studies show that some children reared in orphanages cope rather better than those reared at home. The twins studied by Jarmila Koluchova, for instance, were raised in the poorest of conditions and had no parenting until they were well past the age of five, which is the age that Bowlby thought was essential for establishing attachment bonds. They appear to have recovered well. Neither would children who were separated necessarily suffer if top-quality alternative care – such as that provided by Joyce Robertson – could be provided for them.

Conclusion to the attachment debate

Bowlby claimed that babies make one central attachment to one main caregiver: their mother. Although that caregiver would not have to be the baby's natural mother, in most cases it would be. Bowlby thought that there would be a hierarchy of attachments, with the mother at the top and all other attachments being inferior to that one. In Schaffer and Emerson's Glasgow study, about half of the sample of sixty children had also made attachments to their fathers or other family members within two months of making their first attachment. Each attachment can be of equal strength and equal value for the child.

Barry Lester and his colleagues found that the babies they studied had all made strong attachments with their mothers by the time they were nine months old, but had also attached to their fathers by twelve months. Fathers are often more playful with their babies, whereas mothers are often more nurturant. As we mentioned earlier, fathers offer rough-and-tumble activities. They can also be gentle with their infants, and the infants can form strong emotional ties with them.

Michael Lamb went further. He had noticed how babies choose and use different caregivers for different activities. Babies appeared to prefer their mother's company if they were distressed. They would respond to their mother's soft soothing voice and gentle cuddles. However, they seemed to prefer their fathers for rather more adventurous activities. These three things – tenderness, emotional warmth, and more physical activities – might help babies use their father as a safe base from which to explore the world.

Dan Stern has shown that babies can signal their needs to their parents and help to regulate the type and amount of contact that they received. This suggests that they are quite aware of their own needs and soon learn how to express them. They interact with other humans for enjoyment. Trevarthen and Richards have shown how interactions between babies and caregivers are like conversations, with each partner taking turns.

It seems that much of the evidence today does not support Bowlby's view that babies make only one central attachment to their mother. Rather it appears they can make several attachments, each of which is of equal value. They may make their *first* attachment with their mother, but soon other attachments can be made.

It is important to note, however, that not everyone agrees that babies are so capable of communicating their needs. Kenneth Kaye believes that this is simply what rather optimistic observers would like to think.

Despite these reservations Bowlby's view of the early importance of mother-child bonds did appear to explain many of the problems that parents and doctors had noticed. What he said about children and mothers seemed to fit the facts. Several professions concerned with children began to change some of their practices to avoid unnecessary separation of mothers and children. For example, hospital wards started to allow young children to stay with their mother for longer periods, if the mother wasn't too ill. In some cases cots were provided so that children could sleep near their mothers. Mothers would be allowed to stay with her child, if the child became ill. Many social workers were taught to regard the separation of the mother from her child as the worst possible solution to a family's problems. Bowlby had claimed that 'a bad home is better than the best institution'. Whatever difficulties stood in the way of the mother and her child staying together, they must be overcome if at all possible.

Children and divorce

Every year it seems that more couples are seeking divorce, and many of these couples have children. There has, however, been very little systematic research into the effects on children of their parents' divorce. For example, we do not know for certain whether it is better for most children to grow up with parents who continue to live together despite being unhappy together, or, following a divorce, with one parent only, or with one parent and a step parent. Michael Rutter found a possible link between unhappy parents' living together and children's showing signs of disturbed behaviour. It appears that step families (often including step brothers and sisters) may be preferable to being reared by a lone parent.

The precise effects that divorce will have on a child will be determined by many things. Here is a short summary of the main ones.

- How close was the child to either parent?
- How old is the child and how much can they understand?

▷
Do not think that a child whose parents have divorced will be inevitably cut off from the parent who has left. This is rarely the case. It could be that the child actually has more quality time with the absent parent following the divorce.

▷

During the crisis phase children feel resentful and angry. Younger children might also blame themselves.

▷

There may be a sex difference in the ways that males and females cope with their parents' divorce, but any effects will be influenced by so many other factors.

• What is the relationship between the parents following their divorce?

Mavis Hetherington has identified the **crisis phase**, as distinct from the **adjustment phase**. For a year or so following the divorce many children feel angry and depressed. They may feel guilty, believing that they caused their parents to divorce. Some become disobedient and resentful. These changes can affect the parents too. Coping with the changes to their own lifestyle is bad enough, but they also have to cope with changes in their children's behaviour. This is the crisis phase. It can be made better or worse by the actions of the divorced parent and the behaviour of other brothers and sisters.

There may be a sex difference here. It is more usual for children to stay with their mother following a divorce. A girl is often closer to her mother than she is to her father and may, therefore, have identified more with her mother than with her father. A girl may feel the loss of a father less than a boy would feel it, as he may have identified more with his father. In Hetherington's own long-term study she found that most daughters had recovered from the effects of the divorce by the end of the second year, but she claimed that many boys took longer to recover. However, other studies have not found any particular differences between the sexes. **M.A. Fine** and her colleagues found that it rather depended on the relationship the child had with each of the parents in the year before the divorce. If a boy was closer to his father then he would feel the loss more intensely.

During the adjustment phase children become accustomed to their new circumstances. They may continue to blame one parent or the other, and wish the two might be together again. These anxieties reduce with the passage of time. The adjustment phase may be achieved more quickly if the children understand that their parents were unhappy when they were together.

Hetherington's study showed that children of unhappy parents were generally happier a year or so after the divorce than children whose parents stayed together. **Judith Wallerstein** and **Joan Kelly** also claim that 'an unhappy couple may well divorce for the good of the children,' and that 'an unhappy marriage for the parents is also unhappy for the children'. As Rutter showed, conflict between parents may lead to emotional disturbance in children. As Wallerstein and Kelly say, 'a divorce that promotes the happiness of the adults will benefit the children as well'.

Exercise on children and divorce

1 Name some of the factors that influence what effects a divorce can have on a child.
2 Summarize Rutter's study and his conclusions.
3 Do children always suffer when their parents divorce? Explain your answer.
4 If parents are planning a divorce, how should they prepare their children so that the children do not feel guilty or resentful?

Summary of the effects on children of their parents' divorcing
Despite increasing numbers of children living in lone-parent families there
haven't been many detailed studies of the effects that their parents'
divorcing might have on them. There are many factors involved, including
the children's level of maturity, their experiences with their parents, the
parents' experiences, and what happens after the divorce. Generally,
children whose parents and home are unhappy are less well adjusted than
children of unhappy but divorced parents.

Social relationships

In the last chapter we examined the first relationships children make with their caregivers. As they become more socially aware, children begin to form relationships with others. We will look at how children's friendships change with age and experience. As people become more aware of others, so their behaviour changes when others are around. They might conform to other people's expectations. In this chapter we will examine these changes, and the evidence for them that has been gathered from studies of obedience in people. Finally, we will look at the factors which influence people's attraction to others.

Friendships in children

As we saw in Chapter 2, the first meaningful relationships in children's lives are with their caregivers – usually their parents. For the next year or two children don't take much notice of other children and haven't really formed friendships. Even an older brother or sister may not be thought of as a friend. Children aged around two years are mostly concerned about themselves. They play on their own, practising and mastering simple skills such as coordination, and exchanging objects, such as rattles, with adults. They don't mix well with other children. Any other child that a 3-year-old does play with might be considered a friend for a few minutes, or even a few hours. The next day that child may be just another person.

▷
The first play activities a child participates in are described as solitary play and involve the child in learning simple skills.

Friendships in young children

If children have brothers or sisters, or if they live in an area where there are many other children, they will learn about friendships sooner than children who don't have the same opportunities. Some children are socia-

Two children who are each playing a
similar game alongside each other are
described as performing parallel play.
After this comes associative play as
each of them begins to recognize the
other's games.

ble and responsive, while others are more withdrawn. These factors will
influence every child's ability to form relationships with others.

Young children will play alongside each other but, because they don't
interact, they aren't forming friendships. They begin to take notice of
each other and may exchange toys or other playthings. Some time
between the ages of three or four, a child may start to form special friendships with particular children. While these friendships last, they are
usually quite intense. Even at this age, children can be fiercely loyal to one
another. Within a day or two, however, the child may meet someone else
and form a new special friendship, and so it goes on. Their play is rather
like two individuals playing together, although separately. Both want to
do the more interesting or exciting things.

Friendships in middle childhood

By the age of about five, children are highly mobile and have plenty of
energy. They have some idea of their own sex and what is expected of
them. They usually prefer the company of members of their own sex, but
are still unlikely to share and cooperate fully. They have difficulty in
'taking turns', and their friends are liked because of what they will do for
them.

Children choose their friends simply from those people that they see
most often. This is one of the factors that influences older people too, as
we shall see later on. Other things that may influence adults – such as
intelligence, personality, skin colour, social-class background, etc. – are
not normally taken into account by children, unless someone else points
them out.

By the age of six, children are gradually learning to cooperate with each
other. Friendships formed at this stage could last for many years.

Children are forced to be together at school, sometimes for the first
time. Teachers encourage cooperation and sharing, so children's attitudes
towards others shift from using them to helping them. Friendship may
blossom in situations where children have, for example, been seated
together, or where they share paints, pencils and other materials. They
may play on the same side in team games and support one another against
others.

Friendships in older children

After puberty, sex hormones encourage children to take an interest in
members of the opposite sex. Friendships will include opposite-sex
members often for the first time. The circle of friends often widens as
children form gangs or groups and individuals compete to be most
popular. Friends are increasingly drawn from those people who have
things in common such as interests, attitudes, and backgrounds.

▶▶▶ *Activity*
The next time you see children playing, try to identify what kind of play
they are using, based on how involved they are with other children.

Exercise on what makes a friend

In 1979 *Psychology Today* magazine published its findings from a survey of 40,000 readers. The readers were asked: 'what are the qualities you feel are most important in a friend?' Here are their top ten choices, in order of preference.

1 Keep confidences	6 Sense of humour
2 Loyalty	7 Willing to make time for me
3 Warmth and affection	8 Independence
4 Being supportive	9 Good conversationalist
5 Frankness	10 Intelligence

1 Which of these would you agree are important in a friend?
2 Would you add any others? If so what would they be?
3 Rewrite your list in your order of importance.
4 Would you say you love your best friend?
5 If the question is asked about the characteristics of the kind of person you would fall in love with, write your top ten choices.
6 What is the difference between friendship and love?

Summary of friendships

Very young children play alone, or side-by-side with others. From the age of about three they will describe someone as their friend, although have no idea of what that means. When children start school, friendships are usually temporary, and usually with members of the same sex. After puberty, friends from the opposite sex usually become important.

Social facilitation: the presence of others.

Children soon learn that what they do affects what other people think about them and do with them. Bandura says that we need adults to be models for us to imitate, to guide us, to approve of us, and to discipline us. Children learn to give a good impression of themselves as they learn that it is likely to gain them some reward, such as adult approval. Well-adjusted humans learn to be concerned with what other people think about them, and the presence of others often affects their performance. These effects are known as **social facilitation**.

Social facilitation was investigated in one of the first experiments in social psychology which was performed by Norman Triplett in 1898. As a cyclist he had noticed that other cyclists rode faster when they were in company than when they were alone. He thought that they were competing with each other without even realizing it. To test this idea he asked children to wind 150 turns of a fishing reel. He told them that it was not a race and they didn't have to wind quickly. He timed them, without their knowing that he was timing them. Some of the children were tested alone, others in pairs. When in pairs, the children wound their reels faster than when they were alone. The effect was even more pronounced when the

▷ Social facilitation refers to any effect that the presence of other people has on an individual's behaviour.

▷ Triplett concluded that the presence of others speeds performance by triggering a desire in people to compete.

children were told to wind the reels quickly. Triplett said that the presence of other children speeds up performance.

During the 1920s **Floyd Allport** found what he called a **coaction effect**. A coaction group is one where the members work side by side, often performing the same task, or a similar task, but without interacting with each other. Writing a timed essay in class or filling in a test questionnaire are examples of coaction.

Allport asked some people to solve some problems at their own pace. Some of the tasks were simple, such as crossing out all the vowels in a newspaper article. Other tasks needed more attention, such as finding what was wrong in a series of statements. Allport still found that his subjects worked faster when in groups than when alone. However, the subjects made more errors in the more difficult tasks than in the simple ones. It seems that a coaction effect appears to speed up people's performance of simple tasks, but slows down their performance of more complicated tasks. Having people around us interferes with our concentration.

The coaction effect doesn't always occur. People do not always put more effort into a task when there are others performing the same task around them. Sometimes they make less effort. For instance, many children sing less enthusiastically in a choir than they do when they're singing a solo. Knowing that there are others doing the same thing means that any one can get away with doing less. This is known as **social loafing**. It was demonstrated by **Bibb Latané** and his colleagues in the late 1970s. They asked students to make as much noise as they could. Each student made rather more noise alone, than when tested in groups. It takes some effort to make a lot of noise, so each student let the others make more effort! When they were told that their own, individual efforts would be tested, they made more noise again.

Social loafing is more likely to appear under three conditions. First, if you do not feel responsible for the progress or achievements of the whole group you may not make a great effort. After all, who would know that the group's failure to achieve has anything to do with your particular contribution? Second, if the task the group is performing is boring you aren't likely to bother much. If a lesson in school were boring you wouldn't bother to answer any questions unless you had to. Finally, if you think that working harder would only seem to be duplicating what someone else is already doing, then you will think that there's no point in doing so. If other people always answer the teacher's questions, why should you bother to make the effort to take much notice?

It follows from this that if we could reverse some of these conditions we could increase the group's achievements. Try to make the tasks more interesting, try to make each person aware of his or her own contribution, and think that that contribution is important.

▷
Earlier we mentioned parallel play, where children play side by side. This is a form of coaction. Coaction simply describes a situation where two or more people are performing a similar action near to each other. A coaction effect describes any change in someone's behaviour which is brought about by a knowledge of the action of others.

▷
Social loafing refers to the way in which individuals often reduce their effort when they know that others are making sufficient effort on their behalf, and that their lessened effort won't, therefore, be noticed.

Exercise on social facilitation

1 What is the difference between imitation and modelling according to social-learning theorists, such as Bandura?
2 Define social facilitation.
3 Think of another experimental situation in which we could test for a coaction effect. Say how the effect would be measured.
4 Give an example which illustrates Allport's claim for the relationship between the difficulty of the task and the extent of a coaction effect.
5 Think when the last time was that you were guilty of social loafing? What did you do less of than you could?

●●● **Summary of social facilitation**
We often behave differently when we know that we are with others. Their presence might make us compete, or it might interfere with our concentration. We may make less effort if we know that other people are involved in the same task as us.

▶▶▶ *Activity*
Look out for the next time you are guilty of social loafing. I wonder if it will be before the end of your next lesson?

Conformity and non-conformity

▷
There's nothing particularly right or wrong with conformity. It makes life rather more predictable and easy-going. A problem might occur if someone always conforms over everything, and seems to agree with whatever the last person said.

▷
Compliance, internalization and identification are all types of conformity. In themselves they are neither good nor bad. Whether they are likely to be a cause for concern depends on the motives and the extent of their use.

Another area of human social relationships concerns conformity. **Conformity** generally means giving in to group pressures. If a group of female friends wants to do one thing, and one of them doesn't, the odd-one-out may give in just to continue to be accepted as one of the group. She has conformed to the majority wish. If your friends think the film you've all just seen was good and you thought it was rubbish you might just nod when they ask you what you thought, so as not to appear different from them. You have conformed.

There are several kinds of conformity such as **compliance**, where someone goes along with the group view, but privately disagrees with it, **internalization**, where someone comes to accept and eventually believe the view, and **identification**, where someone accepts and believes the group view because he or she wants to become associated with the group. There are also a number of reasons why people conform to the behaviour they see around them. They may publicly agree and because disagreeing would be inconvenient, they may genuinely come to agree and be seen to be agreeing because membership of the group could be useful to them.

Some studies of conformity

The first major research in conformity was conducted by **Muzafer Sherif** in 1935. Sherif used a visual illusion known as the **autokinetic effect**.

Your eyes are constantly moving to keep the cells on your retina active so that you can see properly. The result of this is that a stationary spot of light in a darkened room will appear to move. This is the autokinetic effect. Sherif told his participants that a spot of light in a darkened room was going to move, and he wanted them to say the direction and distance of the movement. In the first **experimental condition** the subjects were tested individually, and Sherif averaged their responses. So one subject might report an average movement of six inches, another of three inches, and another of one inch. In the second experimental condition, Sherif placed his participants into groups, usually of three people, and asked the group to describe the movement of the light. Their responses now were much nearer to an average for the group members. (Just over three inches for our three participants.) Sherif asked if they felt their responses were being influenced by the scores of the other members, and they all said that they were not.

It is possible that we are likely to conform to other people's views when we are not confident of our own. Remember that the spot of light didn't move at all, so that those participating in the experiment could have been sure that they were right. When we agree with others, we might feel more secure that we are in the majority and must therefore be right. If you are uncertain about what to do in a new situation – such as your first day at college – it might be an idea to follow some other students who do seem to know their way around.

In the late 1940s and early 1950s **Solomon Asch** conducted experiments with students to see if they could be pressurized into conforming to a judgement that they could see was not true. He had groups of around seven university students in a classroom. They sat around one side of a large table facing a blackboard. On the left side of the board there was a white card with a single black line drawn vertically on it. On the right side of the board there was another white card, on which were drawn three vertical lines of different lengths. One of these three lines was the same length as the single line on the other piece of card. In total, there were 12 pairs of cards. In each instance, the students had to say which line on the second piece of card was the same length as the single line on the first piece of card. All but one of the students were actually assisting Asch and were going to choose the wrong line on seven of the twelve trials. People who assist researchers in this way are called **confederate participants**.

The other student was seated at the end of the row so that he would always be the last or the second to last person to answer. This way, he would hear the others say which line they thought was the same length, before he gave his own answer. Such people, who do not know what is going on are called **naive participants**.

Altogether, there were almost 123 naive participants and 1500 trials in Asch's early experiments. Confederates agreed on the wrong answer on 861 of those trials. One third of the naive participants conformed to the incorrect judgement of the confederate participants on each of the seven trials. About three-quarters of the naive participants conformed on at least one occasion. Only about 20 per cent of them refused to conform at all.

So why do we conform? According to Asch, people are more likely to

> An experimental condition is one part of an experiment in which the participants have particular experiences in common. These experiences will be different from what happens to participants in other experimental conditions.

> Despite claiming that they were not being influenced by hearing other group member's reports, each subject did conform nearer to an average of their individual scores.

> A trial is a try-out or run through of a part of an experiment. It is really a mini experiment. Taken together, several trials will make up the complete experiment.

▷

Over 30 per cent of the sample of 123 naive participants conformed on all 861 occasions. Only about 20 per cent didn't conform at all.

▷

Crutchfield's subjects were military or business people. Unlike Sherif's and Asch's research they were not students taking part in a psychology experiment.

▷

As in other research into conformity, around one-third of the subjects seemed willing to conform on at least some of the questions.

▷

A person possessing a personality like the one described here could be seen to be quite a weak character. We are probably all rather weaker than we would like to think we are.

conform when they believe that others have already stated their agreement. However, saying that a particular line is of a certain length is not to conform in real life any more than is saying how far a stationary spot of light moves.

In 1954 **Richard Crutchfield** published the findings of his study of military and business people conducted on the final day of their three-day assessment course. They had been grouped into fives and seated side by side in individual booths. They could not see each other, and were told not to talk. Various multiple-choice questions were projected onto the wall in front of them, and they had to give their answers by pressing one of five switches which corresponded to the answer they favoured. For example, if they thought the answer to one question was the fourth alternative, they would press switch number four. They were also told that they would each see the answers that the others were giving. The answers they saw, however, were controlled by Crutchfield. As in Asch's experiment, after some of the questions, they would see wrong or ridiculous answers supposedly being given by the others. Some of the questions involved stating some fact, judgement, or opinion.

Crutchfield found that, on the judgement questions (such as asking whether one figure was larger than another), and on factual questions (such as asking for the next number in a given sequence), 30 per cent of his subjects would conform to the wrong answer when the others were appearing to agree to that as the correct answer. Thirty-seven per cent of the army personnel he tested agreed with the statement: 'I doubt whether I would make a good leader'. When tested privately, none of them had agreed with this statement. It appears that, in certain situations, some people will agree with almost anything at all!

Crutchfield investigated what it was that made some people more likely to conform than others. He found that conformers lack understanding and are less able to apply logical principles. Rather, they are more cautious, or prefer to imitate other people's solutions. They lack confidence in their own abilities too, are less likely to be able to take care of themselves and need the support of others. Their cautious approach and general indecisiveness would make them poor leaders. They tend to have rather strict views of what ought to happen, and what should be done. They tend to have inferiority feelings too, and are generally submissive. They know they lack confidence and competence, and so look to others to be strong and decisive. They will not defend their ideas with enthusiasm and tend to agree with whatever the most determined person in the group says. They have few friends and are not widely liked, although they may be widely tolerated.

Exercise on conformity

1 What is the autokinetic effect?
2 Why did Sherif's participants conform in the second experimental condition?

3 What is the difference between a confederate participant and a naive participant?

4 What explanation does Asch give on why we conform?

5 What explanation does Crutchfield give on why we conform?

Activity
Construct a table summarizing the major studies on conformity described here. Include the column headings 'name of researcher', 'type of participant', 'research claims', 'possible problems'.

Deindividuation

We have looked at Crutchfield's research into the way in which personal factors have some effect on our willingness to follow other people without too much regard for our own view. There are also social factors which may lead us to behave in ways in which we wouldn't usually behave. For example, we may be watching a football match and get caught up in the excitement of the game and the enthusiasm of the supporters. We may start to shout support for the Wolves players and abuse at their opponents. If a Wolves player is criticized by the referee we may hurl abuse at him too. We might even start to lose touch with our own individuality. Instead of thinking for ourselves, we become part of the mob. This loss of one's own sense of individuality is called **deindividuation**.

▷
Deindividuation is a state where someone's self control and sense of identity are taken over by the identity of the mob. In such a situation, people lose control and sometimes do things that they wouldn't dream of doing under normal circumstances.

One of the best known psychological studies of deindividuation was an experiment conducted by **Philip Zimbardo**, which was published in 1972. It has become known as the **Stanford Prison experiment**. Zimbardo found twenty-five healthy, mentally stable students to be his experimental subjects. They were to play the role of being a prisoner or a guard in a mock prison. On the day the experiment began they were blindfolded, and driven to the basement of the psychology department of Stanford University. This had been set out as a prison, divided into small cells, with bars on the doors and windows, and bare walls. It was here that the deindividuation process began.

When the prisoners arrived at their prison they were stripped naked, deloused, had all their personal possessions removed and locked away, and were given prison clothes and bedding. They were given a smock with their number written on it, but no underclothes. They also had a tight nylon cap, and a chain around one ankle.

The guards were also deindividuated. They wore khaki uniforms, and had silver reflector sunglasses, so that it was impossible to see their eyes. They also had short clubs, whistles, handcuffs, and the keys to cells and the main gate. The guards worked shifts and were allowed home in between. They had offices along the corridor.

▷
A clear distinction was to be made between the superior prison guards and the inferior prisoners. Both groups were being deliberately deindividuated.

The prisoners were only to be allowed visits from the chaplain and from their relations. They were to be locked in their cells all the time, except when let out for work, toilet privileges, or head counts. Toilets were only allowed until 10 o'clock in the evening. After that the prisoners had to use buckets. There were no shower facilities. Each cell measured

▷

Deindividuation involves anonymity and dependence.

▷

Most prisons do have lists of rules which are often strictly enforced. Many of them may be quite petty and are probably unnecessary. Rules have a role in deindividuation since they encourage prisoners to become dependent on the guards.

▷

Remember that all these people were educated, were emotionally stable, and had perfectly normal personalities. They had been randomly divided into the role of guard and prisoner.

two metres by three metres, and was to sleep three men. Apart from the cells, there was 'the hole', a small, converted storage cupboard where men could be kept in solitary confinement for fairly short periods if they broke one of the prison rules. To assist in the deindividuation process, feelings of **dependency** on the guards was fostered. The prisoners needed to obtain permission from a guard for almost everything. They were not allowed to smoke, use the toilet, or write a letter (which they could only do on prison notepaper), without a guard's permission. They had no knowledge of the time either. All clocks, radios, etc. were removed.

On arrival, the guards were instructed to maintain law and order in the prison, and to make the prisoners aware of the sixteen prison rules which were to be enforced. For example, there was to be silence after lights out, prisoners were to eat at mealtimes and could not eat at any other time. Tampering with walls was forbidden, and prisoners had to address each other by number only. Meanwhile they had to address a guard as 'Mr correctional officer, sir'. The final rule was that the failure to obey any of the other rules might result in punishment!

Within a very short time both guards and prisoners were settling into their new roles, the guards adopting theirs quickly and easily. Within hours of beginning the experiment, some guards began to badger some of the prisoners. They behaved in a brutal and sadistic manner, apparently enjoying it. Other guards joined in, and other prisoners were also tormented. The prisoners were taunted with insults and petty orders and they were given pointless and boring tasks to do. The prisoners soon adopted submissive prisoner behaviour. They talked about prison issues a great deal of the time. They told tales on each other to the guards. They started taking the prison rules very seriously, as though they were there for the prisoners' benefit and that infringement of any rule would spell disaster for all of them. Some even began siding with the guards against prisoners who did not conform to the rules.

Over the next few days the relationships between the guards and the prisoners changed, with a change in one leading to a change in the other. As the prisoners became more dependent on the guards, the guards became more scornful towards the prisoners. They held the prisoners in contempt, and let the prisoners know it. As the prisoners became more submissive, the guards became more aggressive and assertive. They demanded ever greater obedience from the prisoners, and so the vicious circle went on.

After the experiment had run for six of the planned fourteen days, Zimbardo closed it down. In a debriefing session later, when the players had been shown how they had behaved, they found it hard to believe. The prisoners couldn't believe that they had responded in the submissive, cowering, dependent way that they had, and the guards said that, at the time, they had felt excited by the power, but they couldn't believe how they'd behaved.

Zimbardo was convinced that anyone was capable of the kind of behaviour his subjects had shown. In any situation where one group has power over another, there is a tendency for the superior group to dominate the lower group. The greater the gap between the two groups (as in this experiment), the greater will be the tendency to dominate. At the same time the inferior group will try to protect or improve itself by trying to please the dominant group in any way that it can. However, this often has the effect of making the dominant group treat the inferior group even more cruelly, as their resentment increases.

Exercise on deindividuation

1 Complete this sentence, 'Deindivuation is….'
2 Explain how anonymity and dependency are involved in deindividuation.
3 Name some of the ways in which the participants in this experiment were deindividuated.
4 Outline the relationship Zimbardo found between the behaviour of the guards and the behaviour of the prisoners.

●●● Summary of conformity and deindividuation

The experiments by Sherif, Asch, and Crutchfield have suggested that about one third of people can be manipulated into conforming in some way. However, their experiments are fairly artificial and may not reflect what real people do in their everyday lives. The experiments imply that conformity may be wrong, but if we didn't conform to certain social rules then life would be hopelessly unpredictable. The problem arises when people are over keen to conform, and so their own personality seems to disappear. Deindividuation is one extreme case of submerged personality, where the situation leads some people to lose all sense of their own identity and to behave in uncharacteristic ways.

Factors in Friendships

Most people live as members of many social groups such as a family, a school, a club, a team, a workforce. Several other animal species also live in social groups. For example, many of the male members of monkey troupes establish their position in the social hierarchy of their group by mock battles and displays. Those at the top of the **pecking order** will try to choose which females to mate with, the most desirable living space, and sometimes even the best food supply (and they sometimes succeed!).

A pecking order (named after the way chickens establish their positions of dominance) is often better known as a dominance hierarchy.

Those species which live as members of a group often create a dominance hierarchy. Some human groups also develop dominance hierarchies, which can influence whom we are most likely to mix with and whom we are unlikely to have much contact with.

Humans also have dominance hierarchies, although the ways in which human groups are organized is extremely broad, with different kinds of people dominating different kinds of groups for different reasons. Sometimes the strongest will dominate, sometimes the richest, sometimes the most qualified, and so on. At school, dominance may be decided by fights and gangs, but also by cunning and wit. Later in life, your position may be influenced by your educational qualifications, your occupation, your income, etc. Unlike other species, humans have sophisticated mental processes which allow us to think and have opinions, to experiment and have preferences, and to use our experiences to make our judgements. Many humans also develop consciences and a fine sense of justice, fairness and right and wrong. Friendships and relationships develop and fade in all our dealings with other people throughout our lives.

Most of us like to be liked. Most people like some other people. Some people love some other people. You may love your best friend. You may also love someone in a romantic sense. As we saw in Chapter 2, even quite young babies prefer some people (those to whom they are attached) and are wary of others (towards whom they may show stranger fear). The question arises, why do we like some people more than others? Social psychologists have been interested in the area of relationships for over thirty years. Many studies have explored how friendships are formed and maintained, and have led researchers to identify the main factors, and suggest some theories. Some confusion exists, however, in the extent to which the factors and theories apply to relationships generally, to friendships as examples of relationships, and to romantic involvements as examples of special friendships. We will try to untangle some of the confusion.

There may be a biological need to form friendships. Friends perform essential functions for us. They reassure us, as their ideas are usually similar to ours. They think well of us, helping us to think more positively about ourselves. They socialize us by providing models of how things can be done. They broaden our experiences and give us confidence. All of these are very useful skills for people who live as members of social groups, particularly those who need to interact with others, to form relationships, perhaps leading to mating and child-rearing.

There are many explanations for why we like some people more than we like others, and all have something in common. They all suggest that the relationships we form with friends and partners must be rewarding in some way. If you gain rewards or benefits from your relationships, such as enjoyment, stimulation, support or sharing (see the exercise at the beginning of this chapter), the bond is likely to become stronger. How rewarding you find these relationships is determined by other factors such as how much you see of them, how well you get to know them, how close you live or work to them, and so on. These are some of the main factors which are involved in forming friendships with other people.

Exposure

In order to become friends with others, in whatever social context we find them, we have to become aware of their existence first. We need to see, and/or hear them. We need to be **exposed** to them and they to us. While a young teenager might be exposed to a favourite pop star on video or television, they won't necessarily become friends. There is more to forming friendships than mere exposure, but it is an essential start.

Proximity

Proximity refers to physical closeness. People who live close to each other are more likely to be exposed to each other more often, i.e. we see more of

▷ Is romantic love a special form of friendship, or is it something quite different? Do you think that the answers which males give to these questions may be different from the answers females might give? Compare notes with members of the opposite sex. Look back to the exercise at the beginning of this chapter (see page 58), and compare your answers with those of members of the opposite sex.

▷ You may travel to work on the same bus as someone you find physically wonderful. You'd like to know them much better. At the moment though, you've seen ('been exposed to') them and you hope that they have seen you.

them, and they become more familiar to us. People who sit together in class, who live near to one another, who share a locker or a dormitory, for instance, are most likely to become friends. The most popular students in colleges are the ones whose rooms are nearest the bar, the lounge, the refectory, the common rooms or other social gathering places. People who interact most are most likely to become friends, and those who have the greatest opportunities to interact are also likely to have the greatest choice of friends. Neighbours may become friends because they see a lot of each other or because they share common interests in their area or community. They may also share common problems or benefits.

Familiarity

Leon Festinger studied some married students in a block of student flats. He found that people living next door to each other were much more likely to be friends than those living at the end of the corridor. They had little to do with students living on another floor in the same block. Other studies have found similar results in student halls of residence, old people's homes and in neighbourhood communities.

Proximity can also have the opposite effect if someone tries to become too close to you. An experiment in a library, by **Felipe** and **Sommer**, investigated the effects of strangers and proximity. They waited until a female student sat at a library table, either alone, or with varying numbers of empty chairs around the table. A male experimenter would then sit either next to the subject, or in one of the other seats. In each case when he sat right next to her, the female either moved to another table, left the library, or separated herself from him by putting her bag on the table between them.

Most of us are very cautious about our personal space. We do not welcome strangers getting too familiar, and we try to avoid contact with others in crowded places. If someone you don't know tries to move too close to you, you will feel uncomfortable and may well want to leave. A stranger who invades your personal space is unlikely to become a friend, and during the early stages of friendship it is important to establish acceptable limits of how close you will allow this person to get to you.

A possible explanation for why people who live close to one another are most likely to become friends lies in **familiarity**. According to research by **Robert Zajonc** repeated exposure to the same stimulus produces greater attraction toward that stimulus. So, the more you see of someone, the more likely you are to become that person's friend, or at least to describe that person as a friend. As we may see more of people who live closest to us, we may well learn to like them more than people we see rarely. This doesn't always happen of course. Some people hold **stereotypes** of the kind of people they will and will not like. For example, if you think that you do not like skinheads, then no matter how many times you see a skinhead you are unlikely to be attracted to him or her. Sometimes, people make fairly instant decisions about whether they are likely to like someone or not. Once they've made up their mind, repeated exposure will not make any difference.

▷ Perhaps you should try to sit a bit closer to the person on the bus?

▷ Don't move too close to the person you like on the bus. Just near enough to make sure you are noticed.

▷ By being noticed a bit more on the bus you may become more familiar to the person you're after!

Exercise on factors in friendship

1 Exposure, proximity, and familiarity are the three most important ingredients for a friendship to begin. Define these three terms.

2 Which of these three elements would you say is most important to people generally?

3 Think of your best friend. When, where, and how did you become friends? Do all three of these factors apply?

4 Which of these three factors would you say is the most important for a friendship to survive over a period of years? Explain your answer.

5 Here are some examples of groups of people about whom some people hold unflattering stereotypes. Briefly describe the stereotype.
(a) Football supporters.
(b) Politicians.
(c) Journalists.
(d) Students.

6 To what extent do you think that exposure, proximity and familiarity are important in romantic love? Copy this table and tick the appropriate box, explaining your answer for each factor. Then do another table for friendships.

▷
A stereotype is a fairly simple (and not always flattering) view that some groups of people hold about other groups of people. Because it is usually based on very little evidence it is often wrong or misleading.

	Exposure	Proximity	Familiarity
Essential			
Very important			
Useful			
Unimportant			
Irrelevant			

People are most likely to become friends with those people who are similar to them in some way, for example, if they have similar interests. Let's imagine that you like horses and that you are a competent rider. Although you don't have a horse at the moment you are hoping to buy one eventually. You find that a girl in the class you have just joined at college has a horse of her own and is an experienced rider. As you have similar interests you start talking, perhaps you break the ice by asking the name of her horse. She tells you her horse is called Ben, and you ask how old he is. She says he is 6 years old, and then asks if you like horses. The friendship is possibly beginning.

▷
What similarities in attitudes exist between you and your best friends?

Probably the most influential areas for similarity are in attitudes, values, and beliefs. Similarity of attitudes may help to strengthen the relationship. Your new acquaintance might say that although she loves riding she hates the idea of fox hunting and could never take part in anything like that. You just happen to be a member of the League Against Cruel Sports.

You have met someone who seems rather like you. If she thinks like you then she must be a sensitive, intelligent person.

Similarities in values and beliefs are also important. Values and beliefs are ideas that members of particular societies hold to be important and which they might use to govern their behaviour. They include the belief in justice and the freedom to speak your mind, in fairness and truthfulness, in decency and integrity, etc. You are likely to have much in common with people who hold similar beliefs to you. Having things in common with someone else is also self-reinforcing. You believe that someone who is quite like you must be good, and the similarity shows that you must be good too, as someone else is very like you.

Other similarities that will help in forming friendships are similar ages, similar levels of intelligence, levels of physical attractiveness, and broadly similar experiences. Although it is possible to be friends with people of vastly different ages, most close friendships are formed between people of similar ages. If you have roughly similar intellectual levels, you are most likely to feel comfortable. If the other person is not as bright as you, then you may begin to feel bored and frustrated by not being understood. You make all the suggestions, your friend doesn't seem to contribute anything. Eventually it feels too much like hard work! If the other person is much brighter than you, you may feel inadequate and foolish. You may think that you are being put down, or even worse, you are being humoured.

Similarity is rewarding because it allows us to share our ideas, to further our understanding, to have fun and more experiences with someone like us. Relationships become pleasant and make us happy. We are less likely to feel embarrassed if we make a mistake that our friends will understand. It is also psychologically rewarding to know that, as there are other people quite like us, we can't be all wrong, we must be okay. The opposite is also true. If we meet people who hold very different attitudes from ours we will probably dislike them more than if their attitudes were only slightly different from ours. We may dislike them when all we know about them are some of their attitudes.

▷
We usually like people whose attitudes, values, and beliefs are similar to ours since it shows: first, that they must have excellent taste, ideas, perceptions, etc.; second, we must be okay, as other people are like us; and third, you also have plenty to talk about and should communicate quite well, as you have so much in common.

▷
By becoming more familiar to the person on the bus you may learn what he or she is like as a person. If you find you are similar, then your relationship may develop even more. If you are not so similar, you may have to realize that there's no point going further, as you have so little in common.

Exercise on friendships

1 Think of some of the people you like. Why do you like them?
2 Name some of the things that you have in common with the people you like.
3 Think of some of the people you don't like. Why don't you like them?
4 Do you know if the people you don't like have very many similar attitudes to you?

Activity
Name two of your best friends at the moment. What similarities do you have with either of them? How similar are they to each other?

Do you like people who always succeed in whatever they attempt, who are usually right, and who rarely make mistakes? You might respect them. You might look up to them. You might wish you were rather more like them. You might even like them. But would you want to develop close friendships with them? It's unlikely. Such people aren't like us at all, as we are wrong sometimes. We are clumsy or insensitive occasionally. We have been known to say or do really stupid things. People who are highly competent aren't very similar to us at all and may make us appear foolish by comparison with them. We like people who are human and who have been known to make occasional mistakes.

Experiments by **Eliot Aronson** and his colleagues found that men who had an average opinion of themselves gave a higher rating to a highly intelligent and competent person if he or she did something incompetent (in Aronson's experiment, the mistake was to spill coffee). Perhaps we imagine that highly superior people are more like us if they do something we might do. However, the same was not true of women. They did not like the superior person to make a mistake, regardless of whether the superior person was male or female. Men who regarded themselves as rather superior liked the competent person less after spilling the coffee. They felt let down, and thought that perhaps the person was not so competent after all. This was also true of females.

Knowing that our **appearance** will create an impression on other people is one of the things that makes humans different from any other species. We often take considerable trouble to present ourselves in a particular way to suit a particular occasion. If you dress smartly for an interview you are hoping that the interviewer will gain the impression that you are a smart person. Smart people are perceived as being more capable and reliable than scruffy people. You probably wouldn't go out to meet your friends for a night out dressed in the same way. Different occasions require different appearances. Other animals do not have a choice of what clothes to wear, what make-up or scent to apply, or how to wear their hair.

People judge by appearances. You may only have to see someone for a few moments in order to be able to make all sorts of predictions about them, just based on what they look like. If someone dresses like a 1950s' teddy boy, a 1960s' flower-power dropout, a 1970s' skinhead, a 1980s' punk, or a 1990s' Gothic, would you want to be seen in their company? What might people think about you if you were seen to be a friend of one of these types of person? People may base their opinions of you on those with whom you associate.

▷
Do you make decisions about what people are like based on how they appear? When the question is asked like this, you will probably say 'no'. Would you go around with people who dressed like skinheads? You would probably say 'no' to this too. So appearance does influence your decision about whom you would choose as friends.

Exercise on further factors in friendship

1 Name three of the main areas in which friends are most likely to be similar.
2 Why are these three areas most important to some people? What functions do they perform?
3 Name three other areas of similarity and say why each of them is likely to be important.

4 Summarize the conclusions of Aronson's experiment with people's perceptions of competent people by completing the following table.

	Competent person	Competent person spills coffee
Average ability male's opinion	Liked / disliked	Liked / disliked
Superior male's opinion	Liked / disliked	Liked / disliked
Average ability female's opinion	Liked / disliked	Liked / disliked
Superior female's opinion	Liked / disliked	Liked / disliked

5 Offer any explanations that you can for the opinions given by the subjects in this experiment. Would you make the same choices?

Summary of factors in friendship (1)

There may be biological urges in humans to live as members of social groups, to have allies and partners, supporters and friends. We choose our friends from people we see frequently, or live or work nearby. They become familiar to us, and we get to know and appreciate them. Our friends are usually people who are like us, as we will have more in common with them. We usually like people who appear to be skilled at some of the things they do, and we may appear irritated by incompetence. Physical appearance seems to be especially important to males in their choice of girlfriends.

Darwin claimed that the driving force behind selecting a mate (in those species that do select one) was not how physically attractive the individual was but rather how physically fit, strong, well adapted and likely to contribute strong genes it was. Humans, with their greater cognition and cultural backgrounds put much greater emphasis on whatever physical features their culture finds attractive. Unfortunately, it is true that, in many societies, physically attractive people are more likely to have more friends than unattractive people.

Activity
Define physical attraction. Compare your definition with a friend's. How important to you are someone's looks when choosing a same-sex friend, or a boyfriend or girlfriend?

▷
Different cultures emphasize different features to be signs of beauty. What features does your society rate as important for (a) males, and (b) females? What features do you imagine might be most attractive among male prostitutes (rent boys)?

Quite a few studies in the last thirty years have investigated what rating of importance people give to physical attraction as a factor in someone's desirability, and whether we really do prefer attractive people to less good-looking ones. In one American high school, students were asked to say whether they would rather go out with the dates who were best-looking, most clever, or most active. More than two thirds of the males

▷

The computer-dance experiments were conducted in the 1960s. Imagine that you were a student then and this experiment was conducted on you. Would you mind being rated for your level of attraction without being told that you were being rated, and would you mind having been deceived about the computer-dance experiment?

▷

A correlation is a way of expressing how far two things appear to go together or are related. A positive correlation means that the two things do appear to be related. The more there is of one of them, the more there is of the other. In this study, the more attractive the female was, the more the male partner wanted further dates.

▷

If adults have different expectations of children according to their looks, why should trainee teachers be made very much aware of this?

said they would choose the best-looking females. The figure was more evenly spread between the three for the females.

This emphasis on looks was investigated in a series of experiments called the **computer-dance experiments**. **Ellen Berscheid** and **Enid Walster** conducted the first computer-dance experiments thirty years ago to try to find out how new students choose their dates. New students at the University of Minnesota who had bought tickets for a dance were invited to have their dream blind date chosen for them by computer. They filled out questionnaires which would assess their intelligence and personality. At the same time, and unknown to them, their level of physical attraction was assessed by a group of people who were helping the researchers, and they were divided into such categories as 'good-looking', 'average-looking' and 'not good-looking'.

In fact, their dates had been chosen at random. Half-way through the dance, the students were interviewed by the researchers to discover how they rated their dates. Six months later they were asked whether they had seen their dates again. The results were clear. Neither personality nor intelligence were highly correlated with either the wish to go out with the same person again, or actually having another date. Instead, the **positive correlation** was firmly with the level of physical attractiveness of the partner. Simply put, the more attractive the person was, the more likely the partner was to want another date. Although the subjects of this study were really the males who wanted to date the prettiest females regardless of their own looks, the females also wanted to go out with the best-looking men. This study suggests that people are quite selfish in the way they choose their partners. If they have the chance, they all want the best-looking person they can get, regardless of how good-looking they are themselves. It seems true that you may have more choices if you are good-looking than if you are unattractive. Perhaps, therefore, it is no wonder we spend so much time and money on our appearance!

Bailey and **Schreiber** had American college students rate themselves for their level of attractiveness. They were asked to be accurate, neither boastful nor modest. Members of the opposite sex were also asked to rate each of them. When asked to choose the level of attraction of a date, they mostly wanted to date people who were as attractive, or better-looking than they were. They were also keen that their dates would agree with their own views of their level of attractiveness.

This differentiation of people by their looks is not confined to adolescents. Studies have found that adults also judge children partly by their looks. We seem to expect different things of attractive and less-attractive children. We imagine attractive children are more intelligent, more skilful, and more successful than less-attractive children. Not surprisingly, even children are aware of looks. **Dion** found that children prefer to have attractive rather than less-attractive children as friends

Why should looks be so important when we all know that 'beauty is only skin-deep'. Perhaps we associate beauty with goodness, and ugliness with badness. Perhaps we believe beautiful people make better friends. Other studies have shown that people see beautiful people as also being more intelligent, successful, better-adjusted and happier than other

▷
A principle of contrast refers to the way that, when we see or think about a particular quality (such as attractiveness) we often think about its opposite too.

people. Or perhaps we feel that if we are associated with beautiful people we will appear more attractive too. While this may be true to some extent, a **principle of contrast** might also operate. We may appear even more unattractive if we are with someone who is very attractive.

Steven Duck has conducted a great deal of research into physical attraction. He concludes that '... we react more favourably to physically beautiful people than we do to less-attractive, ugly, or even deformed people'. However, he points out that simply being attractive doesn't automatically lead to being well-liked or being a popular friend to many people. He says that, 'relating to others involves interaction and social processes that can override the effects of initially positive responses to superficial characteristics.' This means that our personality, our knowledge, our talents, our mannerisms, and many other things about us can have more effect on how other people see us than just what we look like.

If a female in a society which puts great value on physical appearance imagines herself to be good-looking, her **self image** may be more positive. Believing in yourself may help you to become more successful. However, there is not much hard evidence for these assumptions.

Exercise on attractiveness

1 Write a description of someone you would find attractive, identifying his or her most attractive features.
2 List these features in order of importance if you can.
3 Outline, in your own words, what happens in a computer-dance experiment.
4 Would you prefer to go out with someone who is good-looking, average-looking, or less attractive? Explain your preference.
5 What does this sentence from the text tell us about human nature: 'Simply put, the more attractive the person was, the more likely the partner was to want another date'?

A reciprocal relationship is one where both partners benefit. **Reciprocal liking** is the belief that someone likes you as much as you like them. We often look for confirmation that the people whom we like and find attractive in some way also like us and find us attractive. Equally, we are least likely to like people who do not appear to like us. This was investigated by **Aronson** and **Linder**. They arranged for their female subjects to meet a confederate (someone who assists a researcher without the subject's realizing it) and then overhear the confederate state the impression he had been given of her. Afterwards the subjects were asked what they thought about the confederate. The confederate's impressions were, of course, all pre-planned.

As you would expect, those subjects who heard the confederate say pleasant things about them were very likely to say that they, in turn, would like the confederate. Those who overheard the confederate expressing an unfavourable impression of them, said they wouldn't want to be friends with the confederate. However, in two of the experimental conditions,

▷
Social psychologists have conducted many experiments using human subjects, who usually were not told that they were taking part in a psychology experiment. In fact, many were deliberately misled. The people taking part in the experiment are called naive participants or subjects, and those helping to run the experiment are called confederate participants.

▷
If the person on the bus appears to like you then you may want to indicate (perhaps with a smile or a nod) that you quite like them.

Aronson and Linder had the confederates change their minds half-way through. Some started by saying good things about their subjects but changed to being negative. The others began by saying unpleasant things but, in the second half of the description, became much more positive.

Those subjects who had heard themselves being described favourably, and then unfavourably, were much more critical of the confederates than those who had been disliked all the way through. Those who had started unfavourably but ended favourably were more likely to be liked more than those who had said positive things all the way through. Aronson and Linder call this the **gain–loss theory of attraction**. This helps us predict that we are more likely to like those people who grow to like us once they learn about us, than we are to like those who have always liked us. A compliment from them will be appreciated more than a compliment from a friend, as we expect our friends to say good things about us. When someone we hardly know does, it's even better. And if our friends turn against us, we will dislike them more than the people we always disliked.

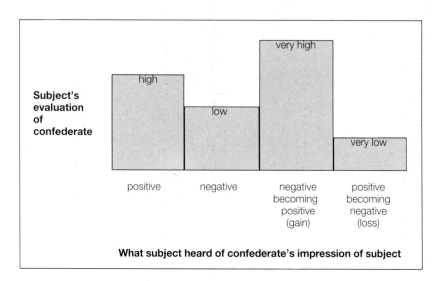

Aronson and Linder's gain-loss theory of attraction

▷
Expectancy effects are well known features of human perception. We often imagine that we are experiencing what we expect to be experiencing.

Backman and **Secord** investigated the **expectation effect**. This is the idea that we are more likely to like someone if we have reason to believe that they will probably like us. They told some people who were about to meet a stranger for the first time that the stranger would like them. Others, however, were not given any indication of how the stranger would respond. When questioned after two meetings with the stranger, those who had been told to expect that the stranger would like them said that they liked the stranger too. However, as the meetings went on this changed. After six meetings it emerged that the subjects liked those strangers who actually did appear to like them, not simply the ones they had been told would like them.

We do tend to make an error when thinking about how we feel about others and assuming how they feel about us. We often overestimate the extent of their feelings. So if you like someone a great deal, you assume that they like you as much. Equally, if you dislike someone, you imagine they have the same extent of feeling about you. This isn't usually true.

As we come to know each other better we learn more about each other. If you are learning to like a new friend you will probably describe some of your experiences or aspects of your life to them. In return, they will describe aspects of theirs that are relevant, interesting, or even funny. If you are getting to know them better you may go beyond **self-description.** You may tell them some small aspect of your life that you wouldn't tell everyone else. This is called **self-disclosure**. In return your friend might reveal something rather private to you. They are reciprocating, i.e. returning the favour. If your friend is sympathetic and understanding towards you, and you are the same towards them, then you may reveal something even more personal. You may expect them to reciprocate again. Over time your relationship develops into a strong friendship and more **reciprocal self-disclosure** occurs.

Some evidence from **Sidney Jourard** and others suggests that women self-disclose more than men, generally, and are more likely to do so with friends who are not particularly close. Men do not generally self-disclose anything too personal, but do emphasize or exaggerate some aspects of their lives for amusement (or sympathy!). Men are likely to self-disclose only if they are certain they can trust the person they are disclosing to.

Self-disclosure also occurs in children. Children are much more likely to disclose to warm, nurturant parents to whom they are attached, or to other adults who are warm and nurturant and whom they have learned to trust. They may tell someone something if that person also reveals something personal. This knowledge can be useful to people who deal with children who have any problems, such as suspected neglect or abuse.

Reciprocal self-disclosure is one of the major features of relationships between humans, as it carries with it certain risks. You are putting your trust in another human being. Humans are not always consistent or reliable. Your friend might accidentally reveal one of your disclosures to someone else, who might tell others, or use it against you in some way. Or you may drift apart as you both make new friends, or as one of you moves. People change and what you used to like about your friend might start to irritate you. Or you might simply run out of things to say to each other. Familiarity might start to breed contempt. Can you be certain that your friend will honour your secrets when your friendship comes to an end?

Self-disclosure must also never be rushed. If a stranger starts revealing all sorts of personal information to you during a bus ride you will probably feel very uncomfortable and want to get off the bus as soon as possible. If someone who could have become a friend starts revealing too much too soon, then you will not want to trust them with your secrets.

Reciprocal self-disclosure may be one factor in the development of romantic love. **Taylor** and **Altman** claim that where members of the opposite sex see more of each other they become more familiar with each other. If they like what they find they will be drawn closer together and they may reveal more intimate and personal information about themselves. As this can be a risky business, they may be drawn further together. If they still like what they see, romantic love might result.

▷
Self-disclosure carries the risk that someone might use the information against you. Your only insurance is that your friend has revealed something personal to you. That is why your disclosures must start with fairly harmless, even mildly amusing stories about yourself.

▷
The implication of Taylor and Altman's claims is that romantic love is a specially deep form of friendship. As we shall see shortly this view is not shared by everyone.

Exercise on reciprocal liking and self-disclosure

1 Outline, in your own words, the conclusions of Aronson and Linder's gain–loss experiments.
2 How do the following phrases illustrate the principle of reciprocity: 'my friend's enemy is my enemy too', and 'my enemy's friend is also my enemy', while 'my friend's friend is also my friend', and 'my enemy's enemy is my friend'?
3 What is an expectancy effect?
4 Describe the role of self-disclosure in the formation of relationships.

Complementarity is important in attraction. It involves completing or improving something. Most of us have some skills or qualities. Perhaps you have the ability to plan and predict the best thing to do. You may not, however, be very organized or able to put the plan into effect very well. Someone who has organizational skills would complement your planning skills. They would make a useful friend or partner. Watching and learning from your partner could broaden your experiences and improve your skills.

In the early stages of any relationship, similarity is most likely to be the factor that determines whether you will like someone or not. As the relationship progresses you may take similarities between you and your friends for granted. If you weren't similar in some ways you'd have little in common, so your friendship would probably decline anyway. Complementarity may become more important. If your friends have possessions, skills, knowledge, access to people or things, etc., that you don't have, and while you have equivalent things that your friend doesn't have, then your friendship will probably continue.

Complementarity can appear more important in some relationships even than similarity. This is particularly true where romantic attachment is concerned. For example, someone who is quiet and shy may benefit from having a partner who is more assertive and demanding. Together, they will be able to gain things that the shy partner would find difficult to gain alone. The assertive one will also benefit from whatever other qualities the passive partner has. Overall, however, similarity is probably more important than complementarity in influencing whom most people will like in the first place. On the other hand, complementarity is often more important in keeping a relationship going than similarity.

Shared interests often give rise to friendships. People who meet regularly to play in a sports team, such as football, cricket, or darts, often become friends. People who share the same hobbies, such as racing model cars or watching motor racing, may form friendships. Owners of vintage cars, traction engines, canal boats and all kinds of other things may also become friends. Much of their interaction will result from being in the same place at the same time, talking about the same things, etc. Colleagues who work together sometimes form friendships that extend beyond work. Members of the same congregation might also become involved in Church-related activities that lead to the development of friendships.

▷
When you first meet someone any similarities of attitude, values or belief are likely to influence whether or not you will like that person. It is not automatic, however. They may be very similar to you in many respects, but there may be one difference that stops you from wanting to learn more about them.

▷
Friendships can be temporary. We make friends on holiday, or at college, or in our work placements. We swap addresses and promise faithfully to keep in touch. We rarely do. Friendships can also last for years. We meet some people who just stay with us. They share our personal history and we know quite a lot about theirs.

Summary of factors in friendship (2)

Physical attraction plays a large part in influencing our choice of partners and even our friends, although different people have different attitudes to what they regard as being attractive. We are especially inclined to like people who appear to like us. After all, they clearly have good taste. We are more likely to open up to these people, especially if they reveal things about themselves to us. If they possess skills that we lack, and if we can do things from which they can benefit, the relationship may well become stronger. Friends are drawn from shared-interest or shared-activity groups, and friendships can last for years.

 Activity

Make a list of all the components in choosing friends that we have discussed here. Ask as many people as you can to rank them in order of importance. Add together all the ranks for each component and find the average rank. List the components by their average rank. (If you don't know how to do averages, see page 310.)

4

Prejudice

Prejudice is an attitude. The word prejudice literally means prejudging and leads to forming an attitude about what someone or something is like without much information about them or it. We might hold prejudiced attitudes about certain individuals or groups of people. Someone might think that New Age Travellers are scroungers, that Pop stars are drunks and dope heads, or that all Tories are morons. Or we might have prejudices about objects. We might believe that hot hatchback cars and spiders are dangerous. Or we might have prejudices about events. We might think that being old must be awful or that voting to join the EEC must have been an act of madness. In this chapter we will investigate how prejudiced attitudes are formed, and where they come from, and how prejudice might be reduced.

Activity

Do you have any prejudices that you are willing to admit to? How long have you had them? Have you any idea where they came from? How do you think you could set about measuring how prejudiced people are?

Throughout the world people live in a huge variety of different groups: from collections of nations (such as Great Britain, made up of Wales, Scotland, Northern Ireland and England), to communes of half a dozen people sharing a house. There is enormous variety, too, in many other bases that there are for grouping people, such as the colour of their skin, their sex, their style of dress, language, food, religion, customs, education or training. Many people tend to think that the groups to which they belong are right and good, and that members of any other groups must be, therefore, inferior in some way. This is called **ethnocentrism** and forms the basis for many people's prejudices.

Secord and Backman claim that all attitudes, including prejudiced attitudes, have three main elements. First, there is the cognitive part, which is what you know, or think you know, about someone or something.

> We may hold prejudiced attitudes about people, objects, or events. In each case we don't know very much about them, but imagine what they must be like.

For example, you might think that I am very greedy and eat anything. Second, there is an emotional part: you might dislike people who eat as much as me. And third, there is a behavioural part: you avoid me.

Prejudices are usually fairly fixed attitudes. By this we mean that once formed, they may be slow to change. For example, I might regard students as lazy and workshy. I am quite convinced of this and am not likely to change my mind. These prejudiced attitudes may lead me to behave in a particular manner towards students. Whenever I learn that someone is a student, I will expect them to be lazy. This expectation will be confirmed simply if the student does anything that I can possibly interpret as a symptom of laziness. Even if the student is hard-working I might claim that he or she must be an exception to the rule, as I shall think that everyone shares my view that students are lazy.

Prejudices don't have to be negative (i.e. against someone or something). They can be positive as well. Someone who is prejudiced may favour certain people over others, for instance, people who come from the same background or same area, or who have similar interests might be viewed favourably. I might have Welsh family connections and rather like Welsh culture. If I have the choice to be friends with some people I might be drawn to any from Wales. I might support Welsh Rugby teams and enjoy holidays in Wales.

Some people hold many prejudiced attitudes about many other people, objects and events. They may not have had many experiences of different ideas. Most of their dealings with others will be influenced by their prejudices. They will avoid the objects of their prejudice, perhaps even try to do them harm. Other people may have some specific prejudices about some particular things, but otherwise may be fairly open in their dealings. Some people have very few prejudiced attitudes and are receptive to all sorts of ideas and people. Prejudice isn't, therefore, a thing which someone either has or doesn't have. It is a reflection of the kinds of opportunity and experience that people have had to learn about others.

We can't therefore talk about whether having prejudices is necessarily either a good or a bad thing. Holding any attitude usually leads to a certain behaviour. If you like chocolate fudge cake then you will try to eat it more often than you eat something you like less. If you like a particular person, you will prefer his or her company to the company of someone you like less. Acting differently towards something or someone is called **discrimination**. If having a positive or negative attitude towards someone or something leads us to discriminate in favour of them or against them, then this can become a problem. In my small way I'm positively discriminating in favour of Wales and Welsh people. In this sense, positive discrimination isn't much different from the choices that all of us make, or the preferences we all have. If I ever rise to the position where I employ people and I start to give jobs to Welsh people over equally or better qualified people from other backgrounds, then my prejudice could become more of a problem. There are three common forms of discrimination: ageism, racism, and sexism.

▷ Prejudice is a fixed attitude that someone has formed about others. All members of the target group will be thought of as having the same characteristics, even where there is evidence that some of them do not have these characteristics.

▷ The likelihood of holding prejudiced attitudes varies between individuals and groups. Some people hold more prejudiced attitudes and are more convinced that they are true than others.

▷ Technically, discrimination means to identify differences between things, but more generally it implies treating people differently on the grounds of these differences.

▷ The prejudiced attitude itself is less of a problem than the behaviour that it gives rise to, which might be a social problem.

79

Exercise on defining prejudice

1 What does the word prejudice mean literally?
2 What is the relationship between prejudice and discrimination?
3 What three parts of any attitude do Secord and Backman identify?
   Give an example of one of your attitudes, identifying the three parts.
4 What is the difference between an attitude and a prejudice?
5 Here is a list of prejudices that some people may hold: ageism, racism,
   sexism. Choose one of these and say what someone who holds that
   prejudice thinks about the object of the prejudice.
6 What are the consequences likely to be of holding such prejudices?

Summary of prejudiced attitudes

Social psychologists study the formation of negative and positive
attitudes, and how they relate to actual behaviour. They find that some
people are more likely than others to hold prejudiced attitudes and act in
discriminatory ways. Prejudice is the attitude, discrimination is the
behaviour. The two do not always coincide!

Forming prejudiced attitudes

Prototypes

▷
In this sense prototypes are the first
examples of something that we
experience and take to be typical of
that thing. What were your prototype
teachers like? A stereotype, is a
generalization from the prototype that
other people share.

When we experience something for the first time, such as being in school,
dealing with teachers, eating hedgehog-flavour crisps, or drinking coffee,
we are learning a **prototype**. For example, your first experiences of
college may be rather off putting. You may be nervous and wonder
whether you'll be able to find your way around such a huge place with so
many strange-sounding room names or numbers. You may long to go
back to the security of school. Your prototype reaction may change when
you've been at college for a few days. You meet some new people, make
some new friends, find all the rooms, and find out about student life. Your
prototype has changed. From your experience of your own college, you
may generalize your prototype of college life to all colleges. You're adopting a stereotype.

Your first experience might not be direct, or first hand. You don't need
to be burned to know that fire can hurt you, and you don't need to have
experienced an electric shock to know that touching live electricity cables
isn't sensible. Humans are capable of learning from other people's experiences. If people you know have prejudiced attitudes towards something,
your prototype may be the attitudes they pass on to you. Many prejudices
are learned from parents and friends during childhood.

Stereotypes

Simplifying what we think about other people or other things, and how we relate to them, makes it easier for us to deal with them. We try to sort the experiences we have of people into simple categories, such as whether we like them, can trust them, will enjoy them, can't ignore them, have to avoid them, and so on. Because we can't know or experience all members of any one category, we assume that all of its members are similar. You cannot have experience of college life everywhere, so you assume that other colleges will provide much the same experiences as your own college. Other people are doing the same thing. Where several people share the same, simple attitude towards something, we have a stereotype. (See page 271.)

We sometimes have a problem when we overextend our stereotypes. Over extension describes what happens when we try to apply our understanding of one situation to another situation which is not similar enough to the first. Student life might be similar in most colleges, but it won't be the same in medical college as it is at university. If you think it will be similar, you are overextending your understanding.

Having a stereotyped understanding of how things work or what they are like can be quite useful. We do not have to learn about every example. As long as we don't overextend our stereotypes, they can be useful. However, they are readily formed, and can easily become prejudices which lead to discrimination. **Gordon Allport**, in *The Nature of Prejudice* (1954), gives the following example:

▷
There are many breeds of dogs, types of beer, kinds of meat, etc. I can't hope to experience them all. From my first few experiences I will form attitudes about them which will lead to stereotyped reactions towards them. This helps me to deal with them when I encounter them in the future.

Jane Elliot was a teacher in an American school. She conducted an experiment – using her own pupils – into the effects of prejudice. She told her class that brown-eyed people were superior to blue-eyed people. She said that they were more intelligent and better behaved. Although there were fewer brown-eyed than blue-eyed children, the brown-eyed children were to be given many privileges. For example, they would sit at the front of the class and be given attention first. Blue-eyed children had to sit at the back of the room and wait at the end of the queue. They also had to wear special collars to indicate their lower status. Within hours, the blue-eyed children began to do less well in their schoolwork and began describing themselves as stupid and bad. The brown-eyed children started to insult the blue-eyed children and behave very badly towards them. They soon developed a prejudice which said that superior people dominate and exploit inferior people. As a result the brown-eyed children soon began to discriminate against the blue-eyed children.

The next day, the teacher announced that she had made a mistake. In fact blue-eyed people were superior. The attitudes and behaviour of the two groups on the previous day quickly reversed. The blue-eyed children took their revenge for their humiliations of the day before.

Clearly, prejudices can be triggered by making some people feel superior and others feel inferior. The superior ones dominate the inferior.

(On the third day, Jane Elliot told the pupils what she had done and reassured the children that they were all equal. She had wanted them to experience what it is like to hold prejudiced attitudes against others, and what it feels like to be a victim of prejudice.)

While some stereotypes are acceptable, others are clearly unacceptable. Some have elements of truth in them. For example, we believe that Ministers of the Church are truthful and trustworthy, and that doctors and nurses are professional and dedicated. We think that the armed services are professionally trained to defend our interests. In psychology we have evidence to support some stereotypes. **Maccoby** and **Jacklin** (among many others) have found much evidence that male children are more aggressive than female children. Some stereotyped attitudes have changed. People used to believe that politicians were all honourable servants of their constituents, that all policemen were honest and impartial, and that sport was about fair competition and the love of the game. Public-opinion surveys have found that many people no longer hold these attitudes.

Activity

Take the examples in this text and some others you can think of. Write them as statements (e.g. sport is about fair competition and the love of the game). Ask as many people as you can whether they would agree with each statement. Perhaps they could rate it in marks out of ten for truth. You could combine your answers with other people's and find average attitudes to these stereotypes.

Many stereotypes are clearly untrue. One obvious example of this is the belief that some people still hold, that females are less intelligent than males. Twenty years ago **Feldman-Summers** and **Kiesler** reported on their study which asked male students to judge how important the contributions of some very well known and very successful male and female scientists had been to science. The contributions of male and female scientists were equal. However, the male students said that the male scientists had made greater contributions and that the female scientists were less competent than their male counterparts. When female students were asked the same question they also rated the male contribution as more important. Females also have absorbed the stereotype. Accepting that the stereotype is true can lead to prejudice.

Exercise on prototypes and stereotypes

1 Why do we form stereotypes?
2 Give some examples of stereotypes.
3 How do you think most people would describe the stereotype for joy

riders, public-school students, doctors or tramps?

4   What reason did Jane Elliot give for telling her pupils that those with brown eyes, and then those with blue eyes, were superior?

5   In your own words, what does the research by Jane Elliot show?

●●● Summary of stereotypes

Stereotypes are useful ways of categorizing people, objects and events. They make the world rather easier. I don't need to have experienced every single spider to know that I don't like spiders! Stereotypes can lead to forming attitudes. Where the stereotype isn't based on much experience, or the experience was not fair, we may adopt a prejudice. Prejudices can lead to discrimination, even in children.

Where do prejudiced attitudes come from?

We learn most of our prejudices towards people or things during child-hood and adolescence. For example, we may have observed that females are not as likely as males to achieve the highest positions in society and so we might go on to assume that they are less intelligent than males. This assumption is a stereotype. Someone may learn to have a prejudiced atti-tude towards spiders and stereotype them as harmful. Such prejudiced attitudes can be modified during our lives as we gain more experience.

In Chapter 1 we outlined the main explanations for how we learn. These included **classical conditioning**, where reflexive responses are given to particular stimuli. Just as Pavlov's dogs learned to salivate when they heard a tone, so I may have learned to show fear when I see a spider. I have learned to associate spiders and fear. Following on from this, I may learn an association between my fear of spiders and my having a particular attitude towards them. I'm frightened of them because I imagine they could harm me. This attitude is a prejudice. However, not all of the people, objects, places, events, etc. about which we could hold prejudiced attitudes can be explained in such a simple S–R (stimulus–response) manner. We sometimes hold prejudices about things which we have no knowledge or experience of, or we may even hold prejudices about things between which we couldn't have learned any associations.

As for **operant conditioning** (see page 11), B.F. Skinner said that all other learning was the result of what happened the previous time we behaved in a similar way. If what we did brought us some benefit then we are likely to do it again. If it didn't benefit us then we will probably try something else next time. So, if we gain some benefit from our prejudiced attitude towards spiders, such as feeling safe when we avoid them, then the benefit would become a reinforcer that would encourage us to behave in the same way again. I will avoid spiders as much as possible in the future. However, we may hold many attitudes about things of which we have had no experience, and therefore we couldn't have been reinforced for holding those attitudes.

▷
Classical conditioning is the term given to the way that associations can be learned between particular stimuli and particular responses. The response is usually fairly automatic or reflexive. For example, smelling the food as we walk past a chip shop might be a stimulus which triggers the response of feeling hungry.

▷
Operant or instrumental conditioning refers to the ways in which we learn some of our behaviour from our previous experiences.

▷
A reinforcer is anything that increases the chances that some behaviour will happen again. It is important not to confuse this with reward or pleasure.

Albert Bandura said that people also learn through observing and imitating others who are clearly successful at doing something. Watching others behave in a prejudiced way may teach people that such behaviour is appropriate. If I see my parents being wary of spiders, and avoiding them, then I will learn their prejudices. Unfortunately for this explanation, many parents aren't frightened of spiders, although their children are. It isn't unknown for people to hold certain prejudiced attitudes despite their not having observed anyone else behaving in the prejudiced way they appear to be reflecting.

Apart from these general explanations, social psychologists have suggested three possible ways in which prejudiced attitudes arise. First, some early researchers see prejudices as being aspects of some people's personalities. They claim that prejudices develop quite independently of the influence of anyone else. Second, other psychologists think that people learn to develop prejudiced attitudes from other individuals in the groups to which they belong. Third, prejudices may result from competition between people in different groups who are all trying to achieve the same ends. We will go through each of the suggestions here.

Prejudice and the personality

The authoritarian personality

T.W. Adorno and his colleagues left Nazi Germany in the 1930s. They were mostly Jewish and were persecuted by the Nazis. They trained as social psychologists and worked at the Berkeley campus of the University of California. They used Freudian ideas about the development of the personality to understand where prejudices come from. Adopting a prejudiced attitude can serve as an unconscious **defence mechanism** (see page 122). If becoming aware of what someone is like, what they think or how they behave, would produce anxiety in us, we could unconsciously protect ourselves by adopting a prejudiced attitude towards them. If we thought that they would be hostile towards people like us, we could unconsciously regard them as unimportant and easy to dismiss.

Adorno conducted a study of anti-Jewish and other prejudices in 2000 people. They asked their sample about such things as which political party they supported, whether they favoured more right-wing or moderate political views, how they regarded the law, immigrants (including Jews), and other aspects of social living. They also asked about their experiences during childhood. Respondents provided information about how fondly (or otherwise) they remembered their childhood and their parents, whether their parents used punishment, if so what kind of punishment, and for what kind of offences. The answers to these questions could be rated on several scales.

The scores on one scale were particularly interesting. This was what became known as the **F-scale**. (F stood for Fascism, an extreme, right-wing political view held by, in particular, the German Nazis, under Adolf Hitler). Their evidence revealed that people who scored highly on the F-

▷
Adorno conducted a fairly large-scale survey to investigate people's political attitudes and their early experiences. He wanted to see if people who have more extreme attitudes had been more harshly treated when they were young.

scale had been raised by parents who showed little warm affection towards their children. They had tended to be rather strict and disciplined, and used physical punishment to force obedience. Freudian psychoanalytic theory suggests that children whose fathers are strict and use a lot of punishment, and whose mothers are weak, are unable to develop a clear idea of whether they are bad or good. Their idea about themselves (their **self-concept**) is uncertain. As they can't handle this lack of knowledge they repress it into their unconscious minds. **Repression** is an unconscious means of removing things which would cause us great anxiety from our conscious mind and burying them in the unconscious. When they grow up, they may project onto others the hostility they feel towards this repressed part of themselves.

When these children grew up they were described as having an **authoritarian personality**. Such a person sees the world in very simple terms. To them, it is divided into those people who have the same attitudes as them (the 'in-group') and everyone else (the 'out-group'). They loyally support the in-group who want such policies as an end to immigration and non-white Americans sent back to their own countries. They want Jewish businesses to be taken over by non-Jews, and Jews discriminated against. They want the police and other authorities to have far more power, and people who commit crimes to go to prison for longer. Anyone who is not in the in-group is to be suspected and investigated. The people not in the in-group are despised, discriminated against and regarded either as weak and inferior, or strong and a threat. The in-group members are intolerant of other's weaknesses and submissive towards authority.

Authoritarian parents may not pass on their prejudices to their children directly, but probably do so indirectly. Children who are treated harshly probably learn that the world is an intolerant place, and that only a narrow range of behaviour is acceptable. Conforming to that narrow range is seen as good, and anything else is bad. When they grow up, this general attitude may produce their authoritarianism and their prejudices.

Adorno's theory doesn't explain all prejudices, however. As we said earlier, many people have some prejudiced attitudes, even people brought up in loving homes by caring parents. At some points in their lives many people express prejudices. At other times they lose these prejudices and may learn others. Prejudices come and go. Our child-rearing style didn't. Some people in minority groups, whom Adorno suggests will be regarded as weak and useless, are often highly prejudiced against people in other minority groups, blaming them for their inferior status. There have also been some societies where the majority of people have shared similar prejudices, For example, in Nazi Germany and pre-war Austria there was widespread anti-Semitism (hatred of Jews). Freud frequently commented on anti-Jewish feelings, even in Paris. Surely whole populations couldn't have been reared by strict, punishment centred parents?

The open and closed mind

Adorno's 1950s research found authoritarian personalities only existed among those people who were politically extremely right wing. This

▷
If you wrote as complete a description of yourself as you could, including a description of your personality, this would be your self-concept.

▷
Adorno produced a description of the authoritarian personality which he suggests is a product of the way the person was brought up. This view sees aspects of personality as being the result of social experiences. It supports the nurture side of the nature–nurture debate.

▷
Prejudiced attitudes may be better understood by looking at how much the person expressing the prejudice knows about the target of his prejudice rather than by looking at child-rearing styles.

Ethnocentrism is the belief that the groups that the ethnocentric person belongs to are superior to all other groups.

doesn't seem likely. It implies that everyone who is more moderate or left wing is tolerant and kind, respectful and generous, open-minded and easy-going. This seems highly doubtful. Ten years after Adorno's research, **Milton Rokeach** suggested that some people are either more or less likely to become prejudiced, regardless of their political preferences. Rokeach developed a **dogmatism scale**. Dogmatic people are convinced that they are always correct and refuse to listen to anyone else. They exaggerate their own importance, while being rather anxious about themselves and what others think of them. They are ethnocentric in the way that they exaggerate any differences between the group to which they belong and other groups, claiming that their group is right and any other group must therefore be wrong.

Activity

Define dogmatism in your own words. Look it up in a dictionary. Do you know any people whom you would describe as being rather dogmatic?

If people have a high score on the dogmatism scale, they have a *closed mind* (i.e. they would not take any notice of anyone who disagreed with them), they would be inflexible in their outlook (i.e. they would refuse to recognize that other ways of doing or seeing things might be better than theirs), and they would express authoritarian attitudes and prejudices, no matter what their political views were.

Exercise on individual explanations of prejudice

1 What is meant by the nature–nurture debate?
2 What is reinforcement?
3 Who suggested social learning theory?
4 What does Adorno's F-scale measure?
5 What correlation did Adorno find?
6 Briefly describe the main characteristics of a dogmatic personality.

Summary of prejudiced attitudes

Social psychologists agree that prejudiced attitudes and discriminatory behaviour are learned. Some, like Adorno, think they are learned indirectly from the way parents treat their children. Adorno found a correlation between social factors in child-rearing and aspects of adult personality. Correlations are statistical devices for measuring how far such things are related statistically. They do not show that one causes any change in the other. Rokeach describes highly prejudiced people as having closed minds. His dogmatism scale found closed minds on all points of the political spectrum.

Prejudice and social factors within the group

Conformity

Conformity is a form of agreement. We said earlier that we tend to like people who have the same ideas as us. If people say they agree with us, it helps to maintain our group solidarity. Of course saying that you agree is not the same as really agreeing. You might actually disagree, but to conform to the group may be more important than to voice your disagreement. Conformity is not just verbal; it involves behaviour too. Groups may decide what to do, where to go, how to dress and act, etc. If you don't really want to go along with the group, or if you don't have any strong feelings either way but you do go along with them, then you are complying. **Compliance** means doing things that conform to other people's wishes or behaviour without particularly wanting to.

Most people live as members of many groups. You are a member of a family, a work group, a group of friends, even a tutor or class group at college. Most people want to fit in with the groups they belong to. One way to do this is to adopt, and conform to, the group's attitudes, many of which may be prejudices.

Reich and **Adcock** agree that people will feel a need to conform to group norms and this may lead to their taking on some of the less extreme prejudices. However, they do not accept that the more extreme prejudices and the discrimination that may result from them could result from simply being in a group that had such views. Most of the groups we join are not likely to contain people who all share the same views anyway, although, as we saw in the last chapter, we do tend to make friends with those people who have similar attitudes to us (see page 68). In this case, however, we already have the attitude or prejudice and may want to meet up with people who think the same way as we do. This isn't the same as acquiring our prejudices through conforming to group norms.

One of the most powerful reasons why people would conform to group norms is when their lives might be at risk if they did not conform. Forty years ago a study of a group of coal miners in West Virginia, America, by **Minard** found that black and white coal miners never mixed socially above ground. Black and white people were segregated, i.e. they didn't live near each other, didn't use the same shops, leisure facilities, such as cinemas and theatres, or churches. However they cooperated fully and worked together well when down the pit. The men were conforming, each to the norms of their own group, which were not to mix with the other group socially, but to cooperate for safety and production at work.

Competition and conflict within a group

All groups contain hierarchies of authority. (We described in Chapter 1 the pecking orders that exist in some species of social animals. See page 65.) Some people will have more power to decide what the group will do than others. In a group of friends some will dominate discussions over

▷ Conformity means fitting in with the wishes or behaviour of others. If you don't actually agree, or don't particularly want to go along with them, but don't want to disagree either you are complying.

▷ Conformity to group norms may lead to someone's taking on any prejudices that are part of those norms. ('Norms' are standards of appropriate behaviour that people in a particular group agree to adopt.) If you want to remain a member of a particular group, you may need to appear to adopt the prejudice.

others, some will make more suggestions or be more forceful in pressing their ideas. In groups containing men and women, men often dominate conversations and activities. If people want to be more dominant, they may need to compete with the present leaders. They may express stronger versions of group attitudes, or behave in even more discriminatory ways against anyone the group is prejudiced against in order to appear more important or credible themselves. Some prejudice may result from competition between members of a group.

Exercise on prejudice within groups

1 Name some of the groups of which you are a member. Start with your family.
2 Why did the black and white miners in Minard's study cooperate when underground?
3 Give an example to explain how prejudice and discrimination might grow as the result of competition for leadership within a group.

●●● **Summary of prejudice and conformity**
There are some psychologists who see prejudice as developing from factors within the groups to which people belong. As most people have attitudes, and we choose our friends from people who think like us, it is clear that our friendship groups will contain people who share some of our prejudices too. Conformity to group norms and competition for status within it may contribute to developing prejudices.

Prejudice and competition between groups

The more competition there is for scarce resources, the more hostility there will be between various groups who want them. During the 1940s, **Donald Campbell** found that over 60 per cent of Americans who were most unhappy with their own financial position, and least liked the way the country was being governed, expressed anti-Jewish prejudices. Less than a quarter of those who were generally satisfied showed any such prejudice.

Muzafer Sherif and his colleagues conducted one of the most famous **field experiments** on inter-group conflict and cooperation using twenty-two adolescent white, Protestant boys on a summer camp at The Robber's Cave State Park in Oklahoma. The experiment would last for three weeks and have three distinct phases. There were two groups, and each was comprised of eleven boys. One group called itself the Eagles and the other called itself the Rattlers. Their camps were some distance apart and, for the first phase of the experiment, members of each group mixed and some made friends with boys from the other group. During this time their counsellors encouraged each group to cooperate among themselves to achieve goals, such as preparing food, pitching tents, and conducting a treasure hunt.

▷
A field experiment is one which is conducted in the subjects' natural environment. The subjects' behaviour is going to be manipulated in some way in the natural habitat rather than in the laboratory.

▷ In the second phase of Sherif's field experiment the two groups were encouraged to feel resentment and hostility towards each other. From these feelings prejudices would emerge.

After a few days the second phase began. The counsellors would encourage prejudices and discrimination to develop between members of each group. The Rattlers and the Eagles were brought together and a tournament with sporting events and competitions were arranged for having the best kept huts, etc. To begin with there was friendly competition between the boys, but with a little encouragement (and cheating) from the counsellors this soon became hostility. There were fights, raids on each other's cabins, and flags were burned. The counsellors had fixed it that the Eagles won the contest. The Rattler's stole their prizes and medals.

The Rattlers soon began to stereotype themselves as tough, though friendly, and they were always brave. They described the Eagles as bigheads and untrustworthy cheats. Each of the two groups was becoming clearly defined to itself and clearly opposed to the other. Sherif claims that conflict between clearly identifiable groups arises when there is competition between groups for the same goal. Hostility between the groups will be almost inevitable.

Exercise on prejudice between groups

1 How is a field experiment different from a laboratory experiment?
2 On a new page write the heading Sherif's Robber's Cave experiment. Divide the page into two columns. Call one 'the first phase', and the other 'the second phase'. Fill in each column with the details which relate to developing prejudiced attitudes.
3 Do you think what the counsellors did (under Sherif's guidance) was morally acceptable? Would you think that it is acceptable to do this kind of research? Explain your answer.

●●● Summary of Sherif's findings
Sherif's classic field experiment aimed to show how prejudices can be created and promoted between members of artificially created groups. By encouraging strong bonds of loyalty and friendship and then having those bonds challenged by another group, prejudices grew about what members of each group were like.

Reducing prejudice

We tend to assume that prejudice is a bad thing. In many cases it gives a misleading impression of what people and things are like and can lead to discriminatory behaviour. However it is wrong to think that prejudiced attitudes are always incorrect. I may not know much about heroin addiction, for instance, but I have formed a prejudging attitude that it is something that I wish to avoid. This is a perfectly useful prejudice for me to have. Most of the research in this area of psychology has been on reducing prejudices in those cases where they are destructive.

How can psychology help us to reduce prejudice? There certainly aren't any easy ways to do this. What we need to find out are what factors produce or increase prejudices, and then we need to try to reduce them. Prejudice means prejudging, and you can only prejudge when you are ignorant of the people you are judging. If I don't know any Australians, it is easier for me to hold the stereotyped attitude that they are all beer-swilling, kangaroo-chasing, sheep-shearers who wear hats with corks hanging round them. I might hold prejudices against Australians and want to keep them out of Britain. However, if I meet some Australians, I will find that my prejudices are wrong. The more Australians I meet who do not fit my stereotype, the sooner my prejudices should disappear.

Roger Brown suggests there are two ways in which prejudices may be reduced. One way is to increase the amount of non-competitive contact between members of the groups. If they are allowed to mix, and both have equal status, they should find that they are more alike than they thought they were. A second possibility is to find one group of people who hold a prejudice, and another group who are the target of the prejudice, and provide a task that the two groups can only complete by cooperating. An incentive must also be provided, such as some reward that is really worth having, for them to receive if they complete the task.

> One way of reducing prejudice is to expose people at an individual level to those people or things that they hold prejudices about more generally. We can only prejudge when we don't have any knowledge or experience. Familiarity will reduce uncertainty.

Equal status contact

Having more contact with people about whom you know little (but imagine much) should encourage understanding and tolerance. People should realize that the targets of their attitudes aren't that much different from themselves. It isn't consistent to know and be friends with some people while holding prejudiced views against the group they come from. (If the prejudices are very deep, someone may prefer to break off the friendship rather than abandon the prejudices.)

It is important that the members of the prejudice group and the target of the prejudice group should be of equal status. If they are not, the prejudices may be reinforced. If my only contact with Australians is with those who don't have a similar background to mine, then I might be further convinced that they are all inferior in some way.

Pursuit of common goals

> One way to reduce prejudice is by equal status contact between the prejudice holders and the targets of the prejudice. However, this offers no guarantee for reducing prejudice. Under some conditions the prejudice may be reinforced.

Elliot Aronson found widespread inter-racial tension in an American secondary school. He attempted to reduce it by the **jigsaw-classroom** technique. Children are put into mixed-race groups. Each child is given information about one part of the lesson. He or she must learn the part and communicate it to the others, otherwise the lesson won't make any sense at all. Each one child is therefore as important as any other. The children also know that they are being graded by their teacher on how cooperative they are, rather than simply on how much effort each child puts in. This method seemed to work well. As the children cooperated to achieve the final goal, the racial tensions seemed to reduce.

Aronson claimed that pursuit of common goals has many benefits in school, and between people generally. It improves how children see and value themselves, making them feel more positive that they can make a useful contribution. It also improves their school performance generally. Classmates tend to like each other more and mix more outside the classroom. It breaks down some of the barriers between children from different races.

Sherif had tried something similar during his Robber's Cave experiments (see page 88). In the third phase, which had lasted a week or so, the counsellors tried to reduce the prejudices and hostilities between the Eagles and Rattlers. They stopped all the organized competitions, but this had no effect. They replaced competition with cooperation so that the two groups had to work together. For example, a camp water truck broke down and the only way to save it was for members of both groups to pull it up the hill with a tow rope. Through this activity, hostility did decrease and some members of the two groups became friends. Having to cooperate reduced the stereotypes they held of each other. Sharing the effort and achieving a joint goal led to a breakdown of the distinctness of the two groups. By the end of the experiment, many of the prejudices and much of the hostility had disappeared, and many of the boys were quite friendly with one another.

▷ Where members of a group feel that their group's nature and goals are clearly defined, they are more likely to identify strongly with the group's norms and values. (Values are attitudes, standards, and ideas which members of a particular group feel are important.)

Scapegoating

One fairly extreme way to reduce the tensions, frustrations, guilt feelings, and so on, that an individual or a group feel is to blame someone else for the trouble that they are in. At an individual level, if you are more successful than I am, I might blame my failure on the way you took advantage of my good nature, and how it wasn't possible for everyone to benefit and some of us gave up our opportunities so that others could benefit. I might say you had a better start in life than me, you had opportunities that I didn't, or you were favoured by people and I wasn't. In fact, it is all your fault that I couldn't do well. This is called **scapegoating**. Scapegoats are usually innocent victims who are blamed for other people's failures.

Scapegoating also occurs at group, or even national levels. Governments use scapegoats to divert blame for failure or for being forced to take decisions that will hurt some people. Governments will try to give people the impression that the scapegoats deserve whatever is about to happen to them. They will say it is 'all their own fault'. In Nazi Germany in the 1930s (and in Britain too), the terrible economic conditions were blamed on Jews. They were the scapegoats. In Britain, during the last few years, familiar scapegoats could possibly have been: coal miners, strikers, Trades Unionists, single parents, Local Councils, immigrants, those attending (and running) run-down schools, and public services generally (with the alleged exception of the police and the military).

▷ Some people or groups are more likely to become scapegoats than others. Those most likely to be scapegoated are those who are obviously different from others. If they are weak, small, timid, strange, or different, then they are more likely to be targeted.

Activity
Find some examples of groups who have been scapegoated for other people's shortcomings.

Exercise on reducing prejudice

1 What is meant by the term equal-status contact?
2 Why might simply increasing the amount of contact between those with prejudices and the targets of the prejudice actually lead to more prejudice?
3 Does what you now know about the third phase in Sherif's study make any difference to what you thought about it before?
4 Can you think of any ways in which the jigsaw-classroom technique might be used to reduce any other prejudices?
5 What is scapegoating? Why do you think it sometimes works? What was the result of scapegoating ethnic and national minorities in Nazi Germany?
6 Why do governments use scapegoats?

 Summary of ways of reducing prejudice
Several factors involved in increasing prejudices can be identified. If they can be reversed, this should lead to a reduction in prejudice. For example, increasing friendly contact between prejudiced groups and helping them to cooperate in solving some task should eliminate some of the fears they have of each other. Contact between people of equal status should reduce the fear that we have of the unknown. Making them try to solve common problems for both their benefits should also reduce their concerns. Ultimately, scapegoating is a means of blaming someone or something else altogether for the difficulties that prejudiced group members face.

Aggression

In Chapter 4 we noted how prejudiced attitudes affect people's lives. We looked at the possibility that the attitude might lead to certain behaviour. This isn't always the case. People are very inconsistent and it is not unusual to find people who express a particular attitude, yet behave in quite a contradictory manner. Sometimes we might say what it is about the target of our prejudice that we particularly dislike or like. We may well possess the same characteristics or behave in the same way ourselves. One way in which our prejudices might influence our behaviour concerns hostility or aggression. In this chapter we will examine the main explanations for the nature and origins of aggression and how it might be reduced.

What is aggression?

▷
There are many variations of aggression. Whether it is disapproved of or praised depends on the circumstances under which it occurs. It could be called bullying or violence and punished severely, or praised and rewarded with a medal, depending on who is doing it to whom.

Most definitions of **aggression** include some idea of hostility, such as harming someone or something. The least harmful kind of aggression may be simply calling someone a name. This is **verbal aggression** and is usually intended to be hurtful. **Instrumental aggression** is aggression which is a part of something else, for example someone might knock you over while chasing someone else. The aggression wasn't directed against you. **Hostile aggression** (**violence**) is directed actively towards the person who suffers it. Aggression is generally thought of as being antisocial and undesirable (unless it is used to defend oneself). Aggression clearly isn't an easy term to define or understand!

●●● **Summary of what aggression is**
Aggression is hostile behaviour which is usually intended to harm someone else. It ranges from name-calling to physical violence.

Aggression and children

Supporters of the nature view have emphasized the importance of biological factors in influencing levels of aggression in children. As we shall see later, there are brain structures involved in aggression, and differences in hormone levels that could contribute to aggressive behaviour in children. For the moment we will look at the influences of the family and of other social influences.

The family usually provides the first influences on a child. Ideally, it provides the child with love, security, and a range of discipline. Children need to know that they are loved and cared for, and need to learn how they should behave, and how they must not behave. Parents' attitudes and practices in teaching children right from wrong vary enormously. Some parents are very firm and strict. They make rules and expect their children to obey. If the rules are broken the children will be punished. Other parents are easy-going and do not discipline their children very much. Others still are fair, and carefully explain what behaviour they expect of their children and encourage them to behave properly. They may use some **punishment** if necessary.

Sigmund Freud argued that we obtain our ideas about right and wrong through identifying with our same-sex parent. **B.F. Skinner** claims that our sense of right and wrong results from the way we are reinforced (mostly by our parents). **Albert Bandura** claims that we model our behaviour on parents and others. According to these three major psychological theories, adults, especially parents, carry a heavy responsibility for their children.

It is quite usual for children to start being physically aggressive, towards things rather than people, from around two to four years of age. After the age of four, children are more likely to use verbal rather than physical aggression. This is intended to hurt someone's feelings. From about six or seven years of age, many children channel their energies more into competition and sport. Outbursts of aggression are increasingly likely to be controlled as they grow up. Parents are very important in a young child's life for teaching the child what is acceptable and unacceptable behaviour. There are no rules that apply everywhere and to everyone. Different cultures have different expectations about what is appropriate and inappropriate behaviour.

However parents aren't always **consistent** in the way they respond to their children. Sometimes, if things are going badly for them, they may be aggressive towards their children when they wouldn't have been otherwise. Each parent may not always agree on what is acceptable and unacceptable behaviour in their children. Mum might be more strict about some things, such as climbing on furniture and good manners. Dad may be more concerned with his children's good behaviour outside of the home and that his children do not do anything dangerous. Parents usually treat their sons differently from their daughters, and their older children differently from their younger children.

As we saw in Chapter 1, children learn quite a lot from observing and

Albert Bandura

▷
Consistency refers to responding in the same sort of way to similar sorts of situation. If people's responses are consistent we can predict what their responses are likely to be. This makes it easier for us to live together. Children need to learn what is appropriate and inappropriate behaviour in each situation. They do some of this by imitation. It is important that the role models they have are fairly consistent.

imitating the people around them whom they see as important (see page 15). Parents should be some of the most important **role models**. If children see parents behaving in one way, but saying something else, the child may find it difficult to know what the right thing to do is. Parents may use aggression to have their own way, while telling their children that aggression is wrong. They may use physical punishment (one form of aggression) to teach their children that hitting people (another form of aggression) is wrong. It does appear that parents can allow more aggression in their sons than their daughters. Learning about aggression is obviously rather difficult for children when there is so much inconsistency around. Studies have found inconsistency between the sexes, between the social classes, and between how discipline is used in one situation compared to another.

Activity

Observe some children playing in a park or a playground. List as many examples as you can see of aggressive behaviour. Note whether one sex uses more aggression than the other.

In 1966, **Mary Rothart** and **Eleanor Maccoby** tape-recorded family interactions and analysed them to observe any differences in how parents treat their sons compared with how they treat their daughters. They found that mothers almost always expected their sons to behave aggressively. They tolerated their sons' aggression and were less likely to punish them for it than they were to punish their daughters for it.

Over 25 years ago, **John** and **Elizabeth Newson** found differences between Nottingham parents from different occupational groups (what sociologists call the social classes). They sampled 700 parents of 4-year-old children. Working-class parents were more likely to encourage their children to stand up for themselves and fight if they had to. They were also more likely to use physical punishment if their children stood up against their parents! Middle-class parents were more likely to object to their children's aggression.

One of the most famous studies of aggressive behaviour in children was conducted in the 1950s by **Robert Sears, Eleanor Maccoby**, and **Harry Levin**. They interviewed 379 American mothers with 5-year-old children. They asked them whether they used punishment of any kind and, if so, what kind of punishment, and what kind of things they punished their children for. From this they established the parents' **child-rearing style**. They also rated the children's levels of maturity and aggressiveness. We will look here at the relationships they found.

Permissive parents used very little discipline, and were very inconsistent in the way they used punishment. They allowed their children to do almost anything they wanted to. They said things like 'anything for a quiet life', and 'boys will be boys', as simple excuses for their own failure to discipline their children. Occasionally they used quite severe punishments. The children of these parents were highly aggressive. As the parents gave in to the children's demands, so the children learned that being aggressive and making demands was the way to obtain what they wanted.

▷ Social classes are categories used by government statisticians. The class you belong to is based on your father's or mother's occupation. There are three broad categories – working class (including skilled and unskilled workers), middle class (including clerical and professionals) and upper class (including executives, most senior managers, etc.).

Sears and his colleagues identified a group of parents who seemed to behave in just the opposite way, whom they called **authoritarian parents**. They used excessive discipline, and punished their children for relatively minor faults. Their children were almost as aggressive as those of the permissive parents. These children would feel frustrated at their treatment, and, because their parents modelled aggressive behaviour towards their children, the children learned that aggression was an appropriate way to achieve what they wanted.

A third group of parents seemed to take a more reasonable attitude towards discipline and punishment. They used a **democratic** style of child rearing. They explained to their children what was expected of them, and explained why they expected their children's co-operation. They used some discipline and punished their children's occasional bouts of aggression (without punishing them unduly). Their children were more in control, and were least aggressive.

Six years later, Sears re-visited the children (now 12 years old). The children of permissive parents continued to be aggressive, while the children whose parents punished them excessively had become less aggressive than they had been, but instead had become more anxious and nervous. The children of the disciplined group still showed the least aggression.

▷
The choice of the term 'democratic' has nothing to do with political organization. Unless the authors of the study would like us to think that the American political system is rather like a family with the government being the kind and fair parents looking after their children!

Child-rearing style	At age 6	At age 12
Authoritarian	Very aggressive	Very aggressive but anxious
Permissive	Extremely aggressive	Extremely aggressive
Democratic	Least aggressive	Least aggressive

Diana Baumrind has also studied the relationship between parental child-rearing styles and children's behaviour. Her sample comprised 134 pre-school children and their parents. Each child's behaviour at home, and in nursery school, was observed and rated for sociability, independence, self reliance, self control, achievement, etc. The parents's behaviour towards the children was found to fall into one of three broad categories.

First, there were **authoritarian parents** who make rules which children are expected to obey. If the children obey they are sometimes rewarded. If they do not obey they are punished. Authoritarian parents are very strict.

Second, Baumrind identified a group of **authoritative** (democratic) **parents**. Authoritative parents are firm, but fair. Their children are encouraged to be independent, but the parents make it clear to them those standards of behaviour they will accept, and those they will not. They will be consistent in the way they impose discipline on the child if its behaviour falls below the standards set.

Third, there were **permissive parents**, who do not use sensible discipline at all, or who use discipline inconsistently.

Baumrind found that permissive parents have children with very poor social skills, such as the ability to make friends, share and cooperate. The children of authoritarian parents were almost as poorly socially developed, while the children of authoritative parents appeared to be best adjusted.

Exercise on learning from our parents

1 What three groups of parental child-rearing style did Sears identify?
2 How would social-learning theorists explain the effects of child-rearing styles?
3 Here is an extract from Diana Baumrind's description of the authoritative parent. When you have read it, rewrite the extract in your own words.

> 'The authoritative parent … attempts to direct the child's activities, but in a rational … manner. She encourages verbal "give and take", and shares with the child the reasoning behind her policy …. She balances her own special rights as an adult [against] the child's individual interest.'

4 Here is an extract from Diana Baumrind's description of the permissive parent. When you have read it, rewrite this extract in your own words.

> 'The permissive parents attempt to behave in a non-punitive, acceptant, and affirmative manner towards the child's impulses, desires, and action. [The mother] consults with [the father] about policy decisions, and gives explanations for family rules. She makes few demands … [and] presents herself as a resource for him to use as he wishes, not as an active agent responsible for altering … his behaviour.'

5 Describe the major differences which Baumrind found between authoritative and permissive parents.
6 The studies on child-rearing styles reflect the importance of parental attitudes. What do these studies suggest is the most sensitive way to use punishment?

Comment on parental influences

Children learn many of their attitudes and behaviour from their parents. Parents who are over-strict, or too easy-going, may have children who are less able to control themselves and their demands, less self-reliant and independent, and generally less mature. However, two points must be borne in mind when discussing the relationship between parental behaviour and children's socialization.

First, we must be careful not to over-simplify the ways in which parents treat their children. Parents are not consistent. Even the best parents act out of character occasionally.

Second, with all the talk of parents being the ones who socialize their children, don't forget that it is a two-way relationship. The children's behaviour can have quite a few effects on the parents too!

Exercise on aggression

1 Tick the appropriate boxes in the following table which best express your opinion.

	Yes	No	Don't know
1 There is more violence and aggression on television now than ever before.			
2 There is more violence and aggression shown in films and videos now.			
3 There is more violence and aggression in society now than in previous generations.			
4 A greater percentage of young people are hooligans or thugs than ever before.			

2 What is:
(a) hostile aggression?
(b) instrumental aggression?

3 Put a tick against whichever of the following you would define as containing acts of hostile aggression.

Programme	Aggression? Yes	No
Tom and Jerry cartoons		
Professional Boxing matches		
War films		
Grange Hill / Byker Grove		
Neighbours / Home and Away		
Most Sega / Nintendo Games		
A cowboy punching a card-playing cheat		
News film of a real war		
The consequences of natural disaster such as flood or earthquake		
The result of a bad car crash		
Wrestling		

Summary of aggression in children

The major psychological theories of child-rearing all stress the importance of parents and the ways they treat their children. As parents are not consistent, the messages children receive about what they should and shouldn't do are sometimes contradictory. Generally, boys are expected to behave more toughly than girls, and parents from working-class backgrounds may be more likely than better-educated parents to encourage their sons to stand up for themselves and use aggression to get what they want.

Parents who are permissive of what their children may do are more likely to have aggressive children, although the example provided by authoritarian parents shows that aggression can be the means to achieve what is wanted.

 ### *Activity*

Look back to the activity on page 95. If you observed the children playing, did you find that boys perform more aggressive acts than girls? Did the boys use forms of aggression that girls didn't use, such as hitting or shouting? Or did they both use the same levels of aggression?

Aggression in adults

▷
While aggression and violence may be less widespread than we imagine, and more likely to be found among some groups in society than others, a great deal of psychological research has gone into trying to discover whether aggression is the result of instinctive, biological, even genetic forces, or whether it is learned in some way.

If you read the newspapers you will gather the impression that we live in a very violent world. People are at war with each other all over the world. Terrorists hurt and kill people to have their own way, men attack and rape women, films and television programmes are full of characters displaying aggression (although no one ever seems to be hurt), and the image of Jerry bashing Tom is a lasting one. Yet how often have you personally known adults behave violently? Is aggression and violence so common? In 1993 about 28,000 crimes of violence were reported to the police in Britain. Many of these were drunken brawls or gang-related crimes. Very few actually involved innocent bystanders or victims of criminal assault (the kind of violence that most people worry about). The vast majority of adult aggression is found among young, predominantly male adults.

Summary of aggression in adults

The vast majority of adult aggression is found among young males, often fighting under the influence of alcohol or motivated by a fanaticism for sport. Despite common media images, the vast majority of people are peaceful and cooperative.

Theories of aggression

We have already referred to the nature–nurture debate. The nature side of the debate stresses the importance of genes and biology in shaping our skills and abilities. The nurture side stresses the contributions made by social experiences. No doubt both account for different skills to varying degrees. No doubt they both contribute to explaining aggression. We will summarize both here.

Biological bases of aggression

Our ancestors have used aggression of one kind or another since human life first appeared on the Earth. This has encouraged some psychologists to think that aggression must be part of our biological make up. There is evidence that aggression is, at least partly, biological in origin. It can be seen in animals and humans at quite young ages, and it has been shown to be affected by hormone levels. Brain centres for aggression have been found, and similar patterns for displaying aggressive behaviour have been discovered.

Biological theories look for explanations for behaviour from genetic inheritance, instincts, urges, drives, hormones, structures in the brain, and from studies of animals, both in the wild, and in the laboratory.

Brain structures and hormones

Evidence for the biological basis for aggression comes from research on both human and animal subjects. We know, for example, that there is a part of the brain, called the **limbic system**, which is closely involved with aggression. Laboratory experiments with numerous animals show that aggressive responses can be deliberately triggered by electrical or chemical stimulation of this part of the brain. Animals as large as bulls have been stopped from charging by certain kinds of electrical stimulation of the aggression centre in their brains. By selectively breeding rats and cats who were highly domesticated, laboratory researchers have produced animals who were extremely mild. However, even they would strike out at, and pounce on, things around them when their aggression centres were stimulated electrically. It has also been found that those people with brain disorders involving the part of the human brain which controls aggression, are more likely to be aggressive than others.

W.C. Young found a pregnant monkey who was carrying a female foetus and gave her large daily injections of the male sex hormone called **testosterone**. Testosterone is the most powerful male hormone (although females produce small amounts too). In humans, it promotes tissue growth, genital maturity, the production of sperm, growth of facial (and pubic) hair, voice-breaking, the development of muscles, and it has a role in promoting aggressive behaviour.

When it was born, the infant female monkey behaved in a much more assertive way, much more like a male monkey. It joined in rough-and-tumble games with the other males, and challenged them in fights for its place in the group. Other experiments have shown that monkeys injected with testosterone between birth and puberty developed similar assertive, typically male behaviour.

▷
The limbic system was one of the earliest parts of the brain to evolve. Scientists are a long way from understanding exactly what its various structures do, and much less how they work. They appear to be involved both in emotional states (for example, anger) and motivation, which is the urge to do something about the emotion (for example, the urge to behave aggressively).

▷
Hormones are chemicals produced by glands and by organs in the body which carry messages to other organs to trigger some activity in them.

Comment on brain structures and hormone levels

If aggression were biologically determined in humans, then it would appear at about the same age in all cultures. Research has shown that aggression in males does begin at around two years of age in the cultures studied. Males continue to be more aggressive. This has been explained by the fact that they have higher testosterone levels than females have. However, not all males in any society are equally aggressive, and some males are aggressive at certain times and not at other times. It seems unlikely that biological factors alone could explain such variations.

Exercise on the biological bases for aggression

1 Summarize the conclusions of W.C. Young's experiment.
2 State briefly what hormones are.
3 Complete the following table:

Evidence for the biological basis of aggression	Why we must be cautious about the evidence
1 W.C. Young's experiment.	
2 There are aggression centres in the brain.	
3 It appears at the same age in children in more cultures.	
4 Males are most aggressive than females.	

Psychoanalytic explanations of aggression

Instincts are genetically inherited and are part of our biological make up. We introduced some key aspects of Freud's psychoanalytic theory in Chapter 1. Freud claimed that we inherit several instinctive urges. He said that people are born with aggressive impulses which drive us towards danger, excitement, and risk. These are the **death instincts**. The death instincts are self-destructive. They try to make children expose themselves to danger, and this conflicts with the libido's instincts for preserving life.

If children are not to destroy themselves, they must use defence mechanisms to reduce the destructive urges.

For example, we might displace or sublimate our destructive urge by trying to destroy something (or someone) else. From when we are about three years old, these aggressive instincts must be kept under control. We ought to be brought up (socialized) to think that aggression is usually wrong. If our personality is not strong enough to resist the aggressive instincts, these instincts might break through into consciousness as aggression.

▷
Freud claimed that death instincts drive us towards risk and destruction. The libido is the opposing drive towards success and fulfilment.

▷
Defence mechanisms are discussed in Chapter 6.

Comment on psychoanalysis

There is some evidence that people who grow up being very strictly controlled by adults may bury their feelings. For example, they may never be allowed to express themselves, to be right sometimes, or to win occasionally. Although they may appear quiet and restrained, or even polite and respectful, some may commit the most brutal acts of aggression, as though their need to have power bursts out.

Although Freud's ideas about our unconscious, genetically inherited urges pulling us towards self-destruction on the one hand, or self-fulfilment on the other, seem very attractive, there is, alas, no scientifically acceptable evidence for them. This, of course, does not necessarily mean that they are wrong. Although Freud's views on aggression were never as widely known as his views on sexuality in development, they have been widely discussed.

Exercise on psychoanalytic explanation for aggression

1 Describe briefly Freud's explanation for the origin of aggression in humans.
2 What is the relationship between the libido and the death instincts?
3 What might be the major criticism of Freud's explanation of the origins of aggression?

Ethological explanations of aggression

▷
Ethology is the study of animals in the wild. Television programmes which show animals living in their natural habitat (such as those presented by David Attenborough) are good examples of ethology.

The word ethology, in this sense, is taken to mean the detailed, scientific study of the behaviour of animals in their natural environment. Ethologists use **naturalistic observation** to record every detail of an animal's lifestyle and behaviour, under as many conditions as possible, so that they can build up a picture of why animals do what they do. One of the earliest ethologists was **Konrad Lorenz** who was, from the 1930s, studying several species of animals such as fish and birds. Lorenz wasn't just an early ethologist however. He also conducted numerous experiments on some of the animals he was researching.

▷
Innate refers to inborn, genetically inherited characteristics. A drive is a state of mind in which you feel the need to do something. So, for instance, hunger is a drive that motivates you to eat.

In 1950 Lorenz suggested that humans have evolved an instinct or **innate drive** to be aggressive. His definition of aggression is 'the fighting instinct in beast and man which is directed against members of the same species'. In order to have survived our earlier evolution, humans would have needed to be aggressive in order to catch and kill our food and to defend ourselves against attackers. The urge is usually stronger in the male than in the female in those species which hunt prey because the male may be better at it. (There are some species in which the females do the hunting, e.g. lionesses.) The male may have evolved to be bigger, stronger, faster, etc. In some species males may have to fight to attract a mate, so it follows that the best fighter is more likely to be able to find the best mate.

Lorenz proposed a **psycho-hydraulic model** for aggression which explains human aggression as follows: 'Some of the things that happen to us during our daily lives make us angry'. Lorenz thought that aggressive energies are being stored up within us. As more events occur which make us angry, we become more and more tense. It's rather like water dripping into a tank. He imagined that we had a means of storing these energies like a tank stores water. Some of the aggressive energies will be released naturally. (Some of the water is released from the tank through a tap.) If more aggressive energy is added than is being released it will eventually reach a critical point. (The tank will overflow.) The next thing that makes us angry will automatically trigger the aggressive response. (The next drop of water will cause the tank to overflow.) The energy has to be released. Once the energy is released, the next thing that makes us angry will begin the build-up of aggressive energies again.

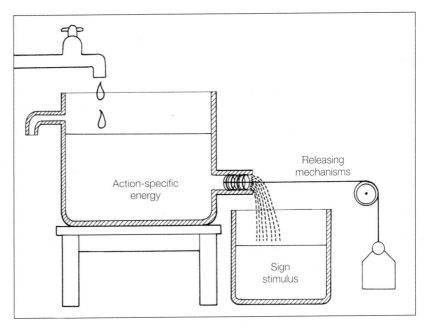

Lorenz's psycho-hydraulic model

Lorenz published his account of aggression in humans, called *On Aggression*, in 1966. In this, he claims that every animal inherits instincts to behave aggressively in order to survive. Like Freud, Lorenz proposes the existence of inherited instincts. There do seem to be brain structures which could be the basis for aggression in humans. They have been investigated experimentally. There is no equivalent experimental support for Freudian death instincts or for the idea that aggressive instincts are stimulated over and over again until they finally show as aggressive behaviour.

Aggressive behaviour will have survival value if an animal uses it to defend itself against attackers, while being successful in attacking its prey (assuming it kills its own food). It must use aggression to defend its territory which contains its food supply and possibly its mate and offspring (assuming it is a territorial species) against invaders. Aggression may even be necessary to attract a mate. As humans are animals too, we would also have inherited such genes. Admittedly, humans do live rather more complicated lives than other animals, but wouldn't you kill to eat (or let a butcher do it for you)? Wouldn't you fight back if someone attacked you? Wouldn't you be aggressive in defence of your children?

The main difference between animal and human aggression is that humans have a vast technology of aggression. Humans don't just fight with hands, heads and feet. Incredibly powerful weapons exist that can remove enemies from each other and have thereby removed the normal ways of **ritualizing** fighting. Lorenz uses the term ritualizing to describe the way that animals fight each other, one wins, the other loses, yet in many species very little real harm is caused to either. They pose and roar, puff out their chests and look threatening, they charge and chase. Soon one appears to realize that if it came to a real battle he would lose, so he gives up. He might hang his head (or tail), expose his throat, lie on the ground, slink away, or use other signs to show that he has surrendered. School children may give in, say sorry, beg for forgiveness or run away from their attackers. These rituals can't happen if you never see the enemy through the sights of your missile, bomb, or gun.

Lorenz suggested that society should provide appropriate channels for our aggressive energies to be released. Active sports, such as team games or boxing, should be encouraged. People should be able to watch others behaving aggressively to help them release their own feelings. Unfortunately, the opposite of what Lorenz claims appears to be true. Far from enabling people to release their energies, to watch others, or to be involved in competition oneself, tends to make people more aggressive.

▷
Ritualizing means performing a sequence of behaviour which has (or had) some specific function or meaning. The behaviour is fairly fixed and inflexible.

▷
Like Freud, Lorenz claims that aggressive energies can be stored and released through catharsis.

Comment on ethology

Most animal responses to any situation are the result of many generations of evolution and adaptation. Aggression may be an instinctive response in some circumstances, such as when fighting off an attacker. However, most animals rarely use aggression against their own species, and only ever really use it for catching food or in some mating rituals. Humans are not slaves to their biological inheritance. We have higher brain centres which can control most of our urges. People across different cultures do not show the same levels of aggression, so it appears that, in humans, social experiences must be important.

Exercise on ethology

1 What is ethology?
2 What is the advantage of naturalistic observation over other methods for studying animal behaviour?
3 Remember that humans are animals too. Name three examples of human behaviour that ethologists could study using naturalistic observation.
4 In your own words, briefly explain how the psycho-hydraulic model explains aggressive outbursts.

● ● ● **Summary of biological bases for aggression**

Hormones and brain centres have been shown to be involved in aggression in several animal species. Freud suggested the existence of instinctive biological urges that trigger aggressive behaviour. Lorenz found evidence that those members of any species that could make a most satisfactory adaptation to the demands of living would survive to pass on its genes to a larger number of offspring. Behaving aggressively may have survival value.

Behaviourist explanations

There are several theories that support the idea that social experiences influence the likelihood of aggressive responses. One, the **frustration–aggression hypothesis**, contains elements of both instinctive and learned behaviour and was proposed in 1939 by **John Dollard** and **Neal Miller**. The hypothesis claims that people are constantly trying to achieve some end, such as to buy a loaf of bread, catch a bus, telephone someone, complete an essay, meet some friends, etc. Things sometimes go wrong. We miss the bus, the shop is closed, we become stuck with the essay, someone isn't in when we ring, and our friends are in a different place. Our goals become frustrated. According to Dollard and Miller, aggression will result from frustration. It is almost automatic.

▷ The frustration–aggression hypothesis says that frustration produces aggression. Frustration means interfering with or stopping someone from achieving their intentions. If you play your stereo too loudly late at night, you will frustrate your neighbour's intention to sleep!

However, frustration does not necessarily lead to aggression. Albert Bandura points out that different people have their own ways of reacting to frustrations. Some of us are long-suffering and very patient. We are tolerant and don't become over-excited. We do not behave aggressively when we are frustrated. However, even some of us might snap if, for example, our child's life is in danger. Others fly off the handle for almost anything. Their normal response to any frustration is aggression. Yet even such people as these are in a good mood sometimes and do not then lash out when frustrated. **Martin Seligman** identified a condition he called **learned helplessness** where people who feel they are constantly being frustrated learn that they can't do anything. This often leads to depression. Learned helplessness is the opposite of aggression.

▷ Learned helplessness has been demonstrated in laboratory animals. If they are repeatedly put in an unpleasant situation and given no chance to escape, they soon learn not even to try. When given an opportunity to escape later, they don't take it. According to Seligman, helplessness has been learned.

B.F. Skinner rejected biological explanations for human aggression, as they were untestable, unconvincing, and unnecessary. Imagine a boy who is playing peacefully when he is attacked by another boy. He retaliates by hitting the other child back. His parents reward him with praise for sticking up for himself. The boy may learn through simple reinforcement that it is acceptable to use violence in certain circumstances. You should recall (from Chapter 1) that Skinner called such circumstances antecedents, and any reinforcements (or punishments) were called consequences.

During the 1960s Albert Bandura and other social learning theorists tried to combine Freudian ideas about how children identify with certain adults with Skinner's ideas on learning, and their own thoughts on observation and modelling. They claim that people who see others benefiting from behaving aggressively, or if they have benefited themselves in the past from behaving aggressively, they are more likely to behave aggressively in the future.

> Modelling comprises the two elements of observation and imitation. Bandura and others believe that it is the fundamental process in socialization. It is not simply that parents socialize their children, it is more the case that children socialize themselves.

Bandura has conducted several experiments to test whether children who observe powerful or attractive models behaving in certain ways are more likely to behave in similar ways themselves. If they see such models behaving aggressively they are more likely to behave aggressively themselves, particularly if they see the model being rewarded for their behaviour. In one experiment, three groups of nursery-school children watched a film of an adult male behaving aggressively towards a large Bobo doll (a rubber toy with weights which made it keep bobbing upright, when pushed). The adult hit and kicked the toy, then threw it around and punched it. The outcome of the film was different for each group. One group saw the adult being rewarded with praise and sweets for his aggression. Another saw the adult being smacked for his wicked behaviour. The third group (the control group) didn't see anything happen to the adult. When given a Bobo doll of their own to play with, the first group and the control group were equally aggressive towards it. The children who saw the adult being punished were much less aggressive.

A bobo doll

In order to test the role of reward, Bandura conducted another experiment in which all the children were rewarded if they behaved aggressively towards the Bobo doll, no matter what had happened to the adult model. They all soon began behaving more aggressively.

Comment on Behaviourism

Some of Bandura's experimental situations have been criticized. It is rather artificial to watch an adult behave in a strange way towards an inflatable toy. In real life people aren't likely to be rewarded with praise and sweets for being aggressive. As the Bobo doll wasn't a toy that many children would be familiar with, can we be sure that they understood that they were being aggressive towards it when they hit it? (You aren't being aggressive to a drum when you beat it, you are simply behaving appropriately. Perhaps some of these children were behaving in what they thought was an appropriate way towards the doll?)

▷
Ethics is about what is acceptable and what is not.

A far more serious criticism concerns the ethics of Bandura's experiments. Bandura deliberately exposed some children to a model behaving in various ways, knowing that they would be likely to imitate it. Some of the children became distressed. Is it acceptable for psychologists to use people, especially children, in this way? We will return to the question of ethics in Chapter 15.

However this does not mean that Bandura's claims aren't essentially correct. If Bandura is correct that we do learn how to respond to any situation from our own experiences, or from the experiences we have seen, then the source of such images is very important. Television is the most widely available and probably the most influential source of images. Could any increasing amounts of aggression in society be the result of aggressive responses portrayed by attractive models in the media?

▷
See Chapter 9.

Exercise on behaviourist explanations for aggression

1 Define the term frustration.
2 Complete the following sentence: 'Learned helplessness is a condition in which ...'
3 What does Freud mean by identification?
4 Bandura found that the children who watched either the adult who was reinforced, or the adult who was not reinforced for his aggression, were equally likely to be aggressive themselves. What was the only thing these children had in common?

 Summary of behaviourist explanations for aggression
The frustration–aggression hypothesis and learned helplessness are intended to expand on the simpler explanations provided by behaviourists. Neither explain all aggressive behaviour. Bandura's Bobo-doll experiments showed the importance of modelling in children, but there's more to human aggression than watching others behave aggressively.

Putting the theories together

Both biological and behaviourist theories have something to offer. They explain different aspects of aggression. Both claim to be able to explain why some people are more aggressive than others, although neither explanation is complete on its own. It might be helpful to combine the two views, rather than see them as separate, opposing explanations.

There are brain centres which are involved in aggressive behaviour, and there are differences in hormones levels. As we learn more about the functioning and structure of the human brain our knowledge of how they link to aggression will be understood more. We also have brain centres which control whether or not to respond aggressively in any given situation. If someone your own age and size pushes you, you may choose to push back. If someone twenty-five centimetres taller and fifty kilograms heavier pushes you, you may think better of it. Retaliation doesn't make much sense if you will definitely come off worse afterwards. Biological brain structures are obviously involved in aggression.

Psychoanalysis, and Lorenz's ethological theories see the urge for aggression building up slowly until it finally breaks out. This implies that the human brain contains storage systems for aggressive energies. Bio-psychologists may want to investigate the existence of such stores. A particular event may trigger the aggression. Nature does provide such triggers. For example, something causes birds to migrate, squirrels to wake up from hibernation and most animals to want to mate. The biological approach would say that certain species inherit a pre-disposition or readiness to behave aggressively. If the necessary event occurs, the aggression will be triggered.

This is all very well for explaining aggression for survival, mating or hunting food in lower-order animals. However, humans are not slaves to their genes or their urges. Our cognitive brain centres can give us messages which will help us to survive, for example, by not responding aggressively. You may plot revenge on someone who uses their superior strength or power to threaten you. You are not automatically triggered to fight back if fighting means you will be hurt badly. You make an assessment of the situation and judge what is the best course of action based on what you know. You acquire this information through social learning. Social learning comes from observation and imitation, from rehearsal and reinforcement, from modelling and identification.

Exercise on aggression

1 What is aggression?
2 What do Freud and Lorenz's explanations have in common?
3 Summarize Bandura's conclusion from the Bobo doll experiments.
4 How would the supporters of biological explanations of aggression explain sex differences in aggression?
5 How do social learning theorists explain sex differences in aggression?

Activity
List as many television programmes as you can which feature aggression or violence. How many are films, soaps, cartoons, dramas, children programmes? Have a class discussion along the lines that social learning theorists would see a link between children's being exposed to violence and their behaving violently, while others see aggression as being biological in origin.

Reducing aggression

▷
One of Moniz's patients must have been rather upset by what the doctor had done to him. He acquired a gun and shot and paralysed the good doctor!

Evidence suggests that the likelihood and level of aggressive behaviour is influenced by a combination of biological (nature) and social (nurture) forces. The biological component could be controlled by such radical measures as deliberately altering hormone levels through brain surgery or drug treatment. However, this is unacceptable in most Western and other societies today. In the past, brain surgery has been used in this way. A Portuguese surgeon named **Egas Moniz** pioneered the use of **prefrontal lobotomies**, which is a surgical operation to cut the nerves which connect parts of the brain. Thousands of such operations were performed in Europe and America between the 1930s and 1960s. The patients can suffer drastic and irreversible personality changes. They can lose interest in things, generally slow down, and their thinking becomes confused. They sometimes have seizures and find life difficult. Psychosurgery might cure their aggression, but at how high a cost?

If socialization explains aggression, then there are several possibilities. If reinforcement promotes and maintains aggression then removing its association with aggressive behaviour should reduce the likelihood of aggression. Praising children for behaving aggressively may lead parents to think that they are teaching their children to obtain what they want, to stand up for themselves, not to be pushed around, etc. If all children receive this message, we simply promote aggression and violence. Reinforcing cooperative behaviour makes more sense. If people learn that it pays to cooperate, we may reduce the appeal of achievement through aggression.

▷
Reinforcement is a powerful motivating force in children. Sadly, parents threaten and punish their children for wrongdoing far more than they praise and encourage them for good behaviour.

If people learn through observing, imitating, and modelling, as social learning theory claims, then we must provide positive, cooperative images of people relating to each other. We should encourage and educate parents (and teachers) to behave less aggressively and more cooperatively. They should try to help children find other means of solving their problems and achieving their ends. Restricting children's access to violent television programmes and trying to reduce the ways in which aggressive acts receive reinforcement could also be helpful.

Parents could also encourage empathy in their children. We will discuss the development of empathy in Chapter 13. Empathy is an understanding that people often have of the feelings and needs of other people. Even quite young children are capable of showing some understanding and sympathy towards others who are clearly in distress. This caring approach could be reinforced.

Exercise on reducing aggression

1 What is reinforcement?
2 How do children learn, according to social learning theory?
3 Explain how a child could be taught to share its toys by a combination of reinforcement and social learning approaches.

4 What is empathy?

5 How might a parent encourage empathy in a child?

 Summary on reducing aggression

It is possible to reduce most undesirable behaviour by removing parts of the brain or administering powerful drugs. However, this is very drastic and not widely acceptable now. Selectively reinforcing desirable behaviour and downplaying undesirable behaviour may be enough to shape someone's behaviour. Teaching and encouraging empathy and providing pro-social models should also help.

Personality

If you asked a large number of people what they thought psychology was about, many of them would suggest the study of personality. To some extent they would be right. Personality is, after all, one of the main ways in which people are different from one another. In this chapter, we will be asking what psychologists mean exactly by the term personality, and we will look at how its meaning has changed over the years. We will also discuss some of the major explanations for personality. We have already introduced one of them, psychoanalytic theory, in Chapter 1. Some theories suggest that many personality characteristics are genetically transmitted and remain fairly fixed throughout our lives. Others say that we acquire our personalities as we interact with and learn from other people during our lives.

Exercise on what you are like

(You may prefer to do this exercise away from other people.)

1 Write down ten statements to describe what you are like, beginning each with the words 'I am ...'.
2 Which of the statements you have just written do you think your parents would agree with?
3 Which would they disagree with?
4 Would they add some others? If so, what else might they say?
5 Which of the statements would your best friends agree with?
6 Which would they disagree with?
7 Which would they add?
8 Mark with a 'B' those of your statements which suggest that you belong to someone or to some group or organization.
9 Mark with an 'I' each of your statements that suggests that you are an individual.
10 What is your ratio of 'B's to 'I's? How does it compare to other people's ratios? Does it tell you anything about how you see yourself?

What is personality?

You may hear people say something like, 'He may not be very good-looking but he has a wonderful personality'. They are suggesting that personality is made up of certain qualities such as being pleasant and helpful, being charming, even being appealing. This isn't quite the way psychologists think of personality, although, as they have been known to describe and explained personality in many different ways, this common-sense usage is probably just as good!

Personality is one of those irritating words that everyone knows, but no-one can fully define. It's rather like intelligence. We all think we know what it is, until we try to explain it to someone else. Turning to the *Penguin Dictionary of Psychology* for a concise definition of personality, we find that 'no coherent statement about it can be made', and that 'we shall not characterize the term definitionally'. There then follows 1,400 words on how the term has been used in no fewer than seven perspectives on psychology. Perhaps, therefore, we should not attempt here to define the term, yet it hardly seems fair to call a section in a book (and a whole area in psychology) personality, and then fail to define it. So, we will offer a rather inadequate definition up front, and try to give more specific definitions as they apply to each theory.

We shall begin, therefore, with the following: 'personality is the particular pattern of thoughts, feelings and behaviour that characterize an individual and influence the way he or she interacts with the environment. It is what makes each person unique and individual'. Just about all established definitions of personality include references to uniqueness of thoughts, ideas, and feelings, and characteristic behaviour patterns which are supposed to be **consistent** over time and in different situations.

The problem is, do you have particular, distinctive, or characteristic thoughts, feelings or behaviour that remain constant over time and across various situations? In other words, do you always respond in similar ways in similar situations? Do you always donate to charities? Do you always do your best? Do you never tell a lie? Do you never become anxious or nervous? I suspect that the answers to these and similar questions will depends on the situation and how you are at the time, in which case you are not particularly consistent. If you do always respond in the same ways then we can know what you are like. We can describe any consistent patterns as your personality. In this case, psychologists can offer explanations for where these patterns come from.

▷ *The Penguin Dictionary of Psychology* cannot give a simple definition of personality because no simple meaning exists. As psychology has grown and new ideas and theories have been advanced, the attitude psychologists have taken towards personality has changed. This varies from a preoccupation with it in psychoanalytic theory, to a dismissal of it by behaviourism!

▷ The term consistent here means thinking or behaving in a way which is constant, unchanging and predictable.

Exercise on whether or not you are consistent

1 What would you do if:
   (a) your girlfriend/boyfriend said she/he loved you?
   (b) a total stranger of the opposite sex said she/he loved you?
   (c) a total stranger of the same sex said she/he loved you?

2 What would you do if:
  (a) a 10-year-old boy hit a 5-year-old boy (you don't know either of them)?
  (b) the 5-year-old is your son?
  (c) the 5-year-old had just kicked the 10-year-old?

3 Would you buy a raffle ticket to support:
  (a) new toys for a local hospital's children's ward?
  (b) a private school's new swimming pool?
  (c) a day at the races for the men in the Social Club in the pub you are in?

Summary of defining personality

Although it is very difficult to define, personality is one of those words that everyone knows the meaning of. Essentially, it refers to those characteristics that are supposed to be fairly permanent, although often they are not.

Activity

Ask some friends to define personality and see what they come up with. The chances are that they won't really be able to answer at all.

How many personalities do you have?

▷
Can you imagine someone who has a fierce temper and who hates practical jokes being set up for a stunt by Jeremy Beadle? Someone must know that the people who are set up can 'take a joke' and that they will play up until they realize what's happened. Perhaps we can predict in general terms what someone is like.

▷
A self-concept is a set of ideas we learn about ourselves, about what we are (a little girl, a baby, a daughter, etc.), and what we are like (pretty, clever, cheeky, happy).

If personality is to do with the unique and characteristic ways in which you think and behave, then it should be possible to predict more or less what you would think and do in just about any situation. This may be generally true, but we will all have been surprised to see someone we know acting out of character. Perhaps you have noticed an abnormal reaction in yourself to something. To say that you acted out of character on a given occasion, implies that you usually act in character. (Character can be taken to mean much the same as personality here.)

Some babies are easy to manage, some are more difficult. Some take time before they start to enjoy interaction, some interact brightly. These differences reflect differences in **temperament**. We are probably born with our temperament. This refers to how we generally react to such things as loud noises, sleep time, feeding, stimulation, contact, etc. Some babies are described as good. They are usually responsive and curious. Others are ordinarily more irritable and cry more. As we grow and are involved in socialization, our personalities develop further. (Later on, we will discuss whether biology or the environment is more influential.)

As a result of socialization we acquire what psychologists in Western countries, such as Europe and America, call our **self-concept.** It has always been assumed that we have just one of these. **John Rowan** disagrees. He has read many accounts of the nature of personality and the evidence from psychological experiments. He has also reviewed the case notes from people under therapy for some personality disorders. Rowan gives the following conclusion:

'It is an extraordinary thing that all personality theories assume that there is just one personality. The questions they then ask are what is the structure of this personality, what are the functions of this personality, what are the origins of this personality, what can we predict about this personality?

But these assumptions are just assumptions, and they are made largely because it is convenient to do so.... Personologists are lazy people, like the rest of us, and do not want the bother of considering that people might be multiple. And other psychologists studying questions like the self, identity and so forth, are only too pleased to fall in with this for their own particular purposes.'

Instead, Rowan (among others) claims that humans have several sub-personalities. The exact nature and function of these sub-personalities is yet to be revealed, but Rowan calls for a radical re-think of our current understanding of the concept of personality.

Comment on personality

Personality has come to describe how people customarily respond to most situations. As humans, we show our temperamental dispositions shortly after birth, and learn what we are like by how others respond to us. This leads to the development of our self-concept. By adolescence we should have developed a personality. However, Rowan suggests that this idea is too simple and is the result of researchers not wanting to have to investigate this potentially very complicated area. He believes we have many sub-personalities which fit our behaviour to particular circumstances and situations.

Summary of the extent of personality

Some people occasionally act in unpredictable ways. This could indicate the existence of more than one sub-personality, which may be active under different circumstances.

Theories of personality

Like all theories, personality theories are statements about what the personalities of certain categories of people are like, where they originated, how they developed, etc. They are theories about how personality works, and they should help us to understand what people are like, and predict what they might do in the future. Inevitably, different theorists who favour different perspectives (such as psychoanalytic theory and behaviourism, discussed in Chapter 1) will not all offer the same theories.

Early psychologists looked for those personality characteristics which make people similar to one another. More recently they have been interested in what makes each person unique. Essentially, personality theories could be grouped into five categories, as follows:

1　personality-type and personality-trait theories, which support the nature view and claim that some aspects of our personalities are genetically inherited;

2　psycho dynamic theories;

3　learning theories;

4　humanistic theories;

5　cognitive theories.

We will describe each in turn.

Biological explanations – trait and type theories

Type theories

When we meet someone for the first time we tend to place them in some category, such as being pleasant, friendly, nice, sarcastic, funny, okay, likeable, big headed, arrogant, etc. We may think they are posh, stupid, a punk, a dosser, a wrinkly, etc. Categorizing or stereotyping people in this way makes our relationships with them more predictable. We may want to avoid them if we think they are stupid, big-headed or arrogant. Or we may want to be with them more if they are likeable, funny, or we feel would like to be more like them. We might tolerate them if they're harmless, or ridicule them if they are very different from us.

In type theory, a **type** refers to a person who is remarkably consistent in his or her attitudes and reactions. Are you an easy-going type, or a serious-minded type? Are you a perfectionist or a near-enough type? A well-known type was first described by Jung. He differentiated introverts from extroverts. Introverts are typically shy and withdrawn. They are more inward-directed. They prefer to avoid company and are wary of strangers. Extroverts are more outer-directed. They enjoy company and seek excitement.

The first types were suggested at around 400 BC. Since then several **typologies** have been suggested, for example, those which linked personality characteristics to body shapes. Fat people are often regarded as rather jolly. Thin people are thought of as serious. The first real attempt to link body shape to consistent personality characteristics was advanced by **William Sheldon** in 1942.

▷
Being an example of one type (e.g. very cautious) usually excludes you from being an example of another type (e.g. a risk-taker). It would be impossible to be an introvert and an extrovert at the same time.

▷
A typology is a classification of types.

Activity
Do you rate others as types? Think about your closest friends. What type, if any, would you say each of them was an example of?

▷

Somatotype literally means body shape, but is always used in psychology to mean a supposed link between body shape and temperament. It is highly unlikely that any such link exists.

Sheldon used photographs of several thousand naked men to see if men's body shapes could be categorized into types. Although no specific body shapes could be called types, he claimed that they all possessed one of three body shapes. Each man could be rated from 1 to 7 according to how much of each body shape he possessed. He called them **somatotypes**.

One somatotype is the round and soft body shape. A man who is round and soft, even inclined to fat, is an **endomorph**. This means he is supposed to be warm and friendly and fond of eating! Someone who is strong and muscular, then, is a **mesomorph**, and therefore supposedly energetic, confident and brave. **Ectomorphs** are tall, thin and weak. They are described as intelligent and artistic, creative and introverted. This is such a simplistic explanation, however, that few people would take it seriously today.

Of course not all men fit neatly into one of Sheldon's categories. They may be a bit of both, or more of one than the others. Here we have the rating for four subjects.

	Subject A	Subject B	Subject C	Subject D
Endomorph	7	1	4	2
Mesomorph	1	7	4	3
Ectomorph	1	1	4	4

Subject A is strongly endomorphic. Subject B is clearly mesomorphic. Subject C is a combination of all of them. Subject D is a bit more of some than others. Think of famous celebrities who would represent each of these categories. Then think of others and describe their characteristics.

▷

Correlation is a statistical test for measuring whether two things are likely to occur together.

An alternative type theory has tried to link personality characteristics to blood type. In Japan **Toshitaka Nomi** claims to have found **correlations** between people with the four major blood groups and certain personality characteristics. If you have type A blood then you are likely to be hard working and peaceful. You have high self-consciousness and pay great attention to detail. If you have type B blood you are said to be original, individualistic and creative. Type O blood correlates with being realistic and aggressive, whereas if your blood is type AB you are thought to be moody and deceitful. It seems highly unlikely that people's temperaments are linked to their blood type. The many environmental and social forces acting upon us are much more likely to shape our personalities.

The type theories described above would be dismissed by anyone except the most determined supporter of the influence of genes and biology on human behaviour. Twenty years ago, **Hans Eysenck** published the findings of research he had been undertaking since the late 1940s. He claimed that, to discover whether there are general personality types, we must first observe people's behaviour to see what patterns emerge. We start at the **specific-response level**, i.e. exactly what do you do under any given circumstance.

▷

At the specific response level, we observe actual behaviour (e.g. we see you donate some money to charity).

Start with one subject. Let's imagine that we observe you behaving in a generous way. Your specific response to being asked for money to help someone in need was to give money. Further observations of you in similar situations show you behaving generously. It seems that you usually behave generously. We're moving from the specific to the more general. This is the **habitual-response level**. It is your habit to behave generously. We also observed your being helpful on several occasions. Helpfulness is another habitual response. So is thoughtfulness. Putting these three responses together, Eysenck would claim to have found a trait. The trait here would be caring. Being caring is one of your personality traits.

Eysenck identified the main personality traits which describe most people's personalities. (Allport found 18,000 or so adjectives which the English language uses to describe personality.) A trait is a simple description of one aspect of the way someone approaches things. Someone might be careful, or thoughtful, or moody for example.

Eysenck statistically analysed the results of personality tests completed by 700 Second World War soldiers, each containing 39 items of personal information. He found that the main traits clustered around two essential dimensions in personality. These are **introversion** and **extroversion** (the E – for extroversion – scale), and **stability** and **instability** (the N – for neurotic – scale). Look at this diagram now.

▷ At the habitual-response level, you help people when they need help(e.g. you shop for some disabled people and carry shopping for an elderly lady).

▷ N.B. the caring trait refers to your general disposition, i.e. the way you are likely to act in a particular situation. It is not an example of your acting in that way. When we see you helping someone to cross the road, we are not observing a personality characteristic, we're observing the behaviour that results from a personality characteristic.

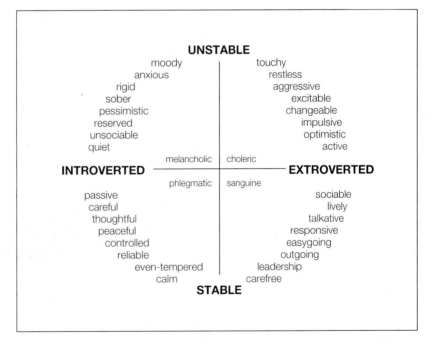

Eysenck's model

▷ Take care not to use the term personality test. A test is usually a set of questions that have right and wrong answers. which you can pass or fail. Personality questionnaires can't be passed or failed, there are no right or wrong answers.

Five years later Eysenck repeated his statistical analysis to see if there were any other personality types. This time he used data provided by patients defined as mentally ill. This may be of interest if the research was only to be applied to people with such problems. It isn't likely to be of much use if applied to people generally. Other research on personality questionnaire data has found evidence to support the E and N scales, but not so much for the P scale, as you would expect in the normal population.

▷
Eysenck claims to have found consistent differences in other aspects of behaviour that correlate with being introverted or extroverted. This isn't surprising. If we find that some people have some things in common so that we classify them as introverted, and others have different things in common so that we describe them as extrovert, then it is to be expected that introverts are different in other ways from extroverts.

▷
Dopamine is a chemical involved in the passage of electrical nervous energy around parts of the brain.

While we said earlier that in a true type theory an individual can belong to only one category, this is not entirely true in Eysenck's explanation. While you could not be introverted and extroverted at the same time, you could be introverted and unstable or introverted and stable at the same time. You could be neither introvert nor extrovert, but either stable or unstable. As these are dimensions of personality, different combinations are possible.

Eysenck has used tests to discover consistent differences in the ways in which introverts and extroverts react to the same situations, For example introverts have lower tolerances to pain than extroverts. Introverts learn quicker when there is little chance of being reinforced and when they are not highly alert. Extroverts need more specific reinforcement or a higher level of alertness. Introverts do not become bored quickly, and a modest amount of stimulation can involve them for quite some time. Extroverts do become bored quite quickly, and need a constant supply of new things to do. People scoring high and low on the stability and instability scale also show consistent differences. For example, the highly unstable types are more likely to react quickly and impulsively to any situation. Those who score at the stable end of the scale take more time to consider their response.

Finding such consistent differences between introverts and extroverts, and stable and unstable people, led Eysenck to conclude that there must be a biological basis for personality. Some animal research has found that highly excitable animals produce more of a brain chemical called **dopamine** than do passive animals. This has been confirmed in humans. Extroverts, who are more active and energetic, produce more dopamine than introverts do. If Eysenck is right, and introversion and extroversion are determined by dopamine (and other) biological activity, then he is assuming that it is the dopamine that causes the extroversion. However, perhaps it is the rushing around and being an excited extrovert which causes the dopamine levels to rise.

Eysenck argues that, as introverts are inner directed they would be easier to condition than extroverts who are more outer directed. In Chapter 1 we considered that most animals, including people, learn by association that some things go together. When one thing occurs, they respond in anticipation of the other. This is conditioning. Eysenck claimed to have found evidence that introverts can be taught the association more quickly than extroverts, and this supports the view that there is a biogenetic basis for introversion and extroversion. However, the evidence for this is far from convincing

Trait theories

▷
If someone usually behaves in much the same way we may think of that person possessing certain traits. A trait is a fairly long-lasting characteristic of a person which explains why they behave in the particular way that they do.

Type theorists suggest that you have either one dimension to your personality or another. Your blood is either type O or it isn't, you are either an introvert or you are not. Trait theorists take a different view. They believe that we each possess a certain amount of many traits, some of which could even be opposing. There are some traits that we all possess to some extent, such as caring, kindness, helpfulness or leadership.

Trait theorists have three aims. First, they attempt to find enough traits to describe most of the characteristics of personality in humans. Second, and like type theorists, they try to devise accurate and reliable ways of measuring them. Third, they look for any relationships among traits themselves, and between traits and specific human behaviour. Different trait theorists have approached these tasks in different ways.

Gordon Allport was one of the most influential trait theorists. He thought that personality consisted of the sum total of all one's traits. It is the exact combination of all your traits, each of which you possess to varying extents, that makes you unique. Allport was not interested in explaining personality generally, but he wanted instead to study each person's individual personality.

▷
Allport was only interested in understanding how traits make up an individual's personality. He was not interested in suggesting principles that would apply to people's personalities generally.

He thought there were three kinds of traits. First, there are **cardinal traits**, which are the major themes around which people organize their lives. For Christians, for example, it may be self-sacrifice and devotion to their God. For soldiers it may be service and dedication to the defence of the land. For politicians it may be the desire for power and glory. Or, as it was for Freud, it may be fame through scientific discovery (although not all people possess such ambitions, of course).

Second, there are **central traits**. These are the main ways in which we think of people. So, if you had to give a brief description of your best friend, you could say she is honest, loyal, and trustworthy. These are her central traits.

Finally, there are the less important, secondary traits. These are to do with people's attitudes to particular things, their styles of dress, the things they prefer, and other behaviour, all of which are not particularly important.

As we said earlier, Allport had counted 18,000 words in the English language which describe personality traits. He and his colleagues reduced this to 4,500 words which were sufficiently different as to have, each, a distinct meaning. During the 1950s, **Raymond Cattell** used a statistical technique called **factor analysis** to reduce this number to about 200.

▷
Factor analysis is a complicated statistical technique which finds terms whose meanings are highly correlated so that repetitions can be eliminated. Only terms whose meanings are sufficiently different and not overlapping remain. These are called factors.

Cattell asked some subjects to rate each of their friends on this list of factors. Many of the friends had many factors in common. These were also subjected to factor analysis and reduced to twelve major personality factors. These included warmth, intelligence, emotional stability, cheerfulness, conscientiousness, sensitivity, suspiciousness, etc. However, rating other people may overlook important traits, so he had a sample describe and rate their own traits. From the analysis of their results, he found four more traits, which were then added to the twelve. These were willingness to try, self-sufficiency, self-discipline, and tension.

Cattell developed a questionnaire comprising 100 questions demanding answers of 'yes', 'sometimes' or 'no', which could be plotted on a graph of the sixteen factors which would give the person's personality profile. This is called the 16 PF Questionnaire (16 PF stands for Sixteen Personality Factors). There are five variations of this questionnaire and it has been widely used in personnel selection, assessment, and in research. It has also been used as a tool in therapy to find what people think of themselves. However, this application may not always be very useful.

People who have difficulties sufficient for them to need therapy, for instance, may also find it difficult to fill out a questionnaire. Their answers may not be judged to be entirely valid.

Summary of trait and type theories

There are a number of other trait and type theories, but those of Allport and Cattell serve to illustrate them. Allport's view, for example, does not explain all behaviour, but only the behaviour of the individual being studied. Personality traits are seen as representing the whole person and can only be seen in terms of that person's whole life. Cattell and others suggest theories to explain how personality links to behaviour in all people.

Comment on trait and type theories

All trait and type theories are criticized for not giving any reasons for why our personality directs us to behave as we do, only correlations between actual behaviour and traits or types. Also, they don't make any suggestions about how personality develops, only what traits and types it consists of. Worse still, those traits and types are the result of statistical analysis of English dictionary entries. Some are the result of self-rating, which may not be a very reliable measure and anyway our personalities are not consistent, we often behave differently depending on how we see the particular circumstances we find ourselves in.

Exercise on trait and type theories

1 What is the difference between a trait and a type?
2 Why do we type people? What does typing help us to do?
3 Name Eysenck's two major dimensions of personality.
4 What evidence led Eysenck to conclude that types are biologically inherited?
5 Outline the difference between cardinal, central, and secondary traits.

Psychoanalytic theories

Psychoanalytic theories attempt to explain the formation and development of personality. They stress interactions between biogenetic factors, such as instinctive urges and drives, and environmental and social factors, such as identification with adults. In Chapter 1 we looked at the major psychoanalytic theories of **Sigmund Freud**. In this chapter we will see how psychoanalytic theory explains adult personality.

One of the most important features in Freud's theory is that of the **unconscious mind**. Freud was convinced that the human mind is like an iceberg, of which 80 per cent is below the surface and can't be seen. The 20 per cent is the conscious part, the rest is the unconscious part. After many years of therapy sessions, asking probing questions, using hypnosis,

▷
Freud was widely criticized for many of his claims. His belief in the existence of the unconscious mind and what it was supposed to do caused some of the fiercest attacks on his theories.

analysing dreams and slips of the tongue, listening to jokes and folklore, myths and legend, of reading widely and imagining and realizing, Freud gradually came to believe that he understood the purpose and structure of the unconscious mind.

Freud claimed that the unconscious mind contained many instincts which urge us to behave in all sorts of ways. Freud identified three major instinctive urges. The first is the **id**, and is rather like the power source for the personality. It is the source of all **psychic energy**. The id is irrational (illogical) and is totally pleasure-seeking. It is based on what Freud called the **pleasure principle**. Throughout our lives, the id is imagined to force us to satisfy all of our needs urgently, regardless of whether we should, or of what might happen to us if we did. If the id wants something, the id demands to have it.

Simply demanding satisfaction immediately is not always going to work, however. If a 2-year-old demands juice without saying 'please', his parents may well not let him have the juice. The **ego** appears when the id fails to be satisfied. The ego is more logical than the id, seeking sensible solutions to the id's demands. Saying 'please' is more likely to lead to the juice being provided, so it makes sense to say 'please'. The ego makes decisions about what will or will not happen. It is based on what Freud called the **reality principle**.

The third part of the personality to appear is called the **superego.** The superego is learned through identifying with the same-sex parent. Freud thought that a son would start to feel jealous of his father for taking is mother's tender love and attention away from him. Of course, he is also afraid that his father might find out about his feelings for his mother. He might resent his father and feel jealousy, guilt and fear. These emotions are called the **Oedipus Complex**. In order to resolve them, the child identifies with his father, and takes on several aspects of his father's personality, including his father's views of what is acceptable or unacceptable, what is right or wrong, what is good or bad. This knowledge becomes part of the child's **superego.** The superego includes the conscience and is based on the **morality principle**.

There will be occasions when the id and the superego are in conflict. You may be hungry, so your id is demanding that you find and eat food. You may be near a sweet shop, but you have no money so you are tempted (i.e. your id is urging you) to steal some sweets. Your superego possesses knowledge about what is acceptable and good. It wouldn't find stealing acceptable. Superego also houses your conscience which will punish you if you do steal. This conflict causes **anxiety**, and will give rise to feelings of being uncomfortable, frightened or worried about what might happen. The ego is the executive decision maker. Freud believed it was sometimes urged by the id and the superego in opposite directions.

The ego has a problem. It needs to find a compromise, and in many circumstances it will be able to find one. There will be some occasions when it can't.

Freud suggested that the ego has three possible ways to resolve this conflict. The aim is to work the conflict through in the unconscious. Dreams provide one way of achieving this. Dreams allow us to fulfil all

▷ The pleasure principle is Freud's idea that the major force driving the development of personality during the first two years of life is the desire to satisfy any wish.

▷ The reality principle deals with children's growing awareness of their environment and the effects that their demands have upon it. Children learn to modify their demands in response to their parents' and other people's reactions to them.

▷ The morality principle describes children's drives towards doing what they 'ought' to do and avoiding what they 'ought not' to do. It leads them to learn all their responsibilities and duties.

those wishes and desires that we couldn't possibly fulfil in reality. Dreaming about being incredibly rich and buying loads of the most gorgeous chocolate bars, sweets and cakes and never being hungry or needing to steal again would be one way to reduce the conflict. Freud regarded the analysis of dreams as one of the most useful tools available to a therapist. If therapists can interpret what you dream, they can understand what is causing your conflict.

Another way to stop the conflict from growing is for the ego to use one of its many **defence mechanisms**. Again, these are quite unconscious (and quite normal). They don't remove the conflict between the id and superego, but they do distract us so that we don't notice the conflict quite so much. It is rather like keeping very busy when you are very upset. It does not lessen the cause of your unhappiness, but it does keep your mind off it. Perhaps the conflict between your id and superego may disappear on its own, maybe you can convince someone that you're not to blame, or you weren't involved, or someone made you do it. The aim of defence mechanisms is to reduce the conflict. The following table lists of some of the major defence mechanisms.

▷
Dreams are one way in which conflicts between what you would like to do and what you know you can do are resolved.

▷
Defence mechanisms are unconscious processes intended to protect the self or ego from anxiety-producing situations.

Name	Description	Examples
Denial	Refusing to acknowledge something that would be too upsetting or frightening.	Your boyfriend hasn't finished with you. A loved one hasn't died.
Displacement	Taking your feelings out on someone (or something) else because you can't express them to the appropriate person.	Your teacher punishes you for something you haven't done so you scream at your younger sister.
Identification	Modelling yourself on someeone else so that you become as like them as you can.	A son models part of his father's ideas, attitudes and behaviour.
Sublimation	Redirecting libido from unacceptable wishes and desires into acceptable and constructive activities. It can also be a direct, intentional act.	Playing football, painting a picture, playing a musical instrument help sublimate unhappiness after a breakdown in a relationship.
Projection	The opposite of identification: you say that someone else has the feelings that would otherwise cause you distress.	Knowing that I was greatly tempted to steal the sweets, when stopped, I blame you for really wanting to steal them.
Repression	The ultimate defence mechanism, forcing a thought or memory that could cause great distress out of consciousness and into the unconscious mind. Therapy may be needed for the person to come to terms with the memory..	Someone cannot remember a major accident that he or she was in.

There are dozens of defence mechanisms. They can be used in various combinations. Unconsciously they protect the ego and provide some time for the conflicts that triggered them to be dealt with in other ways. As such they are perfectly healthy, and to varying extents everyone uses them. However, a danger could occur if they become overused, and become a substitute for recognizing reality. An adult who had lost touch with reality would no longer be neurotic but would be diagnosed as **psychotic**. Psychoses are severe mental disorders where people fail to see things in the same way that most people do. They lose touch with reality. They make obvious mistakes about who people are and what things are for, and continue to make the same errors despite all the evidence against their view.

The third consequence of conflict between the parts of personality is the emergence of some neurotic symptoms during adulthood. This usually occurs because the other defence mechanisms weren't available when they were needed, or because they haven't been completely success-ful. Instead repression has occurred and some emotional energy (libido) has been fixated. This is most likely to happen during childhood. Repression is the first defence mechanism that children use. As we grow older we are better able to deal with our emotions. Young children are more likely to repress conflicts or anxieties.

▷
There are many forms of neurosis. Those which Freud identified are still widely recognized by psychiatrists today.

As an adult our repressed anxieties may emerge through some neurotic symptoms. Freud suggested that there are four main types of neuroses in adulthood (although he added others later). These are:

anxiety neuroses, where adults are particularly sensitive to some things which would upset them;

phobic neuroses, such as fear of snakes, spiders, the dark, cinemas, etc.;

obsessive compulsive neuroses, where adults can't seem to stop thinking about something, e.g. the need for cleanliness, or can't stop behaving in some way, such as washing their hands;

hysterical neuroses, where odd behaviour is a symptom of earlier repression.

Some children will face great conflicts and anxieties over some impor-tant features of personality development. These are caused by their interactions with the environment during the early stages of personality development. Here is a summary:

▷
Someone with an oral character is either overgenerous, overexcited and hopelessly optimistic or aggressive, depressive, and very pessimistic.

The first erogenous zone is the mouth. The libido gains satisfaction through sucking, swallowing, licking, biting, chewing, etc. It is important that the libido achieves adequate satisfaction during this **oral stage**. If children receive too little oral stimulation, their personalities may become fixated (get stuck). As adults, they become rather sarcastic, depressed, and pessimistic. They find it difficult to make friends and are loners. They try to manipulate other people and are selfish and uncaring. As children they may have sucked their thumbs, pens or pencils, talked too much and eaten too many sweets. As adults they may smoke, and still try to dominate others.

If they receive too much stimulation, the libido may still become fixated. As adults they develop a rather higher opinion of themselves than

The desire to exert power lies at the heart of the anal stage. Someone with an anal-expulsive character will probably be untidy, overgenerous, and will agree with whatever other people are saying. He or she will lack discipline and may feel weak and ineffective. Someone with an anal-retentive character is obsessed with tidiness, cleanliness, punctuality. He or she might also be very cruel and rather miserable.

they deserve. They become overoptimistic, overgenerous, and are easily conned by others. They are easily roused and have short tempers. They may rely too much on others to make decisions for them, and might look to others to mother them. All these are symptoms of the oral character.

The second erogenous zone is the anus. Children find pleasure in controlling their faeces during the **anal stage**. They also have some power over their parents, as they can control some of their parents' behaviour. For instance, they can make their parents late by relieving themselves at inappropriate moments! Parents vary in how much discipline they use to potty-train their children. This might interfere with the children's desire to give or withhold their faeces. It may result in some fixation of the libido. If the parents use too little encouragement and the id wins the battle, a personality may become fixated and this can lead to the **anal-expulsive** or the **anal-retentive character.**

From the age of about three, the male sex organ (the phallus) becomes the main source of pleasure for boys. Freud claimed that sons have their first sexual feelings during this stage and the objects of those feelings are their mothers. Not all children have parents who provide ideal role models. For many, the father-figure may be absent altogether, or available only sometimes. For some, their mothers may be too occupied, or too exhausted, to do all of the things other mothers are able to do with their children. Other fathers are too strict or have little understanding of their children's needs. So, according to Freud, some children's personalities may become fixated in the phallic stage. Fixation here may produce adults who are dominant, aggressive, uncaring and cruel. They will have high opinions of themselves and seek to dominate others. They may be very proud and may enjoy danger.

Freud did not claim that everyone will have repressed many anxieties. Most people's early years will be happy and the ego will have successfully resolved whatever conflicts it faced. However, for those who are less fortunate, the symptoms of neurosis include temporary amnesia, hydrophobia, a temporary squint, uncontrollable hand-twitching, a morbid fear of something, temporary paralysis or many distortions of reality.

Comment on psychoanalytic theories

Countless studies have been conducted to test various aspects of Freud's theories. Many have found evidence which supports the character types which Freud described. For example, people who are overconcerned with cleanliness, orderliness, and meanness *do* exist. This does not, however, prove the existence of an anal character. Such people may simply have been socialized by people who were concerned also with these things. Or their own experiences may have made them this way.

Freud is accused of having an answer for everything. It is impossible to confirm or challenge the explanations Freud identified. Driving forces for good and bad, primitive urges, looking for rational solutions, and the emergence of conscience may all be seen in people's behaviour. None of these features, however, supports the existence of the libido, death instincts, id, ego, or superego, despite Freud's claims to have made a scientific breakthrough. His methods of 'free talk', interpretation of dreams, interpretation of slips of the tongue, interpretation of sense of humour, etc., are not scientifically acceptable. Nor were the particular people Freud studied in any way representative of all people. Most of his patients were neurotic, and the majority were middle-class Jewish women living in Vienna between the 1880s and 1920s. Yet despite these criticisms, many people still find Freud's theories and explanations to be temptingly believable and a source of inspiration.

Exercise on psychoanalytic theories

1 Explain what is meant by repression.
2 What are defence mechanisms used for?
3 What would an adult be like who suffered excessive repression in the oral stage?
4 What is the role of the superego in Freud's theory?
5 What are dreams for?

●●● Summary of psychoanalytic views

Unconscious urges, such as the id and ego, are said to drive our personality through various stages, avoiding anxiety and developing our emotions. Excessive or too little stimulation can cause unconscious anxiety, which will need to be dealt with by some defence mechanism if our adult personality is not to be disturbed.

Learning and personality

According to most learning theorists, psychology can and should only be taken seriously if it is a scientific subject. To be scientific it must develop and use scientifically acceptable methods of observation, data collection, measurement, and statistical analysis of results. There is no place in science for guesses about the contributions of biological factors, the unconscious mind, urges and drives. The only area that is worthy of study is that of human behaviour, as this can be observed and measured. So, they claim, we don't really need the concept of personality at all.

Ivan Pavlov had claimed that the vast majority of human behaviour was no more than sets of classically conditioned responses. This was a rather exaggerated claim, as there is much more to human learning than the development of associations between simple stimuli and reflexive responses. **J.B. Watson** first used the term 'behaviourism' in 1913 to argue that most aspects of personality – including fears and phobias of people and things, the usual ways in which we do things, and the conflicts that we face – are no more than classically conditioned responses, just as salivation was a classically conditioned response in Pavlov's dogs. (See page 8.)

▷
Behaviourists reject what they see as non-testable, hypothetical, imaginary explanations for aspects of human behaviour. Many dismiss altogether the usefulness of the idea of mental events. Their motto might be: 'If you can't record and measure it, don't waste time on it.'

B.F. Skinner

Dollard and Miller attempt to combine Freudian and behaviourist principles. They accept the ideas of repression and defence mechanisms.

Not all behaviour, however, is learned by association with a reflex. **B.F. Skinner** was probably the most influential behaviourist psychologist this century. He completely dismissed psychoanalytic references to the unconscious mind, the role of infantile sexuality, drives and instincts. He also disagreed with Watson's view that all behaviour could be explained by classical conditioning. In Chapter 1 we discussed the principles of operant conditioning (see page 11). Skinner believed that those terms which we use to describe personality – such as kind, caring, thoughtful, helpful, generous, etc. – are really only alternative ways of describing aspects of behaviour. Why would you say someone is kind? Because you may have seen that person behave in a kind way. Similarly, someone who is thought to have a generous disposition may have been seen behaving generously.

Skinner believed that there were certain fundamental laws which govern all human behaviour. He was more interested in discovering these laws than in trying to state a theory of personality. In Chapter 1 we discussed Skinner's claims that various types of reinforcement shape our behaviour. We learn to do things because, when we did something similar under similar conditions previously, we were successful.

In Chapter 5 we referred to John Dollard and Neal Miller's explanation for aggression. How aggressive someone is is just one aspect of their personality. Like Freud, Dollard and Miller thought that childhood experiences would influence personality. Young children need food and drink, comfort and stimulation. These needs are usually met by caregivers such as parents. If they aren't met, then repression may occur. Dollard and Miller accept the idea of repression and other defence mechanisms.

▶▶▶ *Activity*

Outline Skinner's explanation for the process of learning, and what he says about how we acquire our knowledge. Then outline Dollard and Miller's frustration–aggression hypothesis. How do the two compare?

As children grow, they will have to learn more complicated behaviour. Freud said that learning and behaviour are driven by the ego's finding acceptable compromises between id and superego's demands. As we said earlier, any conflict will have to be dealt with by dreams or defence mechanisms. Dollard and Miller also accept that many of our habits are the result of these defence mechanisms. For example, I might have found my new secondary school so frightening and intimidating that I started to play truant. My truanting habit was learned in order to avoid the distress that was associated with going to the big school.

Dollard and Miller also suggest that the aspects of behaviour which become associated with personality are learned through the process of **drive**, **cue**, **response**, and **reinforcement**. This idea links Freud's and Skinner's ideas. You are hungry. Hunger is a drive. You go the kitchen and make a sandwich. This is a cue for some behaviour to appear. You eat the sandwich. This is the response. You feel satisfied and your hunger drive has been removed. This is the reinforcement.

Exercise on learning and personality

1 Behaviourist techniques are claimed to be more scientific than Freudian methods. What does 'more scientific' mean?

2 What is science, and how does it differ from non-science?

3 Why does Skinner reject the need for the term 'personality'?

4 Give an example from your own experience of the four-stage process of drive, cue, response, and reinforcement to explain the drive to sleep.

Summary of behaviourist views of personality

Behaviourists claim that most of what we know, we have learned, although some attempts have been made to link Freud's ideas about the existence of instinctive drives and Skinner's ideas about reinforcement. According to Skinner, the consequences of any behaviour will affect the likelihood of that behaviour being repeated. Children are reinforced and punished at different times by different people for all kinds of things. Their personalities emerge from these selective reinforcements.

Social learning theory

Social learning theorists are the first major theorists to say that children and adults are actively involved in their own learning. Supporters of Freud and traditional behaviourists regard the child as reacting rather passively to influences which are beyond their control.

Like Dollard and Miller, social learning theorists following Albert Bandura have tried to merge some Freudian ideas about identification with Skinner's views on reinforcement. They say that we acquire the patterns of behaviour that make up our personality as we gain more experience of our environment. Unlike other behaviourists, social learning theorists do not see people as being passive and only behaving in ways for which they have previously been reinforced. They believe that people's interpretation of their environment is important. People are active in their own social learning.

We don't always behave in the same way in all similar situations. We have to learn the best way to behave in any particular situation. This learning – and therefore what we end up doing – will depend on many factors. These include:

- our (probably genetically inherited) temperament;
- whatever skills and talents we possess;
- our interpretation of the situation we are in;
- the expectations we have of what will happen to us if we behave in certain ways;
- the norms and values which we have learned;
- any plans we have for our future.

If the situation that you are in allows any of these factors to be appropriate, then they will influence your behaviour.

Exercise on social learning theory

See Chapter 5, page 95.

1 What did Bandura demonstrate with his Bobo doll?

2 What are role models, and why are they important in social learning theory?

3 We don't always behave in the same way in all similar situations. From the following list of factors, choose any that would influence you in:
(a) how you answer your mother's question 'do you like my new dress', when you actually think it's awful;
(b) telling someone you love that their pet has died;
(c) asking to borrow fifty pounds from your mum or dad to go on holiday.

Comment on behaviourist explanations for personality development

Watson's claim that all behaviour can be explained in terms of classical conditioning is highly doubtful. It implies that humans are little more than robots who aren't capable of making rational, conscious choices about their behaviour. A similar criticism is made of Skinner's view that all we need is to understand someone's particular behaviour in order to find what it is that is reinforcing that behaviour.

The major problem with psychoanalytic theory is that it offers no evidence for the existence of many of the claims it makes. Nor is it possible to test them. Dollard and Miller's drive reduction theory, and Bandura's social learning theory, include some aspects of psychoanalytic theory, and do allow experiments to be conducted which may find evidence to support their claims. Social learning theorists are the first major theorists to say that children and adults are actively involved in their own learning. Followers of Freud, together with traditional behaviourists, consider that children react rather passively to influences from beyond their control.

Summary of social learning theory

Bandura adapted Freudian ideas about the importance of identification, merging them with Skinner's views on the role of reinforcement. He added the idea of observation and modelling, and claimed that children's personalities result from a combination of identifying certain models, observing their behaviour, imitating it, identifying with some of them to varying extents, modelling their ideas and behaviour, and responding to any reinforcements.

Humanistic views

With the exception of Gordon Allport's trait theory, all the theories described so far have tried to explain personality from the outside, by asking what biological, environmental, or social influences shape an individual's behaviour. Like Allport, humanistic psychologists do not try to predict people's behaviour. They try to explain the behaviour from the inside, concentrating on how people see themselves and how they feel about their experiences.

Probably the best-known humanistic psychologist is **Abraham Maslow**. Maslow rejects psychoanalytic claims for the unconscious mind as well as simple behaviourist assumptions about reinforcement. He believes that human nature is essentially good and positive. Psychology ought to aim to help people achieve their potential and this starts with the process he called **self-actualization**. Maslow studied the characteristics of a number of people at various levels in American society to see what psychological qualities some had and others lacked. He identified a **hierarchy of needs.**

▷
A hierarchy is a series of grades, the most important at the top, and the least important at the bottom.

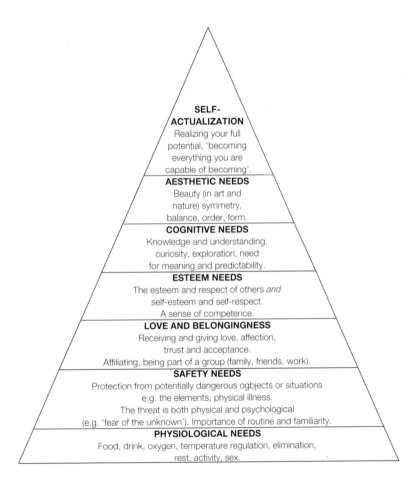

Maslow's hierarchy of needs

Humans have certain essential needs that must be met if they are to survive. The needs which form the base of the hierarchy are the bodily needs for food, drink, and shelter. The second level is formed of safety needs: we need to feel secure and not in danger. Third, there are the needs we feel to belong to something such as our family or friends. Fourth, there are the needs to achieve, to be competent, to have people value us. At the fifth level are our needs to know and understand something of what is happening around us. Near the top of the hierarchy are our needs to appreciate order and beauty, to experience calm and predictability. At the top of the hierarchy are self-actualization needs to feel fulfilled and at peace with ourselves. At any stage in our lives our personality will reflect how far we have moved towards self-actualization.

Carl Rogers is another eminent humanist who believed that humans have two essential human needs. They are the need for self-actualization, and the need to be approved of, respected, even loved, perhaps, by others. Most of us have enough of these two basic needs met. If these needs aren't met, then someone may suffer some psychological damage.

● ● ● **Summary of humanistic approaches to personality**
Unlike the other approaches, humanistic psychology sees personality as emerging from individuals' perceptions of their own experiences.
People need to be approved of, respected, and loved. They need to feel good about their achievements. Someone's personality is an expression of the extent to which these things are achieved.

Cognitive views

Cognition is the process by which we come to know about our world, by making sense of information received through our senses. **George Kelly** believed that cognition is the major force in personality development. We learn about objects and events, and about ourselves and others, through our interactions. If our interactions are positive, then we develop confidence, if they are negative, we develop a lower sense of our own value.

Kelly argues that people behave in much the same way as scientists do in trying to perceive, understand, control, and predict what happens around them. Like scientists, we develop ideas (or hypotheses) which he called **personal constructs**, about what should happen in any situation. When we first experience someone or something, we form an impression of what that person or thing is like. For instance, my first impression of students might have been that they sit quietly and listen to what their teacher has to tell them and obediently take notes and copy diagrams. My next impression was that some try hard with their work and others do not. A further impression is that students are usually pleasant people. So far, my construct for students includes obedience, general reliability, enthusiasm, and possession of pleasant attitudes. Of course another teacher might form a different impression and build up a different construct. My judgement about students in general, or about any student in particular, will be influenced by my overall construct for students.

Our personal constructs are built up from our previous experiences. Positive experiences lead to confident testing of our ideas. As each new situation arises we apply what we think is the most appropriate construct. We then test it. If it is nearly correct (i.e. if what we guessed seemed to work), then we may modify our construct to make it even more appropriate. If it is half right we revise it, and if it doesn't work we reject it. This is just the process that scientific investigators follow. If the construct works

▷ A personal construct is an idea or set of ideas about what something is like. We are constantly trying to apply the most appropriate ones to each new situation we encounter. Personal constructs are constantly being confirmed, modified, or rejected as we confront new situations. They are, therefore, said to be 'dynamic'.

for us, and makes our world more understandable and controllable, then that construct becomes part of our personality.

Kelly is interested in how people use their constructs, by modification, revision, and so on. He is not interested in trying to measure or even describe people's constructs, or in explaining how people developed these in the first place. Instead he is more interested to see how far someone's constructs help them to make sense of their situations.

Kelly used his theory to develop an approach to therapy. He designed the **Role Construct Repertory Test (Rep Test)** to discover the constructs people use in describing what they think and feel about other people. Clients are given a list of descriptions of people's roles and are asked to think of someone they know who fits those descriptions. For example, their favourite teacher at secondary school or the person they most admire at work. When they have completed the test, three of the people they have described are chosen and the client has to say how two of them are alike, and how these two are different from the third. In this way, the clients are explaining their constructs, which will help the therapist understand how the clients see the world.

Comment on humanistic and cognitivist views

Humanistic psychology has been called the third force in psychology, after psychoanalytic theory and behaviourism. It does not aim to provide theories about what things are like but concentrates instead on how individuals see themselves. Allport's trait theory claims that people's personalities are the sum total of their traits. Like Maslow, he didn't offer any suggestions that could be applied beyond the individual being investigated, so offers no overall theory.

Kelly does not say how personal constructs are created in the first place, and nor does he explain how they are developed beyond a vague idea of modification and revising when they are applied and don't entirely work. Perhaps the biggest drawback is that he doesn't show how personal constructs relate to someone's behaviour. However, the theory has had an application in therapy and does take us beyond untested psychoanalytic theory and simple behaviourism.

Exercise on humanistic and cognitivist views

1 What is a trait?
2 In your own words, explain what is meant by self-actualization.
3 What is a personal construct?
4 Match the terms used to the researcher.

    Maslow   personal construct
    Allport   hierarchy of needs
    Kelly   self-actualization trait

 ### Summary of cognitive views

Kelly claimed that individuals create their own personal constructs about what the world is like from experience. They use this knowledge to test their understandings and relationships and it becomes their personality.

Activity

Read the summaries of each of the major psychological approaches to the development of personality. Draw up a table which summarizes, on the one hand, what they have in common, and on the other, how far they differ from each other.

Studies of temperament

▷
(See Chapter 7 for a discussion of identical and fraternal twins.)

We have referred to temperament several times now. It is the general description of how people react to certain kinds of stimulation, such as being touched, being handled, being stimulated. **Jerome Kagan** identifies activity, irritability, and fearfulness as the most widely studied aspects of temperament. Some babies generally respond well to such stimuli, with smiles and coos. Others are usually more stiff or distant. Such differences begin to emerge quite soon after birth, so we tend to think that they are genetically inherited. Personality is seen as being the result of a mixture of temperament and social experiences.

▷
Freedman's research found similarities in the temperaments of babies from different ethnic origins, which suggests that temperament is linked to heredity.

In 1965 **Daniel Freedman** reported his observational study of twenty pairs of twins. He found that there were more similarities among the identical twins than the fraternal twins in their responses towards adult strangers and their social smiling.

This supports the view that temperament is genetically inherited. In the 1970s, Freedman studied some Chinese-American babies and some White-American babies. Their mothers had received similar pre-natal care. The Chinese-American babies were much less irritable, easier to settle, and generally happier than the White-American babies. This also suggests that temperament is linked to heredity.

Alexander Thomas and **Stella Chess** conducted interviews in the mid–1970s with a sample of middle-class American parents to ask them to describe their children. They identified three broad categories of children's temperaments. First, there are the children who are easy to handle. They don't have wide swings in their moods, they are fairly even tempered, and they adapt well to new situations. Second, there are the children described as difficult. They are irritable and have tempers. They dislike change in their routines, and show their dislike clearly. Third, there are the children who are slow to warm up. They are also moody and not very active. They don't like changes in their routines but are more passive than the difficult children.

▷
Be careful not to draw the wrong conclusion here. We are not saying that children who are easy to handle will have a better life than other children. There are all sorts of other factors too which will influence the chances any child will have in life.

Thomas and Chess believe that temperament is modified by experiences. Parents have their own child-rearing styles. Those who encourage their children and are patient with them may find that their child who had been slow to warm up, can learn to do so much more quickly. With sensitive handling, a difficult child can realize that other responses are possible. The influences of a child's early temperaments can be altered.

The differences in the three groupings of children identified by Thomas and Chess are very general and cover many individual characteristics. They may well continue into later childhood, adolescence, or even adulthood. So children who are easy to handle are likely to make an easier and better adjustment to school than difficult children. They may form better social relationships too and be more popular amongst friends. Since success breeds success, the early advantage of a more open, accepting, and easy temperament may well have beneficial effects throughout one's life.

Exercise on temperament

1 What is temperament?
2 What is the relationship between temperament and personality?
3 Do Freedman's studies support the nature or nurture case? Explain your answer.
4 Where would personality come from, according to Thomas and Chess?
5 Will children who inherit an easy-going temperament have a more successful life than others?

●●● Summary of temperament

Temperament is the description of the general ways in which babies respond to stimulation. The main dimensions to have been studied so far include energy, bad temper, and fear. Any differences in temperaments can influence how parents respond to their babies and this can reinforce their tendencies which could last into adulthood. Equally, they can be altered with appropriate child-rearing tactics.

7

Intelligence

Some people are more likely to learn things, and learn them more quickly, from the same environment, than others. In any class at school some pupils will always seem to find learning easier than others. Some adults seem to be able to reason things out more quickly than others. It is tempting to describe some people as being more intelligent than others. In this chapter we will be looking at how our understanding of intelligence has changed, whether it is possible to measure intelligence, and whether intelligence is fixed at birth or can be modified by social experiences.

▶▶▶ *Activity*

Stop and think about what intelligence is. Answer these questions with either 'yes' or 'no':

1   Are you more intelligent than your best friend?

2   Are you more intelligent than your brothers or sisters?

3   Are you more intelligent than people younger than you?

4   Are you more intelligent than most of the elderly people that you know?

5   In your own words, write a definition of intelligence.

Defining intelligence

Intelligence has been one of the most thoroughly researched areas in psychology over the last hundred years, but still we can neither define it precisely nor measure it accurately. There are many intelligence tests, most of which are criticized for one limitation or another. There has always been disagreement among psychologists about precisely what intelligence is, where it comes from, and if it can (and should) be mea-

> Intelligence is an impossible word to define. We know it is to do with how easily we learn and can remember, put ideas together and solve problems. Yet we don't know much about the brain processes involved.

sured. As with some other terms in psychology, we cannot offer anything more than a general description of what intelligence includes.

To put it simply, intelligence includes the following qualities: the ability to learn and benefit from previous experience, to go beyond the information available and predict likely outcomes, abstract thinking, reasoning, problem solving, and all those marvellous skills that humans use to adapt themselves to their environment, and adapt their environment to themselves. When the first human beings found ways to escape from their enemies they were adapting themselves to their environment. When they first made shelters to protect themselves from the harsh weather they were adapting their environment to themselves. Humans have a long history of intelligent thought-directed behaviour.

The *Penguin Dictionary of Psychology* concludes that '... intelligence will be what it has always been, "the ability to profit from experience", and ... what it has become, "that which intelligence tests measure".'

Exercise on defining intelligence

1 Write what you think the definition of intelligence is and, if possible, compare it to someone else's definition.

2 Look up 'intelligence' in a dictionary and see how close your definition came to the one you find there.

3 Look it up in other dictionaries, and and see if each definition:
(a) has something in common with the others, and
(b) contains parts that others do not.

4 Here is a list of qualities that intelligence includes. Complete the table.

Quality	Put into your own words	Could it be tested in an IQ test?
1 the ability to learn and benefit from previous experience		
2 going beyond available information and predicting likely outcomes		
3 abstract thinking		
4 reasoning		
5 problem solving		
6 adapting yourself to your environment		
7 adapting your environment to yourself		

Summary of defining intelligence

Intelligence is a description of how easily we take in, store, and use new information. It includes the ability to see enough of the elements in a problem, and imagine solutions.

▶▶▶ *Activity*

How do the definitions here compare to your own definition? Look up the word intelligence in two or three dictionaries. Note what the definitions have in common and what differences there are between them.

Are there different kinds of intelligence?

▷ One major area of research since intelligence was first investigated was to discover whether intelligence is a general ability to solve all sorts of problems, or a series of particular skills.

In our everyday lives we need to deal with people, objects, and events which we take completely for granted. For example, we hear, use and comprehend language to understand people's attitudes, and to express our own. We recognize and manipulate objects, such as finding our car in a crowded car park, and driving it home. We perform mental arithmetic when we add up the price of goods in shops or count our change. Just because we take them for granted doesn't mean these are not complex mental challenges. The question is whether humans have a natural mental capacity – a general intelligence – which they use to solve all these specific problems, or do they possess different types of intelligence for verbal skills, number skills, recognition skills, etc.?

In 1904 **Charles Spearman** suggested that there are two types of ability in human intelligence. One is a general intelligence (which he called the **g factor**). This is genetically inherited. The other is a set of specific abilities relating to particular tasks (which he called the **s factor**). This **two-factor theory** is rather simplistic.

Cyril Burt had been a student of Spearman. He also thought that intelligence was partly innate. (Spearman and Burt represent the nature view.) He added another factor between the general and the specific, which he called **group skills**. He thought specific abilities, such as size of vocabulary, understanding complex arguments, verbal and written comprehension, constructing a logical argument, and so on, would all be part of a group of skills called verbal skills. There would be other group skills too, such as mechanical skills, creativity, mathematical skills, etc., which would each contain many specific skills. For example, mathematical skills include mental arithmetic, the ability to approximate and the ability to make predictions based on mathematical probability. General abilities are collections of group abilities which are themselves collections of specific abilities.

▷ There were general factors, specific factors, and group factors. Understanding intelligence was becoming complicated!

In 1938 **Louis Thurstone** published his redefinition of general abilities. He used similar data and a similar kind of analysis to Burt. He identified many skills and aptitudes involved in intelligence. These are called factors. By using a statistical procedure called factor analysis, with many subjects, he identified seven **primary abilities**. None of these need be thought of as genetically inherited, but could be developed from expe-

▷ Factor analysis is a complicated statistical technique for discovering whether aptitudes, abilities or traits generally appear together. If so they may have elements which overlap. These factors may be very similar. It may be that we can reduce some of the factors so that the ones remaining are sufficiently different.

rience. Thurstone's claim represents the nurture view of intelligence. These primary abilities are shown in the table.

Ability	Meaning	Example
1 Verbal comprehension	Meanings of words, vocabulary.	Which is the odd one out: potato, onion, apple, carrot?
2 Number skills	Arithmetic calculation.	What is the next number: 7, 15, 31, 63, 127 —?
3 Spatial relationships	Recognize shapes and objects from different angles.	
4 Perceptual skills	Seeing similarities and differences between objects.	
5 Memory skills	Remembering word meanings.	Put these words in order: flying animal, warm-blooded, pigeon, bird, animal.
6 Reasoning skills	Completing an incomplete argument.	If David is taller than Graham, Graham is taller than Karl, and Karl is not as tall as Chris, could Chris be taller than Graham?
7 Word fluency	Recognizing words quickly, solving anagrams, etc.	Who is this: dumsing drufe?

Thurstone developed several intelligence tests to measure these primary mental abilities. Although they provided useful scores for each skill identified, someone scoring well on one was likely to score well on the others. It seemed that general intelligence is involved in all of them so the tests are no more useful in investigating specific aspects of intelligence after all.

It appears to be difficult to escape the idea that people have general intelligence rather than many specific intellectual abilities. In 1967 **J.P. Guilford** rejected the idea of general intelligence altogether. Instead he thought that we have to understand three distinct processes in intelligence testing. First, there is the **content** of the test item. What are the subjects to think about? Is it a number sequence item or a 'spot the odd one out' question? Second, there is the **operation** that we are asking the subjects to perform. Exactly what mental skill are we testing? What are the subjects to think about? Third, there is the result, or **product.** What kinds of response do we want? Will they move something, fill in a gap, choose from a multiple choice, etc.? Guilford identified four different types of content, five types of operation, and six types of product. He multiplied them together and suggested there were 120 separate mental abilities and set about devising ways of testing each one. About seventy have been produced, although the scores on each are positively correlated, so it is highly unlikely that there are so many different types of mental ability.

Content	Operation	Product
Figural	Evaluation	Units
Symbolic	Convergence	Classes
Semantic	Divergence	Relations
Behavioural	Memory	Systems
	Cognition	Transformations
		Implications

●●● **Summary of kinds of intelligence**
Researchers have, historically, suggested that we have different kinds of intelligence, although this seems highly unlikely. Humans have many different skills and can apply their general intelligence to whatever they are doing at the time.

The information-processing approach

These early theories looked for similarities in intelligence using factor analysis to define which skills were involved in which activities. A more recent approach has been to view human beings as **information processing** organisms. This way of understanding human thinking has parallels in the development of computers and artificial intelligence.

Information can come from two main sources. One is outside the individual, which includes anything which has been sufficiently noticed by our sensory systems (eyes, ears, nose, etc.). This information becomes a perception when it enters our perceptual system. The other source is inside us already. Any idea, thought, hope, imagining, memory, feeling or other mental event can also be information.

▷ Information can be both external and internal. It is processed to make the world meaningful and understandable.

Humans are capable of taking in and storing a vast amount of information, although we need to be selective. This is where the idea of processing is important. A process is a series of steps or stages geared towards achieving some specific goal or end.

So the first stage in information processing could include light falling in various colours and patterns on the cells of the retina in the human eye. This is **reception** or **registration**. It could just as easily be the waves of air pressure converted by the bones in the ear to movements of tiny hair cells inside the cochlea of the inner ear to create a specific sound. Or it could be chemical changes in taste receptors on the tongue, or in changes in activity in any of our other senses.

▷ Each sensory system has its own specialized sense receptors which only detect a specific kind of stimulation. Rods and cones on the retina only respond to light. Hair cells only respond to vibration.

We can't possibly take notice of everything we see, hear, touch, taste, smell, etc., so we need some filtering system to allow **selective attention** to some things and not others. This is the second stage. If the perception is attended to it will need recognizing or interpreting. This is **decoding**. Indeed it may already have been partially decoded before it passed through the filter. This is the next stage. Decoding will need access to memory to discover if we recognize the perception from a previous experience. Accessing storage or **retrieval** is another stage in information processing. At the same time as searching memory for clues or patterns to help understand the perception the new perception is being **coded** for storage in memory. If we don't know what it is now, we might need to retrieve it later. At some point during the processing of new information we will recognize and have some understanding of the perception, even if it's only to admit that we see it, but we do not know what it is. At this point the perception becomes a **cognition**.

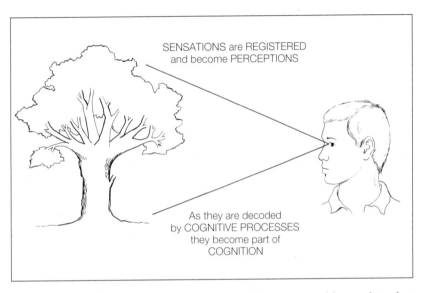

SENSATIONS are REGISTERED and become PERCEPTIONS

As they are decoded by COGNITIVE PROCESSES they become part of COGNITION

Sensation—registration—perception —cognition

If we accept that there is a process at work here we could speculate that intelligence is the product of how quickly and efficiently the process works. If you are quick to understand new situations and can respond efficiently, you may be more intelligent (or perhaps more quick-witted?) than someone who is slower to respond.

One way of applying this approach to measuring intelligence would be to find something that requires fast responses and measure it in a sample of people. Reaction-time tests have been used. People who have faster reaction times also tend to have higher scores on other intelligence tests. Other researchers suggest which of the many stages in the process are responsible for deciding which response we are likely to give. For example, **Robert Sternberg** makes a distinction between the stages in the process and the knowledge we already have. He thinks that our existing knowledge helps us plan and decide how to respond, making us better at organizing ourselves.

Summary of information processing
Human beings take in great quantities of information through their senses. They can store enormous amounts in their memories. They can also retrieve vast amounts, although what comes out isn't necessarily quite what went in. Intelligence may be to do with how efficiently these information-processing systems work.

Activity
Make notes on the differences between the early theories and the information-processing approach to intelligence.

Intelligence testing

Many psychologists have invented ways of measuring all sorts of human skills, abilities, aptitudes, knowledge, personality and achievements. Humanistic and individualist psychologists suggest that such attempts are a waste of time as each human is unique and our skills are best regarded as matters of quality not quantity.

The area of psychology which deals with the testing of human mental abilities is called **psychometrics**. Humanist psychologists such as Allport and Maslow did not think it worthwhile to test someone's intelligence. Cognitive psychologists such as **Jean Piaget**, for example, totally rejected the idea of intelligence being tested, as he did not believe that intelligence is a thing which can be tested and measured. Instead he regarded intelligence as a quality. We will examine Piaget's theory in Chapter 10.

The term intelligence test is really very misleading, as intelligence is not one single thing which can be measured. Instead, an intelligence test is simply a test of a sample of abilities. Many tests exist, some are individual tests (where one person is tested by one tester). Others are group tests (where larger numbers of people can all be tested by one tester at the same time). Which type to use depends largely on what the results are to be used for. To survey the progress of all children in a class requires one kind, to evaluate the extent of brain damage in a particular patient requires another.

Intelligence tests involve someone working through a series of questions. Therefore they can only be used with subjects who can stay alert for some time, who understand language, can read and write, and who can follow instructions. Babies, young children, and adults with some mental or behavioural problems can't do these things, and so intelligence tests aren't used with them. Young children's progress is measured on developmental scales. These are not intended as measures of intelligence as such, but rather as measures of a child's physical development.

Developmental scales

These are a range of tests which measure the progress of infants and pre-school children towards achieving certain developmental stages. They involve children doing something or answering questions and then rating them. The score a child makes on a developmental scale is called a **development quotient**, or **DQ**.

During the 1920s and 1930s **Arnold Gesell** and his colleagues observed hundreds of children in order to establish **age norms** of what

Age norms are simply descriptions of lists of behavioural or mental skills that the majority of children at given ages have.

average children were achieving at given ages. Gesell's scales are simple descriptions and do not suggest anything about the origin of intelligence or the factors which affect it.

Nancy Bayley's scales consist of three types of test aimed at measuring the abilities of young children from the age of two months to 30 months. There is a mental scale which measures things like perception, learning ability, following direction, searching for a mising toy, memory, and simple problem solving. The motor scale measures coordination skills such as are used in sitting, walking, manipulating objects, throwing a ball or climbing stairs. The infant-behaviour record measures social and personality development, persistence, attention span, etc.

The McCarthy Scales are aimed at children between two-and-a-half and eight-and-a-half years old. There are eighteen tests which rate children on scales of verbal skills, perceptual skills, mathematical skills, memory skills, and general cognitive skills. **Cognitive skills** are usually taken as a measure of intellectual development.

David Wechsler has devised a whole series of intelligence tests which are very widely used today. The Wechsler Adult Intelligence Scale (WAIS) has been modified for use with 6- to 16-year-olds as the Wechsler Intelligence Scale for Children (WISC). The Wechsler Pre-school and Primary Scale of Intelligence (WPPSI) is for children below six years and give two scores, one for verbal, and one for nonverbal performance.

One of the main problems with developmental scales is that children develop at their own pace, regardless of any norms laid down by psychologists. Categorizing children as being advanced or slow on some range of skills according to some test isn't, therefore, very useful.

▷ Cognitive skills include mental processes such as taking in and interpreting perceptions, attention and memory, language, reasoning, thinking, etc.

Exercise on developmental scales

1 What do developmental scales measure?
2 What are developmental scales used for, and why?
3 Say, in your own words, why scores gained on developmental scales may not be good predictors of scores on intelligence tests.

●●● **Summary of developmental scales**
Developmental scales are attempts to discover the ages at which children are capable of various tasks. Unfortunately the tasks have little to do with intelligence!

Intelligence tests

The first intelligence test was designed by **Alfred Binet** (1857–1911) in Paris in 1905. It contained thirty items. The French government had asked Binet to devise a way to identify those children whose intellectual abilities were so low that they would need special education. It was thought that having low-ability children in a class might hold back the average and bright children.

Binet believed that mental ability matured as the body matured, so he spent many hours conducting naturalistic observations and experiments to find out what skills average children of various ages possessed. He produced a long list of skills which most 5-year-olds had mastered, another list of the typical abilities of 6-year-olds, another for 7-year-olds, and so on. These skills included things like reasoning and deduction. Binet's tests do not attempt to measure the whole of a child's intelligence, just some aspects of it. Binet never claimed that his test could assess general intelligence, or that they could be used as general tests for all children. They were simply intended as a practical way of discovering children who had some learning problems in some particular skills, such as arithmetic or language.

Other researchers either ignored these reservations, or tried to overcome them. Binet's original test was modified at Stanford University, in California for use with American school children. The **Stanford Binet test** gave an individual score for each child. It soon became popular and has been revised many times since it was invented, and it is still used today. It consists of a series of subtests which are arranged from easiest (for youngest children) to hardest (for older children). There are subtests for every half-year from two to five-and-a-half, then for each year from six to fourteen, and then there are four adult levels. The idea is that an average person of a given age could pass all the tests set for those younger or the same age, but could pass none of the tests set for someone older.

For example, an average 10-year-old could pass all the tests which are meant for 10-year-olds, but could not pass any of the tests for 11-year-olds. Of course, some brighter children would be able to pass some of the older children's tests, while others couldn't pass all of the tests for their own age group. Binet used a simple formula to give each child a score. He distinguished chronological age (CA), which is actual age in years and months, from mental age (MA), which is worked out from the number of correct answers given to the subtests. Unfortunately, Binet's tests assume that particular skills only appear at specific ages.

So if a 5-year-old girl (CA = 5) could do all the tests of a typical 5-year-old, she would have an MA of five. Her abilities are those of a typical 5-year-old. She is average for her age. If she could do all the tests of a 5-year-old, and all those for a 6-year-old as well, she would have a CA of 5 and an MA of 6. She would be well above average.

Binet did not intend to provide a test of intelligence across the whole range, but only to identify those children whose abilities were below an acceptable level.

Intelligence and IQ

A German scientist called **William Stern** invented the idea of a mental ratio. He found that dividing one's actual age into one's mental age would give a figure which could be used to express one's level of intelligence. So mental age divided by chronological age was used to express one's level of intellectual capacity as a number. Someone who was aged four, but had a mental age of four-and-a-half would have a mental ratio of:

By 1927 Spearman despaired of trying to measure intelligence at all. He called intelligence 'a word with so many meanings that finally it had none'.

$$\frac{4.5}{4} = 1.125$$

However, 1.125 isn't a very attractive way of communicating a measurement of someone's intelligence, so two further steps were taken. These were developed by **Lewis Terman** at Stanford University in 1916. The number could be expressed more simply by rounding it down to two decimal places, for example, 1.13, and it would look much neater if we could lose the decimal point, so Terman multiplied it by 100. This produced the intelligence quotient (IQ) of 113. Terman expressed Binet's findings as the formula,

$$\frac{MA}{CA} \times 100 = IQ$$

Applying this formula, a 17-year-old who can answer all the tests for someone aged seventeen, but none of the tests for anyone over seventeen will have an IQ of:

$$\frac{17}{17} = 100$$

The average IQ score is 100. Similarly, a child of five with a mental age of 5.5 would have an IQ of:

$$\frac{5.5}{5} \times 100 = 110$$

Comment on IQ testing

Three points could usefully be made here. First, different intelligence tests measure different mental abilities. Although there would be positive correlations between people's scores on different tests, we should be careful about describing someone as having an IQ of a particular number without knowing which test was used to produce it, and what mental abilities that test covered.

Second, IQ scores do not show the amount of anything which someone has. Someone with an IQ of 125 doesn't have 125 units of intelligence. The IQ is simply a way of indicating someone's average stage of mental development, as measured by the particular test.

Third, recent evidence suggests that the average IQ, as measured on a range of tests, has increased since Binet's time, by about 13 points. As people's diet, housing, and experience of life has improved, so has the average IQ. Few psychologists today believe that intelligence is fixed at birth and never alters throughout life.

Exercise on IQ

1 What is the difference between mental age and chronological age?
2 Briefly describe how an IQ score is calculated.
3 Work out the IQ score of a 7-year-old who could do the test items for a 6-year-old, but none of the tests for older children.

4 Find the IQ for a 6-year-old who can do all the tests for a 6-year-old and below but no others.
5 What is the IQ of a 4-year-old who could do all the tests for a 5-year-old?
6 Read the comments on IQ testing and say whether or not you think they have any value.

Summary of intelligence testing
Intelligence has always been a difficult idea in psychology. We aren't sure what intelligence is, and therefore attempts to measure it have not been particularly successful. For those who believe that it is useful, many different tests have been identified and a formula has been devised to state intelligence as an IQ score which can then be used to compare one person's ability on the test to another's.

Activity
At the beginning of this chapter you answered yes or no to some questions in which you compared your intelligence to that of other people. How could you tell whether your answers were correct?

The curve of normal distribution

If we were to take a massive number of people, for example the 1000 million people who live in India, and we were to measure how tall each one of them was, we would find that a few are very short, and about the same number are extremely tall. Some would be smallish, and about the same number would be tall. The vast majority would, of course, be of average height. There is a statistical device called the curve of normal distribution which allows us to predict the percentage of the population who will be of any particular height. Binet assumed that there would be roughly equal numbers of very intelligent people and very dull people, and the same number of fairly bright and fairly dull people. He thought intelligence would also follow the curve of normal distribution. If it did it could be useful for predicting the percentage of people in the population who would obtain various ranges of IQ scores, as shown below.

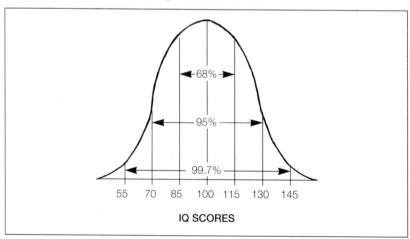

The curve of normal distribution

The value of intelligence testing

We have said that it is extremely difficult to define intelligence, so psychologists often assume it means that which intelligence tests measure, for example, logical problem solving, numerical ability, nonverbal reasoning, ability to understand time and space, etc. Many psychologists now prefer the term 'intelligent behaviour'. At least this can be measured to some extent.

Intelligence tests are widely used in many areas of life, such as in schools, in personnel selection for managers, and the military for officer selection. In Britain, educational psychologists still use them to identify particular areas of difficulty a child might be having, such as failure to recognize words or an inability to understand number relationships. What value they have, however, is simply the value that those who administer them think they have. If someone believes that performance on a particular test is a useful indicator of an effective manager, then that test has value to them. Other people may find the test less useful.

Exercise on intelligence tests

▷
If you are in a class, take a vote over whether members of the group support the use of IQ testing in school. Try having two groups of people. One will be in favour of using IQ tests in school, another will oppose it. Each group has to find as many reasons as it can to support its own case, and present its arguments to the other group. At the end of the presentation take another vote to see if people have changed their minds.

Intelligence tests do not measure the whole range of abilities that people have – merely a sample of them. Here are a few examples of some of the skills which modern IQ tests do measure. (The answers are on page 161.)

1 Seeing relationships between series of things:
   (a) What is the next letter in the sequence A D G J?
   (b) What is the next letter in the sequence Q P M L I H?

2 What do these pairs of words have in common:
   (a) wood and coal
   (b) apple and peach
   (c) ship and car.

3 Taking words from a scrambled sentence and putting them into the right order:
   'school back we Monday it's so go tomorrow to'

4 Vocabulary, such as find a word which means the same as:
   stake and mail.

5 Which is the odd one out:
   tootap, prinut, tintek, otrrac?

6 Unscrambling words. Which of these towns is not in England:
   grothnib, yuqtora, drifcaf, hercest, sheeldiff?

Other skills which IQ tests may attempt to measure include memory span, number ability, copying shapes, finishing sentences, pointing out illogicalities, following a maze, completing a jigsaw, assembling coloured blocks into a particular pattern, etc. It is important to remember, however, that

IQ tests can only really measure our ability to deal with items in the particular test.

Are intelligence tests accurate?

To be accepted as accurate, IQ tests must be **standardized measures of psychological functioning**. This rather grand phrase simply means that each item on the test must be given to many hundreds of people (called the standardization sample), who have been chosen as a representative cross-section of the people for whom the test is intended. If it is meant for adult males it should be tested so that it gives a score for what typical adult males can do. If it is intended to measure children's abilities there would not be any point in standardizing it on adults.

IQ tests must give consistent results. If you score 120 today and 95 tomorrow you wouldn't have much faith in the test. Scientists say a test is **reliable** if it gives consistent results. Tests must also be **valid.** This means that the test really should be measuring intelligence and not something else, such as general knowledge. Questions must be clear and easy to understand so that everyone taking the test knows exactly what the questions mean. Unfortunately, some IQ tests fail in one or more of these areas, and none is likely to be entirely accurate, as we cannot know exactly what intelligence is. All the tests give is an indication of an individual's general level of ability.

Here is an example that illustrates the problems that many items in intelligence tests have caused (adapted from A.M. Colman *Facts, Fallacies and Frauds in Psychology*, Hutchinson, 1987).

> Here is a problem of a type that will be familiar to most people: 'Which of the following is the odd one out: cricket, football, billiards, hockey?' This problem first cropped up in an IQ test that formed part of a school entrance examination in England. It provoked a puzzled parent to write a letter to *The Times* newspaper:

> 'I said billiards because it is the only one played indoors. A colleague said football because it is the only one in which a ball is not struck by an implement. A neighbour says cricket because in all the other games the object is to put the ball in a net; and my son, with the confidence of nine summers, plumps for hockey because it is the only one that is a girl's game. Could any of your readers put me out of my misery by stating what is the correct answer, and further enlighten me by explaining how questions of this sort prove anything, especially when the scholar has merely to underline the odd one out without giving any reason?'

> The four-sports problem stirred up a lively controversy in the correspondence columns of The Times. One correspondent thought that 'billiards is the obvious answer … because it is the only one of the games listed which is not a team game. … I should have thought it a very suitable question for an intelligence test'. Another suggested that 'football is the odd one out because … it is played with an inflated ball compared with the solid ball used in each of the other

▷
When applied to a psychological test, 'standardized' means that all the items and procedures which are a part of it, e.g. the questions asked, the instructions given, the conditions under which the test is conducted, must be the same for all the people taking the test. Otherwise some of the results may be explained by the differences in the way the subjects were treated.

games'. An eminent philosopher … began by commenting that 'billiards is the only one in which the colour of the balls matters, the only one played with more than one ball at once, the only one played on a green cloth and not on a field, and the only one whose name has more than eight letters in it' – but he went on to argue that equally logical reasons could be given for any of the other games.

Summing up the controversy in his book, *The Tyranny of Testing,* the mathematician Banesh Hoffmann noted that the correspondents to *The Times* had offered excellent reasons for choosing cricket, football, or billiards, but that their arguments for choosing hockey were dubious at best. At first he thought that hockey was therefore the worst of the four choices, and that it could be ruled out. But then it occurred to him that 'the very fact that hockey was the only one that could thus be ruled out gave it so striking a quality of separateness as to make it an excellent answer after all – perhaps the best.'

The controversy over the four-sports problem illustrates something that applies to all IQ test questions of the odd-one-out type: logically valid arguments can often be found for any of the listed options. The problem is to guess which of the answers the test constructors had in mind.

Comment on the use of IQ tests

Here are some points to consider about the use of IQ tests.

1 To justify the use of any intelligence test we have to accept two main assumptions. First, that there are some identifiable abilities which make up intelligence. Second, we must assume that these abilities can be measured by some questions that can be asked in a test. Many psychologists reject one or both of these assumptions.

2 According to Binet, intelligence is both fixed at birth and distributed normally throughout the population. Many psychologists dispute both of these beliefs too.

3 IQ tests do not measure all the skills we may have. Tom may be especially good at verbal reasoning and have a large vocabulary, but be less good with numbers. Tracy may have good number skills but not be so good with language. If the test has lots of questions which involve verbal reasoning then Tom will have an advantage over Tracy. To give one IQ score is, therefore, misleading. (Some people with quite severe mental handicaps have some exceptional abilities.) The belief that intelligence consists of many abilities has led psychologists to devise many tests of specific ability such as aptitude tests for things like mechanical ability and musical capabilities.

4 A person's IQ score does not remain constant over time. The reasons for this are that our abilities vary according to the environment we grow up in, and an individual would take different tests which measure

different skills. There is no reason to imagine that your average score for one set of skills when you are 6 years old should be the same as your score for some different skills when you are 20 years old.

5　If intelligence were something we were born with, which couldn't change, and if IQ tests were accurate, then it wouldn't be possible to be trained to pass an IQ test (e.g. the old 11-plus exam, which was used to help decide which type of secondary schools children should attend. Many primary-school children were taught how to tackle the 11-plus.)

6　IQ tests try to measure some of the skills someone has, but do not indicate anything about where such skills come from.

7　The relationship between the person administering the test and the person taking it might influence the performance. The examiner may appear bad tempered and frightening, or kind and helpful.

8　The mood the person taking the test is in: whether or not the individual feels motivated to do well. This may depend on why they are taking the test in the first place. If it is for a promotion that they desperately want, they will be highly motivated. It also works the other way round.

9　IQ tests usually work best when the people taking them share the same ideas, norms, values and cultural background as the person who sets and administers the test. They do not always work satisfactorily with people from different cultures who may have different experiences, attitudes and abilities.

10　They are not accurate!

Exercise on the uses of intelligence testing

1　What is an IQ test?
2　What do IQ tests measure?
3　When applied to intelligence testing, what do the terms reliability, validity, and standardization mean?

●●● Summary of the usefulness of IQ testing

As we cannot know exactly what constitutes human intelligence we cannot know how useful attempts to measure it are likely to be. Despite this, tests are widely used in many areas of life such as in schools, in personnel selection, and in the military for officer selection.

▶▶▶ Activity

Does this section make you think any differently about your answers to the questions at the beginning of this chapter?

Gender and intelligence

▷ Sex is a biological description of the differences between males and females. Gender is the combination of socially learned roles about how people of each sex are expected to behave.

▷ There are obviously differences in male and female behaviour. They are probably better explained by differences in socialization than any supposed differences in their brain structures.

Although there are no differences in the average IQ score for boys and girls, there are some slight differences in particular skills. None of the differences is very marked, and there are many exceptions to them. Some do not appear until the teenage years. Up to about the age of six, girls are slightly ahead in basic arithmetic, although on average boys take over some time after that age. Most girls develop language skills slightly ahead of boys, and stay slightly ahead. By the time they reach adolescence, boys are slightly better at artistic abilities such as thinking about abstract shapes, whereas girls are slightly better at verbal reasoning, such as solving word puzzles. There are two possible reasons for these slight differences.

First, it is possible that there are differences in the ways in which boys' and girls' brains are organized. This reflects the nature side of the nature–nurture debate. The language centres may be slightly more efficiently organized in females, whereas the parts of the brain concerned with processing numbers may be better in boys. This explanation seems fairly unlikely however, because the overall differences are very small, and there is tremendous variation between individuals. (See Chapter 8 for a fuller discussion of whether there are differences in male and female brain structures.)

Second, boys may be socialized into thinking more about science, mechanics, and things which involve numbers. This reflects the nurture view. Girls may be encouraged to be more talkative, more sociable and cooperative, and generally to use language more.

The importance of parental expectations and roles on children's achievement has been studied by **Jacquelynne Parsons**. Parsons asked some American parents of children of secondary-school age about their attitudes towards various school subjects. Most of the parents said that they thought maths and science subjects were more important for boys than for girls. They also thought that maths was easier and more enjoyable for boys than for girls. Parsons found that the children's expectations of their abilities were in line with their parents' expectations. Girls who had similar abilities and scores in maths compared with boys, said that they didn't think they had the same potential or aptitude for the subject as the boys claimed they had. When girls did well at maths their parents might say that it was because they had worked very hard at maths. When boys did well their parents said that they had ability. Not surprisingly, such attitudes were found to influence the children's perception of their own abilities.

Exercise on gender

Write two paragraphs each outlining one possible explanation for why more girls tend to do arts, humanities, and English subjects at school, while more boys tend to do maths, physics and chemistry.

Summary of gender and intelligence

There are very few differences in the IQ-test scores between males and females. Any differences that do show consistently may be the result of differences in the ways the two sexes' brains operate, but is much more likely to be explained by differences in socialization.

Is intelligence genetically inherited or acquired socially?

Although we can't measure intelligence very accurately, no one would deny that some people seem more able to do certain things than others. We've all heard people say that someone is very bright while someone else is rather slow. An important question is: how do these differences between people come about? More specifically, are there any measurable differences between the intelligence of individuals that could be (or need to be) explained by genetic inheritance? Alternatively, could all the differences between people's intelligence be explained by their social experiences?

There are two obvious possibilities. First, intelligence could be acquired genetically, and therefore fixed at birth. If so, there's nothing much we can do to alter it. Second, and alternatively, intelligence could be acquired socially through our experiences. If so, then changing the amount of stimulation people have would alter their intellectual abilities. These two options form the core of the nature–nurture debate on intelligence.

We will look here at the arguments for both sides.

Activity

If intelligence results purely from biological inheritance from our parents would there be any point in having remedial education classes? Do the Bulldogs Bank and Koluchova studies discussed in Chapter 2 support this idea?

Nature – the case for heredity

This argument can be traced back to **Charles Darwin**. Darwin was a famous nineteenth-century biologist who found evidence to support his view that all species of living things on the earth, including human beings, would have to evolve in order to survive. Those species which could not evolve would die out. He thought that most of the differences between most members of a species were the result of differences in their **genotypes**, and this would include the differences in intelligence between people. Here is some of the evidence for these claims.

Many human characteristics are fixed at conception

As we said in Chapter 1, when a male sperm fertilizes a female ovum the egg will contain twenty-three chromosomes from the sperm, and twenty-three chromosomes from the ovum. Chromosomes carry thousands of

▷
Genotype is the word used for all the influences that we inherited through our genes and which will determine what we are likely to become. Our sex, colour, shape, and even our temperament are influenced by the genotype.

Chromosomes carry the particular species' genes. Each species has its own number of chromosomes.

genes, each of which will trigger when and how parts of the body will be formed. Supporters of the nature view argue that intelligence is also triggered in this way. During pregnancy, however, some things could happen to the mother which might also affect the child's intelligence. For example, taking certain drugs, suffering from particular diseases, or having some kinds of accident, could all affect how the foetus develops.

Selective breeding

Racehorse breeders try to breed their best mares and stallions so that their foals might inherit their parents' speed. Most animal breeders try to mate their adult animals so that their offspring will possess the characteristics which the breeders want to emphasize. We hear people say that a child has her mother's eyes or his father's nose. But these are physical characteristics. Can we breed other characteristics selectively too? Can we breed intelligent animals to see if their offspring are more intelligent?

In the late 1950s **Cooper** and **Zubeck** took a sample of rats, and put each in turn into a maze. They counted the number of mistakes each made, and timed how long it took them to complete the maze. Those who made the fewest mistakes were called the 'maze-bright' group, and were only allowed to breed with each other. Those rats who made most mistakes were called the 'maze-dull' group, and they were only allowed to breed with each other too. After a few generations, the descendants of the 'maze-bright' group were much better at running mazes than their ancestors had been. The descendants of the 'maze-dull' group were much worse than their ancestors had been at running mazes. Maze running may be selectively bred.

Animals with different temperaments have also been selectively bred. For example, aggressive animals have been bred and their offspring were found to be more aggressive. Very placid animals also have more placid descendants. However, there are two problems in using selective breeding as evidence for the nature case. First, we can't really know what intelligence means in animals. It certainly cannot be compared to human intelligence. Second, inter-breeding in humans seems more likely to produce a child with some disability than to produce a genius.

Animals who possess a certain talent or feature can be selectively bred, we have first to choose a pair that possess that talent. However, intelligence is not a thing like speed of running, or skill at maze-running. It is more like a process. It wouldn't be easy to know that we have selected intelligent animals and bred them for their intelligence.

Identical-twin studies

For every 1,000 babies born, about twelve will be twins (i.e. six pairs). There are two major types of twins: fraternal and identical. Fraternal twins occur when two male sperms fertilize two female ova at the same time. A fertilized cell is called a **zygote**, and fraternal twins are called **dizygotic twins** (DZs for short). Two babies develop in the womb. The only other thing they have in common is that they are born at about the same time. They are just like ordinary brothers and sisters. Identical twins occur when, for some unknown reason, the single zygote divides into two virtually identical halves. They each have the same chromosomes carrying the same genes. Because they come from a single zygote they are called **monozygotic twins** (MZs for short). MZ twins must have just about identical genotypes. If intelligence is the result of our genotypes, then MZs must have just about identical intelligence.

One possible way to discover the contributions of the environment and of genetic inheritance is to study the IQ scores (taken on the same tests) of three groups of people of the same age. Two of the groups need the same heredity (i.e. identical twins). Some pairs need to have shared the same environment, i.e. been brought up together. They have both heredity and environment in common. We would expect their IQ scores to be similar. If they're not, then neither heredity nor environment consistently contributes to IQ.

Other MZs need to have been reared separately. They have the same heredity but different environments. If they have different IQs then it could be that the differences in their social experiences would explain their intelligence. If they have similar IQs then intelligence could result from heredity.

A third group comprises pairs who have different heredities but share the same environment. Step brothers and sisters or pairs of adopted children living as part of the same family could be used. If their IQs were similar it may be that the environment is contributing to the similarities.

Exercise on genetic inheritance

1 What do MZ twins have in common?
2 What do DZ twins have in common?
3 To be absolutely sure of the influence of heredity and environment we would need the following four samples:

MZs		Others
Reared together.	Reared apart.	Reared together.
Same heredity, same environment.	same heredity, different environment.	same environment, different heredity.

4 Explain why comparing the IQ scores of these samples (assuming they are of the same age and the same tests were used) should help us to solve the nature–nurture debate on intelligence.

It isn't difficult to find people who have grown up in the same environment. Most twins do, to a large extent. Finding people with identical genotypes (i.e. identical twins) isn't so easy. A small number of identical twins who have been brought up separately have been found. They have been studied in three main surveys. All three found a high positive correlation between each member of the pair of twins' IQ score. This supports the idea that intelligence is innate. We will return to this idea later.

Activity
A positive correlation means that an increase in the amount of one variable is accompanied by an increase in the amount of another. It does not mean that one is causing a change in the other. Studies which find that two variables occur together are sometimes called concordance studies.

Not everyone agrees that the similarities in monozygotic twins is evidence that intelligence is a result of heredity. **Leon Kamin** has summarized the evidence against this view. He questions the most widely quoted of the studies – by **Cyril Burt** – which found a high positive correlation between the IQs of MZs reared apart. There are some doubts about whether Burt's research can be trusted, and Kamin suggests that we should ignore this study. He also claims that those twins who were separated were often reared in very similar homes and treated in similar ways. They may have been reared separately, but they weren't reared differently. For example, two-thirds of the twins in the study by Shields were raised by the same family, one twin by the mother, and the other by the grandmother, aunt or other relation. Most were treated similarly, attended the same school, and saw a great deal of each other.

Another problem Kamin identified is with the nature of the IQ tests the twins were given. In each of the studies the twins were given different IQ tests, some of which were not properly standardized for the group taking the test. For example, most of the twins in Newman's study (1937) were female (as were the majority in each of the studies quoted). Newman used the Stanford Binet test (1916) which hadn't been properly standardized for adults, or for females. As we know, different tests measure different skills anyway so we shouldn't really compare IQs for people if they have been measured using different tests.

A final problem concerns the unrepresentative nature of the twins studied. Most had answered advertisements in the media asking for twins who had been reared separately to contact the researchers. Each sample was therefore self-selected. We can't be sure that self-selected samples are typical, although the total number of separated twins is very small.

Exercise on concordance studies

1 What does standardization mean? Why is it important that test items should be standardized?
2 The following table lists Kamin's main objections to research on intelligence in MZ twins. Complete the second column to explain how each challenges the nature view.

Kamin's objection	Challenge to nature view
Similarities in upbringing	
Non-standardization	
Selection of sample	

Summary of the nativist claims for intellectual development
Many human characteristics, such as hair and eye colour, are inherited genetically. It is possible to breed animals to emphasize some of their features. However, much evidence for the importance of genetic inheritance comes from studies of people with identical genotypes. They appear to have very similar IQs. However, there are many problems with these studies.

Nurture – the case for the environment

The case for the environment appears to be rather stronger than the case for genetics. Animals and children whose environments have been changed and whose IQ has changed, provide support for the argument that environmental factors affect intelligence.

Activity
If people's surroundings and experiences affect their intellectual abilities would there be any point in remedial education classes? Is this view supported by the Skeels and Dye studies reported in Chapter 1?

▷
Impoverishment and enrichment studies have been conducted in the past on both animals and children. Such research would not be permitted now.

If intelligence is affected by the environment, then someone brought up in an **impoverished** (unstimulating) environment would not be capable of very intelligent behaviour. **Enriching** (improving) the environment should lead to an increase in their intellectual skills. Although psychologists cannot deliberately impoverish children's environments the same restrictions have not always applied to animals. However, there are some problems with applying findings from studies of animals to human intelligence. There are two main problems. First, what exactly do we mean by intelligent behaviour in animals? Second, can we generalize from the behaviour of animals to the mental functioning of people?

Exercise on impoverishment and enrichment

1 Why would conducting impoverishment and enrichment studies help us untangle the influences of nature and nurture?
2 Write a paragraph outlining as many reasons as you can think of for why it wouldn't be possible to use children or animals in impoverishment studies.
3 Would each of these reasons apply equally to conducting enrichment studies?
4 Imagine that you have just been made director of an under-equipped orphanage where there are many under-stimulated children. Identify some of the kinds of experiences that you would provide for them. Say how each would contribute to cognitive stimulation. Remember that you have a limited budget.

Studying animals isn't really of much use in untangling the role of nature or nurture in intellectual development in humans, as we don't know what intelligence means in animal species. We can't deliberately manipulate children's environments to see if their levels of intellectual functioning alters. However, some children have been raised in depressing, unstimulating orphanages. We could see if there are any differences in intelligence scores between those children when compared with the scores of children in more enriched environments, such as better-off orphanages. If the average IQ score for children in well-staffed and well-equipped orphanages was greater than that of children in poor orphanages, then it may be that the environment affects the intellect.

This still wouldn't entirely support the claim that the environment has a greater effect on us than heredity, because we could not match the children in the different institutions for the key variables like age, intelligence, health, etc. If those children in the better-equipped orphanage did turn out to be more intelligent than the others, we do not know that they might have been more intelligent to begin with. A number of such studies have been conducted however, all finding much the same results, that environment has a major effect on intellectual growth.

Some studies of children in orphanages have been made which could help explain the effects of impoverishment and enrichment. Until 1956 adoption of illegitimate children or those whose parents could not cope was not legal in the Lebanon. In 1955, just before adoption was legalized, **Wayne Dennis** measured the intelligence (both DQ and IQ as appropriate) of a group of children in the deprived environment of a Lebanese orphanage. Their average score was fifty-three. (Remember that the average DQ and IQ score is 100.) Dennis also measured the IQ of some teenagers who had been in the institution for some years, and found that they too had scores well below average. An impoverished environment did correlate with poor intellectual and social development in the children, i.e. those children raised in the least well-equipped orphanages had the lowest DQs and IQs.

After 1956 many of the children were adopted, some by American couples. Fifteen years later Dennis traced and retested the children. Almost all the children showed an increase in their scores. Those who were the youngest when they were adopted showed the greatest increase. Dennis suggested that Lebanese children, who were adopted by two years of age, could catch up with normally reared children. If adopted after two years of age their intelligence stayed behind by the number of years spent in the orphanage after the age of two. A child adopted at five, for example, would remain around three years behind in its intellectual development. Dennis suggests that around two years might be the time marking the end of the **sensitive period** for intellectual development for these children. He says, '... there is a period near the second birthday which is critical with respect to complete recovery from the effects of ... deprivation upon intelligence. Those adopted before age two recover completely ... among those adopted later there is a marked persistence of retardation.'

If impoverished environments restrict intellectual development, then enriched environments should encourage it. Dennis provided increased stimulation for some orphanage children, giving them more to play with, things to watch, etc. He found that the extent to which the child progressed was determined by its state of maturation. More stimulation

▷ There are practical, moral, ethical, and legal reasons why we can't conduct research that could harm children. The same reasons may also apply to using animals. Unfortunately, both humans and animals have been used in the past, however, before many people became concerned about such things.

▷ Remember that DQ scores are measures of physical functioning. It was thought that intelligence developed as children grew. Those who had not matured would be least well-developed intellectually too. While Dennis did find this relationship, there were probably other reasons for their lack of intellectual development.

▷ A sensitive period is a length of time after birth when an animal is particularly sensitive to certain kinds of stimulation, usually involving the sights, sounds, and smells of their mothers.

would not improve motor or intellectual skills unless the child was maturationally ready.

A second major series of studies of children whose environments have changed was conducted by **Harold Skeels** and his colleagues. Most showed a corresponding change in their intelligence. In a 21-year **longitudinal study** of two groups of children, Skeels found that those who lived in the most stimulating environments increased their DQ and IQ scores over those who did not. Skeels knew about two children in a state orphanage in America who were so backward it was decided to put them in a special institution for backward children. One had an IQ of 35, the other's IQ was 46. A few months later they were retested, and now showed dramatic increases to 87 and 77 respectively. It seemed that the other children in the institution, and the staff, 'mothered' the new, younger members of the group and gave them lots of stimulation and attention. Within two years both children were fostered, having IQs which were just below average. This observation suggests that intelligence can be influenced by the amount of stimulation a child's environment contains

Skeels and Dye decided to test this more thoroughly. They found the DQs of twenty-five 19-month old orphans in a rather deprived and overcrowded orphanage where there was little to do or see. Thirteen of them had such low DQs that they were considered unadoptable. They were then moved to an orphanage for slightly subnormal older girls who cared for the children for much of the time, acting as subparents. Eighteen months later the babies's DQs had risen on average by twenty-eight points, from around sixty to nearly ninety.

The twelve babies who remained in the first orphanage acted as a kind of **control group**. They lost up to twenty-six DQ points. Their DQs were now the same as the first group before they were moved: around sixty. Two-and-a-half years later the differences were still there, and when Skeels tested them again when the two groups were 21 years old, those from the more stimulating environment were still ahead.

▷
Remember that DQs are not necessarily anything to do with intelligence.

▷
A control group is a group that is not being manipulated in any way. The behaviour of those in the group will be normal. If psychologists can measure the control group in the same way as they measured the behaviour of the group they are manipulating, they can compare the two groups. If there are any differences we may assume that the differences are caused by the manipulation.

Exercise on orphanage studies

1 What is meant by the phrase 'sensitive period'?
2 What is a longitudinal study?
3 What sensitive period did Dennis suggest for intellectual development?
4 What is maturation?
5 Why did Skeels use a control group?

●●● **Summary of orphanage studies**

Dennis's study of Lebanese orphans suggests that there may be a sensitive period of around two years during which children should be stimulated emotional and intellectually. Otherwise they may never achieve their full potential. Skeels and Dye found that children placed in more stimulating environments made considerable gains in their intellectual development.

Activity

What does the research of Skeels and Dennis actually show us about the effects of early experience on intellectual development? If you attempted the earlier Activities, consider now what these studies tell us about what intelligence is.

Some large-scale enrichment programmes have been attempted. During the 1950s and 1960s in America, many children were leaving school with very little education and no qualifications. Many came from the ethnic minorities and the poorer home backgrounds. The fact that they were unqualified, and the general shortage of decent jobs for unskilled people meant that many were living on welfare benefits, and some were turning to crime.

Oscar Lewis suggested that their lack of success in education was due to the fact that many lived in deprived neighbourhoods which did not have the usual facilities such as libraries, parks, theatres, etc. These children often spoke their own native language at home so their American English was poor. Lewis concluded that their culture was deprived when compared to that of normal American children. This deprived or impoverished culture would hold those groups of children back in later life. This would be bad for them, and bad for America as a whole, as they could end up in dead-end jobs, or on welfare, or in prison!

In response to this, and as a part of a much wider government policy to combat poverty – called the War On Poverty, – the government made a massive attempt at enrichment, to improve the culture of these children. It spent seventeen billion dollars on a series of **compensatory education** programmes for disadvantaged children. Some of the programmes emphasized social development, some emphasized cognitive development. The general aim was that deprived children would receive some pre-school remedial education. One of the best known programmes of compensatory education was called **Operation Headstart,** which started in the summer of 1965.

The people running the many Headstart programmes often had different ideas about what the children needed. Some of the centres were very education-centred, with children being taught discipline as well as basic skills. Others were more child-centred, trying to help children be more sociable, cooperative, or confident. Most of the children in Headstart, and in similar programmes, would go on visits to parks, and have people come into their neighbourhoods, even into their homes and teach them about road safety and where to play. They had extra teaching in English and maths, they received free medical and dental checkups, and generally were encouraged to absorb the competitive atmosphere that dominates American schools. In this way, it was argued, they would be academically as prepared for junior school as their native American classmates, and they would be able to join in the games, the competitions, the individual achievements etc., too.

▷
Lewis proposed that the reason why many people lived in poverty was because they had developed a culture of poverty. Their expectations were that they would live in poverty and so were unlikely to escape using the acceptable forms such as hard work and educational or other qualifications. This explanation is criticized for failing to explain why people became so poor in the first place.

▷
Operation Headstart comprised dozens of small-scale attempts to improve the life-chances of their children.

▷

Although the Headstart children were not all making the progress in school that had been hoped for, some were. Studies showed that the main factor that those who were most likely to succeed had in common was the involvement of their parents in their experiences.

▷

More recent studies of those who went through Headstart are more encouraging. Although the children may not have benefited in the ways that were intended, they do seem to be more likely to be successful citizens, committing fewer crimes, holding down a job, finishing school, less likely to become pre-maritally pregnant, etc.

▷

Compared to Headstart, the EPAs were not well funded and supporters claim they were not given an adequate chance.

Most of the children benefited from their early enrichment. However once they were in school many of the Headstart children started to fall behind their better-off classmates. Many coped better than they may have coped before, at least for the first few years of schooling, but very few actually improved very much by the end of it. By nine or ten years of age, the vast majority had slipped behind their better-off American classmates.

So why didn't more of the children who went through these compensatory education programmes improve in their schooling? Perhaps the influence of the home and family as the children grew was greater than the influence of spending a few hours each day in the programme when they were young. Those Headstart programmes that involved parents did seem to be more successful than others. Enrichment only seems to have any real chance of success when all the areas of one's life are affected, for example when a child is removed from one institution, such as a poor orphanage, and reared by loving parents. A few extra hours of enrichment could not begin to outweigh the disadvantages of being brought up in a poor, deprived environment.

In Britain something on a much smaller scale than Headstart began in the late 1960s. Children in some inner-city areas were leaving school with few qualifications and little chance of worthwhile jobs. Many lived in sub-standard housing in run-down areas. The government recognized that there was a link between children's social experiences and their chances of success in education, and directed some money into intervention programmes to improve school buildings and encourage teachers to work in these areas by giving extra pay. Four areas were identified as **Educational Priorities Areas** (EPAs). These included parts of Liverpool, Birmingham, London and Yorkshire.

These programmes of compensatory education aimed to raise reading and writing skills in children of pre-school age and in primary schools. The results were disappointing, as they had been with Headstart. EPAs did not lead to improvements in academic qualifications or employment prospects. As with Headstart, without involving the parents, and even the wider community in education, specific programmes of education alone are unlikely to succeed in improving the life chances of children.

Exercise on intervention programmes

1 How does the culture of poverty explain the continued existence of poverty. What kinds of norms and values would maintain this culture?
2 When and where did Operation Headstart begin?
3 What was Headstart's main aim?
4 Give some reasons under these two headings:

Headstart didn't help as many children achieve educational success as was hoped	Headstart was successful in other ways

5 Do the findings of these intervention programmes support
   (a) the nature view,
   (b) the nurture view,
   (c) both, in part, or
   (d) neither the nature nor the nurture view.
6 Explain your answer to question 5.

●●● **Summary of the nurture case**

Improving or worsening people's environments makes an important difference to their intellectual performance. Studies of children removed from unstimulating institutions and reared in more stimulating homes leads to a rapid increase in their IQ scores. Intervention programmes can also have an effect, but this is limited by the time they are able to spend in the stimulating environment compared to the time spent at home.

▷
The Minnesota study publicizes the many curious similarities that were found between twins who were reared apart. Many psychologists would disagree that these differences are the result of genetic influences. If they are nothing more than curious coincidences, then why should similarities in their IQ scores be anything more than coincidence too?

Studies which nativists claimed showed that identical twins have almost identical IQs were discussed earlier. Here we will summarize the nturist's objections to these claims. It is obvious that there will be similarities between identical twins. The question is whether these similarities have much to do with genetic inheritance. A study of twenty pairs of identical twins who were reared apart, conducted at Minnesota University in America, reports the many similarities in the lifestyles before they knew about each other. For example, both members of one pair of male twins who had not grown up together always visited the same holiday resort every year, and had a white wooden bench around the tree in their garden. They both enjoyed woodwork and smoked the same brand of cigarettes. Both had owned a dog named Toy, both married a girl called Linda, both had vasectomies and haemorrhoids. Apart from the fact that thousands of people visit the same resorts, smoke the same cigarettes and enjoy woodwork, and many more thousands have haemorrhoids, are we supposed to believe that these coincidences have anything to do with genetic inheritance? Are we to imagine that we inherit genes which direct us to the name we choose to give our dog or the girl we will marry? This seems pretty unlikely. If it's true, it means we don't have much free will at all, and that we are prisoners of our genes.

We are informed of the many similarities between the twins, but what about the many differences between them that we aren't told about? Perhaps one twin was a deeply religious person and the other was an atheist. Perhaps one twin always started the day with a large glass of carrot juice and the other twin hated carrot juice. We are only told about the startling similarities, which imply that there must be something mysterious about them.

In 1981 **Peter Wilson** published his findings having analysed the available information on studies of twins. He is not convinced that the similarities have anything to do with genes. He suggests that parents often treat identical twins in very similar ways, doing the same things with both of them, dressing them in similar clothes, and emphasizing all the similarities between them. Once established, this early bond may be hard to break. The individuals are treated as a unit and similarities in their

159

behaviour, tastes, expectations, etc., may well stem from this. The twins may become dependent on each other, and their socialization will not be ordinary.

Exercise on twin studies

1 Why are monozygotic twins so called?
2 How do dizygotic twins occur?
3 Does the fact that some identical twins have a number of similarities mean that their intelligence will also be similar? Explain your answer.
4 How does Peter Wilson explain the similarities often observed between twins?

Summary of twin studies
Studies which claim to have found incredible similarities in aspects of the intelligence of identical, separately reared twins can be criticized for ignoring many points of difference between them. It seems unlikely that there will be genes for every aspect of our functioning, including our intelligence.

Activity
Have a class discussion to decide whether the idea of intelligence is very useful. Ask which members of your class think that intelligence is a useful concept, and which do not. Divide the rest of the class so that each point of view is supported by half the class. For homework everyone should summarize the evidence for their particular case. In class the teacher can then pick a couple of members of each group to argue their case.

Conclusion – the nature–nurture debate

Attempting to untangle whether human intelligence is the result of genetic or environmental factors is both impossible, and a complete waste of time. We do not even know whether intelligence is something that we possess more or less of, or a process that we apply, with more or less success, to thriving in our environment. It is almost certain that both environment (nurture) and heredity (nature) are involved in it.

Combining the two views

One explanation of intelligence suggests that our genetic potential for behaving intelligently can be thought of as a rubber band. Rubber bands come in different sizes and the amount of potential each of us inherits will vary too. Some people inherit lots of potential (a long rubber band), others rather less (a short rubber band). Some people will grow up in stimulating environments with lots of good experiences. Others will not have so much stimulation. The amount of stimulation reflects the amount the rubber band is stretched. The following table summarizes the possible outcomes. People who could be intelligent have long rubber bands, while less bright people have shorter bands. The environment in which we grow up influences how far our band is stretched.

	Stimulating environment	Unstimulating environment
Long rubber band	Very intelligent behaviour	Quite intelligent behaviour
Short rubber band	Quite intelligent behaviour	Not very intelligent behaviour

Exercise on combining nature and nurture.

1 What is the average IQ score?
2 Can someone with a low genetic potential ever achieve a higher IQ than someone with a higher genetic potential?
3 What sorts of things provide enrichment or stimulation?

Answers to the intelligence test items (page 145).

Answer	Explanation
1 (a) M	A [B C] D [E F] G [H I] J (K L] = M
(b) H	H I J K L M N O P Q are from the alphabet. (Reading backwards we have QP, missing the next two gives ML, missing the next two gives us I and H.)
2 (a) Wood becomes coal if kept under pressure for long enough. (b) Apple and peach are both edible fruits. (c) Ship and car are both forms of transport.	
3 It's Monday tomorrow so we go back to school.	
4 Post means the same as stake and mall.	
5 Kitten	tootap = potato prinut = turnip tintek = kitten otrrac = carrot
6 Cardiff (is in Wales, not England)	grothnib = Brighton yuqtora = Torquay drlfcaf = Cardiff hercest = Chester sheeldiff = Sheffield

Gender

Sex refers to the biological differences between males and females. The most obvious are the organs for sexual reproduction. Although we are born with our sex, we have to learn our gender. As children are socialized they learn to be those things which are appropriate to being a male or a female in their culture. Some of the differences will be in their ideas, attitudes, thoughts, and expectations, such as members of each sex preferring some activities over others, having a distinct **self-concept**, developing certain **personality traits**, having different interests, etc. Other differences will be in the behaviour that members of each sex will show. For example boys may be expected to be more active and energetic, girls more quiet and caring.

▷
Our self-concept is the general set of ideas we each develop about what we are like. It is what we think we know about ourselves.

▷
A personality trait is a fairly permanent and fairly characteristic way in which we respond to a particular stimulus.

 Activity
List as many differences as you can in the ways in which boys and girls of (a) five years of age, and (b) ten years of age, are expected to behave.

The process of learning what behaviour goes with being your sex is called **sex-typing**. Sex-typing is the process through which males and females learn the appropriate attitudes, expectations and behaviour for people of their sex. The result of it is that children acquire their **gender concept**. In their early years children learn that they are called a girl or a boy, a daughter or a son. They learn that certain behaviour is expected of boys and girls. By the time they are around three years old they have acquired their **sex identity**. This is the knowledge of which category they belong to. Some familiar categories include mum, dad, uncle, son and daughter. Over the next year or two they develop some understanding of what kinds of behaviour are expected of them as individuals, female or male, what they can and cannot do, what they will be praised for or allowed to do, and what will lead to punishment. At this stage, they are learning their **gender identity**.

Activity
*How do you think children acquire their sense of gender identity? Think of the explanations that could be offered by **two** of the following: Freudians, Behaviourists, social learning theorists, Piaget.*

▷
A chromosome is a tiny piece of protein that carries several thousand gene cells. Genes are the building blocks from which our bodies develop.

▷
Traditional stereotyped male and female roles have decreased very rapidly during the last forty years in many parts of Europe and America. Women's awareness of their life chances has led to feminist movements raising female consciousness and demanding fairer treatment.

At the moment of conception in humans twenty-three **chromosomes** from the sperm form a chain with twenty-three chromosomes from the female. Chromosomes are tiny elements of protein, and can be of two main types, described by their shape as X and Y. The exact arrangement of these will determine our sex. Those who support the nature side of the nature–nurture debate argue that much of the behaviour that is associated with being male or female is also largely determined by biological factors. Supporters of the nurture side claim that every society has evolved expectations about aspects of male and female behaviour. In the West the male has traditionally been thought of as a strong, active and determined provider for his family. The female has been regarded as weak and passive, and grateful to her male partner for looking after her and the family. Supporters of each side of the nature–nurture debate have looked for evidence for their view from studies of males and females from many cultures. We will discuss each of their claims.

 Activity
List four things about yourself which you think you would have acquired through socialization, and four which you think have resulted from your genetic inheritance.

▶▶▶ **Activity**
If you woke up tomorrow morning as a member of the opposite sex, list as many ways as you can in which your life would be different.

Biological explanations of sex differences

The word 'sex' refers here to the many differences between males and females. For example, there are differences in organs such as the sex organs used for reproduction. There are also different hormone levels that trigger male and female functioning such as changes with puberty. Research shows that gender identity in girls changes as they reach puberty. Speculation about how certain instincts explain certain aspects of gender behaviour have been made. We will look at each proposition. It has also been suggested that there are differences in some of the structures and functions in male and female brains. However, a great deal of modern evidence shows that, while there are large differences in the ways individual brains are organized, there are no consistent differences between male and female brains.

Sex differences in children

There are differences between male and female babies and young children. In the West, on average, boys are heavier, more active, more irritable, more demanding, less hardy, sleep less well, and are less easy to comfort than girls. On average girls are walking and talking before boys too. Over the next few years these differences largely disappear and there is no evidence that these early differences explain much of the person's sex-linked behaviour later. Also there are wide individual differences within these group averages. Some boys will be more intellectually and socially advanced and easier to raise than some girls. On balance, by puberty, the two sexes are equally sociable, have similar levels of self-esteem, and are similarly motivated by achievement.

Early appearance of sex differences

Male babies are usually bigger and heavier than female babies. They often sleep less, cry more, and are generally more active. They are usually more irritable, and are harder to comfort than females too. Female babies tend to be rather hardier than boys. Many start to talk before the average male baby does, and they usually reach physical maturity sooner too.

Similar patterns in primates

Several experiments have investigated the influence of hormones on sex-role behaviour in animals. For example **W.C. Young** injected a pregnant monkey who had a female foetus with the male hormone **testosterone** every day from the forty-second to the one-hundred-and-twenty-second day of the pregnancy. The development of the female foetus was influenced by the androgens. As the female offspring grew, so her behaviour became more like that of a male monkey. She was assertive, challenging others for a place in the group, she started fights, and she was more independent. When mature she even tried to mate with another female!

Many experiments with lower-order animals have shown how altering androgen and oestrogen levels affect the extent of sex-linked behaviour. Increasing oestrogen levels in males produces behaviour more typical of females while increasing testosterone in females produces more male-like behaviour. However the environment also influences the amount of hormones released. Monkeys who won their battles against challengers seemed to produce more testosterone than they had before, while the testosterone levels of those who lost went down.

▷ Male babies are generally heavier, more active, more irritable, less easy to manage, and more susceptible to illness and disease than female babies. They are also slightly less likely to survive into middle childhood!

▷ Testosterone is one of the main androgens.

Comment on sex differences

It is often tempting to generalize the findings of carefully constructed experiments on nonhuman animals to human beings. If this were possible then we could explain sex-role behaviour and aggression rather simply in terms of our hormones. Hormones are important (as anyone who has benefited from hormone-replacement therapy will tell you). However, humans have higher brain centres that can override our biological urges and influences.

Differences occur everywhere

As we said earlier, there are many physical differences between male and female babies. Being stronger, males are more likely to perform most of the heavy work, while females occupy less physically strenuous roles. Males are more aggressive, so it might be suggested that we would only expect to find male warriors. This isn't true either. There have been famous female fighting forces in the past, and in many armies women have front-line fighting roles.

Summary of sex differences
There are sex differences in size and weight between males and females and these differences occur in many different species of animals and in most human cultures.

Hormones

Hormones are chemical messengers which are released by various glands and organs in the body at certain times. They trigger activity in other parts of the body. The main male hormones which are responsible for such events as the onset of puberty, the adolescent growth spurt, becoming biologically fertile, and so on, are called the **androgens**. The **oestrogens** are important female hormones which control the timing of biological maturity and menstruation. It could be that these, and other sex-linked hormones, also affect psychological development. Both sexes have androgens and oestrogens, males having more androgens, and females having more oestrogens.

One of the most critical factors during pregnancy is the amount of androgen hormones that are produced. Androgens are responsible for developing male genitals. If the mother has a male foetus and produces enough androgens, her son will have normal male genitals. If she is carrying a female foetus and has too much androgen her daughter may also have developed male sexual characteristics. This condition is called **Androgenital Syndrome (AGS)**. Such cases are extremely rare, and the error is usually quickly corrected.

Some studies by **John Money** and his colleagues have been made of AGS girls whose mothers were given extra amounts of androgens during their pregnancy (to reduce the likelihood of miscarriage). The daughters tended to be more aggressive and tomboyish, and less what our society might call 'feminine'. They preferred male activities with male company, and expressed more interest in having a career than in having a family. This research strongly supports a link between hormone levels at critical times and psychological aspects of gender.

▷
The activity of hormones during pregnancy can affect how the body matures, but it cannot change the foetus's sex. This is determined by the type of chromosomes it inherits.

▷
'Masculine' and 'feminine' are creations of particular members of society at particular times (particularly media figures, advertisers, and fashion designers). They are not shared by members of all societies.

Summary of hormone differences and gender
Oestrogens and androgens control biological changes in females and males. Both sexes have some of each hormone. Altering the balance between them makes the individual behave more like a member of the opposite sex.

Instinct

After the Second World War **John Bowlby** (see Chapter 2) claimed that mothers develop a maternal instinct to care for their babies and children. He placed great emphasis on mothers, as though fathers and other care-givers have little impact on the child. As babies need to form emotional bonds with their mothers (or substitute mothers), Bowlby claimed that mothers would have instinctive urges to form emotional bonds with their children too, and that these maternal instincts will appear in all females some time after puberty. Such a claim is not widely believed now. If all females had instincts to have babies then all females who could give birth would probably do so. Many females choose not to have children, however. Also, if their instincts are to care for their young, how could any female neglect or abuse her children (which, sadly, some do)?

Bowlby claimed that females have a maternal instinct to have and care for their young. In most societies child-care roles are performed by females. Freud explained the emergence of gender differences as being by social identification with the same-sex parent to resolve the Oedipus crises of early and middle childhood. Freud's claims for the concepts he created have been attacked for not being open to testing and therefore being unscientific. Instincts and identification are just ways of thinking about some behaviour, the processes they represent may not actually exist.

If gender roles are genetically transmitted then it seems reasonable to imagine that any differences between the sexes would appear soon after birth, they would be the same in all societies, and that they may even appear in some of the other higher primate species.

▷ Instinct is a difficult idea to understand, as it has several different meanings. In the simplest sense, (which will be perfectly adequate here), it refers to some unlearned responses which members of a particular species (human females) will give towards a particular stimulus (a human baby).

▷ Freudian psychoanalysis is introduced in Chapter 1.

▷ Cognition is the process that humans have by which they take in information about their environment from their senses and can use it to help them know what is going on, and what to do in that situation.

Comment on biological explanations of gender-role behaviour

In all societies sex differences in behaviour can be seen by about two years of age. However, humans aren't simply the prisoners of their hormones or instincts. We have **cognition** and can make predictions. If I know that you are bigger stronger, and more aggressive than me, then wanting to fight you does not make good sense. An animal in this position might leave and try its chances elsewhere. Instead, I might try to think of some way to outwit you, or may have a position whereby I can outrank you, or I may be able to appeal to your sense of fairness or justice. Because I have knowledge and understanding, intelligence and communication skills, I can control my own behaviour. My cognitive skills ensure that I do not have to obey any sex-linked biological urges.

Exercise on biological influences on behaviour

1 What is testosterone and what are some of its effects?
2 What is oestrogen and what is it responsible for?
3 What is the difference between sex and gender?
4 Evaluate each of the following for how far it supports the biological explanation of gender-role behaviour, on a table like the one shown.

	Supports biological explanations	Does not support biological explanations
Sex differences		
Hormones		
Instinct		

 Summary of the contribution that instincts make to gender
Instincts are supposed to be genetically inherited forces that make animals behave in certain ways. Humans are supposed to have maternal instincts although this seems highly unlikely.

 Activity
Draw up a list of factors that support the biological case for acquiring our sex roles. For each point note any problem with it which may make it less certain.

Social explanations of gender differences

Supporters of the nurture case claim that biological forces do not force us to behave in definite ways, they can only make it more likely that we might. They would say that the experiences humans have had will influence whether they are likely to act in those ways. For instance, you may be a female with more androgens than others, but if you are raised to be a feminine person then you are likely to be quite feminine. You may be a male with plenty of testosterone being produced in your body. Whether you usually behave in an assertive way will be influenced by your socialization and cognition rather than simply by your hormones.

Those who see a major role for nurture in developing gender roles identify the main influences on a child (sometimes called the main agencies of socialization). These are:

(a) the family and the ways in which the child is reared,
(b) the influence of the peer group, and
(c) the impact of the media.

Exercise on social experiences

1 Adults give children toys to play with. Sort the following list into girls' toys, boys' toys, and toys for both sexes:

doll	cuddly toy	sports equipment	drum
bicycle	nurse's outfit	skipping rope	pram
gun	skateboard	toy shop	chemistry set
ball	equipment	construction set	

(a) Which of your three lists contains the greatest number of 'active' toys?

(b) Which contain toys that will be played with caringly or lovingly?

(c) Does any list in particular contain significantly more toys which will stretch the imagination?

2 Here is a list of nicknames which parents have called their children.

darling	*tiger*	*boxer*
angel	*daddy's favourite*	*pretty little thing*
matey	*cowboy*	*tough guy*

(a) Which sex would each apply to?

(b) Add to the list any nicknames which you know of. What do they show about the differences that parents will expect to find between female and male children?

3 Mention one way in which male and female babies are dressed differently.

4 What sort of thing do you suppose a parent might say to comfort a daughter who has hurt herself? Might the parent say anything different to a son when he hurts himself?

5 In view of your answers to the previous questions, describe any differences between the ways the two sexes are being treated by parents.

6 If a girl behaves like a boy she may be called a tomboy. What would you call a boy who behaves like a girl? Which of the two do you consider to be more of an insult?

Child-rearing

In any group of people there will emerge certain roles that some people need to perform. For example, the job of organizing the group, trading with others, defending the group, and rearing the young are all important social roles. Albert Bandura has shown how children learn their roles from those influential models they observe around them, particularly from their parents. If the two sexes are treated differently, and have different expectations made of their behaviour then they will learn to behave differently. Many parents do treat their sons differently from their daughters, and differences in children's behaviour can be seen from a very young age. Boys may be regarded by parents as more sturdy than girls, and so are more likely to be offered rough-and-tumble-type play. Girls are more likely to have cuddles and gentle treatment. This might be preparing them for the kind of social roles that they may find themselves in later.

Beverley Fagot studied twenty-four American families, each with a child between twenty and twenty-four months old. She visited each family five times, observing parents interacting with their children for an hour on each visit. She was looking for examples of the kind of behaviour parents encouraged and discouraged in their sons and daughters.

Generally, girls were encouraged to ask for help when it was needed, to follow and stay near to a parent, to dance, to take an interest in girls' clothes, and to play with dolls. Girls were usually discouraged from running around, jumping, climbing, and being too active, being aggressive and playing rough games, and manipulating and exploring objects. Boys

▷ Fagot conducted a naturalistic-observation study. She visited families in their own home and noted particular aspects of their interaction, i.e. what behaviour was to be encouraged and discouraged in each sex.

were encouraged to play with and explore toys such as trucks and building blocks in an active, manipulative way which would help build strong muscles. They were strongly discouraged from playing with dolls, asking for assistance, and anything the parents considered feminine. Fagot also noted that boys and girls were not treated equally in the activities they were discouraged from beginning. Boys who started any feminine activities were more severely criticized than girls who played in a masculine way.

Goldberg and **Lewis** interviewed the mothers of thirty-two male and thirty-two female babies of six months to discover if there were any differences in the ways boys and girls were treated. When they were thirteen months old (and toddling), the babies and their mothers were observed in a laboratory setting. The laboratory contained a chair for the mother, and nine toys. Some of the toys (e.g. drums) encouraged active or noisy play. Others (e.g. dolls) encouraged more passive and quiet play. When settled in the play room, the child was put onto the floor to investigate the toys. The mother was to behave normally. The mother's activities, and those of her baby, were recorded for fifteen minutes.

These observations were compared to Goldberg and Lewis's earlier observations. Some interesting differences emerged. Girls tended to choose quieter toys and play nearer their mother, involving her in their games. Boys tended to choose more active toys and appeared more independent.

••• Summary of Goldberg and Lewis's observations

	Reactions to play	Reactions to mother
Girls	Preferred passive toys which were played with near to mother wanting help, involvement and conversation.	Seemed quite dependent
Boys	Preferred bigger, noisier toys or those which could be investigated in detail.	Generally more independent and played further away from their mothers.

In another play session, Goldberg and Lewis tested the children's responses to frustration. They waited until each child and his or her mother were separated, and quickly raised a barrier between them. The mother was then asked not to go to the child immediately, but to wait and see what the child would do. The girls generally approached the barrier, looked at their mothers, and, presumably realizing their way was blocked, started to cry. The boys tended to approach the barrier, explore it to see if there was any way through or around it, and, finding none, only then begin to cry.

Combining their earlier interviews and observations with the observations that were used during the experiment at thirteen months, Goldberg and Lewis were able to draw some conclusions about the effects of child-rearing on gender-role behaviour. Girls had been treated more gently than boys. They were more likely to have been breast fed when younger.

▷
Let us be clear about what researchers on sex differences have found. They do not claim that males and females are so extremely different that they may be virtually members of different species! Far from it. Most males and females have similar genetic inheritances, similar socialization, similar environments, etc. Not surprisingly, they are, therefore, quite similar! Some researchers have found differences in some responses made by male and female participants in some studies.

They were more likely to be picked up and cuddled, and the amount of time they were held was also longer than for boys. They were spoken to in a softer tone of voice. Boys were generally treated more robustly. Goldberg and Lewis felt that these differences would have explained some of the differences in the boys' and girls' behaviour at thirteen months.

Exercise on Goldberg and Lewis's experiment.

1 Why did Goldberg and Lewis interview the mothers of the children when the children were six-months-old?
2 The sample size in this study was sixty-four. What does 'sample size' mean?
3 Who were the subjects of this study: the mothers, the children, or oth?
4 Explain your answer to the previous question.
5 Can you think of any reasons why parents discourage their sons from playing what are thought of as feminine roles more than they might discourage their daughters from playing masculine roles?
6 Summarize Goldberg and Lewis's conclusions.
7 How does this research contribute to our understanding of the origin of gender roles?

Occasionally a pregnant female may have an imbalance between her oestrogen and androgen levels. As we saw with W.C. Young's experiment, hormone levels during pregnancy can affect foetal development. A mother with excessive androgen can give birth to a daughter who has secondary sexual characteristics and could be wrongly identified as a boy. The baby has Androgenital Syndrome (see page 165).

As we mentioned earlier, **John Money** has conducted research in this area. He found that if the error was realized before the child was about eighteen months old, then appropriate surgery or hormone treatment and changed socialization could be given, and the girl shouldn't suffer any major problems. If the error went undiscovered until the child was three years of age or older, then there could be serious problems. Money reported the case of one AGS girl who was thought to be a boy. She was reared as a male until 'he' was three-and-a-half years old. The parents decided that the risk to the child's personality was simply too great to risk changing, and the decision was taken to continue to raise the child as a boy. With appropriate surgery and hormone treatment the 'boy' continued to behave like a boy, joining with the other boys in active play, and taking a healthy interest in girls, etc.

Money also reports the case of a seven-month-old Jewish boy (one of identical twins) whose penis was damaged by faulty equipment during circumcision. As he wouldn't, therefore, be able to function as a male it was decided to make him into a girl. At seventeen months he had surgery, and a course of hormone treatment began. With female socialization, the child soon started behaving like other girls in Western society. By the age of five, the differences between the twins was considerable. The 'daughter' enjoyed feminine things such as playing with dolls, having her hair brushed and her face washed. She disliked being dirty, moved carefully

▷ Such a case as this is extremely rare, and decisions about a child's sexual future could only be made following careful discussions involving the child's parents with medical and other professionals.

and gently, and spoke softly. If gender roles were determined by innate forces then such a change in behaviour would not have been possible, as this child was genetically male.

 ### Summary of the effects of child rearing

Parents take different approaches to rearing their children. As children learn by observing, attaching, modelling, reinforcement, etc., the ways in which they are treated will affect their particular development. Goldberg and Lewis found differences in male and female reactions in toddlers, and John Money showed that gender roles can be changed by socialization.

Cross-cultural studies – Margaret Mead's research

If gender roles were biological in origin then we would expect that males and females everywhere would have similar roles and expectations. In the 1920s and 1930s, **Margaret Mead** conducted some **anthropological cross-cultural** research among various societies living on some Pacific Islands. She found dramatic differences in the ways boys and girls were treated, and in the personalities and behaviour of the adults which appeared as a result. In one society there were no gender differences in the behaviour of the two sexes, in another the traditional sex roles were reversed, with women being dominant. Although Mead's research has been criticized for sometimes relying on second-hand reports which may have been exaggerated, she does provide some evidence that gender roles result from childhood social experiences.

The Arapesh Indians were poor, gentle, cooperative people. All jobs (including child care) were shared equally by husband and wife. The children were also treated with respect. Aggression was virtually unknown in either sex. They were a humble, caring, loving people.

The women of the Tchambuli people socialized their male children to be artistic, creative, and sentimental. The adult males would sit around the village gossiping, making themselves look pretty, and arranging entertainment for the women. The women took the lead in all matters. They were competitive, efficient and conducted all the group's trade and commerce. The men's lives revolved around the women.

The Mundugumor people's males and females, both adults and youngsters, were aggressive, argumentative, and suspicious of everyone else. They were forever spying on each other, making alliances and truces, and fighting. Children were not welcomed, as they might form alliances against one of their parents. The wives tended to rear their sons, and the fathers reared their daughters although neither parent paid much attention to their children, and the children learned that they had to fight for everything they wanted.

Exercise on Margaret Mead's anthropology

	Boys	Girls
Traditional view of the West	active, competitive, independent	passive, cooperative caring
Arapesh people	unassertive, caring and cooperative	unassertive, caring and cooperative
Mundugumor people	aggressive, impatient and irritable	aggressive, impatient and irritable
Tchambuli people	artistic and gentle	competitive and assertive

1 In which of the four cultures are there differences in the ways boys and girls are raised?
2 What is a cross-cultural study? (Look back to Chapter 1 if you need to refresh your memory.)
3 Describe one problem that researchers conducting cross-cultural research face, which wouldn't be encountered when studying a single culture.
4 Does the evidence in the table support or contradict the view that gender roles are genetically inherited? Explain your answer.

Comment on Margaret Mead's studies

No one disputes that important biological differences exist between males and females and that these differences will have an impact in shaping the behaviour of members of each sex. However, if such enormous differences exist between male and female behaviour from three societies, then children's social experiences must play an important part in learning gender roles. Mead's work has been criticized for overstating the extent of some of the differences she claimed to have found, and some of her information may have been exaggerated.

Summary of Margaret Mead's cross-cultural research

Mead found striking differences in the ways that males and females in different societies were reared, and the differences in the adult personalities that resulted. Although doubts have been cast over some aspects of Mead's research, such broad differences in child-rearing style and adult personalities do exist in different cultures.

Peer group influence – Michael Lamb's studies

It's not just adults who provide their children with models for appropriate gender-role behaviour. Other children do too. **Michael Lamb** studied three- to five-year-old boys and girls playing with a variety of toys. When

▷
Peers are equals. A peer group is a group of people who are equal to each other.

the children played with their toys in a way that was appropriate to their sex the games were inventive and enjoyable. If a child picked up a toy which its same-sex **peers** thought was a cross-sex toy (for example, if a boy started to play with a doll), then they became very critical and the doll would soon be abandoned as the child rejoined its friends.

The effects of the media on gender roles

In Britain and many other countries, children's books, stories, films, and television programmes all used to present a very similar picture of the roles of boys and girls. They were stereotypes.

Exercise on the media

1 Complete the following nursery rhymes. Each of these could give children some ideas about what girls are like. What are these ideas?

   Polly put the kettle on ...

   Mary had a little lamb ...

   Mary, Mary, quite contrary ...

   Little Miss Muffet ...

2 Complete these rhymes. What impressions might little boys learn about what boys are like from these rhymes?

   Little Jack Horner ...

   The Queen of Hearts she baked some tarts ...

3 What would children of both sexes learn from such games as *He Man, Master of the Universe*, *She Ra*, *Sonic the Hedgehog*, and *Super Mario Brothers*?

If you ever read Enid Blyton's children's books, or almost any of the books for children from earlier this century, you may notice how almost all have certain themes in common. The most important figure is a male or group of males. The males are more active than the females. They take the initiative and make the decisions. They receive most of the credit too. Girls are portrayed as supporters of boys. They tend to go along with the boys, run errands for them, use their charm for them, and generally look out for them. Boys are determined and practical, while girls tend to be more weak and indecisive. While the boys are entering dangerous or forbidden territory, girls are outside keeping watch.

Even in girls' comics there were rarely many major adventures. Girls were shown as being more interested in pony clubs and ballet classes. Or, like Minnie the Minx, they were little horrors. Romance, concern with relationships, and preparation for a caring, domestic role dominated the pages of girls' books. These stereotyped ideas have largely disappeared now (particularly since more women are involved in producing women's media now).

Activity

Think of some children's soap operas or fictional adventures on television now. What roles do the males and the females play? Are they more equal now, or are the roles still stereotyped?

Summary of other influences

Other children and the media also provide powerful models from which children draw their ideas about what to do and think. Lamb showed that gender-role socialization was established before children start school. These ideas may have been influenced by comics, television and other media showing male and females performing certain roles.

Psychoanalytic theory of gender roles

In Chapter 1 we mentioned how Sigmund Freud thought that people's personalities, including their understanding of themselves, were influenced by unconscious, instinctive urges. These urges would determine our feelings and behaviour. As a child would be having different feelings at different ages, so Freud talked about different stages of personality development. It was during the third stage of personality development that a boy experiences his first sexual feelings. These would be towards the person who loved him and cared for him: his mother. Freud called this the **phallic stage** of personality development and it occurred between about three and five years of age.

The problem with being drawn to one's mother is that she already has a partner, the child's father. Unconsciously, Freud claimed, the boy resents and hates his father for taking his mother's attention away from him. Unconsciously, he will feel guilty and afraid that his father may find out how he feels. This creates something of a conflict in the child's mind. Loving and hating someone at the same time, feeling guilty and feeling frightened are described as the **Oedipus Complex**, after a character in an ancient story (see page 229). The way to resolve these conflicting emotions could be to become as much like his father as possible, including adopting his father's gender role behaviour. If the father is weak, or isn't always available, the boy will be unable to identify strongly and will remain unsure about his own masculinity.

Comment on psychoanalytic explanations for gender

No hard evidence for any of Freud's ideas exists. The supposed phallic stage and the emotions that go with it are part of Freudian interpretations of the symptoms of some disturbed adults in Vienna during the early decades of the twentieth century. Freud's references to sex as a theme which underlies personality development has attracted a great deal of criticism and ridicule.

Exercise on psychoanalytic explanations

1 What is the role of the libido in Freudian theory?
2 During which stage is the child said to experience Oedipal conflict?
3 What is Oedipal conflict?

 Summary of psychoanalytic views of gender roles
During the phallic stage (3–5) boys are unconsciously drawn to their mothers in a pre-genital way. This causes anxiety in the child about what his father's reaction would be. This anxiety was described as the Oedipus Complex. Boys resolve it by identifying with their fathers, including taking on their gender roles.

Kohlberg's cognitive development theory of gender roles

Lawrence Kohlberg disagrees with Freud that gender roles have anything to do with sexual drives, and with social learning theorists such as Bandura that they emerge from observing role models. He claims that children acquire their gender roles in the same way as they acquire their other **cognitive skills**. Research into how children process information suggests their thinking skills change according to how they can perceive objects and events. Kohlberg identifies three stages of development.

The stage of basic gender identity

By the time they are about three years old children have learned their basic gender identity. They can describe themselves as a girl or a boy, but have little idea about what that means, or that their sex won't change during their lives. Knowing that you are a little girl will encourage you to play with other little girls. This will reinforce your definition of yourself as a little girl. You will know that there are such things as little boys, but they won't have much real meaning for you.

The stage of gender stability

During the next few years children mix with members of their own sex and ask questions about what boys and girls do. Parents will say 'boys don't cry' and 'girls are pretty' and the child slowly realizes that little boys and little girls do some things, and those things are different from the things the others do. They gradually realize that their sex is fixed for life and will not change. When they know this they have **gender stability**.

Knowing that one's own sex is fixed for life doesn't mean that children have the same understanding about other people's sex. At four and five years of age children are still largely making their judgements of what things are like from what they look like. So, if a child knows that girls have long hair, then they may well describe a man as a girl if his hair were long.

The stage of gender consistency

By the time children reach six or seven years old they will have spent many hours in the company of other people of their own sex, and probably someone they fancy. They will have heard adults refer to people using familiar words such as man and woman, boy and girl. They will stop using appearance as the main feature in making judgements and will have realized that gender can't change. They now have **gender consistency**.

Comment on cognitive explanations for gender development

Kohlberg sees a child's understanding about sex and gender roles developing in the same way as other aspects of the child's understanding develop. Essentially this is through a series of stages. One of the main differences between Kohlberg's and other explanations for learning about gender is that they see gender roles emerging as a result of imitation and identification with other members of one's sex. Kohlberg sees those things being the result, not the cause, of acquiring one's gender.

Summary of Kohlberg's views

Kohlberg suggests that children learn their sex and gender roles through the same cognitive process by which they learn other things. As their understanding of the world, and as their cognitive skills develop, so their knowledge of the expectations of their sex increases.

Conclusion – Combining the Explanations

The nature–nurture debate has dominated many researchers' ideas throughout this century. To say that some features of our psychological make up such as our gender roles are the result of either genetic or social forces seems a rather old fashioned debate now. Surely most of our psychological skills and qualities are the result of both? A better understanding of gender-role behaviour would be gained by asking how our nature and our nurture contribute to our acquiring gender roles.

Throughout this chapter we have talked about the ways in which many children acquire their sex and gender roles and identities. However, many others have quite different life experiences and acquire their ideas and behaviour in quite different ways that are beyond the scope of this book.

Comment on theories of gender roles

Main points	Comments
Biological theory There are sex differences which are the result of conception, and of hormone balances during maturation. Biological forces do act on us, because we are human animals.	Gender roles vary between people, between cultures, and between members of the same sex in any one culture. If biological factors explained gender behaviour such wide variations would not exist.
Social learning theory Even very young children can imitate role models. Their behaviour can also be conditioned in quite informal ways, by other children, as well as by adults.	Although the behaviour which is generally associated with boys and girls may vary according to their socialization, the extent or depth of it may be explained by hormone levels.
Psychoanalytic theory Freud saw a child's knowledge of its gender roles being acquired through the process of identification with its same sex parent as a part of resolving the Oedipus Complex. This was a radically different way of looking at gender role acquisition.	There is no evidence to support the existence of the Oedipus Complex, and gender socialization and gender roles are learned by children who do not have a same-sex parent with whom to identify.
Kohlberg's cognitive view Kohlberg sees gender socialization occurring in stages, as other aspects of cognitive development occur. If cognition does develop in ways like those suggested by Kohlberg then it seems logical that other aspects of knowledge, gender, would too.	Not everyone agrees that (a) any aspect of development, including cognition, occurs in stages, and (b) that the distinctions between the stages that Kohlberg identifies are specific enough to be of any value in understanding like gender rule socialization.

The development of the self-concept

You are a conscious, thinking animal. Humans are probably the only species that have consciousness. By having consciousness you are able to think and have ideas and feelings. You have an idea about what kind of person you are, and you have feelings about whether you like being that person. For example, what do you quite like about your personality, and what would you like to change? You have ideas about other people, such as your friends, relatives, acquaintances and enemies. What aspects of your friends' personalities do you like, and what don't you like about your enemies? You have thoughts and feelings about objects and events too. What do you think about some of the soaps on television, the price of CDs, or student grants and loans?

Humans are the only animals to have such ideas about what and who they are. Your self-concept is simply the total of all your ideas, feelings, and attitudes about yourself, others, and objects and events. If you wrote as many statements as you could beginning with 'I am ...' you would have a good description of your self-concept. In this chapter we will examine how self-concept develops, what it comprises, and what factors affect its development.

 Activity

Write 10 statements beginning with 'I am ...' that describe your personality. How many of your statements include other people? How many describe your personality? Put them away in a safe place and don't look at them until you have left college. When you read them again see if you've changed.

Humans are the only animals to have any idea of who and what they are, their thoughts and feelings, and of the impression they make on others. These ideas form their self-concept.

Where does the self-concept come from?

There have been a number of theories to explain the development of the self. Around the turn of the century **Charles Cooley** claimed that we learn what we are like from what we see of how other people treat us. He said 'The self ... is a reflection, largely from the minds of others.' He calls it a **looking glass self**. (A looking glass is an old fashioned phrase for a mirror.)

▷
The looking glass theory suggests that people learn about their self-image and self-esteem by experiencing how other people react towards them, and by trying to change themselves.

Thirty years later **Gordon Herbert Mead** extended Cooley's idea. He claimed that our ideas about ourselves are constantly changing as we meet new people who treat us in new ways. Also we can change ourselves. If we don't like what we think we are like, then we might decide to try harder to change some of our attitudes and behaviour. He calls this **self-interaction.** It is quite common during adolescence and early adulthood. As we grow older and become less concerned with other people's approval, self-interaction is claimed to become less important.

▷
Mead says that the self-concept consists of all the ideas that we have formed about ourselves from the ways people have treated us, and so isn't a thing at all. It is one aspect of our understanding about the world.

During the 1950's and 60's some psychologists and psychiatrists favoured humanistic psychology's approach (see chapter six). Humanistic psychologists believe that every human being is unique with their own particular ideas and views about themselves and their situation. **Carl Rogers** saw people as largely rational, sensible creatures, who usually have some reasonable understanding about their self. Rogers sees the self as the very centre of the individual.

Rogers agrees with Cooley and Mead that the self develops from the interactions people have with other people. Rogers thinks that our self-concept leads us to behave consistently. If you learn that you are a caring person from the way that other people respond to you with their troubles, then you may well try to behave in a caring way. Some problems for people can happen when what they think that they are like is different from the way that other people think of them. For example, if Karl believes that he is likeable and popular, but other people seem to ignore him, Karl may realize that there is a difference between his self-concept and reality. This could lead to Karl having a personality problem which may need discussing with a therapist.

▷
Rogers thinks that people are generally logical and rational creatures who try to behave in consistent ways. When a gap opens up between their perception of who they are, and how others seem to treat them, it may be necessary to help them face their true selves.

Activity
If you dare, try this little exercise in total honesty. Write down how you think your best friend would describe your personality. Ask them to write how they think you see theirs. Make the descriptions as detailed as you can. If you're good enough friends, swap papers. Beware though, this can be quite a strange experience. If you are slightly unsure about this, don't do it.

Gordon Allport also disagreed with the early ideas about the self-concept being a thing that simply develops through interaction. He rejected those theories which try to explain why some people's personalities are similar. Instead he claimed that each individual is unique, and has had a unique set of experiences which shape the way she or he understands the world.

▷

Allport uses the word proprium to mean all those things that we learn which become part of our self-concept.

(However we each learn about what the world is like through our interactions with others.) He also thought that the concept of self has become confused since different writers mean different things by it. Allport invented the term **proprium** to replace the self. Proprium consists of such dimensions as our body image and our self-image generally, our wish to succeed in life, our attempts to improve ourselves, our sense of identity, our knowledge of what things belong to us, and 'the knower' which is the overall cognitive ability which knows about all the other parts of self.

Exercise on theories of self

1 How does Cooley explain the origin of our knowledge about our self?
2 What does Mead mean by self-interaction?
3 How does a humanistic psychologist regard people generally?
4 Rogers says that humans are rational creatures who try to behave consistently. What does he mean by this?
5 What does Allport mean by proprium?

▷

When you were very young most of your thoughts and feelings were about yourself, about what you needed, what you could do, and what happened when you did things.

At what age do infants start to have their own personality? We said in chapter two that babies are born with a temperament, a set of ways in which they usually respond to certain kinds of stimulation. For example a caregiver is holding a baby and smiling at it. This is the stimulation. The baby smiles back. This is the baby's usual response. It reflects the child's happy, good-natured temperament. As the child gains more experience its personality emerges. The personality might be an extension of the temperament, or other factors might intervene. As the child acquires language and simple thinking, after the first year or so it starts to learn about itself. This is the origin of the child's self-concept.

▷

Egocentric thought is thinking which only really takes the point of view of the thinker into account. It appears to ignore anyone else's needs or ideas.

For the first few years of their lives children's thinking is described as **egocentric**. That is they behave only in ways which bring them pleasure. They are unable to imagine what effect their behaviour, or even their presence, is likely to have on someone else. Their behaviour may bring them praise or reward, or punishment. The child must learn what it should do, what it can do, and what it mustn't do, in all situations. The most important factor in determining how it learns appropriate and inappropriate behaviour is probably through what happens to the child when it has behaved in one way or another.

We'll take two extreme examples, Graham and David. Like most parents, Graham's parents only want what's best for their son. They believe that their son is able to understand their wishes as long as they are carefully explained. They expect him to try to control his own behaviour and follow their wishes. They explain to him why he should eat all his food, and why he should not hit his sister. When he clears his plate and helps his sister they reward him with praise. They say that he's 'a good boy'. He feels good about himself. Graham acquires a positive idea of what he is like and develops a **positive self-concept**.

On the other hand David's parents leave him to get on with things. They say it teaches him self-reliance. They ignore him unless he is doing something dangerous or disturbs other people. Then they smack him and tell him to stop being silly. He learns that he mustn't bother others and doesn't want people to know that he is silly. David's self-concept is rather negative. Two things have happened here, in order for these children's self-concept to start developing. One is that they are becoming able to control their own behaviour, the other is that they can understand how other people respond to them.

▷ The self-concept begins to develop when children realize that some people, (e.g. parents) have power over them. and they begin to be able to control their own behaviour.

Most of us live in groups with other people. We live in family groups, friendship groups, school groups, work groups, etc. Some groups are fairly permanent, others constantly change. Different people in different groups will react to us in different ways. A particular child's family will probably be more helpful and supportive towards it if it needs help. The child learns that it will receive help if it has problems. A child in another class at school is not likely to be as helpful. The child now learns that only certain people can be relied upon to be helpful.

The child can't expect everyone else to do what it wants all the time. It will have to learn to agree to live by certain rules, such as cooperating and sharing, helping and not stealing, thinking about others and not just itself. These ideas also become part of its self-concept. Whilst the child is developing its own ideas of who and what it is and what it is like, it is also getting ideas about who and what other people should be like too. (We usually think that other people should be rather like us!) The child's self-concept is quite complex, especially since it is constantly changing.

▷ The child's self-concept changes and expands rapidly throughout childhood as it gains more experiences of what other people think and feel.

The child's perceptions of how others react towards him or her is very important to developing the self-concept. Bandura and other **social learning theorists** have shown (see Chapter 1) that children learn a great deal about themselves and others by observing and imitating important models such as parents. When the child begins school teachers become important role models, stressing what the child should think and do. We will return to this when we look at **Jean Piaget**'s theories of how children's thinking changes as they grow in Chapter 10.

▷ Albert Bandura's Social Learning Theory stresses the importance of observational learning and modelling. As children grow they learn to adopt more social roles.

Exercise on the self-concept

1 What is the self-concept?
2 What is a temperament?
3 What is a personality?
4 What is meant by egocentric thought?
5 Name some of the groupings that human beings form themselves into.
6 What are the main features of social learning theory?

●●● **Summary of the origins of self-concept**
Since we aren't born with the ability to recognize, much less know anything else about ourselves, then we must learn who we are and what we are like. Part of this knowledge comes from our perception of how other people treat us. During adolescence and adult hood we might try to change what we are like to make us appear more attractive to others.

Humanist psychologists believe that each person develops their own unique personality through interaction with others, and that we can be made aware of ourselves and can influence what we are like.

The three parts of the self-concept

Your self-concept comprises three major forces. These are the image that you have of yourself (your self-image), how much value you place on yourself (your self-esteem), and what you wish that you were really like (your ideal self). We will go through each here.

Self-image

Your self-image is the description that you would give of the person that you know you are, or imagine yourself to be. The most obvious features of your self-image are your name, your sex, your age, what you do, and what you look like. It also includes what you know about your behaviour and personality. Look at the following activity:

Activity
How far are the following descriptions true of your behaviour and personality?

	I'm not very	I'm usually fairly	I'm very
1 Confident			
2 Friendly			
3 Generous			
4 Hard working			
5 Helpful			
6 Loyal			
7 Polite			
8 Thoughtful			
9 Truthful			

Another important part of your general self-image is your **body image**. Would you describe yourself as very good-looking, okay, or rather plain? Are you too thin or too fat? Is your hair too coarse, too fine, or quite manageable? Are you too tall or not tall enough? When we looked in Chapter 3 at why certain people are attracted to certain others, we noted the importance that people often put on physical attraction. Millions of pounds are spent in the West every year on cosmetics, hair styles, fashion-

Body image is important in many cultures. How successful you think your body image is can affect how you feel about yourself in many other ways too.

able clothes, and even cosmetic surgery. Clearly, our body image is very important to many of us, particularly to younger people who are concerned about how they appear to others. What we look like is often the first thing anyone finds out about us. The way people react to us will have an effect on what we think about ourselves.

In some cases, distorted body image might lead to **anorexia nervosa**. This is an eating disorder where a person becomes obsessed by the thought of food. A sufferer may hoard food, talk about food, even prepare food, but will not eat it. Over eighty per cent of anorexics are females between the ages of puberty and thirty, and it is estimated that about one in every five females suffers from an eating disorder of some type at some point in her life. Although the causes of eating disorders are unknown, many anorexics say that they think of themselves as being overweight, even when they are near to death by starvation.

►►► Activity

How important is body image to you personally? What would you change about yours, if anything?

A third component in self-image concerns our **social roles**. We all have different social roles. I could be a spouse, a parent, a grandparent, a teacher, a member of the darts team, a member of the British Psychological Society, a friend, and a Samaritan. Each of these is a social role, and each contributes to how I think about myself. If I think that I am being successful in my roles, my self-image can be quite positive. If I am sometimes unsuccessful I might think that I've let myself or others down. If I start to believe that I'm not being effective in one role, I might want to change it if I can. So I might be effective as a grandparent and a parent, but be losing my edge at darts. Perhaps its about time I dropped out of the team. If I carry on and keep on losing I'm just going to become more depressed and miserable.

Most people live as members of a society. I am a member of British society. As societies evolve over the centuries their members start to associate certain behaviour with certain people. In Britain, children are supposed to be curious and adventurous. Adolescents are expected to be a bit rebellious and do their own thing. Parents are expected to be straight (and boring, according to young people). Students are expected to be hard working but fun loving. The rich are expected to consume a lot and live in big houses and have flashy motor cars. These social roles emerge as a result of living in society, and the more complex and industrial the society is, the more complex the roles within it are likely to be.

Your social roles might include being a student, a daughter, a son, a friend, a shop assistant, a bus passenger, or a library user. There are undoubtedly many more. Do you think that you are usually successful and effective in the way you perform these roles? Are you often unsuccessful through some fault of your own? Do you just muddle through, or are you fairly competent in the way you handle people and situations? The way you perform your social roles will affect how other people respond to you.

Just because we have social roles does not mean that we are necessarily

▷ Social roles are the roles that we play in society. Each society expects certain behaviour of certain people. These behaviours become social roles.

▷ Self-image is your knowledge of your own personality and behaviour, your appearance and the effect you (and it) have on other people. It includes your social roles and how you play them.

going to play them as we are expected to. Some students may be particularly hard-working and dedicated. Some parents might be quite trendy. Some grandparents might be young at heart, some punks might be quite caring and responsible. Being assigned social roles is no guarantee that people are going to play those roles. What they actually do will determine how other people respond to them, and this will be absorbed into their self-concepts.

Activity
List some of your social roles. Give yourself marks out of ten for how successful you are in playing each of them.

Exercise on self-image

1 Name some of the most obvious features of your self-image.
2 Define the term 'body image', as used by psychologists.
3 What is the first thing that many people find attracts them to others?
4 What are social roles?
5 Where do social roles originate?
6 Name some of your social roles.
7 Briefly mention the behaviour that is expected of each of your roles.

Summary of the self-image
The major components of your self-image are your knowledge of your personality, your body image, and your knowledge of what you do, Any of these understandings could become distorted and you might lose touch with who you really are.

Self-esteem

Self-esteem refers to how much people value themselves. Some children will have been encouraged to be curious and adventurous, to explore and investigate, and to try things out. If they have been rewarded (or reinforced) for their efforts, they build up a positive view of what they can do. As adults they may think that they can achieve certain things if they set their minds to those things. They feel good about themselves and the contribution they can make to society. They are said to have high or **positive self-esteem**. Children whose achievements are largely ignored, or who are punished for making a mess, asking too many questions, getting in the way, and so on, are likely to stop trying. They may develop a low or negative self-esteem.

One of the most useful studies of self-esteem was conducted by **Stanley Coopersmith**. Beginning in the 1950s, Coopersmith conducted a longitudinal study beginning with nine- and ten-year-old boys. They filled in questionnaires concerning how they felt about themselves, their families, their friends and their school work. He asked their teachers to rate them according to how they responded to success and failure, how motivated they were, what they were like with other children, how they responded to the teachers, etc. He identified two groups, those who had high self-esteem and those who had low self-esteem. Those who had high self-esteem had more friends, felt generally confident about their progress in school, were easily motivated, were confident in their judgements, and were happy at home. The boys with low self-esteem were self-conscious and nervous, reluctant to join in, unsure of their contributions and self-centred. They didn't expect to do well in school, and generally didn't achieve much. They passed fewer exams and went on to gain lower status jobs.

Coopersmith also found that children who regarded themselves positively were more likely to have parents who regarded themselves positively too. He gave questionnaires to the boys' parents and interviewed them about how they treated their sons. They treated their children as individuals who could take responsibility for their own actions, who were treated with respect, who were encouraged to achieve and rewarded when they made a good effort.

Some of the people in Coopersmith's study had developed negative self-esteem that applied to every area of their lives. Most of us have some strengths and some weaknesses. We may be hopeless at spelling but good at maths and science. We may feel that we cannot mix with other children very easily, but feel that we are making progress with our music lessons. The low self-esteem group in Coopersmith's study became isolated and unhappy.

Some of the main factors involved in developing self-esteem are intelligence, competence, degree of emotional adjustment, and popularity. If you believe yourself to be intelligent (and most people probably would think of themselves as fairly bright), then you may think that you make sensible and appropriate responses. You usually do the right thing. You are usually competent You can solve most of the problems that ordinary people are likely to face. Only specialist things that ordinary people wouldn't be expected to know will defeat you. You regard yourself as emotionally mature too. You don't go to pieces over small things. Although you do have feelings, they are usually under control. These qualities lead to you being admired and liked by others, as they appreciate your friendship, or even look up to you.

Ask yourself questions rather like those which follow as a guide to help you understand your level of self-esteem. How do you feel about your self-image (your personality and general behaviour)? Do you approve of yourself? How valuable a member of the human race do you think you are? How realistic are you about your successes and do you learn from your failures? How do your answers to these questions make you feel about yourself? How do you feel about your appearance? You may want to change things, but how do you feel about what you've got? How do you feel about your social roles? Do you think that, on the whole, you're a pretty good daughter, student, and friend? Do you have a generally high or generally low opinion of yourself? How do you feel about yourself?

$\triangleright$
Coopersmith has found a correlation between how parents treat their children and how the children feel about themselves. Another correlation exists between how children feel about themselves and how successful they are in school and subsequently in their careers. We must remember that a correlation only shows that the factors are statistically related, not that one necessarily causes the other.

$\triangleright$
'Self-esteem' refers to the amount of value you give to yourself. In some areas you may consider yourself worthy, while in others your self-esteem may be low. No other animal has self-esteem.

Exercise on self-esteem

1 Name some of the things that parents can do to encourage high self-esteem in their children.
2 What sorts of thing should parents avoid in order to minimize the risk of their child developing low self-esteem?
3 Why do you think it is important to have a reasonably high level of self-esteem?
4 Name some of the main factors in self-esteem?
5 Choose a couple of them and show why they contribute to high or low self-esteem.

Summary of self-esteem

Where self-image is your knowledge of you, self-esteem is how you rate it. You could have a positive or negative self-esteem, or be positive over some things and less so over others. Coopersmith found a relationship between parents and their children's levels of self-esteem. Some of the main factors in developing self-esteem are intelligence and ability, popularity and emotional stability.

Although the ideal self can include appearance and social roles, it is usually thought of comprising aspects of character or personality.

Ideal self

Ideal self refers to what you really wish your personality was like. People who are sure that they are just about perfect and don't need to change at all are probably mentally unstable! We probably all know people who have personality characteristics that we wish we had ourselves.

Activity

Here are some characteristics that people find desirable in themselves and others. How do you rate yourself against each one?

	Quite content	Wish I was more	Not bothered
1 Confident			
2 Truthful			
3 Generous			
4 Loyal			
5 Good with people			
6 Caring			
7 Outgoing			
8 Thoughtful			
9 Quick witted			
10 Hard working			

▷ Freud described ideal self (ego ideal) as one of two parts of the superego, the other being conscience.

If we could find all the characteristics that you personally thought were desirable, and could measure how you rated yourself on each, we would have some assessment of your ideal self.

Exercise on ideal self

1 Define the term 'ideal self'.
2 Name some of the main personality characteristics in people's ideal selves.
3 What does Freud mean by ego ideal?
4 What do you think someone might be like who has a large gap between his or her self-image and ideal self?
5 Explain your last answer.

 Summary of ideal self

Ideal self is the description of the person you might really like to be, We would hope that your ideal self would be fairly close to your general self-concept. If there were a huge gap between what you think you are, and what you would like to be, then you may be rather unhappy.

The factors which influence the development of the self-concept

Now that we have looked at the main components of the self-concept we can describe the main factors in its development. According to **Michael Argyle** there are four major factors which influence the development of the self-concept. We have already touched on some of them. They are:

- first, the ways in which other people react towards us,
- second, how we think we compare to others
- third, our social roles,
- fourth, the extent to which we identify with other people.

We will describe each of these four factors.

The reactions of significant others

We are members of many different groups. In some groups we will be important members, for example, in our family or among our closest friends. In other groups we will be significant. In class you may make useful contributions to discussions. As a member of the class you are significant, but not as important as you are to your parents. In other groups we are quite anonymous. As a bus passenger you are just one of many as far as the driver is concerned. You regard some people as more important too. These are your **significant others** just as you might be a significant other to your parents, friends, etc.

The ways in which significant others react towards us are important in

▷ A significant other is any person whose ideas you like or respect, someone who has some kind of power or influence over you. Someone by whom you want to appreciated.

developing our self-concept. If parents always treat their son as though he were stupid, then the child's self-esteem will suffer. You wouldn't want to wear anything you know your friends would really dislike, you wouldn't want your teacher to know that you cheated in an exam, you wouldn't want your parents to know that you told them a deliberate lie to get yourself out of trouble. These people may well be among your significant others. While we don't mind too much if someone we hardly know doesn't seem to like us, we will be quite upset if we find that a significant other has said something unflattering about us.

Activity

Make a list of your significant others. Also list their sex and approximate age. Do they come from both sexes and across the range of ages? If not, what factors do they have in common?

▷
Young children generally think of their parents as being significant others in all areas of their lives. Adolescents are rather more concerned with what their friends think about some aspects of their lives (such as the kind of clothes to wear) than what their parents think.

▷
The reactions of significant others towards us is quite important to the development of our self-concept. However, this is not necessarily true for people who are suffering some kinds of mental disturbance and who are unaware of the effects they are having on other people.

▷
Gergen's research can be criticized for the way he deliberately set out to deceive and manipulate his participants' behaviour. This kind of research would probably not be allowed now.

One of the earliest observations in this area was by **Edwin Guthrie**, an American college professor, from sixty years ago. He noticed that one of his female students was regarded as quite unattractive by the boys. She sat alone and had little to do with the others. As a joke, some of the males decided to draw lots to see who would take her out. By the fourth or fifth date, she appeared to have become rather more attractive and other males wanted to date her. It seemed that she became popular by being treated as though she was a popular person.

In the 1960s **Kenneth Gergen** showed how the reaction of a significant other could influence people's self-esteem. Subjects were asked to talk about themselves as honestly as possible to a clinical psychologist. The clinical psychologist was to be regarded as a significant other. Half the sample had their revelations rewarded by the psychologist. He looked interested, nodded, smiled, and generally approved. The statements of the other subjects were treated negatively. The psychologist appeared to disagree, he looked unimpressed, even bored. When questioned later, all the subjects appeared to have been influenced by the psychologist's reaction to them. Those in the negative group were more doubtful about themselves and their ideas, those in the positive group were more confident. These differences continued for some time.

Earlier we described Coopersmith's important correlational study of the relationship between parents' attitudes towards their children and how they treated them, and their children's level of self-esteem and achievements. Although correlational studies cannot show a cause between factors, it does seem highly likely that parents who provide warmth, encouragement, support, help, discipline and the motivation to achieve, will have children who feel positive about their abilities and opportunities. Parents are our most significant others. Coopersmith's study sampled boys. **Robert Sears** found that if only one parent was warm and encouraging, then girls would have higher self-esteem.

Exercise on significant others

1 What makes other people 'significant'?
2 Name some kinds of people that might not be significant others to a particular child.
3 Why might significant others have more influence over a child's development than non-significant others?

Comparisons with others

When a teacher tells you that you are doing well, what does she mean? Usually that, compared to the other students in the group, or compared to the average standard, that you are making a good effort or good progress. She doesn't mean that compared to a bunch of university professors you're doing well. If you think you're broke because you're down to your last pound, don't you mean that, compared to someone who seems to have plenty of money you're quite poor? Compared to someone with no money at all, of course, you're quite well-off.

Parents sometimes compare their children to others. 'You're the prettiest girl around', 'You're the toughest little chap I know', 'You're brighter than the child over the road'. Unfortunately, the comparisons aren't always favourable. 'Why can't you be clever like your brother?', 'Why aren't you good like your sister?', 'Why don't you help me like Sophie helps her Mum?' During adolescence it's not just adults who make the comparisons. Young people frequently compare themselves with others, even if they aren't always entirely aware of what they are doing. Are you as kind, as generous, as thoughtful, as intelligent, as hard-working, as good-looking, as stylishly dressed, etc., as other people in a similar position to you?

As long as the comparisons that you make, or other people make about you, are between yourself and people in the same sorts of position as you, then this seems a reasonable way in which the self-concept may continue to develop. However, if you make unrealistic comparisons, between yourself and someone who has much greater talents or opportunities than you, then you will appear inferior and develop an unnecessarily negative self-image. For instance, you can't be as popular as the latest pop idols, you can't afford the kind of clothes that a top footballer can afford, you can't lead such a glamorous life as a catwalk super model. If you only compare yourself to these people, you will become pretty depressed!

▷ Comparisons are always relative. They can be relative to someone else, or to ourselves on another occasion, we are now either better or worse off than we were last month.

▷ Comparisons between us and others can be made by all sorts of people. If they are made by our enemies we aren't usually too bothered about them. If they are made by one of our significant others the comparison can have much more of an effect.

Exercise on comparisons with others

1 According to Albert Bandura, how do children learn about themselves?
2 What are role models?
3 Who are the most significant others to a child of between one and ten years of age?

4 Why should these people be careful when they make comparisons between their children and others?

5 Explain how comparisons with others can contribute to our self-concept.

Social roles

> A social role is a part someone plays in society. It involves their doing and not doing certain kinds of things. A shop assistant should do certain things (such as help customers choose their purchases, operate the cash register, give change, etc.), and should not do others (such as plan a holiday during work).

Earlier we said that our social roles involve our behaving in certain kinds of ways. A shop assistant's role is characterized by serving customers, stocking shelves, taking money, giving change, etc. Here are some examples of social roles: student, daughter, husband, grandparent, spectator, competitor. We have a good idea of the kinds of behaviour that are associated with each of these roles. If we know that someone plays a role, we know what behaviour to expect of them. So when you tell a stranger that you are a student, that person has a whole set of expectations about what you are like and what you do.

▶▶▶ *Activity*
List as many aspects of the behaviour and attitudes of each of the following that you think people would hold: student, mother, pensioner.

As a child you were a son or a daughter and a schoolchild. You may have belonged to a club such as the Brownies or Cubs. As you grow, you take on more roles. As a teenager, you may became a student and become associated with other clubs too. You may also have become a boyfriend or girlfriend. Later still you take on roles associated with jobs and other things that you do. One of the first things we like to know about strangers is what roles they have. It helps define them for us. We gain an idea of how important they are (compared to us and to other people we know). We know how we might be expected to behave around them. If, as a teacher, I were introduced to a student, then I might talk in a way which is very different from the way in which I would talk and behave if I were introduced to someone who is a doctor.

The roles we play are particularly important in influencing how other people see us, and eventually how we see ourselves. What kinds of reaction do motorists generally have towards traffic wardens? The images are usually fairly poor. Lollipop men and traffic wardens often complain that motorists aren't always very respectful towards them. This lack of appreciation and respect may become part of their self-concept. Some may compensate for this lack of regard by applying, in an inflexible way, the rules which are there to make things easier, thus increasing their own sense of importance. They become a 'jobsworth', a name which comes from 'It's more than my job's worth to break the rules to let you do that', by Jeremy Taylor:

> Jobsworth, jobsworth, it's more than my jobsworth
> I don't care, rain or snow, whatever you want, the answer's no
> I can keep you standing for hours in the queue
> And if you don't like it, you know what you can do.

Exercise on social roles

Read the words from the chorus, on the previous page.

1 Name some of the roles that Jeremy Taylor may have been thinking of when he wrote this chorus.
2 What kind of impression might some of the people who play these roles form of themselves and what they do?
3 Explain how their feelings about themselves might lead to the attitude expressed in the song.

Nurses and doctors are held in quite high regard. As people are respectful towards them, however, they may start to think of themselves as rather superior. Some hospital patients have complained that their consultants seem very superior and distant, not even talking to the patients at all but rather talking about them to the other medical staff, as though the patients were not there at all.

Erving Goffman observed people in a variety of roles. He noted that when people take on a new role for the first time they often hide behind it. A teacher who is threatening to ask to see a child's parents might hide behind the school rules. He has to see the parents to report the child's absences. He may sit behind the teacher's desk too, almost using it as a barrier between himself and the youngsters. A more experienced teacher is used to the arguments and complaints and less likely to need to hide.

▷ Social roles can become a mask that we can hide our true personality behind. We can blame the rules or the boss or the organization for their behaviour when it affects other people badly. (When others benefit from it we usually take whatever credit we can!)

Labelling

The way in which people label us can affect how they and others think of us, possibly even how we think of ourselves. The idea of labelling has been used to criticize psychiatrists and mental-health professionals. We still do not understand a great deal of what is called mental illness. Psychiatrists are accused of applying an appropriate label, such as 'schizophrenic' or 'manic depressive' to someone, without first really understanding the symptoms of each particular patient. Having been given a label, the person can then be treated with some drugs or be offered counselling. For example, if we know that Miranda is a schizophrenic, then we may not know exactly how she will react to anything, so we will be rather wary of her. We may avoid her, or talk to her as though she were five years old. The label can lead to a **self-fulfilling prophecy**. A prophecy is a statement which we think will be seen to be correct. Miranda will begin to think of herself as rather odd, particularly as people treat her as though she is. This will reinforce her odd behaviour. The prophecy that Miranda is a schizophrenic, and that the label is therefore correct, is supported by her behaviour.

Self-fulfilling means that it happens automatically, as a result of itself. Imagine you decided that you could not understand a subject at college and that you were never going to pass the exam. Then you failed the exam. Your prophecy has become self-fulfilling. You stated something that came true because (probably unknowingly) you made it come true.

Here is an example. Let's imagine that I am Alexandra's teacher. I

▷ As humans have cognition (i.e. they think and reason), and because we hate 'not knowing', we often make statements to explain something that we don't really understand. When we make the statement (even to ourselves) we will behave in ways which make that statement appear true. This can lead to a self-fulfilling prophecy.

notice that she is a hard-working student so, of course, I will encourage her all that I can. I will talk more enthusiastically to her because I can see that she is interested. I will offer her extra support. I will write glowing reports about how good she is. She will feel good about her progress in my class, and about herself generally. I've told her truthfully that she could do very well in my subject. This makes her want to try even harder, so she works harder still. Eventually she passes with good grades.

So why did she pass? Would she have worked so hard without so much encouragement? I prophesied that she could do well. She did well. Ultimately she did well because she worked hard and deserved to. So why did she work so hard?

This also works the other way around. If I constantly ignore someone or make unflattering remarks such as 'it's no good asking Roger, he always gets it wrong', or 'I'll bet that is Roger messing about again', then it is not surprising that Roger will make less effort in my class. He will know that whatever he does he won't get much encouragement so it becomes a waste of time to try. He will probably do badly. My prophecy that he is pretty hopeless has been confirmed, thus proving that I was right to treat him the way I did all along.

Sometimes it isn't even necessary to know the child in order to start a self-fulfilling prophecy. We could do it on the basis of a stereotype. (See Chapter 4.) **Judy Gahagan** defines a stereotype as a belief about the characteristics that a group of people possesses, and therefore all members of that group must possess them.

I might recall that I taught Elyse Atkins a couple of years ago, and I remember her to be a little horror. 'She was always up to something she shouldn't have been. I was glad to be rid of her when she moved up at the end of the year. Now I see I've got her brother, Daniel, starting in my group in the new session. I can imagine what he'll be like. Blood is thicker than water after all. I'll be keeping an eye on him. The minute he steps out of line I'll have him straight up to the head teacher.' So poor Daniel is being doomed to a hard time, and possible failure, even before he starts in my group next session! His only sin was that he is a member of a particular family.

We form impressions of people either before or after we have met them. Some people form impressions very quickly, and they place a lot of importance on their first reactions to them. They may know whether they are going to like this person, or at least be able to cooperate with them, within a few moments of first meeting. Other people like to take a little more time to learn more about people they meet before deciding what they think and feel about them.

▷
The ways in which our significant others treat us, and the things they say about us, can have quite an effect on our self-concept. If they treat us in ways that they think we deserve then their ideas about us may be fulfilled.

Activity
Are you someone who develops instant impressions of people, or do you like to take your time? It has been found that the first five to ten minutes of a first meeting are the most important time for forming good impressions on occasions such as job interviews. So try not to do or say anything silly during the first ten minutes of your interviews!

We may describe someone as a bit of a clown, a nice person, a serious person, a funny person, a chatty person, a friendly person, a cold person, an aggressive person. Where such simple definitions suggests that we wouldn't like that person because he or she is different from us and not the kind of person that we would like, then we are **labelling** that person. Labelling is a process related to making self-fulfilling prophecies. Having labelled someone as some kind of deviant, we will then treat that person accordingly. If other people also respond in a similar way, the person's self-concept will include the knowledge that he or she must be like the label, and so that person's behaviour may indeed get worse.

Exercise on other people's reactions

1 Explain what Goffman means by a social mask.
2 Define the following terms: social role, significant other, self-fulfilling prophecy, self-concept.
3 Name a social role and an important significant other to the person who holds that role.
4 Look at the two people you have named in answer to question 3. Explain how a self-fulfilling prophecy held by the significant other could affect the role-holder's self-concept.
5 What is a stereotype?
6 What kinds of people are most likely to be labelled?
7 Take one example and show how being labelled can affect that person's self-concept.

Identification with others

In Chapter 1 we described Albert Bandura's claim that children learn by observing and imitating certain role models. These models are usually attractive and powerful. Children model their behaviour on the adults' behaviour in order to learn about what they can and should do. Freud thought that children of three or four years of age learn what their same-sex parent is like in order to become more like them. If they are more like their same-sex parent they will be even more wanted and loved by the opposite-sex parent. They identify with their same-sex parent.

Identification and modelling continue throughout adolescence and into adulthood. If you start college on a particular day it may be helpful if you knew someone who was already a student who could show you around. You could watch and copy what that person does, as he or she has experience that you lack. If you go to a posh restaurant for the first time, you may want to see if you can spot someone who looks experienced in the art of what to do in posh restaurants. You could try to copy that person, as you don't want to show yourself up by looking inexperienced or stupid.

Identifying with others is important to our self-concept. If we are successful and identify with the right people, we can develop a positive regard for ourselves. We are competent and confident. Identifying with appropriate others is a shortcut way to discovering what you should and

▷
Modelling is a means of learning appropriate behaviour. Identification is a means of learning appropriate ideas such as what the parent thinks is right and wrong, good and bad.

▷
Identification here means observing and imitating someone's behaviour (modelling), and taking on their attitudes and ideas. It is a shortcut way to learning what to do and think in new, unfamiliar situations.

shouldn't say and do. Identifying with the wrong people, or being misled by the right ones, can result in terrible embarrassment and lowered self-esteem.

The three components in our self-concept (self-image, self-esteem and ideal self) develop together, largely from the ways in which other people treat us. Constantly telling a child that he is hopeless, useless, or thick will lead to his absorbing that message into his self-concept. Knowing that he will fail, will probably stop him from even trying. Equally, a child who has been told that he is brilliant at everything is likely to develop an unrealistic self-concept.

So far we have been describing our self-concept as though it were a single thing, like personality or intelligence. Personality certainly includes our self-concept. When we looked at the development of personality in Chapter 6, we suggested that we may have sub-personalities that appear on different occasions. Few people always behave in the same way. We all act out of character on occasions. John Rowan suggested that we have several personalities (see page 114).

Exercise on identification

1 Social learning theory is one theory within the behaviourist approach. What is behaviourism?
2 Outline what social learning theorists mean by observation, imitation, and modelling (in that order).
3 Freud used the term identification to mean a process of learning to be like one's same sex parent. Why do children identify, according to Freud?
4 Why would identification be important in helping our self-concept to form?

 Summary of factors affecting the development of self-concept
All of us have some people who are more important to us than others. Parents, friends, colleagues, etc., all influence our understanding of who we are. People compare us to others, and we compare ourselves to others too. The roles that we play, and the way we interact with people while playing those roles, influence who we think we are. The extent to which we identify with certain people also affects our understanding of who we are.

Cognitive development

Humans have highly advanced cognitive skills. Cognition is the process by which many living things learn about and come to understand their environment. We pay attention to some sources of stimulation rather than others. We might look at a smart car in the street in front of us or turn when we hear someone call our name. The first stage of cognition is taking information in through our senses. We then interpret that information and make it meaningful. We search our memories to appreciate the looks of the car or identify who is calling us. In addition to de-coding information from the senses, the process of cognition includes everything from intuition and insight, through reasoning and making educated guesses, to solving complex mental problems.

▷
The twentieth century can be thought of as 'the century of the child'.

Until the twentieth century, it was widely believed that children were simply 'small adults' who would eventually grow up to think and behave like adults. A great deal of research has been conducted in the last 70 years or so into many areas of child development, including developmental psychology. One of the most influential researchers and theorists was a Swiss geneticist named **Jean Piaget**. We will study his theories in this chapter.

Jean Piaget's theory of cognitive development

In Chapter 7 we described how intelligence testing developed from the pioneering work of **Alfred Binet** in Paris very early this century. In 1920 Piaget was helping to standardize an intelligence test at Alfred Binet's laboratory in Paris. Piaget was a biologist and had little interest in children. However, he decided to investigate why so many of the children who had taken the test gave the same wrong answers to various test items. His research convinced him that children are not little adults simply waiting to grow up, but rather they view things in ways quite different from those of adults. This observation has led to one of the major contributions to our understanding of how children think. Piaget spent over fifty years studying children's thinking, until his death in 1980.

Exercise on cognitive developmental psychology

1 What is cognition?
2 What do you think cognitive developmental psychology is concerned with?
3 What is the average IQ? (See page 143 if you need to refresh your memory.)
4 What does the term average IQ mean?
5 What is intelligence?

Jean Piaget

Piaget's methods

Piaget observed children playing naturalistically, both alone and together, to see how they understood the rules of their games and how they responded to one another. Naturalistic observation is the name given to the method of watching your subjects behaving normally in their everyday situations. He asked the children questions such as could another child join in? Where did the rules of their game come from? Could the rules be changed? What would happen if they were broken? Piaget was looking for similarities in the children's answers which would suggest similarities in their thinking. If, in answer to the question 'who made up the rules?', most five-year-olds replied 'God', but most eight-year-olds replied 'we were taught them when we were young', then Piaget had found that the way in which younger children think is different from the way in which older children think.

 Activity
If you have access to young children, ask them the same questions that Piaget asked. You may be surprised at their answers.

He also asked children direct questions. He asked about how certain things compared to other things. For example, he would show them a stick and a length of string and ask them which was longer. He would then curl the string and ask once again if it was longer or shorter than the stick. He would show the children balls of plasticine and roll them into different shapes and ask whether the amount of plasticine changed when the shape was changed.

Piaget was one of the first researchers to employ the story-telling method. He told children stories about other children acting in all sorts of ways, often in naughty ways. He then asked them what they thought should happen next. The stories could be interpreted in different ways which would reveal how children's thinking about right and wrong, crime and punishment, obedience and disobedience worked. Over a period of years Piaget developed his cognitive theories, largely influenced by his knowledge of biology, which attempted to provide a model for how children think, and for intelligence.

Exercise on Piaget's methods

1 Name three methods which Piaget used for studying children's thinking.
2 Why was Piaget interested in discovering how children of certain ages answered his questions?
3 Why did Alfred Binet want to find what questions most children at particular ages could answer?
4 Can you think of any other method Piaget could have used to investigate cognitive development?

As we saw in Chapter 7, intelligence has been one of the most widely researched areas in psychology. The early views saw it as a group of things which each of us is born with, and which could be measured to see who had more or less of these things. Binet believed intelligence could be seen in an individual's ability to make reasoned judgements and adapt easily to new situations. Louis Thurstone identified 'general' intelligence, which we applied to most things we do, and 'specific' intelligence, which we apply in particular situations. Philip Vernon argued there were three components:

1 'Intelligence A', which is innate;

2 'Intelligence B', which we develop as a result of Intelligence A and our interactions with the environment; and

3 'Intelligence C', which is what intelligence tests measure.

Piaget rejected all such ideas. He thought that intelligence was an ever-changing process which each child is constantly developing through their own direct experience, especially during their first ten years or so of life. Each child interprets what things are like and what the child can do with them through its own personal experiences. Intelligence, therefore, cannot be measured, as it would be impossible to invent any means of measuring such a process. Intelligence isn't really a 'thing' at all. It is a word we use for communicating with each other, as we all imagine that we know what we mean by it, but it doesn't really mean anything at all in itself.

Summary of Piaget's methods

Piaget naturalistically observed children playing games, he told them stories and asked them questions. From this he built up an idea of the way children reasoned.

Basic cognitive processes

Piaget believed that babies are born with a few basic mental images or

▷

Reflexes are involuntary responses to particular stimuli. Much animal behaviour is reflexive and helps the animal to survive. Reflexive responses could be exhibited much more quickly than learned responses.

ideas which he called **schemas**. As a biologist, he knew that there must be structures of nerves in the brain which are responsible for each piece of knowledge that we possess. Each schema has its own mental structure. There are three types of schema which appear as a child matures. The first schemas are the 50 or so **reflexes** which human babies are born with. Breathing, sucking, grasping, crying are fairly obvious examples. They involve actions or behaviour and are called **action schemas**.

Exercise on reflexes

1 What is a reflex?
2 Reflexes may have some survival value. What does survival value mean?
3 Name three reflexes that human babies are born with, but which disappear by adulthood.

▷

Symbolization is the process by which children gain their understanding about objects and relationships. Children should be encouraged and helped in their symbolization, especially through actual experience.

▷

Schemas are basic ideas or mental representations of how to deal with something. Some schemas are fairly simple (for humans), such as eating with a knife and fork. Some are more complex, such as playing various games. Others are more complex still, such as playing a musical instrument or driving a car. Operations are more logical ways of combining schemas and do not appear until middle childhood.

Action schemas will be joined by **symbolic schemas** from the age of around two years. A symbol is simply anything that we allow to stand for something else. So a green traffic light stands for carry on, a pelican crossing means cross here, and a referee's red card means 'get off'! As symbolic schemas develop, the child can let one thing (such as a doll) stand for another (such as a mummy or a baby). The whole of language is just a collection of symbols. Children of this age are learning the meaning of new words every day. They learn that 'spoon' is a sound which represents an object, so they can 'hold the spoon'. They also learn that the sound of the word can also involve actions such as 'put the spoon in the ice cream'. Later, children will learn that the letters S–P–O–O–N spell 'spoon'. All these are symbols. Different languages have different symbols for spoons and for other objects. Learning symbolization is very important to children's cognition.

Five years or so later children's thinking changes to become more logical, or, as Piaget calls it, **operational**. **Operational schemas** allow children to realize that rules can be changed, that things aren't always what they seem, or that problems can be solved if they think about them. Piaget described schemas and operations as having **variant mental structures**, because everyone's cognition varies.

●●● **Summary of the main types of early schemas**

Schema	Age	Examples of behaviour
Action	birth–2	Practising by repeating actions until the behaviour is mastered.
Symbolic	2–7	Role plays for learning about feelings and ideas, communicates through language.
Operational	7 onwards	Plans ahead, cooperates and shares, predicts a logical outcome for behaviour.

▷
Human babies are born with a few unconscious capacities. One is to develop schemas about those things of which we have some experience. Another is to organize smaller schemas into more complex ones so that we can make some sense of what is happening around us. Everyone has different experiences, so each person's particular schemas will be different.

Human babies are genetically prepared to develop schemas and to **organize** them mentally in such a way as to be able to build new experiences on old ones. For example, a child develops the schema for reaching towards an object such as a rattle. Reaching out often results in being given the object. At first, the child may drop the object but eventually develops the grasping schema. Moving the rattle around makes a noise so the child develops the schema for shaking the rattle. The three schemas for reaching, holding, and shaking become one larger schema so that the sight of the rattle will trigger the 'reach, grasp and shake' schema. The inborn capacity to combine individual schemas into larger ones is called **organization**.

	Cognitive change	Behaviour
Schema	Develop a schema	Crawling on the floor
Organization	Link it to another, related schema	Hurts when bumped into a wooden table leg
Adaptation	Adapt thinking and behaviour accordingly	Recognize table legs and avoid crawling near them

▷
Assimilation and accommodation leading to adaptation are the central ideas in Piaget's theory. Other people use the term 'intelligence' to describe an individual's general or specific abilities. Piaget prefers the term cognition and sees it developing as the result of this process.

There is another genetically inherited ability which humans possess, according to Piaget. This is the ability to modify our knowledge and behaviour as a result of the newly combined schemas. Piaget calls this process **adaptation**. It has two parts, **assimilation** and **accommodation**. Assimilation means taking notice of someone or something and using an existing schema to understand that person or thing. Accommodation refers to modifying existing schemas to take account of new information. For example, a three-year-old boy may have a schema for 'dog' which contains the elements: four legs, head at one end, and tail at the other. The first time the child sees a horse he assimilates it, that is to say he applies his most appropriate schema, and so describes it as a big dog. The general schema for 'dog' works to some extent. The object is more like a dog than a plate or bus. But it isn't accurate. The child will need to accommodate his schema for dog to exclude four-legged things with a head and a tail which are horses. As well as refining one schema he has begun to develop another for horses. Later this will be wrongly applied by describing, for example, a giraffe as a big horse.

Reflexes	Assimilation	Accommodation	Adaptation
Grasp, suck gaze, reach the figure	Apply basic schemas	Modify schemas by new information	Respond more appropriately in

It is important that the process of assimilating and accommodating is given enough opportunity to become established. If it is interrupted then existing schemas will not have become properly modified and the child

▷
Equilibration refers to the balance that
needs to exist between a child's ability
to absorb new information
(assimilation) and modify it
appropriately in the light of new
experiences (accommodation).

▷
Knowing or having cognition is
described as a state of equilibrium
between what children know and
what they need to know.

will continue to give an inappropriate response. Clearly there must be a balance, called **equilibration**, between the number of new experiences that the child needs to assimilate and his or her capacity to accommodate those experiences.

Younger children have a great deal to learn about their environment. When they have learned all that they can from their existing environment there will be a balance between their knowledge and the information the environment can provide. Children's cognition is said to be in a state of **equilibrium**. Inevitably, there will always be new things for younger children to learn. The state of cognitive equilibrium doesn't usually last very long. When children have successfully assimilated, accommodated, and made appropriate adaptations, they now know how to respond in the future.

Assimilation, accommodation, and adaptation are three stages in the process of cognition. Most living organisms are genetically programmed to take in certain things about their environment, and to make appropriate responses to them. If a rabbit has made an adaptation to features in its environment (such as increasingly loud noises and the ground shaking beneath its feet), it will be able to make an appropriate response (running to escape the approaching tractor). Although we have described assimilation, accommodation, and adaptation as though they were separate processes, they are actually three aspects of the same process. They always function together. Children may assimilate anything which is there to be assimilated, and this inevitably triggers accommodation and adaptation.

Summary of Piaget's assumptions

All children acquire their own ideas and insights about their environment from their own experiences. They start with some basic mental structures for simple reflexive responses. As they assimilate new information, their schemas expand to accommodate the new ideas. Thus they develop increasingly complex schemas through the process of organization.

Exercise on schemas

1 What did Piaget mean by a 'schema'?
2 What are operations?
3 What did Piaget mean by 'variant mental structures'?
4 What is assimilation?
5 What is the relationship between assimilation and accommodation?
6 What is adaptation and why can it only occur after assimilation and accommodation?
7 What is equilibration and why is it necessary?
8 Here is a description of a five-year-old child's activities at school. From this, identify the aspects assimilation, accommodation, adaptation, and equilibration.

Rebecca wanted to play with the skipping rope, but Kim and Caroline were holding the rope while Nicola skipped. The other girls were older than her and were quite good at skipping. Rebecca had tried to skip a week earlier but the rope was too long and she had tripped. Her mother had helped her at home and said she was getting quite good. The teacher asked the big girls if they would let Rebecca try. They turned the rope slowly and Rebecca timed her jumps well. After a short while she asked the girls to go faster, but when they did she could only just keep up, and soon missed her skip, tripped over the rope and banged her knee. The teacher said she thought Rebecca had had enough skipping for one day.

Piaget's stages of cognitive development

Piaget found that the ways that children think are different from the ways that adults think, and that the principles they use change as they mature. The principles are genetically inherited and linked to maturation. Four distinct stages of the development of thinking were identified by Piaget. He claimed that all children pass through the same sequence of stages, although the ages at which they enter and leave each one does vary widely. The four stages of cognitive development are **invariant,** that is, they always occur in the same sequence, as they are dependent on the state of maturation. Progress through them cannot be speeded up, as it is controlled by genetic forces and maturation. At each stage the kind of information that can be assimilated and the kind of accommodation possible is more complex than at any previous stage.

The sensory motor stage (0–2 years)

Babies are born with some limited use of their senses and some limited abilities to move parts of their bodies. During this stage both sets of skills develop, as do the babies' abilities to connect them. Some major advances in cognitive development are made when a baby learns to use one to affect the other.

For the first month after birth children's behaviour is mostly reflexive. For example, they grasp and suck, breathe and sleep. They repeat actions that they find satisfying. By four or five months, babies do things with objects which will not directly satisfy their basic needs, but are stimulating in some other way. They may wave toys around, throw or drop them, look at them and put them in their mouths. If they can't see the object, they may show no further interest in it. By eight months of age, children are accommodating schemas for objects in their environment being 'real', and still being present even though they cannot see them. By twelve to eighteen months of age, children will follow the movement of an object as it disappears from view, and look for it in the place where it was last seen. Between about eighteen months and two years, children first show signs of insight, the ability to solve problems in their head (i.e. symbolically).

The sensory motor stage has two main themes. The first is the arrival of action schemas through accommodation and adaptation of earlier reflexive schemas. The second theme is the appearance, at around eight months, of **object permanence.** Piaget believed that very young babies would not be able to tell the difference between themselves and other people or other objects. So when a baby girl becomes aware of an object such as a rattle, she does not realize that the rattle exists separately from herself. If she can't see, hear, or touch it, then she acts as though the object no longer exists. The rattle has ceased to exist until the next time the child experiences it. Object permanence is the child's knowledge that objects and people do exist separately from themselves, and they continue to exist even when hidden from view.

Activity

Hide a toy which a young baby is looking at under a cover and see if the child looks towards the cover, or quickly loses interest.

We said in Chapter 2 that babies in the West start to form emotional bonds called attachments with their special caregivers at around six to eight months of age. By this time they have realized that some people exist separately from themselves. They have achieved object permanence at least for these people. Not everyone agrees with Piaget that object permanence doesn't appear until the infant is eight months old. **Tom Bower** has conducted experiments with babies of between one and four months in which an interesting object was placed in front of them. When their attention had been caught, the object was hidden by a sliding screen. The object was removed while unseen by the babies. The screen was pulled back and the babies' reactions were observed. If they showed surprise that the object was no longer visible, then they probably have object permanence. Many babies did show surprise. Bower also showed them an object which they might try to take. When they started to reach for it the lights were turned off. Observations with an infra-red camera showed the babies continued to try and reach for the object, despite not being able to see it.

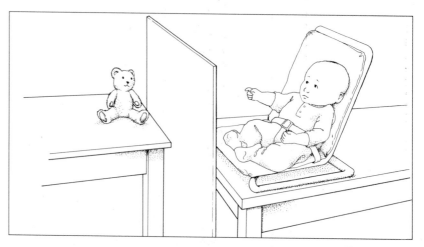

Bower's experiment

A. Mundy-Castle and **J. Anglin** sat a number of four-month-old infants in front of a board which had two viewing holes (A and B). An object travelled behind the apparatus so that it appeared at the bottom of viewing hole A travelling upwards, and at the top of viewing hole B travelling downwards. The researchers watched the infants eyes. After a few revolutions of the object the babies started to look for the object to appear in the next viewing hole. These infants had object permanence

Mundy-Castle and Anglin's experiment

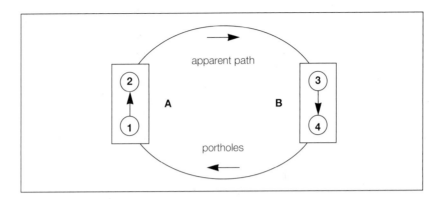

Mundy-Castle and Anglin's experiment

Exercise on the sensory motor stage

1 Outline the first stage in Piaget's theory of cognitive development.
2 What is object permanence?
3 At what age did Piaget claim that babies acquire object permanence?
4 Outline the evidence that disputes Piaget's claim for acquiring object permanence.

●●● **Summary of the sensory motor stage.**
The first schemas concern action as infants learn what they can do with the world and what they can make the world do for them. Their senses provide information and their muscles and limbs respond. This is the sensory motor stage.

The pre-operational stage (2–7 years)

▷
Piaget has been criticized for his rather negative view of the thinking of the two- to seven-year-old child's thinking. Children of this age can be inventive and imaginative. Some of their reasoning may not be the same as that of an adult, but it is often consistent and logical for their purposes.

Piaget reasoned that, compared to children's illogical, irrational thought processes, adult thinking was more ordered and logical. He described adult thinking as **operational thought**. To describe children's thinking at this stage as pre-operational suggests that children are not able to accommodate new experiences in the way that adults would and so their thinking remains rather illogical and unadaptable. According to Piaget, limitations in children's thinking in the pre-operational stage are caused by their lack of maturity. The problem is that children of this age cannot learn by being taught by someone else. They can only learn from their own direct experience.

Between the ages of two and four years children's thinking is described as **pre-conceptual**. Pre-conceptual thought is thinking which concentrates only on objects that are real, such as toys, and dolls, and which are in the same place as the child. If a toy is near the child, or somewhere that the child can fetch it from, then the child can get it, think about it and play with it. The child could not imagine playing with the toy unless the toy were present. The child's pre-operational thinking is dominated by unrealistic ideas such as **animism**. Animism is the name given to children's idea that everything must have similar qualities to the qualities that they have themselves. For example, as children have feelings, then all things must also have them, including inanimate things. 'Smacking the naughty

▷
Animism is the idea that nonliving, nonhuman objects possess the same ideas, wishes and beliefs that children possess.

table' for hurting the child who bumped into it, or 'scolding the naughty dolly' for getting itself lost are examples of the pre-conceptual thinking of a four-year-old child.

Activity
Ask a four-year-old where the sun goes at night and she may well say 'to bed because it's tired'. (Although this may be because some children's books encourage this kind of thinking.)

Another example of pre-conceptual thinking is **egocentrism**. This is the inability to take anyone else's needs into account, or to see things from someone else's point of view. The egocentric child is the centre of his or her own thinking. Things are only important in so far as they affect the child directly. Such children can only answer questions from their own viewpoint. An example of egocentric thought would be asking four-year-old Kathryn if she has a sister (assuming that she does). She says 'yes, my sister is called Lianne'. Ask if her sister has a sister and she may well say 'no'. Kathryn can't imagine what it would be like to see family relationships from her sister's point of view, only from her own. Of course, if her caregivers have often talked about Lianne's sister, Kathryn, then she will probably say that her sister does have a sister called Kathryn. She may not fully realize that she is the Kathryn in the answer.

Children have to assimilate and accommodate many more experiences before they can stop thinking of themselves as the centre of their own concerns, and that no one else matters very much. Piaget thought that children learn to **decentre** some time after seven years of age. Decentring is the name given to the ability to see things from someone else's viewpoint, as children learn not to centre on themselves as the only important thing around.

Piaget conducted a rather complicated experiment to demonstrate egocentrism. He made three model mountains from papier mâché. Each was a different shape and had something different on the top. A child stood in front of the model and a doll was placed in a different position at the foot of a mountain. The child was shown ten pictures taken from different positions around the model and asked to choose the one which showed what the child thought the doll could see. Children under the age of eight were unable to do this, often choosing the photograph corresponding to what they could see. Piaget concluded that children below the age of eight cannot decentre, but, this may not necessarily be the case. It is just as likely that children under eight couldn't really understand what was expected of them. Piaget's experiment has been criticized for being unnecessarily complicated. It is likely that the children would have had more chance if the experiment had involved them in a more interesting task.

Later in the pre-operational stage children's thinking is less dominated by egocentrism and animism and more concerned with the most obvious feature of any object – what it looks like. This is **intuitive thought**. Intuition means knowing about something by being aware of its most obvious, direct features that do not need any conscious thought or effort

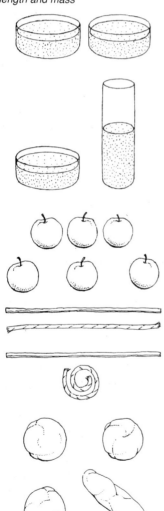

Conservation of volume, number, length and mass

to understand. Between the ages of four and seven, children concentrate only on those features they know by intuition, and ignore others. This is called **centration**.

Conservation tasks are the best known examples of intuitive thought. Young children do not realize that changing the appearance of something does not mean that anything else about it has changed. Show a child two identical balls of plasticine, roll one into a sausage shape, and ask if the balls contain the same amount of plasticine. The intuitive, pre-operational child will say that the sausage shape has more. This is because it looks bigger. Present two identically spaced rows of five buttons. The child will agree that both rows have the same amount. Spread out the buttons in one row. The child who cannot conserve will now say that there are more buttons in that row.

One of Piaget's most famous conservation tasks involved two identical tall, thin jugs (Jug A and Jug B) each containing the same amount of liquid. The contents of one of the jugs (Jug A) is emptied into a smaller, wider jug (Jug C). The child is asked which jug now contains the most liquid, Jug B or Jug C? The pre-operational child who has not learned to conserve will say the tall thin jug (Jug B) contained more. We know that this cannot be true, as no liquid has been added or removed. Jug B and Jug C must still hold the same amount of liquid. If you then ask the child what the level of liquid in Jug A would be if the contents of Jug C was poured back into it, this would require the child mentally to reverse the process of pouring the liquid from one jug into another. This is called **reversibility**. Piaget claimed that mental **reversibility** will not appear until a child is around eight years old.

▷
Conservation is the ability to hold in the mind an image of what something is like, even though its appearance has changed.

▷
Reversibility is the mental process of reasoning what would happen if a sequence of operations were reversed.

Exercise on egocentrism

1 What does Piaget mean by egocentrism?
2 Evaluate one way in which Piaget investigated egocentrism.
3 What does Piaget mean by decentring?

Comment on Piaget's research

Piaget was the first person to make such detailed observations or conduct such ingenious experiments. He identified the essential features of cognition, but also provided a detailed description of the stages and sub-stages of its development. Whenever scientists reveal their findings, others try to reproduce them. The original findings are supported, refined, or rejected. Not everyone agreed with Piaget's judgements about the ages at which some features occur, as we saw earlier with object permanence. The ages at which children stop being egocentric, and can conserve and decentre have also been challenged.

▷ This experiment was probably more interesting for a young child than the one involving some model mountains and a bunch of photographs. It is more like a real game in which the child can become involved.

▷ These were rather simple tasks. Tasks requiring abstract thought would be impossible for such young children. These two experiments are not saying that children aged between two and four years could decentre in more complex issues.

In the 1970s **Martin Hughes** made a model with four walls forming a cross, and some dolls which could be moved, by the experimenter or by the child, into various places behind or in front of the four walls. There was a policeman doll, and a boy doll who was hiding from the policeman. The game was to place the boy doll in various positions and ask if he could be seen by the policeman. Hughes found that children as young as three and four could put the dolls where each couldn't see the other. This showed that they could decentre and imagine what it would be like to see things as the doll saw them. Even when more walls were introduced, and more dolls, still over ninety per cent of the children could decentre.

John Flavell showed some three-year-old children some cards with a drawing of a cat on one side and a drawing of a dog on the other. Holding the card vertically between himself and the child, so that the child could see the dog, he asked what the child could see. These children had no difficulty in saying what they could see.

Children between two and a half years and five years were then seated on the opposite side of a table to a researcher. On the table was a 'Snoopy' doll. The children were asked to close their eyes, and then answered questions like 'Can I see you?', 'Can I see your head?', 'Can I see your arm?', and 'Can I see Snoopy?'. The youngest children were not sure whether the researcher could see them, although most said he could see their arm or head. Yet all said she could see Snoopy. Clearly these children are not completely egocentric.

McGarrigle and Donaldson used Piaget's conservation-of-number task. They had two rows with the same number of sweets in each row. A glove puppet called **Naughty Teddy** spread out the sweets in one of the two rows, while not moving those in the other row. The four- and five-year-olds sampled may have felt that the experiment was an enjoyable game, or they may have had sufficient language skills to understand what was happening. Or it may be that children are constantly amazed at what strange things adults can do. Of the eighty children tested, fifty could conserve number. When the adult moved the sweets, rather than the teddy, only thirteen out of eighty said there were the same number.

Naughty teddy

Activity
Ask children of different ages 'which is heavier: a ton of lead or a ton of feathers?' How old are they before they consistently answer correctly?

Many experiments have shown that children can conserve when they have been taught how to. Children can learn that there are still the same number of objects in two rows, even when the objects have been spread out in one of them. The amount of water does not change, just because it is poured into a different container. Children do not simply know how to conserve when they become maturationally ready (which doesn't occur until later childhood). Whatever maturation is necessary has occurred by the age of four or five. What is then needed is training and practice, and these are socially acquired. **Dorothy Field** trained some four-year-olds in one conservation task. She found that they could conserve correctly. Also they could apply their new skill to other conservation tasks in which they were not specifically trained.

 Summary of egocentrism and conservation
Piaget concluded that children below seven years of age were not maturationally ready to decentre or conserve. When children are mature and experienced enough, then decentring and the ability to conserve occur. More recent research has suggested that Piaget was too pessimistic. Some of his experiments may have been too difficult or boring for testing children below seven. When the task is made more interesting and relevant, children aged three or four can decentre, and, with training and practice, children aged four and five show they can conserve.

Exercise on conservation

1. What does Piaget mean by conservation? What exactly can children who can conserve do which children who can't conserve cannot?
2. Why could children in the McGarrigle and Donaldson experiment conserve number?
3. Why could children aged four and five decentre in Martin Hughes' 'walls and dolls' experiment, when eight-year-olds in Piaget's model mountains research could not?
4. In the following table, put these features in the thinking of sensory motor and pre-operational children into the correct column. Action schemas, pre-conceptual thought, acquires object permanence, animism, egocentrism.

Sensory motor	Pre-operational

The concrete-operations stage (7–11 years)

By seven years of age many children will be in school and learning to compete and cooperate in play and other activities. Decentring is necessary to be able to cooperate in team games. Children use objects and events that they have experienced (or at least imagined) in their play. These objects and events are a real part of the child's experiences. This is what Piaget means by concrete-operations. For example, arithmetic has formal rules which must be learned in a logical way. One of the first things to be learned is adding up. A child who is about to learn to add will want to know what are we adding up? Children can see the point of adding 3 apples to 2 apples to see how many apples there will be. It makes sense. They have schemas for apples. This need for concrete, real objects to manipulate is what Piaget means by concrete-operations.

During the concrete-operations stage children's conservation skills develop. Some things are easier to understand and conserve than others, and these will be learned first. Conservation of number, for example, only requires the child to consider one thing when making the judgement about whether there are more or less of it. Piaget claimed six- and seven-year-old children could conserve number. An object's mass is a combination of its size and density. Conserving it means the child will have to consider both size and shape. This will take longer to learn. Weight requires size and mass to be considered, whilst volume requires an understanding of shape, size, and mass. Children will need to be ten or more before they can conserve weight, according to Piaget.

▷
Concrete means real, actual objects. Concrete objects can be touched. The opposite of concrete is abstract.

▷
Conservation is simply the knowledge that the fundamental properties of a substance, object, or event do not change merely because its appearance changes. Conservation skills are acquired during the concrete-operations stage.

●●● **Summary of the concrete-operations stage**
As children start to understand the relationships between things, such as whether there are more or less, 2 and 3, longer and shorter, they need real objects to practise with. They learn to conserve number, weight, mass, volume, time, etc. during the concrete-operations stage. They also realize that if they take away a number of things which they had added to another number, they end up with the number they started from. This is reversibility. Egocentrism is supposed to give way to decentring during this stage, when children learn to see things from other people's points of view.

The formal-operations stage (11 years onwards)

During the concrete-operations stage children were learning to think about objects or events, as long as they had some experience of them. Formal-operational thinking does not need this direct experience. They develop abstract ideas about justice, freedom, and conscience. Formal-operational thinking is more flexible, rational, and logical. Formal-operational thinking allows solutions to 'what would happen if', and 'if this then that' type questions. In this stage children have ideas about right and wrong, good and bad, what should and should not be allowed to happen. They are often concerned with saving the planet, preserving nature and the countryside, and seeing fair play.

Such mental skills take several years to achieve, and not everyone fully achieves them. It's quite possible to think formally about some things, but not others. Piaget thought that most people would have acquired most formal-operational thought by the age of fifteen or twenty. Not everyone agrees that formal-operational thinking is the last stage of development. It could be that there are stages above that which only certain gifted people (like Piaget himself) would reach.

Summary of operational thought

Piaget believed that children acquire operational thought some time after the age of seven, although Piaget's methods have been criticized for being inadequate, and others have found at an earlier age in children the kind of thinking which Piaget described, and not everyone acquires fully operational thought in the Western sense.

Exercise on operational thought

1 What do the words 'formal' and 'operational' mean?
2 Name some of the things that children in the last stage can think and talk about that children at earlier stages of cognitive development could not.
3 Outline the main differences in the thinking of children above and below the age of seven, according to Piaget.

Piaget and education

Although Piaget didn't specifically apply his findings about children's cognitive development to education in the classroom, it is not difficult to see that there are implications. Pre-operational and concrete-operational children learn by manipulating real objects. They discover what an object is like and what they can do with it. Transforming water into paint, sand into buildings, paper into aeroplanes, etc., challenge a child's imagination. All these are examples of an active process of discovery. The application of Piaget's work to education is referred to as Discovery Learning.

The role of the first-school teacher in discovery learning

Children are naturally curious and active. The primary school teacher can take advantage of this to help them to learn. As they progress from pre-operational to concrete-operational stages, so the kinds of experience they are offered should be altered to suit their cognitive needs. It is not possible to teach young children in the same way that older children are taught, because children do not think operationally until they are seven, and even then they are only beginning to think logically.

Summary of 'The first-school teacher should . . . '

1 provide a safe, warm, secure environment in which the children can feel comfortable;

2 provide the kind of materials which are appropriate to children of the age in the group;

3 encourage the children to explore and to think about what they are doing with the materials, and how else they can be used (assisting assimilation);

4 encourage different activities which provide variety and keep the children interested (assisting accommodation);

5 provide new materials when the child has fully explored the old ones (assisting adaptation), and encourage but not push the children, as they may not be able to learn from things for which they are not maturationally ready;

6 encourage children to discover things for themselves by letting them observe or compete with others, for example by arranging pairs or small groups of children to work together;

7 ensure that the children move into the next stage by knowing exactly what stage of development each child is in, what skills a child in that stage is capable of, and what skills will be mastered in the next stage (this is called the readiness approach);

8 provide an alternative way of doing something if the method children are using has no chance of success, as knowledge of their success is important to children.

The role of the child in discovery learning

The child should be enthusiastic, active, curious, and adventurous. It should regard school as a fun place, because learning should be fun to young children. It should see school as a place of adventure and stimulation. Sadly this isn't always true of primary school children, and is probably much less likely to be found amongst secondary school children. The role of the parent is obviously to encourage these ideas about school in the child.

Activity
What advice would you give to (a) the parents and (b) the teachers about applying ideas from Piaget's theories to the education of young children?

Comment on the discovery method

Piaget suggests that the way children think changes at around the age of 7. Teaching should reflect this change.	Other research has shown that the mode of thinking can be changed before the age of 7, and that progress could be held back by waiting until that age.
Discovery learning provides a logical and practical guide to the abilities of children at various ages.	Piaget concentrated on 'the average child'. Strict application of the theory will inhibit many children.
It provides a model for teachers in the first school.	We do not know exactly what to look for, what skills are involved in or are beneficial to any stage.

Evaluation of Piaget's theory

Children are incapable of logical, operational thought.	A rather pessimistic view not supported by much research.
Logical thought is the most advanced form of thinking.	People use a variety of forms of thinking. Logic isn't the only one, or even the most widely used
Formal operational thought develops from puberty.	Many adolescents and adults do not think formally.
Cognitive skills change at 2, 7 and 11.	They probably occur before these ages.
Piaget gave children particular tasks and asked them particular questions.	The tasks may have been too difficult or boring.
Piaget claims cognition develops through four distinct stages.	Piaget is unclear about why one stage ends and another begins.
Piaget describes what the average or typical child of a particular age can do.	There are wide variations in individual children's abilities.
Piaget emphasized the importance of the child's relationship with the environment for cognitive development.	The children's relationships with other people may be very important too.

Development of perception

Many animals, including humans, have perceptual skills. Perception is the process of taking in information collected by our senses so that our brain can work on it in some way. Humans are said to have five main senses, although psychologists think several others, such as the sense of balance and the muscle senses which tell us about the position of our arms and legs should be added. Of all the perceptual senses sight is probably the most widely used and provides most of the information that people take in. We will discuss the origins of visual perception in this chapter.

The human sense of vision is highly evolved with about 126 million light-sensitive cells, 120 million rods and six million cones on the retina of each eye. The retina is at the back of each eyeball and comprises several layers of cells. Rod cells are stimulated by quite low light levels and provide our impression of black and white. There are three types of cone, which operate in brighter light and provide our colour vision. There are other layers of cells on the retina which are involved in organizing our perception and they transmit information about what we have seen to the visual cortex at the back of our brain.

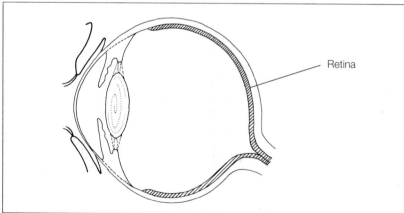

Retina

The eye

Although we appear to know what we see almost immediately, this knowledge is actually the final stage in quite a long process. These are the major stages:

Activity	Example
Detecting sources of stimulation around us.	Rods and cones on the retina detect light.
Converting perceptions into mental, nervous energy.	Optic nerve sends information to the visual cortex in the brain.
Interpreting this for meaning by consulting memory.	Recognize the patterns of nervous activity as (for example, 'people in a busy place').
Paying more attention to some information and filtering out other information.	Selecting one person to look at by recognizing some familiar feature.
Making sense and becoming aware of this information (for instance, achieving cognition).	Recognizing the person as a good friend.
Having thoughts and feelings about this information which allows us to respond in several ways.	The wish to speak to this person so call their name to attract their attention.

Human vision includes a number of abilities such as the ability to recognize shapes. This is **pattern perception**. You would recognize a cup from whichever angle you saw it. You know that objects do not grow larger or smaller just because they appear to change size. A cup held right in front of you appears to be larger than a cup which is 3 metres away, but you know that it isn't. This is called **size constancy**. Things don't change their colour either. The dark-blue cup may appear black when the room is dark, but you know that it is the same dark-blue cup it was when the room was lighter. This is **colour constancy**. You also have the ability to make judgements about distance or, if you're looking down, depth.

There are three possible explanations for the origin of these and the other visual skills. I'm sure that you could guess that these explanations reflect the nature–nurture debate.

First, you may have had these visual skills since you were born. To illustrate this, **Robert Fantz** showed that chicks can instinctively recognize food-shaped objects right from birth (as we shall discuss shortly). However, we must not generalize from animals to humans. If you did have these visual skills from birth, they were probably inherited genetically.. Even of they didn't appear until later the ability might still be genetically transmitted but only appear when the human is maturationally ready.

▷
Constancy means unchanging. Piaget gave the term 'conservation' to the knowledge that objects do not change their essential features when their appearance changes.

Exercise on innate perception in animals

1 Why might there be survival value for chicks in being able to recognize food?
2 Would this skill help human babies?
3 What do human babies 'eat' (or drink)?
4 Are human babies able to recognize their food?

As human visual skills are so highly developed, and the result of all this processing is virtually instant, it may seem that some human visual skills are probably innate. Robert Fantz, Genevieve Carpenter, and others (see Chapter 2) have investigated the human baby's preferences for human sights and sounds. We concluded that babies do appear to enjoy looking at some shapes and patterns more than others.

Second, such visual skills may be learned. We learn to recognize objects as we gain experience of them. As we learn that objects do not change shape, size, colour, weight, volume, mass, etc. (note here some of Piaget's investigations into conservation skills) so we are able to generalize to other objects.

The third, and most likely, explanation is that, like so many of our other skills, some visual skills are genetically inherited, some are learned, and some are the result of a combination of both.

In this chapter we will examine the evidence for all three of these possibilities.

The nature view – perception is innate

Pattern perception

Patterns are whole shapes. Do infants perceive objects as whole shapes? Do they have any preference for looking at one pattern of colours, lines or textures rather than another? Research into these areas has inevitably used animals, as it is difficult to design experiments suitable for human babies and it may be difficult to find samples of parents willing to allow their babies to be used. The first experiments were conducted 30 years ago by **Robert Fantz**. He hatched some chicks in total darkness. Because chicks will peck at grain soon after birth, and well before they could have learned that grain is their food, it seems reasonable to assume that they have an instinctive knowledge of what their food looks like. Fantz gave his chicks eight tiny, different-shaped objects and recorded the number of times they pecked at each of them. The objects were different shapes ranging from small round objects, similar to a grain, to pyramid shaped objects. The chicks pecked ten times more often at the round objects than at the ones which didn't look anything like grain. Fantz concluded that chicks innately recognize round shapes and objects with three dimensions. This supports the nature view that shape recognition in chicks is innate.

Fantz's chicken food

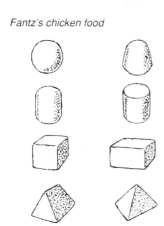

Because chicks appear to be genetically programmed to peck at food-shaped objects it may be that humans infants may inherit a preference for looking at things which could have survival value for them. Fantz designed some apparatus called a **looking chamber** which would allow him to film children's eyes and to time how long they looked in a particular direction. He thought that children would gaze longer at things they found interesting, but would quickly look away from things they find uninteresting. He could also judge their facial expressions and body movements to see if they appeared interested.

▷ Fantz claimed to have shown that babies as young as one week can perceive form or pattern and that, during the next six months their vision improves so that they can see increasingly complicated patterns of lines and shapes.

Various objects and pictures could be placed in the looking chamber. Fantz tested thirty infants at weekly intervals, from when they were one week old, until they were fifteen weeks old. He showed them different shapes and patterns such as a bull's-eye pattern, stripes of various thicknesses, a cross, a chessboard design, plain triangles and plain squares. Fantz found that even the youngest infants generally preferred the more complicated shapes, such as the bull's-eye and the chessboard. Some degree of form perception may well be innate, therefore. This led Fantz to investigate whether human babies inherit a preference for looking for the human face genetically. (In Chapter 2 we noted that Ahrens had suggested that they did. See page 32.)

Exercise on form perception

1 How did Fantz measure the babies' ability to recognize and show if they preferred any particular pictures?
2 What sample size did Fantz use?
3 What did Fantz conclude about the origin of form perception?
4 What did Ahrens conclude about the infant's abilities and preferences for the human face?
5 List three difficulties that researchers might face when wishing to use babies as subjects in psychological experiments.

Fantz's face shapes

Fantz showed three particular pictures to babies in the looking chamber. The first was a face clearly drawn on a plain background. The next was the same as the first but the features were all jumbled up, and the third was a face-shape without any features except for the hair. He showed these pictures, in every possible combination to forty-nine infants aged between four days and six months. Most of the infants ignored altogether the face without features. The infants aged around six months barely glanced at it. The children up to about three-and-a-half-months of age seemed interested in the scrambled features. The infants all appeared slightly more interested in the picture that was closest to a real face. Although the differences were quite small, Fantz did conclude that human infants are born with a preference for looking at the human face. This claim appeared to support those psychologists who believe that babies have innate capacities to recognize, and attach to, their caregivers, although by six months of age infants have had plenty of experience of looking at faces!

Age of baby	Face shape	Scrambled features	No features
Up to 3 months	Some interest	Some interest	No interest
3 to 6 months	Some interest	No interest	No interest

Comment on Fantz's research

Fantz's claim that this looking-chamber research suggests that human babies have an innate preference for looking at the human face has been attacked at a number of levels. Although he provided an ingenious way of experimenting on babies and recording their responses, some of the material he used, such as the pictures of the faces, let it down. First, they were two-dimensional black and pink drawings which didn't move. Human faces are always changing expression. Would Fantz's drawings really look like animated human faces to a baby? Second, the difference between the babies' reactions to the different pictures was small. Other researchers have used Fantz's methods and repeated his experiments, but either have not made similar findings, or have offered other explanations for them.

Exercise on pattern perception

1 Imagine that you were repeating Fantz's experiment. Make a list of each of the stages he went through, in the correct order, noting what the students were to look for at each stage.
2 Why might the ability to recognize the human face, and to show some preference for it contribute to survival value in humans?
3 Evaluate Fantz's contribution to our understanding of the origins of form or pattern perception in humans by filling the spaces in the table on the page opposite.

Summary of pattern perception
Early research suggested that babies are born with the ability to recognize the human face. Such an ability might appear to have survival value. Innate visual recognition of food and other shapes has been demonstrated in some animals, although it seems highly unlikely that humans would be able to recognize a face.

Good point	Bad point
Interesting topic to investigate.	
Original idea to construct a looking chamber.	
Useful way of measuring what babies looked at and for how long.	
Careful experimental design.	

Depth, distance and direction perception

Another original piece of apparatus was designed by **Eleanor Gibson** and **Richard Walk** in 1960. They wanted to see whether human infants' abilities to judge depth was present soon after birth (in which case it is probably genetically inherited), or whether it had to be learned later. One principle of evolutionary adaptation suggests that animals evolve those skills which they need in order to thrive in their environment. The animal will show those skills when it is mature enough to use them. If so, then it is unlikely that human babies would have depth perception soon after birth. As they cannot move around on their own, and cannot do anything to stop themselves from falling even if they could perceive depth, it does seem unlikely that they would have inherited any ability to judge it.

On the other hand, the ability to judge depth and distance is very important to visual perception. The majority of things you look at will have depth. People and things will be nearer to or further away from you. How could you reach for something and pick it up if you couldn't perceive distance? In this case it does make some sense that the ability to judge depth and distance might be present from birth, just waiting to be used.

Gibson and Walk constructed some apparatus known as the **visual cliff** which comprised a sheet of non-reflective glass covering a table top. Half of the table top had been removed. A piece of chequered cloth covered the remaining table top, fell to the floor where the top was removed, and lay along the floor The illusion would be that the apparatus had a shallow side and a deep side. A shelf was placed along the edge between the deep and shallow sides.

Some new-born animals were placed on the shelf, and Gibson and Walk recorded their responses. Would they move all over the glass? Would they look down? If they saw the cloth on the floor under the deep side would they refuse to move onto the glass above it? If they have innate depth-perception they would probably not move onto the deep side. Most of the animals tested would not move over the deep side. Even one-day-old chicks never strayed onto the deep side. Lambs and kids placed on the deep side refused to stand, and kittens either froze or circled backwards. Rats were the only animals that would venture onto the deep side. Rats rely on their whiskers as guides and so touch is more important to them than vision. When the researchers trimmed their whiskers and they were

▷ Even very young babies will try to reach and grasp things that are offered to them. Within a few months they have learned what sort of things they can grasp and what they cannot.

The visual cliff

forced to use vision, they also wouldn't move onto the deep side. This seems to confirm the view that animals have innate depth perception.

Just because other animals have innate depth perception does not mean that humans have. The problem for Gibson and Walk in testing humans is that their apparatus needs the subjects to be mobile, to see whether they would cross onto the deep side. Humans aren't mobile before six months or so. By this time they could have learned about depth and distance. However Gibson and Walk did try thirty-six human infants on the visual cliff. They were between six and fourteen months of age. They were placed on the shelf between the shallow and deep sides. Their parent called them from one side, then from the other. Nine infants refused to move at all, but the twenty-seven infants who did would crawl to their parent over the shallow side, and only three would crawl over the deep side. Some crawled away from their parents when they were being called from the deep side, others just cried because they couldn't reach their parent. Some of the infants fell onto the glass on the deep side, and started to crawl towards their parent until they looked down. Once they saw the chequered cloth at some distance below them they became distressed. Before looking down these babies were presumably using their sense of touch, which told them that the surface they were crawling over was safe. As soon as they looked down their sense of touch must have been over-ruled by their sense of vision.

▷
Experiments that are likely to cause children any distress are carefully examined before they are allowed to go ahead. Parents have the absolute right to remove their children if they appear to become distressed.

Comment on depth perception

Gibson and Walk's clever experiments do not allow them to claim that depth perception is innate in humans. The visual-cliff experiment requires that the subjects can crawl, so they have to be six months old or more. Much learning occurs during the first six months of life so the babies could have learned depth perception. Gibson and Walk did say that the results support their view that depth perception is innate in animals.

Exercise on depth perception

1 What was the purpose behind the visual-cliff experiment?
2 Name some of the animals used.
3 What was the sample size for children?
4 What evidence is there in the passage to suggest that perception may be innate in animals?
5 Explain why these findings may not be used to solve the nature–nurture debate on depth perception in humans.
6 Do you think that encouraging their babies to crawl over a cliff will help in the formation of attachments between mothers and their infants? If not, can you comment on the ethical implications of this study?

Distance and direction as cues for perceiving depth

Tom Bower has also devised some ingenious experiments to investigate babies' visual abilities to judge distance and direction. We said in Chapter 10 that babies are born with about fifty reflexive responses. Doctors use one of them, the defensive reaction, to test whether babies are blind. In this test, an object is moved towards an infant's face. If the infant is blind, she will not react. If she (or he) can see the approaching object, she will try to lean out of the way or lift her arms to protect her face. This suggests that the ability to judge direction is innate. Judging direction of movement is an essential ingredient in judging distance or depth. So why do babies lift their arms or try to move away from the oncoming object? There are two possibilities. Either the ability to judge direction is innate, or they are responding to the movement of air towards their faces as the object approaches. Bower tested this possibility. He arranged three experimental conditions.

Condition 1: A cube is slowly moved towards the baby's face (and the air around it is displaced in the normal way). This produced the classic defensive response.

Condition 2: The air was displaced but there was no object. The baby appeared to take no notice.

Condition 3: A film was shown, depicting an approaching object. Obviously the film is two dimensional and no air was being displaced. The baby showed no defensive reaction here either.

Bower's experiment supports the view that the ability babies have to judge direction is innate. They show distress if an object appears to be heading straight for them, but do not show concern when the same object would miss them, even by just an inch or two! The defensive reaction is also probably innate. This would make sense, as it could have considerable survival value.

These experiments also indicate some of the limitations of babies visual systems. Babies can take in a great deal of information, but cannot process it as quickly as an adult can. Piaget said that babies have relatively few schemas and those that they do have are quite limited. If the object in the defensive-reaction experiment was heading for them at any speed, then the babies didn't respond at all. The information would probably have been sent to the brain, but the brain isn't mature and well organized enough to respond very quickly.

We mentioned **size constancy** earlier (see page 213). Size constancy is the knowledge that something which you can see nearby isn't going to become smaller when you see the same thing some way off. The fresh-cream cake that you just bought, held a few centimetres in front of your face, will cast quite a large image on your retinas. It cast a much smaller image when you saw it earlier, in the cake-shop window across the street. You know that it is still the same cake. This is known as size constancy. There are other visual constancies too. You know that something doesn't change its shape just because you see it from different angles. You know the colour of your front-room curtains doesn't change according to whether you see them on a sunny day or in the middle of the night.

In 1966 Tom Bower conducted an experiment to investigate whether size constancy was innate or learned. Nurturists argue that infants could not show size constancy because they would not have learned it. Nativists argue that infants would show size constancy because it is an innate ability. One at a time, babies of between six and twelve weeks of age were placed on a table in a comfortable cot from which they could see a screen. Behind the screen is a 30-centimetre cube which is about one metre from the babies. When the screen was moved and the babies saw the cube they were called by their mothers who were to one side of the infants. If they turned to look at their mother she would pop up and say peek-a-boo and tickle the child. The babies enjoyed this form of reinforcement. Here, Bower is using operant conditioning to teach the babies to perform a simple task, turning their heads to one side when they see the cube in order to gain a reinforcement. After several **trials,** the babies were conditioned to turn their heads towards their mothers when they saw the cube.

Bower had three other experimental conditions. In the first, the 30-centimetre cube was moved back until it was three metres away from the babies, and the screen was removed. If the babies had size constancy they would look at the cube, recognize that it was the same cube as before, and turn their head to receive their reward. The number of head turns was counted.

In the next condition the original cube was removed and one which was three times as large (measuring 90-centimetres) was placed three metres from the babies. It would now cast the same size image on their retinas as the original 30-centimetre cube had at one metre. If the babies perceived this new cube to be the same as the original cube, they should turn their head for their reward.

In the third condition, the 90-centimetre cube was placed one metre from the babies. Such a cube would look three times as big as the original cube. Would the babies think that this was the original cube and turn their head for their reward?

So, the experimental conditions compared a 30-centimetre cube at one metre with:

1   a 30-centimetre cube at three metres;

2   a 30-centimetre cube at three metres;

3   a 90-centimetre cube at one metre.

In each experimental condition the number of times the babies turn their heads for a reward is used as a measure of how similar the infants thought the cube was to the 30-centimetre cube at one-metre distance that they were conditioned to turn from.

If the nativist view is correct and babies are born with size constancy, they should respond most to condition 1, as it uses the original cube. They should respond rather less to condition 2 and least to condition 3. If the

▷
A trial is a run-through of an experimental procedure.

nurturists are right and babies have to learn size constancy, then the babies should respond most to condition 2, as this cast the same size image on their retinas. Condition 1 and condition 3 should trigger the fewest head turns. Bower's results are shown in the following table:

	Average number of head turns
Control condition a 30cm cube at one metre	
Experimental condition 1 a 30cm cube at three metres	58
2 a 90cm cube at three metres	22
3 a 90cm cube at one metre	14

Bower's findings appear to support the nativist view. The babies seemed to recognize the 30-centimetre cube as the original stimulus, and turned their heads most for their reward. Less than half that number of head turns was recorded for the 90-centimetre cube at three metres. Less than a quarter of that for the 90-centimetre cube at one metre.

Exercise on Bower's experiment

1 Summarize Bower's conclusions from the distance and direction experiment.
2 What would Bower's hypothesis for this experiment have been?
3 What would Bower's hypothesis for the size-constancy experiment have been?
4 'Bower is using operant conditioning to teach the babies to perform a simple task.' What is meant by operant conditioning and how would Bower have used it here?
5 In view of the results Bower found in these two experiments, would you say that he would favour the nativist or nurturist view of these aspects of perception?

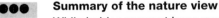 **Summary of the nature view**
While babies may not have many innate recognition skills they may have some other visual skills present from birth. Depth perception is difficult to demonstrate in humans, although they do seem able to predict direction and appear to have an understanding of relative size.

The nurture view – the case for learning

If perceptual skills have to be learned, then people who had been blind since birth, who then had their sight restored, would take some time to learn to recognize all the things that normally sighted people recognize straight away. A normally sighted person will have the various constancies we described earlier, whereas people who have their sight restored through surgery may not. Studies of sight-restored patients find that they do take some time to learn to judge depth and distance, etc. This appears to support the nurture view. However, just because adults can learn visual skills, such as judging distance, this doesn't mean that babies have to learn them.

If human visual skills have to be learned, then they can be relearned. This idea is tested in **readjustment studies**. Altering the way in which someone perceives the world, for example by making them wear goggles with lenses that distort their view, shouldn't cause long-term difficulties. They should be able to learn to adjust their behaviour. The following experiments seem to suggest that this is true.

A readjustment study is usually an experiment in which people have some aspect of their normal routines changed to see whether or not they can adapt their behaviour, and how long it takes them to do so.

George Stratton (1897) wore a patch over one eye so that he couldn't see anything through it, and an **inverting lens** over the other eye, which made everything he looked at appear upside down and left to right. Objects that were to his right looked as though they were on his left. He walked into things which he was trying to avoid, and looked to his right to try to recognize a noise he could hear coming from his left. He wore the lens for eight days to discover if he could make a visual adjustment. By the fifth day he was able to walk around without bumping into things. While he was moving around everything appeared okay. When he stopped, and concentrated on an object, it appeared to be upside down. Stratton claimed that his eyes had adjusted to his altered perceptions, but many researchers were not convinced.

J. and J. K. Peterson (1938) used inverting lenses on both eyes of a sample of people, and found similar results to Stratton, although not all of the subjects could adapt to their new perception. Eight months later they retested their subjects and found that they adapted to their upside-down world more quickly than before. They quickly learned to avoid furniture and do most things that others could do. Clearly, learning is involved in perception. In another study an Australian professor was so confident in his new skills that he used to ride his bicycle to college. When a subject in this type of research was asked whether what he was looking at really appeared upside down he replied, 'I wish you hadn't asked me. … When I recall how they did look before I put on these lenses, … they do look upside down now. … Until you asked me I was absolutely unaware of it.'

Thirty years ago **Ivo Kohler** wore different lenses which distorted his sight in several different ways. Some had different coloured lenses, some turned the line of sight slightly to the left or to the right. After a few hours

▷
An inverting lens turns everything one sees upside down and also reverses left and right.

of wearing each of his distorting lenses he was able to adapt his behaviour to cope with his changed visual experiences.

Activity
If you can find some three-dimensional (3-D) spectacles, with different-coloured lenses (or make some from coloured cellophane), wear them for an hour. When you take them off, close one eye and note what everything looks like. Then close that eye and look through the other. What do things look like now? Then look at the colour of the lenses for each eye. What do you find? Do you have any ideas for an explanation?

These readjustment studies seem to support the nurture view, that perception results from learning. If it were innate then we would never be able to adjust it. However, things are not quite as straightforward as they seem to be. People do seem able to make some adaptation to changes in their visual experiences. These adaptations are in their responses, not in their perceptions. They do not start seeing the world the right-way round, but they begin to learn how to behave in an upside-down one. In other words, it isn't their vision that is readjusting, it is their behavioural response to it. They are simply learning what to do to compensate for their visual distortions. For example, you know that your lenses make everything on the right appear to be on the left. So if you see something on your left, you know you have to turn your head to the right to see it.

> All of the experiments discussed so far have failed to provide a solution for the nature–nurture debate. It is unlikely that any ever will. Human perception is very complex and is bound to be affected by all sorts of influences.

Summary of the nurture view
Studies of blind people who have their sight restored show that they quickly learn to recognize things. Readjustment studies show that humans can adapt their behaviour to take account of new visual experiences, although this isn't the same as making a visual adaptation.

Combining the two views – the need for biology and learning

So far we've reviewed the case for the nature view, and the nurture view. Most modern psychologists would think that visual perceptual skills result from an interaction between the two. For the first few months of life a baby's visual system isn't fully developed. The nerves in those parts of the brain involved with vision take time to develop their insulating layers. The result is interference (a bit like a radio that isn't quite tuned properly). Some of the signals are lost, others are confused. The baby's vision is blurred. As the baby's visual system matures so its ability to see will improve. Biology influences perception at this early stage.

Despite these limitations, babies can see reasonably well right from birth. We can do tests to measure how far a baby can see, and even what sorts of things it can see. However, we cannot know what the infant makes of the things it sees. **Genevieve Carpenter** showed that by two weeks of age babies may have learned to recognize their mother or father, and will expect her or his face to move and change expression. Learning from early experience is also necessary for infants to make sense of what they can see.

The research so far has either used adults or children. There are inevitably problems in using humans in this type of research. One way to investigate the contribution of biology and learning is by experimenting on animals. In the past, experiments have used animal subjects instead. Now there are very strict guidelines concerning the use of animals.

Deprivation studies with animals

In 1950 **A. N. Reisen** reported his study in which he kept a male and a female chimpanzee in the dark, so depriving them of sight, for their first sixteen months of life. If perception is innate this early deprivation won't make any difference, they would still be able to see well enough. When they were exposed to light after sixteen months they couldn't open their eyes like normal monkeys, they appeared scared by bright lights, they had no blink reflex when something moved towards them quickly, and they had no interest in their toys unless they touched them first. This suggests that perception isn't entirely innate.

▷
Deprivation studies such as these were carried out before people became more concerned with animal rights. They probably would not be allowed now. The British Psychological Society provides guidelines for research with animals. These say that any suffering must be kept to a minimum, and a very few animals are allowed to be studied.

One chimp remained in the normally lit conditions. Over the next five months its visual skills developed until its sight developed normally. It had good hand-to-eye coordination and could recognize objects by sight. The other chimp was returned to the dark for another sixteen months. When exposed to normal light it behaved in the same way as it had earlier. Its abilities improved slightly over the next few weeks, then declined.

It seems that chimps (and presumably other animals) need light during the first year or so, for their eyes to develop normally. If this is correct, then it would be necessary to rear subjects who can see light, but not see objects. Reisen reared another chimpanzee who was made to wear a translucent mask which allowed one-and-a-half hours of diffused, unpatterned light to enter the eye each day. (Like looking through grease-proof paper.) The mask was removed at seven months. This chimp also did not develop normal sight.

▷
Translucent means that light can pass through, but distinct patterns or shapes cannot be seen.

However, Reisen's experiments were often carried out on very few subjects (and sometimes only one) and so we must be cautious about any generalizations we make from them. His subjects did have some visual experiences too. He turned the light on for 45 seconds each day to allow the chimps to feed.

▶▶▶ *Activity*
Try making a mask from tracing paper and wearing it while you try to recognize your friends.

Thirty years ago **Colin Blakemore** and **Grahame Cooper** reared some kittens inside large drums which were painted on the inside. One drum had vertical black and white stripes, while the other drum had horizontal black and white stripes. When they stood up the kittens reared in each drum could only see either vertical or horizontal black and white lines. The critical period for kittens developing visual skills was thought to be from three to fifteen weeks of life. Blakemore and Cooper tested their visual abilities from when the kittens were five months old.

If visual skills are simply innate, then their early experience wouldn't have much influence and the kittens would be able to see normally when they were removed from the drum. If it was the result of nurture they wouldn't be able to see anything different from the lines inside their drums. At first the kittens could not recognize anything with edges that were different from the ones they had seen inside their drum. However this does not entirely support either side of the nature–nurture debate because it could be that all of the cells necessary for normal vision are present at birth but need stimulation from light in various patterns to make them work.

There is another problem. Like most kittens, the subjects in this experiment would have rolled around in their play. A vertical stripe will appear to be horizontal when the kitten is lying down. They would have seen the stripes from many angles. Several independent judges could not tell which cat had been reared in which drum.

At the same time as Blakemore and Cooper were rearing their cats **Richard Held** and **Alan Hein** had designed some apparatus to overcome the problem of the cats' movement changing their visual experiences. Their apparatus, called the **kitten carousel**, made two kittens share the same visual experiences, although only one of them could move fairly independently. They were connected by pulleys and strings so that the movements of the active kitten were transferred to the passive kitten.

▷
A critical period is a period of time, usually shortly after birth, during which something must be experienced if normal development is to follow.

The kitten carousel

The kittens were allowed three hours each day for several weeks on the apparatus. When their paw-to-eye coordination was finally tested, the active kittens had far better abilities. For example, after 30 hours in the apparatus, all of the active kittens could move their paws deliberately in a particular direction. None of the passive kittens could. It seems that experience in the environment is necessary for normal visual development.

Comments on animal readjustment studies

There is a major problem with all experiments which involve animals behaving in some way or another after we have altered some feature of their environment. We can describe what they do, we can't know whether they are capable of doing other things. Just because an animal behaves in one way does not mean that it can't behave in another way.

Summary of combining the two views

On many occasions when psychologists have re-examined the contributions of either biology or the environment they have concluded that both are involved and there's little to be gained from trying to decide which is responsible for what. This is true here. Rather than trying to claim some skill for biology or the environment it makes more sense to see how the two interact to produce the skill.

Conclusion

Human babies have impressive visual skills such as depth perception, size constancy, and pattern recognition. They also have the ability to imitate facial expressions and to copy behaviour. If, for instance, a mother sticks her tongue out, the baby may well return the gesture. Although this simple copying may seem fairly obvious, it really is quite amazing. How does the infant know what is being stuck out, and how does it know what part of its own anatomy to stick out?

It is unlikely that there will ever be a simple solution to the nature–nurture debate. Most psychologists now support the **nature modified by nurture** view. Babies are probably born with the capacity to develop all the visual skills that they will show later. If the environment they grow up in allows those skills to develop, then they will.

Exercise on the nature – nurture debate

1 Summarize the evidence for each side of the nature–nurture debate on size constancy.
2 Describe some of the evidence which suggests that the environment may be necessary for the development of visual perception.
3 Describe three different techniques that have been used to study the perceptual skills of babies or young children.

The development of moral behaviour

I n the last chapter we talked about the emergence of the self-concept. An important part of the self-concept is the knowledge of what members of the particular society in which the child lives regard as right and wrong. In this chapter we will be looking at one of the features that separate human beings from other animals: their moral sense. Children must learn those expectations, rules, and laws which govern what they may do, what they must do, and what they may not and must not do. Moral awareness is an essential part of the personality and so we shall describe the main theories which try to explain different aspects of it. We will look at the role of children themselves, and the major influences on them, their parents and their friends.

Exercise on moral development

1 Give two examples which show the difference between what children must do and what they may do.
2 Give two examples which show the difference between what chilren must not do and what they may not do.
3 Where does our understanding about right and wrong come from?
   (a) From God.
   (b) From some instinct.
   (c) From some inner knowledge.
   (d) From our upbringing.
4 Does your answer to question 3 suggest that you are a supporter of the nature or nurture approach?

Five approaches to moral development

Children develop their ideas about what is good and bad behaviour in society generally, and what is right and wrong for themselves personally, largely during childhood and adolescence. There are many explanations for how children learn right from wrong. We will describe three of these explanations here. Each relates back to theories we discussed in Chapter 1.

Psychoanalysts, starting with **Sigmund Freud**, are interested in the ways in which children's feelings affect their personality development. Human emotions are very complex. Behaviourists, particularly **B. F. Skinner**, are more concerned with what children do rather than what they feel. They regard children as little adults who will learn appropriate behaviour by reinforcement. **Albert Bandura** adds the notion of modelling. Cognitive psychologists, such as **Jean Piaget** and **Lawrence Kohlberg**, are interested in how children's thinking and reasoning about moral issues change as they grow. They believe that children's ability to make moral judgements develops as their cognitive skills develop generally. We will go through each of these views in turn.

Freud's psychoanalytic theory of moral development

▷
Chapter 6 looks at how psychoanalytic theory explains adult personality.

Sigmund Freud was an Austrian doctor who advanced psychoanalytic theory to explain children's personality development. He once claimed that one of the hardest tasks for parents was the moral development of their children. By three years of age most children are quite skilled at walking, running, and handling things. They can communicate quite well through language, and they can understand much more than they can say. Freud imagined that there were three unconscious urges which direct our behaviour. The first one is the source of all psychic energy, the **id.** It is present from birth and unconsciously drives us towards satisfying our needs for food, sleep, comfort, and pleasure. The second unconscious urge is the **ego** which has to find socially acceptable ways to satisfy the id. If a child simply takes food without asking, or urinates when having made no attempt to use a toilet, then he or she is likely to be punished in some way.

▷
The id and ego are the first two parts of personality development in traditional Freudian theory. The death instincts and libido are the two instinctive urges which prompt particular behaviour.

A child will experience pleasurable feelings through different parts of the body at different stages of development. These parts of the body are called the **erogenous zones**. Sometime around the age of three, during what Freud called the **phallic stage** of personality development, a son will start to have intensely loving feelings towards his mother. She bathes him, dries him with a towel, dresses him, and kisses and cuddles him. Freud claimed that the id will unconsciously draw the boy to his mother and want her to love him in return. Unconsciously he will see his father as a threat as his father shares with him his mother's time and affection. In the boy's unconscious the **death instincts** will be triggered to make him feel jealousy and hatred towards his father.

▷

In the Greek mythology, Oedipus was the son of the king and queen of Thebes. He returned home after many years, fell in love with a woman whom he didn't realize to be his own mother, killed his father, and married his mother.

So, Freud claimed, the boy now has another problem: what if his father discovers how his son feels towards him? This produces more anxiety in the boy. At the same time as hating his father the son loves his father too. Wanting to destroy someone he loves will produce further anxiety in his unconscious mind. All of these anxieties combine into what Freud called the **Oedipus Complex.**

The unconscious anxieties that make up the Oedipus Complex can be overcome. First, the child must stop being aware of his feelings towards his mother. He does this by **repressing** his feelings about her. Repression is an unconscious **defence mechanism**. Freud thought that we possess many unconscious means of protecting our self-concept and our personality. He called these our defence mechanisms. We may deny that we have these feelings, or blame someone else, or transfer our feelings onto someone else, we conveniently forget unpleasant experiences and channel our energies into other activities. All these are descriptions of defence mechanisms.

▷

See Chapter 6 for a discussion of defence mechanisms.

Repression is an ultimate defence mechanism. It is quite unconscious. Its function is to stop ideas that would cause negative emotions – such as guilt and fear, anxiety and hostility – from reaching consciousness.

Second, a boy may try to become as much like his father as possible. If he is like his father his mother will want him instead of his father. Anyway a father is less likely to be angry with a child who is rather like him. Freud called the process by which children become like their same-sex parent **identification**.

▷

Identification is an important idea in Freud's theory. It is a mental process by which we try to think like someone else. We copy them and aspects of our personality become like theirs.

Freud's explanations for how girls acquire their moral feelings are even more unlikely than those he developed for boys, and they are not taken seriously now. Freud outlined what he called the **Electra Complex**. A girl is supposed to imagine that she once had a penis, but that it was cut off by her mother as punishment for something she had done in the past. As a result of this belief, she is supposed to suffer from penis envy. This unconsciously draws her to her father. Being with her father is supposed to satisfy her unconscious urge to have a penis. This produces unconscious anxieties about her relationship with her mother. In order to reduce these anxieties, the girl represses her feeling toward her father and identifies with her mother. (It is easy to see why no one takes this view seriously now!)

▷

Electra was a character in another Greek legend whose father was murdered by her mother's lover. Electra urged her brother to kill her mother (and her lover) in revenge.

The result of children **identifying** with their same sex parents is that they learn to think, act, and feel in similar ways to those of that parent. Each child will build up a mental picture of how its parent would think and what its parent would do in different circumstances. Unfortunately children don't always do what their parents want them to. It may be much more exciting to do something which parents wouldn't approve of than something that they would. If the parents find out the child may be disciplined in some way. If the child does things it knows its parents wouldn't like it will feel guilty and anxious that they might punish the child if they find out. These anxieties and fears become the **conscience**.

▷

The conscience here refers to the unconscious urge to make the child feel fear and guilt if he or she does something known to be wrong.

The conscience is a major part of the third part of personality to appear, the **superego**. The superego is the result of successfully resolving the anxieties of the Oedipus or Electra complexes. It provides the moral component in personality.

Summary of identification

The process of identification is most important in understanding Freud's theory of moral development (particularly for boys). Here are the stages in acquiring the moral component of personality.

1 The boy experiences (pre-genital) sexual feelings towards his mother.
2 Unconsciously, he feels angry at and jealous of his father.
3 The ego unconsciously drives the child to become more like his father so that his mother will want him and he will be able to show his feelings for her.
4 Partly to overcome the feelings of guilt about his feelings towards his father, (and the anxiety that these feelings produce), and partly to appear more desirable to his mother, the child will want to become like his father.
5 The child identifies with his father, taking on his father's ideas, beliefs, attitudes, etc. (i.e. his father's personality).
6 An important feature of his father's personality is his ideas about moral conduct. The child acquires his superego (conscience) largely from his father.

Evaluation of Freud's claims for the development of moral feelings

Contribution	However
Freud offers a complete theory to explain the origin of moral feelings.	There is no evidence that it is true.
Some of the ideas he offers, such as identification, are useful.	Others, such as penis envy, seem simply ridiculous.
Children do identify with their same-sex parents and learn their morality from them.	Not exclusively. Males reared by mothers in lone-parent families are not necessarily less moral than males reared by both parents.
Freud thought that an understanding of right and wrong would be complete by the end of the phallic stage (that is by the age of six or seven).	Teenagers sometimes still have confused feelings about moral issues (for example towards their family).

It is true that children do learn the difference between right and wrong, and we may well choose to call their ideas a conscience. There is no evidence that consciences have anything to do with identifying with one parent because the child has pre-genital desires about the other parent.

Exercise on Freud's explanation for moral development

1 Name the first three stages of personality development in traditional psychoanalysis.
2 At what ages does the third stage begin and end?
3 Outline what Freud meant by the Oedipus Complex.
4 What did Freud mean by identification?
5 What is the superego?
6 How do we develop our superego?
7 Fill in the blanks in the following table with a brief description of how a sensitive parent responds to his or her child's personality during the third stage of personality development.

	Mother	Father
Son resolving his Oedipus Complex		
Daughter resolving her Electra Complex		

Summary of psychoanalytic theory and moral development

Freud claimed that boys take on their father's feelings about right and wrong through the process of identification as a part of an attempt to resolve their Oedipal conflict. there is no evidence for any Oedipus Complex it is probable that children do take on aspects of their parents', and other important people's, personality.

Jean Piaget's cognitive view of moral development

Jean Piaget was a Swiss biologist who devoted his long life to studying cognitive development in children. He thought that both the kinds of thing that children think about and the ways in which they can think about them, change as they gain more experiences of the world. Here is a summary. (For a fuller discussion of Piaget's theory of cognitive development, see Chapter 6.)

Age and stage	Mental activity	Major concerns
0-2 sensory motor	Pre-conceptual (i.e. before the child can think). Actions influence mental representations of them.	What any action can do for the child's mental activity.
2-7 pre-operational	Thought concerns one main feature of objects which can be brought near enough to be explored by direct manipulation.	Thinking is egocentric and dominated by the child's own experiences. The child cannot understand other people's experiences. (continued overleaf)

7-12 concrete operational	Several properties of an object as long as the object is near enough to be manipulated directly.	Learns to think about objects and events from different points of view.
12+ formal	Wider issues requiring several points to be held in mind at the same time.	Learns to apply logical and consistent reasoning to a variety of issues.

Operational means applying sensible principles in a logical sequence in order to reach a rational conclusion.

Operational thought is an important idea in Piaget's theory. Below the age of seven Piaget described children's thinking as pre-operational, i.e. illogical (at least according to adult rules of logic!).

▶▶▶ *Activity*
Ask a child whether a ton of lead is heavier than a ton of feathers.

Piaget and children's attitudes to rules.

Piaget became interested in children's responses to moral issues quite early in his long career. He published his book *The Moral Judgements of the Child* in 1932. He had investigated children's responses to moral issues in several ways. He told them stories which involved some issue which could be interpreted in different ways. He played games with children – such as marbles, which had rules that everyone knew – and asked them where the rules come from, and what would happen if they tried to change them. Generally, pre-operational children are egocentric. They believe that rules are imposed by some superior authority which must not be disobeyed. Children in the concrete-operations stage are more willing to invent new rules and discuss whether or not existing rules can be changed.

Age	Attitude to rules
2–3	No understanding of rules. Play was random and unstructured.
4–5	Some imitation of other children, but claimed blind obedience to the rules, while breaking some of them.
6–7	Beginning to realize that it is possible to get away with breaking some rules since punishment does not always follow automatically.
7+	Children who can de-centre begin to negotiate the rules.

Piaget found that children in the early pre-operational stage had no understanding of rules at all. They played with the marbles in any way they wanted to at the time. By four or five years of age they were starting to imitate each other's games, although their thinking was still egocentric. When they were taught some of the rules of marbles they followed them obediently, as though the rules were laws which must not be broken and cannot be changed. When asked what would happen if someone did break the rules the children replied that that person would be punished quite severely. Even though they said this, some of the children were quite content to break the rules to suit themselves anyway.

By the time they reach the concrete-operations stage (from about age seven onwards), children still insist that the rules must be obeyed, although not quite so unthinkingly as they had before. Children who can decentre are more willing to accept that the rules of the game are there for the benefit of the players, and that rules can be changed, as long as the change is seen to be fair to everyone.

Exercise on egocentrism and decentring

1 What did Piaget mean by egocentrism?
2 What did he mean by decentring?
3 Name two games, other than marbles, that young children play.
4 How does either of these games reflect that children's thinking is egocentric?
5 Name two games that operational children (over the age of seven) play.
6 How does either of these games show that the players are able to decentre?

Comment on Piaget's investigations of attitudes towards rules

Piaget talks about rules as if they were a single, fixed thing. However, there are different kinds of rules. Some are more important to children than others. If an adult gives a direct command, then it must be obeyed. Children who know that they must not hit other children should know that they have behaved badly if they then do hit another child. They should expect to be punished for breaking this moral rule. This knowledge is learned by quite young children if their parents are strict about not hitting others. There are also social rules about what you can and can't do. If an adult hasn't directly commanded a child not to do something, then doing it isn't nearly so bad as if the child has been made to understand that it is wrong but does it anyway. Children are much less likely to obey social rules than Piaget imagined.

Piaget and children's attitudes to telling the truth

In order to find out what children of various ages thought about telling the truth, cheating, stealing, and similar bad behaviour, Piaget developed the **story-telling technique**. For instance, he would tell children two stories. One story concerned a child who told a big lie, although no one could possibly believe it. The other concerned a child who told a lie that could have been true, and which could have had unfortunate results. This technique investigates whether children are aware of the consequences of an action.

So, for instance, in one story a little boy says that his dog is as big as a horse, and the postman won't come to their house because he knows he

▷
The problem with the story-telling technique is that you have to assume that the child understands the story, and what children say in response to a story probably bears little resemblance to what they actually think.

will be eaten alive. This is a silly lie that no one would take seriously. Saying that a dog is as big as a horse was seen as quite a big lie.

In another story a little boy tells his father that their dog has just run off down the street. He waits until his father is ready to go out and search for the animal before admitting that it hasn't really run off at all, but has been taken for a walk by his mother. In this story there is a deliberate lie. The father may have become concerned about the dog and spent some time getting ready to go and find it. He could have wasted more time searching. This lie could have been true, it could be thought of as quite a small lie.

The pre-operational children judged how wicked the lie was by how big a lie it was, not by the possible seriousness of the consequences. They said that the child in the first story was more wicked than the child in the second story because what he said was obviously a big lie, while the child in the second story told a small lie.

Here's another example showing how pre-operational children can't take consequences into account. This story concerns behaviour rather than speaking. A little boy is called to come downstairs for his meal. He rushes downstairs and flies into the dining room, as he always does. He doesn't realize that there is a tray holding fifteen cups and saucers on a chair behind the door. The tray is knocked off and all the crockery breaks.

In a second story another child climbs onto the furniture to reach some food, despite having been told not to by his mother. In reaching for the food he breaks a cup and saucer.

▷
Piaget is arguing that children differentiate between a big lie and a small lie. Can you think of any other explanation for their answers?

Exercise on pre-operational reasoning

1 Which would you say was the naughtier child?
2 Why?
3 Which child would a pre-operational thinker say was the naughtier?
4 On what do pre-operational children base their judgements about right and wrong?

Pre-operational children can't take intentions into account either. In the first of two more stories a little boy stole a loaf of bread from a shop to give to his friend who was very poor and was starving. In a second story a little boy fancied a cake so stole one from a shop.

In the first story the dishonest act was committed for a good reason. In the second it was committed for a selfish reason. However, a loaf of bread is larger than one cake, and pre-operational children judge by appearances. Being egocentric they can't understand intentions either. Many claimed the child in the first story was more wicked than the child in the second story.

Piaget claimed that children from around the age of seven are acquiring operational thought. They are becoming able to take other things, such as consequences, motives, and intentions into account when making moral judgements. They can see that deliberate lying is worse than exaggeration or accident.

Comment on Piaget's story-telling technique

Piaget told children stories and asked for their responses. He did not find out whether the children really understood the point of the stories. If all they understood was that one child broke fifteen cups and another broke one cup, then it isn't surprising that they thought that the first child was more wicked than the second. They don't need to be able to tell the difference between a big lie and a small lie in order to say that one child is naughtier than another. Perhaps they thought that telling a lot of people that their dog was as big as a horse is worse than telling one person that it has run away. Recent research has shown that even 3-year-olds can take someone's intentions into account when making judgements, if the intentions are explained to them.

Piaget's two stages in the development of moral reasoning

Piaget suggested two stages in the development of moral reasoning. The first is the stage of **heteronomous morality**, (or the stage of **moral realism**). The stage of heteronomous morality reflects pre-operational and concrete-operational thinking. Children accept that all rules are made by some authority figure. Breaking the rules will lead to immediate and severe punishment. They think that rules cannot be changed, and have always been the same as they are now. Heteronomous children believe that all behaviour will be judged by its consequences, regardless of the intentions or reasons for that behaviour. Between seven and ten years of age, children start to learn that rules can be changed by agreement, or by trial and error. Children begin to realize that if they behave in ways that appear to be wrong, but have good intentions, they are not necessarily going to be punished. A child who can decentre can take other intentions and circumstances into account when making moral judgements.

As children gain more experience they should acquire the rules of logic. Piaget calls this formal-operational thought. Children's thinking changes to become more philosophical. They talk about what should happen, and what shouldn't be allowed. They realize that there are often many sides to an argument and things aren't always quite as clear and simple as they seem. When judging their own and other people's behaviour they may take several factors into account. Children should be becoming able to control their own reasoning and behaviour. Piaget calls this the stage of **autonomous morality** (or **moral independence**).

Piaget's methods and the theories he developed are still regarded as a revolutionary step forward in our understanding of how children think. Many researchers have repeated Piaget's studies and attempted to refine and improve his methods. They have shown that children's moral reasoning does change as they grow up, and distinct stages of development may well exist. However, Piaget's methods have been criticized for being rather overcomplicated and difficult for children to understand. If children give consistent answers to questions perhaps they are not saying what they really know, but rather they might not understand the questions.

▷
Heteronomous means from the outside. Rules are made from outside the child and the child cannot change them and must obey them.

▷
Decentring refers to being able to think about one particular position or point of view from different positions and points of view.

▷
Autonomous means controlled from within.

Comment on Piaget's theory of moral development

Children's moral thinking does appear to change as they gain more experience.	The methods used for studying these changes are rather subjective and based on interpretation.
Piaget links distinct stages of moral thinking to changes in thinking in other areas too.	The general theory has been criticized for being too pessimistic about children's mental abilities.
The idea of rules are important to children and Piaget links this to cognitive development.	There are different kinds of rules and children's responses to them varies.
The stage of cognitive development and children's abilities to make moral judgements are linked.	Other research finds that much younger children have the skills if the task is explained to them.

Exercise on Piaget's view of moral reasoning

1 Outline Piaget's explanation of how pre-operational children view rules.
2 Outline Piaget's explanation of how operational children view rules.
3 What does Piaget mean by heteronomous morality?
4 What does Piaget mean by autonomous morality?
5 At what age does the change from heteronomous to autonomous morality generally occur, according to Piaget?
6 Why does it occur at this stage?
7 Write a paragraph to outline how parents and teachers should help children develop their moral reasoning.

Summary of Piaget's view of moral development

Piaget identified the stage of heteronomous morality where moral reasoning was largely absent from the child's thinking. Instead children believe that rules are imposed from outside and are not negotiable. As they become able to decentre, children realize that rules can be negotiated and punishment doesn't automatically follow some behaviour. This is autonomous thinking.

Kohlberg's cognitive theory of moral development

During the 1950s and 1960s an American social psychologist named **Lawrence Kohlberg** set out to improve on, and extend, Piaget's ideas. Kohlberg was interested in the development of pro-social reasoning. He developed Piaget's story-telling technique, but used it in a rather different way from Piaget. He told people stories involving **moral dilemmas**. In each story he presented a choice to be considered, for example between the rights of some authority and the needs of some deserving individual who is being unfairly treated. Piaget used stories to investigate the ways in

▷
A dilemma is a problem which has two or more possible solutions, neither of which is totally satisfactory. Kohlberg uses dilemma stories to investigate pro-social reasoning.

which children reason; Kohlberg is after the explanations and justifications for that reasoning.

One of the best known of Kohlberg's stories concerns a man called Heinz who lived somewhere in Europe. His wife was dying from a particular type of cancer. A new radium treatment had been discovered by a local chemist and the husband tried desperately to buy some, but the chemist was charging ten times the money it cost to make the drug and this was much more than the husband could afford. Heinz could only raise half the money. He explained that his wife was dying and asked if he could have the drug for the money he could raise or pay the rest of the money later. The chemist refused, saying that he had discovered the drug, and was going to make money from it. The husband was desperate to save his wife, so later that night he broke into the chemist's and stole the drug.

Kohlberg asked a series of questions such as:

- Should the husband have stolen the drug?
- Why
- What should happen to him?
- Would it have been different if the woman had been a very important person?
- Should the chemist have refused to sell the drug?
- Should the police arrest the chemist for murder if the woman died?

▷ This is a dilemma story because it is possible to judge Heinz's behaviour at a number of levels. By asking questions, Kohlberg was able to discover how people use their reasoning.

By studying the answers from people of different ages to these questions, Kohlberg hoped to discover the ways in which moral reasoning changed as people grew.

Kohlberg's analysis found some differences in children's pro-social reasoning compared to Piaget's theory. First, Piaget claimed that young, pre-operational children believe that rules are made by some authority figure who must be respected and obeyed. Some of Kohlberg's younger children said that theft is always wrong, and that the husband should be punished severely. They said this not because they respected the authority, but rather because they feared the punishment.

Second, Piaget said that moral reasoning was just about complete by the time children achieve autonomous morality, soon after puberty. Kohlberg found that it continued to change right into adulthood. The reasoning behind their responses continued to adapt as they gained more experience of the world.

▷ Asking people to respond to stories isn't necessarily going to reveal how they reason in real-life situations. However, there are very few ways in which children's moral development can be investigated.

Activity
Tell some people this story and ask them to answer the questions here. Make a note of their answers and compare them with other people's answers.

Kohlberg told several dilemma stories and asked many such questions to discover how people reasoned such moral issues. Starting in 1964 he published several scientific papers outlining his findings. Kohlberg identified about thirty aspects of moral thought which develop through three distinct levels of moral reasoning. People can only pass through these levels in the order listed. Each new stage replaces the reasoning typical of the earlier stage. Not everyone achieves all the stages.

Kohlberg's levels of moral development

Level One – The level of pre-conventional morality. Moral reasoning hasn't started yet. Children believe that their responses are imposed from outside themselves. Whether the answers to Heinz's situation favoured what he did or not, they were justified on the grounds of their consequences. (They would say, for example, that he took only a small amount of the drug, or that stealing is always wrong.) Their ideas about right and wrong are specifically bound up with concern for their own well being, avoiding physical pain or seeking physical pleasure.

> *Stage One* – Younger children are only concerned with the results of people's behaviour and do not take their motives into account. Their own main concern is avoiding the pain of physical punishment. They have no real understanding of pro- and anti-social behaviour.
>
> *Stage Two* – Older children make judgements according to what gives them, or their favourite people, pleasure. Behaving pro-socially is good if they think they will gain some physical benefit from it in the future. The child is beginning to recognize the intentions which lie behind an act although its seriousness is still mostly judged by its consequences.

Level Two – The level of conventional morality. The concern here is more to do with psychological rewards, such as winning approval from adults, peers and other social groups. There is also some concern with maintaining social order. If social order isn't maintained their own psychological security might be threatened. (They said things to do with Heinz's behaviour being justified if it was what others would approve of, or the law simply must not be broken if we are to live in a civilized society.)

> *Stage Three* – Young teenagers are keen to win approval from others so their judgements take into account what they think will make them popular. They want the psychological approval of being a good boy or good girl. They are able to take intentions into account in their reasoning of social and anti-social behaviour.
>
> *Stage Four* – Many rules exist which govern how people can live together. These benefit most people so must not be disobeyed. It's not so much because they fear punishment but rather that they want to preserve the psychological benefits of social stability.

Level Three – The level of post conventional morality. Decisions about what is right and wrong are becoming entirely personal. Others may agree, but that is less important than knowing that one is right. Not everyone reaches this high moral stage. Answers here go beyond the law and refer to what each person thought was acceptable weighed by what would be in society's interests.

> *Stage Five* – The interests of the wider community are becoming recognized, and sometimes may have to be put before the interests of

▷
Conventional means a way of doing something or thinking about some thing that most people in a particular group would find acceptable.

the individual. Ideas about justice and fairness, democracy and what should happen are more usual. People in this stage believe that injustice should be challenged.

Stage Six – Anyone who reaches this stage will have a wide experience of social life and will have thought deeply about it. They have developed a set of personal, ethical guidelines and a clear and strong conscience. Reasoning about pro- and anti-social behaviour comes from their own perceptions of the situation.

Exercise on story-telling

1 What is a moral dilemma?

2 How did Kohlberg's stories differ from Piaget's?

3 Why may the story-telling method not reveal what the subjects really think?

4 Summarize the conclusions of Kohlberg's research on moral development.

Comment on Kohlberg's theory

1 Kohlberg has claimed that he told people stories including moral dilemma and asked them what ought to happen to some of the characters in the story. However, whatever they say is not actually going to happen because the story and its characters are invented. If asked about real situations, people's answers might well be different. So are these answers really showing us how people actually reason? Kohlberg thinks so, and anyway it wouldn't be possible to make them face real dilemmas for all sorts of legal, moral, practical and ethical reasons. Telling them stories may be the next best thing.

2 If Kohlberg is right then the stories must have been interesting enough to keep the people involved, and detailed enough to provide sufficient information so that the point of the story is clear. At the same time they must have been told in words that the children could easily understand. A final problem for this technique is that the sample had to be able to express their ideas clearly when answering the questions in order for Kohlberg to assess how they think. The first sample tested were aged between 10 and 16. Their language should have been sufficient for them to express their ideas.

3 Kohlberg's sample comprised only males. **Carol Gilligan** has argued that neither he nor Piaget have any idea about how girls reach moral decisions. She says that whilst males use some idea of right and law and order as the basis for their decisions about moral issues, females are more likely to use ideas about kindness and care. Neither style is better than the other, they are different.

4 The dilemma stories have been translated and used in several countries, and support for the levels and stages that Kohlberg identified has been found. Some societies, such as those ruled by powerful dictators or dominated by a strict religion, have fixed rules about right and wrong, good and bad, and people would be actively discouraged from thinking about moral issues for themselves. The model Kohlberg suggests may be useful to understanding moral reasoning in some societies more than others. It might also be that the stories are more appropriate to some societies than others.

5 If changes in moral reasoning are not genetically fixed, but result from socialization there may be differences between the sexes in any one society, since boys and girls are often socialized to have different expectations. In his early research Kohlberg asked boys aged 10, 13, and 16 to respond to his dilemma stories.

6 Further research into moral reasoning, including some by Kohlberg himself, has not supported the idea of stage six amongst people generally. It may not be a stage of development of moral reasoning open to everyone, but a special stage of reasoning only used by certain great thinkers.

7 Kohlberg's theory explains moral reasoning. It doesn't explain why people actually behave as they do when faced with real situations. We often say things that we wouldn't actually do.

8 Children will behave in certain ways, imitating important models, under certain conditions. Reinforcement and modelling are strong influences as we shall see shortly. This doesn't mean that children's moral reasoning does not pass through identifiable stages however, as younger children's statements and behaviour do not always match!

Exercise on Kohlberg's model

1 What is a moral dilemma?
2 Outline Kohlberg's three levels of moral reasoning.
3 Discuss some of the criticisms that have been levelled against Kohlberg's theory of moral development.
4 Evaluate one method used to study children's moral development.
5 What is meant by a stage theory of moral development?

Evaluation of Kohlberg's view of moral development

Kohlberg refined Piaget's views, offering three levels of moral reasoning, each containing two stages. Moral thinking develops to reflect the individual's state of cognitive development. Kohlberg accepts that not all people will pass through all of the stages. This implies that more 'intelligent' people are more moral. This is highly doubtful. The theory is based on interpretations of answers to questions about stories which would only make sense in some countries and not others. Gilligan has argued that Kohlberg's model is of limited use as, at best, it describes only the development of males' moral reasoning. Females use different rules.

Behaviourist explanation of moral development

▷
Although behaviourism takes many different forms, they are all part of the explanation for learning. Some critics say that Skinner's theories are more to do with teaching than learning.

▷
Pro-social behaviour means behaving in ways that support, help, comfort or generally show care towards others.

▷
The major categories of reinforcers are primary (essential to survival e.g. food) and secondary (things associated with primary ones e.g. money), positive (beneficial in some way e.g. access to good company) and negative (avoiding or escaping from something unpleasant, for example, staying out of prison by paying one's taxes).

▷
Skinner and other behaviourists have conducted many experiments on animals to investigate the principles or laws of learning. Humans have far superior mental (cognitive) skills and do not need constant reinforcement. Knowledge of their own results is often enough.

Freud was concerned with the development of children's moral feelings, especially how they feel about themselves. He claimed that children are driven by unconscious urges which must be fulfilled if personality disorders are to be avoided. Piaget and Kohlberg are interested in how children apply their own rules to making moral judgements. This is to do with the cognitive processes involved in reasoning. Behaviourists emphasize the role of the parents and other adults who train their children's behaviour. Parents may encourage their children to give different responses depending on the circumstances. Two possible responses are to behave in **pro-social** or **anti-social** ways.

From Chapter 1 you may recall that behaviourists such as B.F. Skinner claim that all behaviour is a result of **reinforcement.** A reinforcer is anything which increases the chances that certain behaviour will occur again. Reinforcers may be pleasant to most people, for example, praise or encouragement. Or they may be beneficial only to a small group of people, such as a promised visit to a railway yard, which would only be potentially reinforcing to railway enthusiasts. Or they may be individually and personally reinforcing. Knowing that I will be able to play a favourite song on the guitar almost perfectly might be all the reinforcement I need to keep me practising for hours.

Parents and teachers use reinforcement to teach particular behaviour to children. We must be careful to avoid the term 'good behaviour', as what I think is good you may not. Instead we can talk about desired and undesired behaviour. The first thing is to decide exactly what behaviour we want to encourage in our children (and in others). For example, we may want our six-year-old daughter, Cara, to be actively involved in whatever she is doing. Every time she is actively involved, skipping rather than just watching others skip, or swimming rather than sitting on the side of the pool, she will be praised and encouraged. Eventually she should join in without needing to be reinforced with praise by us. Simply knowing that she is doing something that she knows we would approve of should be sufficient reinforcement.

Reinforcement is claimed to explain learning moral behaviour in the same way as it attempts to explain all other forms of learning. If a child is in a situation (what Skinner calls an **antecedent**) then it will **behave** in one way or another. Three **consequences** may occur. The child may be reinforced (either positively or negatively), and this would encourage the child to behave in the same way again. Or the child may be punished, in which case it is less likely to repeat that behaviour in a similar antecedent in the future. Or nothing might happen. Perhaps no one except the child knows what it did. If the child experienced something that encouraged it to behave in a similar way in a similar antecedent, then it was reinforced. If it does not, then it wasn't reinforced.

Antecedents	Any situation in which some behaviour could occur	About to have your first driving lesson
Behaviour	Something that you do	Drive the car
Consequences	The state you are in after the behaviour	Feel good, excited, pleased

According to behaviourists, any act that those in authority approve of should be reinforced, while any act of which they disapprove should be ignored. However, this simply does not happen very much in our everyday lives. During an ordinary day you behave mostly in ways that other people would approve of. Yet how many times are you reinforced during that day? Much of our behaviour goes unnoticed by other people anyway and many of those who do observe us are not in a position to reinforce us. When we do something that authority figures would approve of they still do not necessarily reinforce us. They would expect us to behave in this way so they think we should not need reinforcing.

 Activity
Think of the last time you were actually reinforced for doing something good. Now think of the time before that. How long was the gap between them? How frequently are you reinforced? Compare your answer to those of other people.

Behaviourists say that reinforcement with adolescents and adults needn't come from the outside, simply knowing that you have achieved whatever you set out to achieve is its own reinforcement. Yet how often are you aware of such feelings of achievement when you do 'good things'? Do you feel good about getting washed and dressed in the morning, catching the bus, arriving at work or class on time, doing your job well enough, etc.? Or do you feel good about behaving in ways which are more obviously approved of morally, such as giving money to charity, taking part in a fund-raising activity for Children in Need, or running errands for an elderly person who needs a bit of help? If we are not aware of reinforcing ourselves by feeling good about ourselves, then are we really reinforcing ourselves? In other words, can we be reinforced without realizing it?

 Activity
Consider the last sentence in this paragraph for a moment. 'Can we be reinforced without realizing it?' Is your answer 'yes', 'no', or 'it depends' (or something else)? If you are studying with others, have a debate with someone who disagrees with you. See if you can see their point of view. Maybe you could take a vote.

Behaviourists claim that you must have been reinforced in the past to continue behaving in the way you do. This leads to the conclusion that a reinforcer is anything that leads to a repetition of some behaviour, and any behaviour that is repeated must have been reinforced. So, the definition of a reinforcer is something that reinforces! This isn't a very satisfactory definition at all. It's rather like saying that a perfectly good definition of the word wysiwyg is anything that wysiwygs. Are you much wiser now?

There is no doubt that we learn many things more enthusiastically because we are being reinforced. However, we learn or just come to know many other things without intending to, or for fun, or for no reason that we can think of. Some experiences simply become stored in our brain, so you could say you'd learned them without any need for reinforcement at all.

If reinforcement helps us to learn desired behaviour, will punishment deter people from behaving undesirably (and therefore decrease levels of undesirable behaviour)? Behaviourists say that punishment does not show people what to do, only what not to do. At best, punishment might discourage a few people from behaving in an undesired manner. But, in any case, they claim that if undesired behaviour goes unreinforced it is likely to **extinguish** by itself.

If a response (some behaviour) has been extinguished it will not appear in that context (antecedent) again. It has been learned that the response no longer produces the response that it used to.

Exercise on punishment

1 Define reinforcement.
2 What is the difference between primary and secondary reinforcement?
3 What is the difference between positive and negative reinforcement? (Look it up if you can't remember.)
4 What is punishment?
5 Why do behaviourists generally reject the use of punishment?
6 What is extinction?
7 How does extinction come about?

 Activity
Make a note of some of the things that you have been punished for and answer the following questions. What exactly did you do? Did you deserve the punishment you received? Was the punishment a fair punishment for that behaviour? Did it stop you behaving in that way again?

Behaviourists claim that punishment doesn't work in promoting desired behaviour, as it can only teach someone what not to do. Most parents and many psychologists disagree with Skinner and the behaviourists' view of punishment. As Piaget and others have shown, children are naturally curious. They need to discover what they can do with people and objects around them. Explaining to a two-year-old boy that he must not throw food around will not stop him, as he knows that he can throw food around. The next stage might be to ask the child not to throw his food. If this doesn't work a parent might threaten a smack. The curious child needs to know how far he can go with his parent. The parent might deliver the threat and smack the child. The child may have learned a valuable lesson, depending on how severe the smack was and how it was given. Good advice here would be that if the parent felt it necessary to punish the child, then the punishment should be delivered in sorrow, never in anger.

Reinforcement	Punishment
Leads to an increase in some behaviour.	Decreases the chances of the behaviour recurring in that situation.
Positive reinforcement contributes to a feeling of well being and a positive self-image.	Contributes to feeling miserable and a lowered self-image.
Provides a structure for repeating certain behaviour.	Provides discipline that children need in order to limit their undesired behaviour.

Activity

Think about the phrase 'punish in sorrow, never in anger'. Exactly what might it mean? Put it into your own words and give an example of its use.

If we are to use punishment, when is the most effective time to use it? The ideal time is just before the child performs the undesirable act. The explanation for this is that the child is about to do something which he or she knows adults would disapprove of and might deliver punishment for. The child will feel anxious. If the punishment is then delivered, then the child learns to associate the unpleasantness of the punishment with the anxiety of behaving badly. Also, the child will not have experienced any pleasure or reinforcement in association with performing the undesired act. Clearly, however, the problem is how can you deliver the punishment before the wicked act has been committed?

Summary of behaviourist claims so far

Behaviourists say that children learn their moral behaviour in the same way as they learn anything else, by a process of reinforcement. Any number of studies of child-rearing styles have shown how children who are reinforced for behaving in caring and generous ways are more likely to behave in those ways again (as we shall see in the next chapter). If children are reinforced for behaving in an anti-social way, they are probably more likely to behave in that way again too. The idea of reinforcement is useful, but must not be taken too far. Deriving principles of learning from studying animals – which Skinner and others did – is useful, but the conclusions are not directly applicable to humans since we are far more highly cognitively developed than other animals.

Bandura's social-learning theory

In Chapter 1 we said that **Albert Bandura** and other social-learning theorists have reinterpreted Freud's concept of identification in behaviourist terms. Freud thought that children try to be as much like their same-sex parents as they can in order to overcome the emotional contradictions of the Oedipus Complex. Bandura agrees that children do observe and imitate certain role models, although he doesn't accept the need for references to sexual motives.

Human beings know more than any other animal species. We have some abilities with language and communication, maths, art and literature, science and technology, interpersonal relationships (friendships, etc.) and self-awareness. No other animal has any of these skills. As we aren't born with them, we must have acquired them in other ways. Childhood is the time during which much of this acquisition occurs. Anything which can make this process easier or more efficient would be beneficial. Observing and imitating others who know things and have skills that we do not have is a useful short cut to learning for ourselves. Bandura calls this **observational learning.** The main processes in social learning are observation and imitation. These two processes then lead to the modelling of behaviour.

Children learn much of their behaviour from those important people they see around them. The first important people are usually parents, with teachers and other adults following later. First, they see what the parent does under certain circumstances. This is observational learning. Second, they copy that behaviour, (often under circumstances where it may not be appropriate!). This is **imitation.** Eventually they learn when certain behaviour is appropriate and when it is not. They are not only learning appropriate behaviour, but also the thoughts that go with it. This is **identification.**

Perhaps the best-known laboratory-based research on observational learning was conducted by Bandura in the 1960s. Bandura concentrated on aggressive behaviour, but modelling pro-social behaviour would follow much the same principles. (See the discussion of the Bobo doll experiments in chapter one.)

▷
Human children have a great deal to learn. Humans spend a larger percentage of their life in an immature state than any other animal. During this time they must learn enough to allow them to make their way in the world.

▷
Observational learning is learning through watching someone else perform. It does not require reinforcement or behaviour-shaping in any way. Identification means taking on the ideas, attitudes, beliefs, etc. of important models.

Comment on social-learning theory

When there is so much to learn for oneself, learning by watching someone else achieve is much more efficient than learning by trial and error, or waiting for some reinforcement which may never arrive.

Many skills could probably never be learned without observing and imitating. Learning to speak one's language, or to play a musical instrument, or to learn many sports, probably could not be achieved without observational learning.

Exercise on theories of moral development

1 What does Freud mean by the Oedipus Complex?
2 What is identification?
3 What is social learning?
4 What is observational learning?
5 Do all forms of learning require the use of reinforcers?
6 You have been asked to advise some new parents on how they could help their child develop a strong sense of morality. Write three pieces of advice that you would give.
7 Tick the appropriate box for each of the following theories.

	Development occurs in stages	Development is continuous
Freudian psychoanalysis		
Piaget's cognitive theory		
Kohlberg's cognitive theory		
Skinner's behaviourist theory		
Bandura's social-learning theory		

●●● Summary of social-learning theory on moral development

Watching others behave can be a very useful shortcut to having to learn everything for oneself. Observational learning is most effective if there is some reward or benefit at the end.

Exercise on theories of moral development

How would each theory of moral development (a) explain and (b) deal with the following issues:

1 stealing a small sum of money
2 cheating in the end of year exam
3 sexual activity
4 trying to begin a relationship with a best friend's boyfriend/girlfriend.

Peers and moral development.

So far we have talked about the influences that adults have on children's moral development. Adults are particularly influential with younger children. Freud was the first to show the importance of the parents' role in helping children to develop appropriate emotional responses. By identifying with their parents they acquire an understanding of what is right and wrong, and a conscience that punishes them when they behave badly. Piaget shows that understanding the relationship between things only comes about through direct experience and parents and teachers are ideally placed to provide such experiences. Some of the experiences should encourage decision-making and some of the decisions involve learning what parents see as right from wrong or good from bad. Skinner's explanation also emphasizes the role of adults as providers of reinforcement for children. Reinforcing pro-social behaviour should increase pro-social behaviour in children. Bandura insists that adults are models from whom children learn by observing and imitating. If the models behave pro-socially, then children should model pro-social behaviour.

As children begin school the attitudes of their peers become increasingly important. Peers are people who share the same status as us (i.e. they have about as much power as we do), and whom we mix with quite often. Peers have similar attitudes, beliefs, and behaviour to ours and often share the same hopes and aims too. Peers can play a number of roles during childhood which can influence children's moral development. For two- to four-year-olds, peers can be people to imitate. Although cooperation is rare, they learn by watching each other. If one child is paired with another who has always been encouraged to behave pro-socially then the observer is more likely to behave pro-socially too.

As children mix more at school, after the age of five or so, they learn to cooperate (as they learn to decentre). Now peers can become important role models to children. Being a member of a group of friends is very important to some children and they may go to almost any lengths to stay in the gang. If the gang's activities include pro-social behaviour, then children will be encouraged to behave pro-socially.

During junior-school years, children often become very keen to conform to what others expect of them. Kohlberg identifies this as the second stage of pre conventional morality when children need adult approval. This is also true if the leaders of the gang are older and more competent than the children in the gang. Younger children are often used to running errands, fetching and carrying, and they will generally act in an inferior way in childhood gangs. They probably feel a need to be recognized by their peers. Being an inferior member is better than not being a member at all. Conforming to the group's norms and values would encourage **group solidarity.** If the norms of the group include behaving pro-socially, then children will learn that pro-social behaviour is desirable.

As children pass through puberty, hormone balances within their bodies begin to change. The results of this are both physical and psychological. Before puberty, children's main concerns were with being appreciated by members of the same sex as themselves, as well as by parents and other adults. After puberty most young people want to be appreciated by someone they are attracted to. There are probably many women who have received unexpected help from a young man whose motives weren't so much pro-social as attempting to impress!

Peers are an important source of stimulation for children and adolescents (and adults). Although their capacity to encourage pro-social

▷ Pro-social behaviour includes any behaviour that helps someone else. Giving a stranger directions is pro-social. Doing a sponsored walk for charity is pro-social. Anything which is helpful to society generally or someone in particular is pro-social.

▷ Group solidarity is a feeling which members of a group share that they have bonds with other group members. They belong to a group to which they express loyalty. Conforming to its norms and values strengthens their feelings of solidarity, and makes sure that other members recognize that they are a loyal member.

behaviour is great, the sad fact is that far more of them seek thrills, have adventures, become excited by challenging authority and make sure that no one tells Mum or Dad. The behaviour that is often modelled is more likely to be pleasure-seeking than pleasure-giving. Peer groups can be a powerful source of pro-social influence, but aren't so very often! Organized attempts to foster pro-social behaviour such as the Cubs and Brownies, Scouts and Guides, various Church-based organizations and other groups have been successful, but only a minority of children are involved.

●●● Summary of peers and moral development

From around three years of age, children start to have some influence on each other's behaviour, including their behaviour that adults would define as right and wrong. Peers are most influential throughout the school years, and much of children's moral development can be seen as their need to be accepted and to maintain solidarity with their peers.

Conclusion

Moral development is the result of a complex set of factors. The first are the parents attitudes to right and wrong, and how they intend to rear their child. Their use of discipline and the models they present to their children are important. Children identify with parents and other powerful adults. Later their peers become important both as models and as providers of reinforcement or punishment. We will explore pro- and anti-social behaviour further in the next chapter.

Pro- and anti-social behaviour

In the last chapter we discussed the factors in people's immediate environment that influenced their moral development. These include their parents and other important models, their peers, and themselves. In this chapter we will discuss some other aspects of morality, especially pro- and anti-social behaviour, including the development of emotional reactions to other people, the wider social factors influencing the chances of us helping others in need or distress, and the norms and values that are involved in pro- and anti-social behaviour.

Activity
A possible project could start with writing a definition of pro-social behaviour or anti-social behaviour. You could decide some examples of the behaviour that you have defined in an age range, e.g. five- and six-year-olds, and produce a 'tick chart'. Then observe some children of that age for ten minutes each and record the number of instances of the behaviour that you see.

▷
In one of Kohlberg's dilemma stories investigating moral development a husband broke into a chemist's and stole a life-saving drug. Would you say that his behaviour was anti-social, pro-social, or something else? Sometimes it's not so much the behaviour that is right or wrong, but the circumstances under which it occurs.

We ought to begin by defining our terms. Pro-social behaviour is anything that someone does which has a beneficial effect for someone else. It could be that just one other person benefits, such as when you stop to give directions to a stranger. Or several people might benefit, for instance when you give some people a lift in your car or help some children cross a road. A whole group might benefit, as when you donate money to a charity. Society generally might benefit, perhaps when you pick up some litter or recycle your bottles in the bottle bank. Of course, you may well benefit yourself if, for example, other people come to think more highly of you, praise you, or reward you in some way. Anti-social behaviour is the opposite. It is any behaviour that causes disruption, or harm, to another individual or group. Aggression and stealing are obvious examples of anti-social behaviour.

Most people would probably prefer others to behave pro-socially. Most parents would want their children to cooperate with them and with others, to share and help, to have some understanding of the needs of others. Such feelings are called empathy.

The development of empathy

> Skinner and Bandura were concerned with learning. Piaget and Kohlberg were more interested in the ways in which we acquire and store knowledge generally. They have shown that the ways in which children think and reason changes as they acquire more experience of the world.

As we have said many times before, humans have evolved highly complex cognitive skills. Without deliberately trying, we have learned all sorts of things, and seem to know even more. Obviously we are not all the same, and don't all know the same things. We have learned much of our behaviour from observing and imitating, identifying with, and being reinforced by important models. Albert Bandura, B.F. Skinner, and others have identified the main features in the process of learning. Much of our knowledge of pro- and anti-social behaviour has been learned in these ways too. Piaget has suggested that some time around puberty a shift occurs in the way we think about pro- and anti-social behaviour. Until this point, children imagine that rules governing their behaviour are largely imposed from outside them, by parents and other adults. After puberty we begin to be able to reason for ourselves. The changeover can occur because we have developed empathy.

 Activity

Produce a table with the following headings:

Theorist	Theory called	How do children acquire their moral sense	Comment
Freud			
Skinner			
Bandura			
Piaget			
Kohlberg			

So what is empathy? Empathy is generally the awareness and the understanding that many people have of the feelings and needs of others. If you see that a friend of yours has been crying, you may be sympathetic towards him or her. You may want to offer comfort and see if there's anything that you can do to help. If you were empathic, you might appear to share your friend's feelings. You may have a genuine idea of what your friend is going through. Something similar may have happened to you. It can be so easy to say 'I know how you feel' when you have no real idea at all. If you are successfully empathizing, then you are effectively experiencing the same feelings that your friend is having, and you may be identifying with your friend. Identification is the final stage of empathizing.

> Identification is the process of discovering some of the qualities of another person (or group of people) and absorbing as many of them as possible.

Activity

Find out what the phrase 'a penny's worth of help is worth a pound's worth of sympathy' means? Put it into your own words.

Exercise on empathy

1 What is pro-social behaviour?
2 Give three examples of pro-social behaviour.
3 What is anti-social behaviour?
4 Give three examples of anti-social behaviour.
5 Complete this sentence: 'Empathy is the ...'.

Since the 1960s, **Martin Hoffman** has made several observations of children from less than one year of age through to late childhood, and has noted their reactions to other people's behaviour. The extent to which children will show empathic feelings depends on several factors, such as their age, their state of **maturation**, their previous experiences, the way their parents respond towards them, and, most importantly, their level of cognitive development. Hoffman identified four stages in the acquisition of empathy.

▷ Maturation refers to the ways in which physical, biological structures develop.

Global empathy.

As we said earlier, empathy is showing awareness and understanding of other people's feelings. In order to do this an individual must be able to experience the feelings. Young babies (below one year) have not experienced a vast range of emotions. Most will have experiences of happiness and sadness, possibly anger and, ideally, security (through attachment bonding). Most, however, are not likely to have much awareness of guilt, shame, jealousy, resentment, etc. They do sometimes appear to show empathy towards others who seem to display signs of having emotions of which the child is aware. This usually means copying the behaviour that they see around them. They show distress when someone else is crying, or laugh when someone else is laughing. At this age they haven't really learned that they are separate individuals, distinct from others, so their empathy isn't very much more than copying. If a large group of babies are together, when one starts crying, many others soon join in!

▷ Global means 'of the whole world' so very young babies empathize with everyone around them and their empathy takes the form of copying.

Egocentric empathy

Between twelve months and two years children also develop egocentric empathy. They realize that it is someone else who is in distress but, as they are egocentric, they assume that everyone must feel as they do. They behave in ways that they might hope others would behave towards them. Hoffman reports an observation of a thirteen-month-old girl who offers her favourite doll, from whom she had appeared inseparable, to an adult who was obviously unhappy.

▷ Egocentric means an inability to see things from anyone else's point of view, or take account of anyone else's feelings or perceptions.

Empathy for another

Between two to three years of age, children begin to experience a wider range of emotions, and develop the language with which to describe them. They can show some sympathy and understanding for a wider range of other people's feelings. They can be angry or frightened when they see someone else being hurt (such as a child being given a painful injection by a doctor). They may be quiet and feel guilty when someone else has been punished for doing something that was wrong. They can understand what you mean when you ask them to leave you alone.

Empathy for another's life condition

By seven or eight years of age, children can think of people belonging to large classes or categories. Before this age their thinking of people in groups is restricted to their family group, or the families of others whom they know well. Or they can think about their particular play group, although they can't think in terms of all families or all play groups. As they have difficulty decentring, they are unlikely to think in terms of larger groups of individuals, each with their own ideas and views. Later on in childhood they are able to understand that people can be categorized into such specific groups as the people who work with mummy, the children in the other classes at school, the other people on the bus. They take longer to understand undefined groups such as the unemployed, the poor, all those children without a daddy, the homeless, children spending Christmas in hospital, etc. They can have empathy with whole categories of people whose life condition makes them worse off than they are. Children of this age are often involved in charitable efforts to help those worse off than they are.

▷
Decentring is the ability to see things from other people's point of view and not just to concentrate on what they perceive.

Exercise on the development of empathy

1 Name three ways in which children acquire some of their knowledge about pro- and anti-social behaviour.

2 Briefly outline what happens at puberty in humans.

3 What does Hoffman mean by global empathy? Give an example of global empathy.

4 What can children who can decentre do that egocentric children can't?

5 What does Hoffman mean by egocentric empathy?

6 At what age do children show empathy for another person?

7 Give an example of empathy for someone else.

8 Give an example of
(a) people in a specified group, and
(b) people in an unspecified group, other than ones found in the text.

9 Why are children of eight or nine able to show empathy for other people's life condition according to Piaget?

●●● **Summary of the development of empathy**
Empathy is generally the awareness and the understanding that many people have of the feelings and needs of others. Hoffman identified global empathy, egocentric empathy, and empathy for another's life condition. Some people are more empathic than others, or at least more willing to show their sympathy and understanding.

Socialization, social norms, and pro-social behaviour

▷
Socialization is the name of those processes through which we acquire many of the things we need to know in order to fit in with, and become a useful member of, our society. Some of these things are the social norms of our society.

As any society develops, its people adopt certain standards of behaviour. These standards are learned through the **socialization** process. Let's clear up a few common misconceptions about socialization which are as much to do with what it is not as with what it is. Socialization is not simply the process by which children learn the appropriate norms and values of their society. It doesn't finish with childhood. We continue to learn new things about our society until we die, especially as society is constantly changing. Neither is it something that people 'out there' (such as parents and teachers) do to us. People are active in their own socialization. You had a hand in socializing your parents and teachers too! After all, who taught your parents how to be parents? Finally, people socialize themselves. Almost daily we realize something new, we make a new connection that we hadn't quite made before, we see things in a different way from the way we had imagined them previously.

Socialization lasts for?	life	not just childhood
Who socialized you?	adults and others	myself
Whom did you socialize?	adults and others	myself

As more people adopt the same standards of behaviour, these standards become **social norms**. They are what people generally think of as acceptable and unacceptable behaviour. As public opinion changes, so the norms will change.

Here are some examples of changing social norms:

To own black slaves – making them work for long hours in appalling conditions – was a social norm in some southern states of America 150 years ago. The norm continued until enough white people opposed it and slavery was finally abolished in 1865.

In medieval Britain, people displaying symptoms of what we now think of as mental illness were thought to be possessed by evil spirits. Some were called witches. Belief in spiritual possession was a social norm. All kinds of awful things happened to the unfortunate victims. (Hanging for witches, for instance, was abolished in England in 1736.)

The usual treatments for the insane until well into the last century included chaining them up for the rest of their lives, whipping them, making them vomit, making them bleed, and giving them powerful laxatives. These treatments were accepted by most members of the medical profession to be the best things to do to release the symptoms. They represented the norms of medical treatment for such conditions. We would regard them as cruel and barbaric today (even though some doctors still give patients suffering from severe depression electric shocks as a medical treatment!).

Corporal punishment in schools was an acceptable social norm in Britain until the European Community made it illegal in the late 1980s.

The standards of behaviour that the majority of the people in any society accepts at any one time are called social norms. Some social norms in British society are said to be fairness, decency, justice, democracy, integrity, and truthfulness.

Activity
Define the term social norms, then find a couple of examples of them that are relevant to you. Compare your choice to someone else's and discuss why they are relevant.

Different societies develop different social norms, or similar social norms to different extents. The members of one society may be generally more competitive than the members of another. Members of American society seem to regard competition between individuals and groups as more important than people in Britain used to. However, not all Americans are more competitive than all British people, nor are any of them necessarily always competitive.

Some social norms are written into the law. We may not kill people we do not like, or hurt people just because they are weaker than us. We must not take things that do not belong to us or try to overthrow the government by force. We are supposed to respect our parents and our system of democracy, and we mustn't tell lies. There are social norms for what type of speech, dress and behaviour are appropriate in different situations. Social norms provide each member of society with a clear set of understandings about what they should and should not do under just about all circumstances. However, it would be wrong to think that all members of any society, or of any of the groups within it, conform equally to all of the social norms of that society or group.

Exercise on social norms and pro-social behaviour

1 What are social norms?
2 Give two examples of social norms that children acquire.
3 What is socialization?
4 Who do you think is mainly responsible for socialization?
5 How are social norms changed?
6 Can you think of a social norm that you would change if you could?

A society whose members share, cooperate, and generally behave pro-socially is more likely to thrive than one whose members are constantly in conflict. Social anthropologists such as **Margaret Mead** have studied societies whose members cooperate more than others. Mead studied three native Indian societies on New Guinea in the Pacific Ocean (to the north of Eastern Australia). She found the **Arapesh Indians** to be calm, gentle, unaggressive, responsive to other people's needs and cooperative. They lived in peace and harmony. In contrast, both men and women of the **Mundugumor** Indians were 'aggressive, harsh, and violent'. They were suspicious and jealous and spent hours plotting aggression and revenge against others. Of the two societies, the Arapesh are more pro-social and the people appeared to have been more content. The Arapesh had developed social norms for pro-social behaviour. The Mundugumor appeared not to have! (Do note that some of Mead's studies have been heavily criticized.)

If we want to encourage pro-social behaviour in society we would do well to start with the children, although changing the behaviour of the existing generation is necessary too. We must identify the main social norms which are involved in pro-social behaviour and teach them to our children. This should increase their effectiveness. At the same time we must identify those social norms that discourage pro-social behaviour (or encourage anti-social behaviour) and decrease their effectiveness.

There are several things that society must do. One is to make sure that the laws discourage anti-social behaviour. This is much more difficult than you'd imagine. Simply catching more criminals and sending them to prison for longer may seem to be an effective deterrent to potential criminals, at the same time curing those who were punished. Unfortunately neither short, sharp shocks nor long prison sentences appear to work.

An alternative is to try to make the socialization process as effective as possible so that desirable pro-social characteristics are passed on to the children. The family, the media, and the school are the main agencies of socialization who could be involved here.

Socialization and the family

Children have more opportunity to be socialized if they are in the company of responsible adults for as much of their time as possible. As parents are the first people to have experience of their children, and vice versa, and because children can form attachment bonds with their parents, so parents are in an ideal position to socialize their children. If parents aren't able to stay with the child all the time, then arrangements for others to care for the children will need to be made. Psychologists have shown that providing 'quality time', giving children a sense of belonging and security, encouraging them to be independent and to take responsibility for their actions, to experience and explore, to be active and curious, to think and reason, to be involved and committed are all positive contributions to successful socialization.

▷
Social norms for pro-social behaviour have developed more amongst members of some societies than others.

▷
Whether members of a society should want to change their social norms isn't a matter for psychologists at all really. It is a matter for politicians, philosophers, journalists, and others who inform people. Then it is up to public opinion to urge change. Psychologists suggest how it might be done, it isn't up to them to say whether it should happen.

▷
Despite several government initiatives to get tough on crime, each year it appears that we in Britain send more people to prison. A significant minority have apparently learned anti-social norms.

▷
Children learn a great deal from observing other people. If children are told to do one thing by people who do not do it themselves, this will not improve their learning. The moral is: be consistent.

Socialization and the school

Schools could teach pro-social behaviour through programmes of moral education. Children can learn by observing teachers and others behaving cooperatively, by being encouraged to help and share, and being rewarded for helping and caring. **Urie Bronfenbrenner** has made a detailed study of the Communist Russian education system and shown how it encourages children to share their toys and cooperate with others. They are given toys that require cooperation, such as jigsaws, construction kits or role-play toys. Older children help younger ones. Competition was between groups, not individuals, and any prizes were shared between members of the group.

Socialization and the media

See Chapter 5 for a discussion on the relationship between aggression and the media. There is no doubt that exposing children to a diet of aggression and violence on television will provide them with attractive role models for their possible aggressive behaviour. Whether children actually do see excessive amounts of violence on British television is disputed by **Guy Cumberbach** and others. Seeing attractive pro-social behaviour in the media is as likely to encourage pro-social behaviour. The evidence either way is largely correlational so we can't be sure that observing any kind of role-model causes us to behave in similar ways.

Activity
List your favourite characters from books, TV, film, etc. Mark each out of ten for how much pro-social and anti-social behaviour they generally use.

▷
Pro-social behaviour is encouraged if we feel that the effort we make is of value or benefit. If we feel – or are made to feel – that our efforts are useless or a waste of time, we are less likely to want to make them again.

In order to help both children and adults develop social norms of pro-social behaviour, several other features of the socialization process can be identified. First, people need to feel that they are valued. Children who feel valued develop a sense of **self-esteem** and become more confident to ask their questions and state their ideas. This is equally true of adults. If you feel that your ideas are valuable, that you won't be ignored or poked fun at when you speak, you are more likely to contribute. If your contribution is judged useful you will feel encouraged to make another contribution. If your early attempts to be caring and helpful are successful you will feel positive about making further attempts.

Exercise on socialization

1 Name some of the things that parents could do to help their children to learn pro-social behaviour.
2 Draw a diagram to show who socializes whom. It should include 'parents', 'children', 'teachers', and 'others'
3 What is self-esteem?
4 Where does it come from?

Another feature is **equality**. People, especially children, like to be treated fairly. Do you mind losing if your opponent is simply better than you are, or had a bit more luck than you did? How would you feel if you discovered your opponent cheated in order to win? If people treat us fairly we are more likely to treat others fairly. This is the principle of equality. If I feel that I'm an equal member of a group which is not obviously exploiting me, then I am more likely to help its other members if I can.

In Chapter 3 we discussed exchange theory as one possible explanation for why people make relationships with others. The idea is that we try to obtain as much from our relationships as we can, while avoiding putting more into our relationship than our partner. Another possibility is the notion of **equity**. This says that we don't keep a balance sheet of every time we do something for someone else and every time they do something for us. Even in your closest relationships, such as within a marriage or partnership, you don't expect that every time you make an effort in the relationship, that your partner will make an equal effort. It is far more a question of how fairly, on balance, you each feel the relationship is. On the whole, do you put as much in as your partner, even though you may contribute in different ways? Do you take on more responsibility or make more effort at one time so that others can be free to develop in other ways? You must feel sure that they would make the same effort for you.

We should avoid manipulating and exploiting people for our own ends. If I tell a friend that he or she must behave pro-socially and help me, and every time I benefit and my friend loses out, then understandably my friend will soon start to be suspicious of pro-social behaviour. We should encourage **reciprocity**. This is the idea that we only get out of life what we put into it. Helping someone now will be repaid with help when we need it at some later date.

We mentioned the principle of **reciprocity** when we talked about interpersonal relationships, especially interpersonal attraction. Simply put reciprocity is the idea that if I find that you like me, I am much more likely to like you. After all you must have excellent taste! If you do something for me, I will do something for you. This is a mutual exchange. In 1970 **D.T. Regan** had two confederates try to sell raffle tickets to students. One confederate bought his students a soft drink (Coca Cola) first. He sold far more tickets than the other. Since someone had behaved favourably towards the students they felt more inclined to reciprocate. (Bribery is one form of reciprocal relationship!)

▷ Clearly children are not equals in family life. They lack the experience of power which their parents have. Well-adjusted children will learn to take on the responsibilities of decision making as they are given more decisions to make.

▷ To describe things, such as the contributions that people make to their relationships, as equal, implies that they could be measured in some way. If they can't be measured, how can I describe them as equal? Equity is the feeling of fairness. It doesn't need to be measured.

Exercise on equality and reciprocity

1 What do you have in common with your peers?
2 What was the last thing that you did with a bunch of your friends? Was there any reciprocity here?
3 How would having a positive self-esteem encourage people to behave pro-socially?
4 What's the difference between exchange theory and equity theory?
5 How does equity contribute to pro-social behaviour?

Activity

Show how the principles of reciprocity and equality are important in children's games by constructing and completing a table like this.

Game	Equality	Reciprocity
Skipping		
Cowboys and Indians		

Well-adjusted people in most societies are expected to develop a sense of **social responsibility** to maintain the existing social order. This has several dimensions. Here are four of them.

Knowledge

First, you have some knowledge of your society and the organizations within it. So you know about what school is, what the police force is for, what dentist services provide. You know something about family groups, school groups, work groups, leisure groups, etc.

Appreciation

Second, you appreciate the contributions these organizations make to society. What would it be like without a police force or a health service? Or water companies to provide clean drinking water or electricity companies to provide power?

Feelings

Having some understanding of society and its organizations means that you will develop some feelings about them or about some of the people who do these jobs. So nurses may become angels and doctors saviours.

Behaviour

You know what is appropriate behaviour towards these **social institutions**. You know what to do when you're with your family or with other people's families, when you're in hospital or helping the police, when you're in college or claiming unemployment benefit. You should behave in ways that help maintain the organizations that are a part of your way of life. If you do, then you are showing a sense of social responsibility.

Even if your own particular experiences have been unfortunate, on the whole you may feel that the organizations are good. They maintain social stability. They are necessary for our way of life. They are worth preserving, supporting, helping, even improving if possible.

▷
A social institution is an organization of people. It has some functions or purposes. It may be voluntary, such as the family, or legally required such as school. What are the functions of

(a)   the family,
(b)   the health services,
(c)   school?

Exercise on social institutions

1 What is a social institution?
2 Why are they worth preserving?
3 If someone steals school or hospital property, who is the real loser?
4 Why?
5 If you see someone behaving suspiciously or committing a crime in a hospital how might you react if you were to behave pro-socially?

●●●   **Summary of social norms and pro-social behaviour**
Social norms are accepted standards of behaviour which the majority of members of any society are said to hold. Some societies have developed norms of pro-social behaviour. Their people are likely to be helpful and hospitable. Other societies have not. Their people are more likely to be reserved and distant and even unwelcoming. School, the media, and role models are all important in passing on pro-social images to children.

What is altruistic behaviour?

▷
Defining some behaviour as altruistic can be rather misleading. It is possible to behave in ways that appear to be putting someone else's interests above our own, without necessarily doing any such thing.

We defined pro-social behaviour as helping others. As the ability to empathize develops, so children learn the benefits of behaving in a pro-social way. Altruism is a particular form of pro-social behaviour. One simple definition of altruism is any action that helps someone else to achieve something, to be happy, to benefit in some way and at some cost to ourselves. According to this definition, when we put our friends' interests or needs above our own we are behaving altruistically. If you gave up your lunch-break to comfort your friend you were behaving altruistically. Most people would think that altruism is a desirable human characteristic. Most parents would probably try to encourage it in their children. We will return to this shortly.

Of course, as humans, we have all kinds of motives for what we do. We usually know what we are doing, and we do things for all kinds of reasons. For example, giving some money to charity may well be altruistic behaviour. However, if you were with someone whom you were keen to impress, and you gave generously, would you really be behaving altruistically? The effect of your behaviour is that someone else benefits at some cost to you. According to the simple definition of altruism given above this would qualify as altruism, as someone else had benefited at some cost to you. However, you know that your intention wasn't altruistic at all. It was quite selfish: you wanted to impress someone. So another definition of altruism might be behaviour which is intended to help someone else, and from which the actor gains no benefit. According to this definition of altruism, then, we need to know something of the motives of the altruist in order to decide whether the behaviour is truly altruistic.

Even with this definition, we still can't be certain that some behaviour is truly altruistic in humans. If I give money to charity when I am not with

▷

There is some difficulty in defining altruistic behaviour in humans. As we have cognition and know the effects our behaviour has on others, we may sometimes do something charitable in order to create a good impression. Is this altruism?

anyone, there's no one to be impressed by my generosity, then I appear to be behaving altruistically. However, I might be rewarding myself by feeling very noble or virtuous. I feel good about myself. I must be a terrific person to give so generously. So am I being altruistic or selfish? What if I have recently done something awful? I found a purse containing twenty pounds, and although I know I should have handed it in, I spent the money on some new shoes. Now I feel dreadful about it. I don't know who the purse belonged to so I can't make it up to them. I can give twenty pounds to charity though, and this is what I do. I hope my guilty conscience will go away. Is this donation an act of altruism?

Even though defining behaviour as altruism is slightly tricky, acts of altruism and heroism are, surprisingly, not rare at all. Strangely we may do little to help ourselves if we are in trouble, but we would often try to help a stranger. This seems to be quite contradictory. Surely most people would be expected to put their own needs above other people's needs? After car, train, and plane crashes, ordinary people who had never thought of themselves as brave, help others, even though there is a good chance that they themselves will be injured by doing so. When an American passenger plane crashed into the icy waters of the Potomac river in January 1982, ordinary people went into the frozen water to help. One passenger gave the harness that had been lowered from a rescue helicopter to four other people who were immediately winched to safety. He died in the freezing river. Why didn't he save himself?

Exercise on altruistic behaviour

1 How is altruism different from pro-social behaviour generally?
2 Name one way in which someone might behave seemingly altruistically.
3 Name one way in which a parent might encourage altruism in a child.

Activity
Conduct a survey to discover the extent of altruism by asking your friends if they can tell you whether they have behaved in any altruistic ways during the last week. Make sure that you explain to them what altruism is. (The first two sentences in the summary here should do.)

Summary of altruistic behaviour
Altruistic behaviour involves doing something that helps someone else more than it helps you. It might even cost you a great deal. The problem for psychologists is that we can never be completely certain about whether someone is behaving altruistically or not.

Psychological studies of altruism

Social psychologists began to be interested in whether people would help others in difficulty about thirty years ago. Helping someone whom you see needs some help is called **bystander intervention** because you intervene on someone else's behalf. This is pro-social behaviour. Simply looking on without doing anything to help is called **bystander apathy**. During the 1960s in America there had been several news reports of people who had been attacked while others simply looked on and made no attempt to help.

An example of bystander apathy

On March 14th 1964, in Queens (a borough of New York), a 28-year-old manager of a bar was returning home at 3.20am. She was Catherine Genovase, whom everyone knew as Kitty. Having parked her car, she walked the remaining 30 metres to her apartment block in a pleasant, tree-lined, middle-class avenue. As she walked, she was grabbed by a man, and she screamed. Lights went on in a ten-storey apartment block, and people looked out to see what was happening. She screamed, 'Oh my God, he stabbed me, please help me.' One man shouted, 'Let that girl alone.' The attacker walked off, but returned moments later to continue the attack as Kitty tried to drag herself to her apartment block. She was stabbed again. More lights went on. A bus passed. The attacker hid, but returned a third time and finally stabbed her to death. In all, the attack had lasted 35 minutes. Thirty-seven people later admitted to having seen at least some of the attack. No one reported it to the police.

These inspired the first researchers to investigate bystander apathy, or bystander intervention. They were **Bibb Latané** and **John Darley**. Some of the major factors that have been identified so far can be represented in the series of questions shown below. Answering no at any stage will cause you to proceed no further and, therefore, not lead you to behave altruistically. To answer yes to all the questions shows you may well act altruistically.

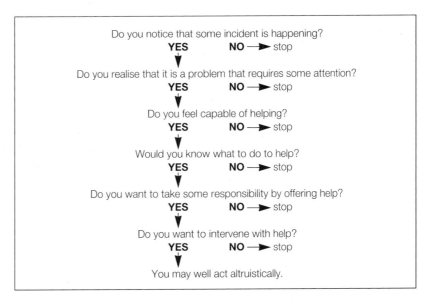

Do you notice that some incident is happening?
YES   NO ⟶ stop

Do you realise that it is a problem that requires some attention?
YES   NO ⟶ stop

Do you feel capable of helping?
YES   NO ⟶ stop

Would you know what to do to help?
YES   NO ⟶ stop

Do you want to take some responsibility by offering help?
YES   NO ⟶ stop

Do you want to intervene with help?
YES   NO ⟶ stop

You may well act altruistically.

A decision tree

Have you observed an incident?

In many social situations there are a number of things going on at the same time. The more people there are involved, such as in a football crowd, the less likely we are to notice an incident that may spark off some trouble. Or we may be a long way from it. If we cannot see or hear a commotion then we are not able to decide whether the incident is any kind of emergency. We may be busy with our own concerns. In an airport or train station we may be more preoccupied with organizing our luggage or the details of our journey than in noticing everything else that is going on. Some people are simply more observant than others, but if we haven't noticed anything happening then we can't respond to it in any way.

Have you defined it as an emergency?

Even if we are aware that something odd is occurring we may not define it as an emergency. Bibb Latané and John Darley have conducted some ingenious experiments in which they have created conditions that could be defined as an emergency. In one experiment, for instance, there were three experimental conditions. In each condition subjects were asked to sit in a room and complete some questionnaires. Shortly after they began some artificial smoke blew into the room in gusts through the heating vents. In the first condition, subjects were tested on their own. Three-quarters of them went to find help within a few minutes of noticing the smoke. Clearly they had no difficulty in defining the situation as an emergency and were able to act. In the second condition there were two subjects. One or both of them reported it in half the experiments. The other half sat there filling in the forms, possibly hoping that the other might do something.

In the final condition there were three people in total. One was the real subject, the two others were helping Latané and Darley. The real subjects are described as naive, as they do not know what is going on. The helpers, who pose as real subjects, are called **confederates**. The confederates had been instructed to ignore the smoke and keep on filling in the questionnaires. When it completely filled the room so that they couldn't see their papers they were to fan it away from their eyes. Ten naive subjects were tested in this condition. Only one tried to report it.

This experiment suggests two things. First, people are more likely to interpret a situation as an emergency and act accordingly if they are on their own. Where there were two naive subjects the emergency was only defined in half the **trials**. Where there were three it dropped to 10%. Second, there is a question of self-confidence. If other people do not appear to define as an emergency a situation in which they are just as likely to be involved, then can that situation really be an emergency?

Latané and Darley's early experiments have been criticized. **Russell Clark** and **Larry Word** say that they were not really testing people's responses to an emergency at all. As people in the room filling with smoke could see two others who were calmly sitting there filling in their forms, the situation couldn't have been defined as that desperate a situation. In

> Naive participants are unaware that they are involved in psychological experiments. They do not know that the others are confederates who are actually assisting the experimenter by behaving in some particular way.

> A trial is a single run through of an experimental procedure. Each time a subject (or group of subjects) is tested under a particular experimental condition is called a trial.

the early 1970s, Clark and Word tested their idea that people's involvement is far more to do with how obvious the emergency is and how dangerous it is for someone to become involved.

They tested both ideas in a series of experiments. They had an actor playing the part of an electrician who appeared to receive an electric shock from a faulty control box, and fall from his ladder. There were three experimental conditions. First, he was in full view of some subjects. He called for help before passing out. They called this the **unambiguous condition**. Unambiguous means that it was clearly and obviously an emergency. Second, he fell behind a counter, but was still heard asking for help. This was the **moderately ambiguous** condition. Although it seemed likely to be serious the subjects couldn't be certain that it was a real emergency. Third, he fell behind the counter, but although people could hear him fall, he made no sound afterwards, so he may or may not have been seriously hurt. This was the **ambiguous condition**. Onlookers wouldn't know whether there was an emergency situation.

Clark and Word tested the danger element by having the electrician in the unambiguous situation fall onto a live wire while still holding the faulty control box. He may have had the live electric current running through his body, and anyone who touched him could also have received a jolt! This was the **high-danger condition**. Alternatively, he dropped the control box and fell some distance from the live wire so wouldn't have posed any danger. This was the **low-danger** condition.

Here is a summary of Clark and Word's findings. Where there is little risk to ourselves, we are more likely to offer help. We will still offer help where the danger is higher, as long as the situation is clearly an emergency. The less obvious the emergency appears, the fewer people will offer help if it involves risk to themselves.

| | Number of subjects who assisted | |
	Low danger	High danger
Unambiguous	100%	over 90%
Moderately ambiguous	over 50%	less than 50%
Highly ambiguous	50% if in pairs	Very few if alone

Exercise on defining the emergency

1 How do Latané and Darley explain the results of their smoke experiment?
2 How do Clark and Word explain it?
3 What two factors do Clark and Word think are most important in explaining the chances of bystander intervention?
4 Does the table of their results support Clark and Word's claim for the two factors outlined in the previous question?
5 Explain your last answer.

How do you see the victim?

There are two main factors in how we see the victim which affect people's likelihood of intervening and offering help. First, does the victim appear to deserve help? Is the victim young, old, weak, or inexperienced? Has he or she had an unfortunate accident? If so, we are more likely to help. Or is the victim partly responsible for the situation? Second, if the victim is someone who has certain characteristics in common with us, such as similar style of dress and a similar cultural background, then we are more likely to feel that person is 'one of us', and we are more likely to offer help.

Irving Piliavin and his colleagues conducted some interesting field experiments during the late 1960s and early 1970s. The experiments generally involved students falling over in subway trains in New York. In one experiment the students dressed up as infirm or disabled people, using a walking stick. They were helped by other passengers on 90 per cent of the trials. When they wore a jacket that smelled of alcohol, and were carrying a bottle in a brown paper bag when they fell over, they were only helped on 20 per cent of the occasions. In the first experimental condition they were seen to deserve help. In the second they are seen as at least partly responsible for their own misfortune. Another possibility here, though, is Clark and Word's idea that perceived danger is a factor. If, as a bystander, you think the drunk might hit you or be sick on you or something equally unpleasant, then you may not want to help.

In Chapter 3 we said that psychologists have found that physical attraction is an important factor in how people respond to each other. In Berscheid and Walster's computer-dance experiments the male students seemed to rate appearance as the most important factor in choosing a girl to date. Piliavin tested the effects that appearance had on levels of helping. In another experiment the students were made up to appear to have an ugly birthmark covering half their face. The offers of help fell from 90 per cent to 61 per cent.

Our perception of our commitment to the victim is also important. If you knew that someone was attacking a close friend or a member of your family, you would be more likely to stop them if you could. We feel a commitment to friends and family. There are many areas of our lives where we are encouraged to feel commitment. Children are usually encouraged to feel that they belong to their house at school, their school generally, their clubs, their neighbourhood, etc. Later, we may feel loyal to our football club, our social groups, our workplace, our Trade Union, our society. Many people find comfort in feeling that they can identify with others.

A commitment may be very strong, such as to close friends and family members, or quite weak, such as to people we hardly know. Yet even what seems to be the weakest commitment can still make the difference between helping and not helping. In an experiment by **Robert Moriarty**, people were asked to keep an eye on someone else's belongings for a few minutes while they were away. A confederate of the experimenter then attempted to steal the possessions. The majority of those who had agreed to look out for

These are field experiments. The subjects who are being tested are the subway passengers. Their natural habitat was the subway. The effect that their perception of the victim would have was being measured by the likelihood of their offering help.

It seems a sad finding that people's looks, over which they have little control, is such an important factor in levels of pro-social helping. Yet it provides further evidence that looks are important in interpersonal perception.

If you agreed to keep an eye on someone's belongings, and someone else tried to steal them, would you be likely to intervene in some way? What might it depend on? What would you do?

the other person's belongings did intervene directly, or went to find help. When people had not been asked, few of them attempted to stop the thief.

Does anyone else have any responsibility?

If you cause an accident, for example if you knock a couple of tins of baked beans off a supermarket shelf, you are (hopefully) more likely to pick them up and put them back than anyone else. It is clearly your responsibility. You know that you knocked them down. If someone else is reaching past you, and it could just as easily have been them that caused the tins to fall, you may well still pick them up, but you might expect that the other person should at least offer. The responsibility for the accident is shared between you. If someone in front of you knocks them off, but doesn't pick them up, you may pick them up if you are a true altruist (or a friend of the shop owner!). People are more likely to intervene when they feel they are directly responsible. Where the responsibility is shared between lots of people the chances of any one of them acting are usually rather less. This is called **diffusion of responsibility**.

In the late 1960s Latané and Darley conducted an experiment to investigate diffusion of responsibility. They thought that if you believe that you are the only person who could help another, then you would. If, as one of several people who are all equal, you are made aware of some emergency, then the chances of you helping are rather less. You – like the others – would feel that the others should be partly responsible for acting too.

Fifty-two students agreed to take part in research into how difficult they found college life. To avoid any embarrassment, they would sit in separate rooms and talk by intercom. In one of the experimental conditions, each naive participant was told that there would be him and one other student. In a second condition, each naive believed there were two others. In the third, each believed there would be six people in the group. They were told that the other subjects were seated in nearby rooms.

Each person had two minutes to describe their problems. When each had spoken they would discuss what had been said. In fact it wouldn't go that far because the other students's voices were actually tape recordings! What would actually happen was that one naive would hear one or more taped reports, believing them to be other students. The voice on one of the tapes began by saying that his problem was that he had epileptic seizures when he felt stressed. Within a few moments he began to have one. The question Latané and Darley were interested in was how many of the naives in each experimental condition would go to look for the person having the fit, and how quickly they would respond.

The results appear in the following table:

▷
Diffusion means spreading something widely (or thinly). It's the opposite of concentration. Is money diffused throughout your family, or concentrated in some member's hands rather than others?

Experimental condition (size of group)	No of trials	% quick response	% eventual response
1 naive + victim	13	85	100
2 naive + 1 other + victim	26	62	85
3 naive + 4 others + victim	13	31	62

▷
In this experiment the subjects (tape recordings) had to be kept separate from naives, so that they may not have immediately defined the situation as an emergency. Also, they may not have known what to do in such an emergency and so didn't intervene to avoid getting in the way.

▷
Even though many naives in intervention experiments do not become involved, many do still care about what is happening.

The number of other people who could also respond is the important thing here. When subjects thought there was just them and the victim (experimental condition 1) they all went to help. When they believed there were four others (experimental condition 3) only 62 per cent went to help. The presence of the others seemed to be a major factor in determining whether any one of them defined a situation as an emergency. After all, if it really was an emergency, then surely one or more of the other four people would be rushing about trying to find out what the problem was and helping to sort it out?

There are other differences between this experiment and the first one Latané and Darley conducted. For example, in the first experiment the subject was also the potential victim. If the smoke situation had turned out to be more serious they would have been at risk. So the naive's behaviour would have helped himself or herself as well as the others. In the second experiment naives were tested to see if they would help a stranger (whom they had never met).

Exercise on intervening

1   Summarize the conclusions of Piliavin's field experiments in your own words.
2   What is meant by commitment to the victim?
3   What effect does shared responsibility have on pro-social behaviour?
4   What are confederate participants?
5   Why do social psychologists employ confederate participants?
6   Some of the things that the psychologists did involved deceiving, misleading, or tricking ordinary people in some way. Make a list of these features in Piliavin's research. Do you think that this reseach is acceptable?

What are the costs of helping?

Before deciding whether or not to intervene many people may briefly estimate the costs of intervening compared to the benefits. The costs include wasting time if the situation is not a real emergency, or even if it is and I can't help, I'm going to feel embarrassment if I fail. Or the danger may even be physical. If I don't help I might feel guilty and ashamed, and others might blame me for not trying to help.

Earlier we referred to exchange theory (see also Chapter 3), and said that any relationship involves costs. You have to make an effort. Costs can be in time, effort, and money. Ideally, a cost to yourself will also have its rewards. You enjoy the company of a friend. He cooks you good meals or you have a laugh when you go out with him. If the rewards you receive are greater than the costs involved, then you are in profit and are more likely to want the relationship to continue. If you are making a loss, because the costs are greater than the benefits, then you may want to end the relationship. Something similar may occur in helping someone to decide whether to behave pro-socially or not. If the rewards of behaving pro-socially are

▷
Low-cost altruists are people who will behave altruistically for as long as the costs to him or her are not high. Giving directions to a stranger, holding the door open for someone, letting someone go in front of you in a queue, lifting a bag for someone, helping someone to cross a road, are all examples of low-cost altruism.

greater than the costs involved, then someone is more likely to behave that way. Research generally finds that people are low-cost altruists.

Latané and Darley had psychology students ask 1500 New Yorkers various questions to test whether they were low-cost altruists. For example, some were asked for a dime (a few pence) without giving any reason for wanting the money. A third of the citizens gave the money straight away. When the students explained to other subjects that their wallets had been stolen and they needed the money to make a phone call the response rate went up to 72 per cent.

Another cost of helping might be that you have to become more involved and this could take your time. Piliavin increased the potential seriousness of the subway-helpers experiment. The student who would fall over had a capsule of red dye in his mouth. When he fell he bit the capsule and the fake blood would trickle down his chin. Clearly this becomes a serious situation. The victim is in trouble and needs help. The problem is that if you help you are making a commitment to look after the victim. You may need to call the guard, or give a statement, or even accompany the victim to the hospital. The offers of help fell from 90 per cent to 60 per cent (i.e. someone offered help on 60 per cent of the trials), although others looked around to find someone else who might be more useful in a medical emergency. If the emergency involves blood, people might be less inclined to help, because of increased awareness of AIDS.

Exercise on bystander intervention

1 Outline the principles of social-exchange theory.
2 How does social-exchange theory differ from equity theory?
3 What are low-cost altruists?

Summary of factors affecting intervention
Psychologists have studied bystander apathy and bystander intervention and identified several factors that influence the chances of someone's behaving in one way or another. These factors include whether some behaviour was observed in the first place, whether it is defined as an emergency, how great would be the costs in helping, and whether the observers believed that they were in a position to help.

Activity
List these main factors which are involved in the chances of someone's behaving altruistically and see if any of the factors apply to the last times you behaved altruistically.

Is altruistic behaviour instinctive or learned?

▷

It may be that there are genetic impulses within us to behave pro-socially. They would contribute to our well-being and so to our survival. Pro-social behaviour may be observed in some animal behaviour.

If pro-social behaviour were innate then the vast majority of people would show it. They probably do. There are wide individual differences in many of the skills or abilities that we accept are largely genetic in origin. For example, some people are generally quite aggressive. Others are quite passive. Others are usually passive, but behave aggressively sometimes. See Chapter 5 for a discussion of the origins of aggression. There are probably wide individual variations in the extents to which people would help others too. This explanation stresses the **nature** side of the nature–nurture debate.

Latané and Darley conclude that the likelihood of our behaving altruistically depends less on genetically inherited instincts but rather more on three social factors. First, do we, as bystanders, define the situation which we are aware of as an emergency needing action? Second, do we think it is up to us or someone else to provide the help required? Third, if it is up to us, what are the likely consequences of our becoming involved? This stresses the **nurture** approach to an explanation. As with most of the skills and abilities we've mentioned before, whether to behave in pro- or anti-social ways probably depends on an individual's unique mix of factors. It also depends on an individual's religious faith, attitudes and values, beliefs, personality, etc.

Exercise on instinct and learning

1 What is meant by the nature–nurture debate?
2 Give an example of what you think might be altruistic behaviour in animals.
3 Is pro-social or altruistic behaviour:
   (a) instinctive,
   (b) socially learned, or
   (c) probably both?
4 How might pro-social behaviour have survival value?

Summary of the basis for altruism
People in many different societies behave in altruistic ways. This doesn't mean that there is a genetically inherited basis for altruistic behaviour, although it is reasonable to imagine that such urges would contribute to our survival. If we all help each other we're all more likely to survive.

14

Construction of social reality

Humans have inherited their abilities to perceive, think, feel, imagine, and predict as a result of hundreds of thousands of years of evolution. We also learn from our own experiences during our socialization (one of the ways in which we socialize ourselves). We find what certain people are like from how they look and sound and from what they do. Because humans usually live in groups it's important that they can make predictions about their own and other people's behaviour. If we never knew what might happen next then we would be very confused and unable to achieve much. We each build up (construct) our own ideas (theories) about what is going on in other people's minds, and what they are likely to be doing and thinking. Each of us is a conscious human being, and each of us has had a unique experience of the world, so we will each have our own ideas, views, and theories. Added together these become our perception of our **social reality**. In this chapter we will look at how we form our impressions of others, and what determines what information we have or do not have in order to make our perceptions.

Activity

Look up the words perception and evolution in a dictionary. Put them into your own words if you prefer. Now put the first two sentences of this chapter into your own words.

Exercise on social reality

1 What is socialization?
2 Why is it important that humans can make predictions about people's behaviour?
3 What is meant by social reality?

Forming overall impressions of others

Activity

Split into pairs. One of you read the following story about 'Jim' in the order presented (paragraph 1 followed by paragraph 2). The other one of you must read paragraph 2 first, followed by paragraph 1.

<u>Paragraph 1</u> 'Jim left the house to get some stationery. He walked out into the sun-filled street, with two of his friends basking in the sun as he walked. Jim entered the stationery store, which was full of people. Jim talked with an acquaintance while he tried to catch the clerk's eye. On his way out he stopped to chat with a school friend who was just coming into the store. Leaving the store he walked towards school. On his way he met the girl to whom he had been introduced the night before. They talked for a short while, and then Jim left for school.'

<u>Paragraph 2</u> 'After school Jim left the classroom alone. Leaving the school he started on his long walk home. The street was brilliantly filled with sunshine. Jim walked down the street on the shady side. Coming down the street toward him, Jim saw the pretty girl whom he had met on the previous evening. Jim crossed the street and entered a candy store. The store was crowded with students and he noticed a few familiar faces. Jim waited quietly until he caught the counterman's eye and then gave his order. Taking his drink, he sat down at a side table. When he had finished his drink he went home.' (A.S. Luchins, 1957)

1 Now write down (each of you separately) your first impression of Jim

2 Would you describe Jim as friendly?

3 Compare notes with the other person in your pair.

We will return to Jim later.

▷
If you prefer tall women, then one of the things that you will notice first about a stranger is how tall she is. If you prefer thin men to fat men, then you may notice a person's size. Having made an observation like this, we have formed an impression.

When we come into contact with someone for the first time we notice certain features of theirs. If they are speaking on the phone we note the sound of their voice. Which sex are they? How old do they sound? Do they sound sensible? Do they sound interesting? If we see them we observe their sex, how attractive they are, what they are wearing, how they stand or sit, what they are doing and how well they appear to be doing it. We interpret these things according to our previous knowledge or prejudices about that feature. This is a part of the process of interpersonal perception called **impression formation**.

The result of impression formation is that we have some idea about what someone is like, and how they compare or relate to us. We have an idea of whether we are going to like someone, or to be able to get on with or dislike someone. Even though our judgements are sometimes wrong, we still make them each time we meet someone new. These judgements are called **inferences.**

An inference is a judgement based on a limited amount of information. We go beyond the information available to us and make an educated guess (or inference). We make inferences when we imagine what someone is like based on our previous experiences or knowledge of what similar people were like. We cannot study every person we ever notice to discover what he or she is like. Luckily for us, people often become members of identifiable groups such as business people, police officers, or nurses. If we think we know what members of a group are like, and we see someone who is a member, we will assume that they are similar. These ideas are called **stereotypes**. Sometimes our ideas about what group members are really like is based on very little actual contact with them. (How many hooligans, rappers, business people, and politicians do you know personally?) You may still hold stereotyped attitudes about them.

> Stereotypes are simple, overgeneralized statements about the psychological characteristics (such as attitudes, beliefs, and behaviour) of a whole group of people. Stereotypes exist for categories of people which can be easily seen.

Exercise on stereotypes

1 Briefly describe the stereotyped attitudes that some people might have of:

vegetarians   hippies   nudists

students   teachers   the mentally ill

2 How accurate do you think any of these attitudes are?

3 Where do you think any of these stereotypes might have come from?

Quite a number of research projects have examined how and why we form impressions of others and have identified some of the main factors involved. The first area of research led to the suggestion that we have evolved the ability to form instant impressions about what other people are like. This approach is called **implicit personality theory**. We each have our own understanding of what people or things are like. Stereotypes are the result of people having rather similar theories about some people or things.

Implicit personality theory

Implicit personality theory says that people are intuitive. Intuition is a direct and unconscious way in which people simply know and understand without needing explanations. Piaget suggested that children develop this style of thinking during the pre-operational stage of cognitive development. We simply observe and know who we will and will not like, or who will be helpful and who will be a threat, etc. We take on a whole impression of a person from this first meeting.

> We rate some physical or personality characteristics as more or less likeable than others. Which person would you rather have as a friend: Mandy, who is rather forgetful and untidy, or Toby, who is well-organized, but sometimes tells lies (assuming that they are similar in all other respects)? Most people probably dislike liars because they can't be trusted.

Nearly fifty years ago **Solomon Asch** applied the principles of **Gestalt psychology** to an experimental procedure that has been successfully applied many times since. Gestalt is the German word for pattern, form, or whole. In this case it implies that we use all the information available to us to form an overall impression of what someone is like, and that some of

271

▷
Peripheral means at the edge or of secondary importance. Central means of primary importance.

▷
A trait is a fairly permanent characteristic that someone might possess, which can help explain why they usually behave in a particular way under specific circumstances.

the information will be more important than other information. For example, if you see someone who is tall and slim you might think they are sporty, that they try to keep fit, or that they are just lucky! If the first two are correct you've been able to predict something about what they are like. Knowing that someone is sporty, however, doesn't really tell you much about what kind of personality that person has. Asch would describe sportiness as a **peripheral trait**. On the other hand, if you knew that someone was warm you would be able to make many other inferences about what else they would be like and whether you would be likely to get on with them. Warm and cold are described as **central traits** that people use to evaluate others.

Activity

Imagine that you are meeting someone for the first time. Which of the following characteristics would you want to know immediately, and which are less important that you know straight away?

friendly	*treacherous*	*generous*
truthful	*manipulative*	*tall*
Welsh	*trustworthy*	*loyal*
decent	*hard working*	*reliable*

Add any more that you think are important to you.

Asch identifies two types of **personality traits**. The first are descriptive traits which simply describe what people are like. The others are evaluative traits by which we are able to decide how we feel about the people who possess them. One immediate problem here, of course, is that what you may regard as merely descriptive, I may regard as highly evaluative. For example, I would evaluate Ben highly as a hard-working student. You may regard his effort at schoolwork as a descriptive trait. At the same time I would agree that Ben would be considered extremely good-looking. To his male friends his looks are merely descriptive. We discussed the research on interpersonal attraction in Chapter 3 (e.g. the computer-dance experiments. See page 72.) which showed that levels of physical attractiveness can be highly evaluative!

According to Asch, evaluative traits are more central or important to whether we judge someone well or not than descriptive traits. To test this Asch gave a group of students a list of adjectives (called the stimulus list) which was supposed to describe an imaginary character. They are then asked to choose other words which describe people's personalities from another list of words (the response list). Altogether, Asch used five groups of subjects in his experiment. One had a list of what Asch thought were peripheral traits. This was the control group. The words on their list were:

intelligent	skilful	industrious
determined	practical	cautious

The other four groups were the experimental groups. They all had the same list as the control group, but two of them had a central trait added.

Group A had intelligent, skilful, industrious, **warm**, determined, practical, cautious.

Group B had intelligent, skilful, industrious, **cold**, determined, practical, cautious.

The other two had an extra word, but not a central trait.

Group C had intelligent, skilful, industrious, **polite**, determined, practical, cautious.

Group D had intelligent, skilful, industrious, **blunt**, determined, practical, cautious.

Asch believed that 'warm' and 'cold' were two of the more powerful evaluative traits. To be described as warm meant that the person was kind and considerate. They would be tender and caring. If someone was cold they would be distant and reserved, unfriendly, unhelpful, and uncaring. If warm and cold are important evaluative traits, then the students in Groups A and B should form quite a different impression of what the imaginary character was like. Asch asked the students to write a paragraph describing the imaginary person. He also gave all of the subjects a response list of eighteen other personality traits and asked them to choose which would also describe the imaginary character.

	Control group %	Group A (warm) %	Group B (cold) %	Group C (polite) %	Group D (blunt) %
Generous	55	91	8	56	58
Happy	71	90	34	75	65
Good natured	69	94	17	67	56
Wise	49	65	25	30	50

▷
According to Asch, warm and cold are important evaluative traits because they allow us to make clear predictions about whether we are going to like someone or not. People who are warm will help and support us and will have survival value. People who are cold would not contribute to our survival.

Asch claimed to have found evidence that warm and cold are central traits. Group A (warm) thought the imaginary person would be extremely generous, happy and good natured, and fairly wise too, compared to the control group, who had not had the 'warm' trait. Group B thought he would be the opposite. The polite and blunt groups didn't make such extreme judgements as Groups A and B. Both groups A and B described the imaginary character as reliable, good looking, persistent, serious, restrained, strong, honest, and important.

Some support for the central peripheral distinction has been found by other studies. For example, a few years after Asch's first study, **Harold Kelley** described to some American college students a guest lecturer who would be teaching them. For this, he used Asch's warm and cold lists. Half of the students were given Asch's Group A list and half were given Group B's list. They were also told that they would be asked to evaluate the lectur-

▷

Evaluation means to point out the value or contribution of something. This is a balanced process between the good points and the limitations.

er later, which they did by choosing from Asch's response list. On average, those students who had heard him described as 'warm' evaluated him more highly. Kelley also checked to see if their evaluations would also reflect their behaviour. The students had all been invited to stay behind after the lecture and ask questions. Over half of the students from the 'warm' group stayed behind to talk to him compared to less than a third of those who'd heard him described as 'cold'.

Not everyone agrees with Asch's insistence on the central–peripheral distinction. **John Wishner** gave Asch's lists of traits to his psychology students and found similar results to Asch. However, when he changed some of the descriptions he found that the 'warm–cold' effect disappeared. If someone was also described as popular and sociable then it seems likely that they would also be warm. If this is the case, there wouldn't be much point in including the term. Students evaluated this imaginary person more highly. It seems that being described as warm or cold were only central when other related terms were also included. Wishner does not believe that evaluative traits are more central than descriptive traits. There are other explanations for how we form our impressions of others.

▷

Do you make instant judgements about whether you are going to get on with someone within the first few minutes of meeting them? Or do you prefer to get to know them a little before deciding if you're going to like them or not?

In real life many of us make our judgements about what other people are like on the basis of the first things we find out about them. Within just a few minutes we can have decided what we think, long before we could know many of someone's qualities. First impressions are important. Therefore the order in which someone finds out about your attributes is important. If the first impression you give is positive, with such desirable qualities as generosity, thoughtfulness, caring, a regard for the truth, etc., then you are more likely to be liked than if other, less desirable qualities appear first, and the more desirable ones appear only later. The first impressions that we give are called the **primacy effect**. The later impressions are called the **recency effect**.

Exercise on implicit personality theory

1 What is intuition?
2 How does the idea of intuition relate to implicit personality theory?
3 Briefly explain what gestalt psychology is.
4 What are personality traits?
5 Summarize the differences between the results for Groups A and B and those for Groups C and D in Asch's central- and peripheral-traits study.
6 In your own words, outline what this study shows.

The primacy and recency effect

Solomon Asch was one of the first to investigate the primacy effect. He used a similar method as before, presenting two lists of adjectives which describe an imaginary person to his subjects, and asking them to rate the person being described. The adjectives were the same, but the order in

Industrious means hard working, impulsive means quick to react.

which they were presented differed. One group heard the person described as intelligent, industrious, impulsive, critical, stubborn, envious. The first three words are positive and good, the second three are negative and unflattering. The other group heard the descriptions the other way round: envious, stubborn, critical, impulsive, industrious, intelligent. Here the first impression is that the person is unpleasant, while the later impression is that they are rather better. People who heard the desirable qualities first evaluated the imaginary person much more highly than those who heard the unflattering descriptions first.

▶▶▶ **Activity**
Copy Asch's list onto one sheet of paper, and the reversed list on to a separate sheet. Give one sheet or the other to as many people as you can and ask them to say what they think about the person described. Will your results confirm Asch's conclusions. There is scope for some coursework here.

How did your findings from the Jim story compare with the other member of your pair?

Further research into the primacy and recency effects was conducted by **A.S. Luchins** over thirty years ago. He had two paragraphs which described an imaginary student named 'Jim'. (You may have read them at the beginning of this chapter. If not, go back to page 270 and read them now.) One paragraph described Jim as a sociable, friendly person (an extrovert). The other showed him to be a shy, solitary person (an introvert). Half of Luchins sample would hear Jim described as an extrovert first, the other half would hear Jim described as an introvert first. They were all then asked whether they thought that Jim was friendly. Over three quarters of those who read paragraph 1 first said that he was, whereas less than 20 per cent of those who read paragraph 2 first thought that he was friendly.

Would this primacy effect still appear if there was a delay between the first impression and the later impression? In one experiment Luchins asked his subjects to spend 15 minutes reading a comic after reading one paragraph and before reading the other to see if the delay made any difference to their ideas about Jim. It did. Those who had read the extrovert paragraph before the comic, and the introvert paragraph after it were more likely to describe Jim as an introvert. If they read the introvert paragraph first and the extrovert paragraph most recently they described him as an extrovert. This demonstrates the recency effect.

▶▶▶ **Activity**
There's some scope for a coursework here by repeating Luchin's experiment. You could test the existence of the primacy effect, or see if you could eliminate it by creating a delay.

Luchins explained his results by claiming that we believe that the first information that we discover about someone must be the truth. This is especially true where the first information is negative. If the first impression that your teacher had of you was that you were lazy and not very interested, then they come to believe that you really are those things.

▷

Luchins didn't really look at long term impressions, so it's not surprising that he thought that first impressions were so important! We form our impressions of people when we first meet them, and modify these impressions as our knowledge of them grows.

▷

Negative first impressions are extremely difficult to remove. This may be one reason why some groups (such as homosexuals, some cultural minorities, even women sometimes) are more likely to be treated as inferior if this is the impression that is a part of the norms, values, or traditions of any society.

Later information may contradict those earlier impressions, but it's hard to shake our belief in the truth. Your test marks and essay results may be higher than your teacher might have predicted, but the teacher is more likely to explain this as you being lucky, or having cheated in some way. So we tend to ignore later contradictory information, thinking that we know better.

Luchins thought that i f this explanation is correct then warning people against making snap judgements before giving them all the information ought to eliminate the primacy effect. It did, particularly if the warnings came between the two inconsistent pieces of information. So reading one paragraph about Jim, being warned against making their minds up, then reading the other paragraph, eliminated the primacy effect.

Most of the early research in this area has been conducted on imaginary characters or confederates doing repetitive tasks. In 1982 **Donald Pennington** reported the findings of his important experiment in the effects of primacy and recency. He asked people to play the part of jurors in an imaginary rape trial. They were all given a detailed summary of the evidence. They all read the same accounts with the same evidence, however some of them read the prosecution witnesses present their evidence that the man was guilty first. The others read the defence case that he was innocent first. When asked whether they would find him guilty or not, those who had heard the prosecution case first were much more likely to say yes.

In all the research so far the subjects did not know the people being discussed since they were strangers. The primacy effect was evident in each case. However Luchins believes that the recency effect is more likely to operate with people who we already know. If you think you know your best friend very well, and you discover something awful about them that you never knew, then this recent knowledge can alter the way you think and feel about them. This could be for the better or the worse, depending on what you discovered and when it happened.

Exercise on the primacy and recency effects

1 What is a primacy effect?
2 Describe your primacy effect when you first encountered your head teacher at school.
3 What is a recency effect?
4 Outline any differences between your primacy and recency effects of your headteacher.
5 Why is it important not to do something stupid in the first minutes of a job interview? Refer to the effects described in the text.

 Summary of impression formation
We make inferences about people from what we know about people generally and what features we know about each one we come across. We build up mental stereotypes to help us classify people, and resopond to

some traits more positively than others. When we don't know someone, or the group to which someone belongs at all we are likely to affected by the first impressions we gain of them. If we know them better then the last things we learned are likely to influence us more.

Filters of Information

We spend most of our lives in familiar situations. We are often with people we know. Millions of things happen all around us, some of which we notice, some we look out for, some we find out by accident, and some we never know at all. There is just so much information out there that we have had to evolve the capacity to filter out many things and concentrate on a few at a time. You couldn't hear every conversation that is taking place in a cafeteria, but you can hear the talk at your own table (and perhaps the one next to you if you try!). At the same time, it's important that we don't filter out those things which we need to know, such as the police car siren right behind our car when we are blocking the road as we try to park.

We will summarize the effects of two types of filters here. The first are **personal filters.** These include what things each individual pays attention to, the particular ideas or attitudes that we have about what things are like, and the automatic way we behave and expect others to behave in familiar situations. In each case they make us more likely to respond to people or events in one way rather than another. The second are **social filters.** These include the ways in which people are only exposed to certain ideas, or are exposed to ideas in particular ways, for instance through the mass media such as the newspapers, television, etc.

Personal filters

We will take three aspects of personal filters. These are selectively attending to some information rather than other information, developing our own personally constructed views of what things are like, and the seemingly automatic ways that we expect familiar events to occur.

Attention

Let's take a familiar situation – a class of students studying psychology at a school or college. Let's say that you are in this class. (You should be able to answer some of these questions easily, others will be rather more difficult.) What is the room like? How big is it? Is it quite old or fairly new? Is there a modern white board or an old fashioned chalk board? These are easy. You have noticed the information needed to answer them because it is obvious.

How many people are in the class? Do you know all of their names? Do you know much else about many of them? These may be a bit more difficult. How much of what happens during the lesson do you actually take in? You don't see everything that everyone else does, you don't hear everything that everyone says. In order to make sense of the lesson you have to take in a fair amount of what the teacher has said. If you want to know what your friends are talking about you will have to pay attention to them. The subject of paying attention has been studied by psychologists for about fifty years.

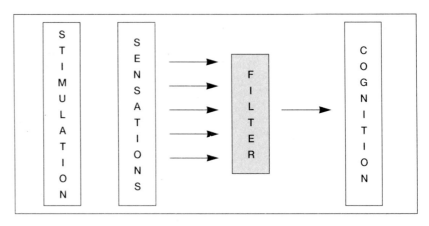

Cognitive filter

▷
Paying attention to some stimuli rather than others is called selectively attending. It is an essential first stage in the process of cognition whereby you come to know about things.

If you don't notice someone or something you can't pay attention to them or it, and you can't behave in the same way as you would if you had noticed them. If you don't notice your teacher standing behind a cupboard while you start to moan about him to your friend you might suffer for your lack of attention later! If only you had noticed that there was someone there and paid attention to who it was you could have avoided the aggravation. If only you had known that your teacher often sorted his books out by that cupboard, if only you'd remembered that the distinctive smell was the aftershave your teacher used, if only you'd noticed your friend shaking her head like mad to shut you up!

Obviously we can't pay attention to everything that our senses pick up. During your lessons cars may have passed outside, planes may have flown overhead, your heart may have beaten 1000 times, but you may not have paid attention to any of them. Since your brain couldn't process all the information that your senses could detect it's just as well that you only pay attention to a small amount. You must have some mental system that allows some information to pass through to your brain for processing and other information to be filtered out. There is a limit to how much your brain can process. Some tasks take a lot of mental effort to process and make sense of the information. For example you need to concentrate on what you are doing in your early driving lessons or when you are studying some written material for a test. These activities take most of your attention. You may not see your friend waving from another car, or hear the telephone when you are studying hard.

▷
We might think of mental effort as being the amount of biological activity that may be going on in parts of the brain. The assumption is that we only have a certain amount of biological mental energy in the same way as we only have a certain amount of physical energy.

Other tasks are quite simple and need very little attention. You can eat a burger and watch television at the same time. Neither takes much mental effort. You can walk in the park, talk to your companions, watch the ducks, and listen to the birds, all at the same time. These are fairly low order skills. You can pay attention to several of them at the same time. Experienced drivers can drive a car and hold a conversation at the same time. Driving needs rather more attention, but with practice you learn to switch it around your various activities. If someone steps out into the road the driver will immediately concentrate their mental effort on their driving and will ignore the conversation until the danger passes.

This idea that we have a certain amount of attention that can be switched around to meet the various demands of our senses was developed by **Daniel Kahneman** in his theory of attention over twenty years ago. There are several parts or processes in this theory. They are not difficult to understand and may explain why we respond to some things rather than others.

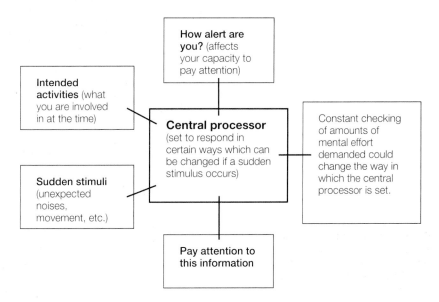

Kahneman's model of selective attention

First, If you are wide awake you'll have more mental energy and therefore a greater capacity to attend to things than if you're half asleep. Your mental energy for selective attention decreases as you become tired. So you can attend to more simple things or concentrate harder on one or two when you are alert. It's not a good idea to drive (which requires a lot of mental energy), particularly over unfamiliar or dangerous roads (which requires more), especially if the weather is bad and visibility is low (which needs even more concentration), when you've been awake for a long time.

Second, what you do take notice of depends on the way in which your central processor (the parts of your brain involved in perception and cognition) is set up. In the cinema your brain is receptive to the usual kind of things that go on in cinemas. Those things will be attended to, processed, and passed through into consciousness. If you're in class, those parts of your cognitive system to do with what happens in class will be receptive to such things, process them, and pass them through into consciousness. Your attention is being allocated in the central processor to the particular activities that you are involved in at the time. Hopefully you are trying to watch the film or follow the lesson.

Something might happen in any situation that could grab your attention whether you wanted it to or not. Would any of these stimuli make you pay attention: a loud noise (the fire bell going off while you're working in the library), a sudden flash of light (the usherette's torch while you're deeply engrossed in the cinema), something brightly coloured (a lime green and shocking pink Mini Metro parked by the kerb), something completely unexpected (someone in a Batman costume standing on the roof of a bus)? During the lesson a late student might burst in through a door. In the cinema someone might push past you.

Exercise on attention

1 Define 'attention' as used by psychologists.
2 What is selective attention?
3 Name two things that you have deliberately selectively attended to in the last half an hour.
4 What was the last thing that you unintentionally selectively attended to?
5 What is the role of the filter in selective attention?

Personal constructs

What do you know about people such as members of your family, your neighbours, your colleagues, your workmates, your friends? What do you know about things such as shopping, dancing, riding a bike, swimming, politics, being assertive, behaving altruistically? What do you know about events such as celebrating Christmas and birthdays, going on holiday, starting college or a new job? The answer is that you probably know an awful lot about most of these things if you thought about them. You've probably learned about some of them, often from experience. Other material you just seem to know about.

Babies are born with different temperaments. Everyone, even identical twins, has had different experiences during their socialization. Although the ways in which the cognitive parts of our brains work may be much the same for everyone, the material they have to work with varies greatly. During the course of our lives we have countless experiences of different kinds of people, objects, and events. We have learned how to look at such things, to decide what aspects of them are important or interesting. We have developed ideas or theories that help us to understand what things are really like. For example we have all been quite close to a fire and felt its heat. We don't need to actually put our hand in it to know that such extreme heat would damage us. We have a theory about fire, heat, and damage to our body.

George Kelly was an American psychiatrist who disagreed with both Freudian and behaviourist views about the ways in which humans think. He believed that people develop ideas about how they can predict what will happen next, how they can control their situations so that they will be safe, secure, happy, productive, successful, and all the other things that many people want to be. In particular circumstances we think, 'if I do this, then that should happen.' These predictions are **hypotheses**. A hypothesis is an idea about how things link together, whether one causes the other. You know that as you approach the fire you become warmer. If you continue you become hotter. A simple hypothesis would be that if you stay too close you will burn. It isn't necessary (or wise) to test this hypothesis! Yet you still know that being too close to a fire results in burning.

As our hypotheses are supported, partly supported, or even rejected throughout our lives we are developing what Kelly called **personal constructs**. A personal construct is an idea that you have developed, either as a result of some first hand experience, or, more likely, through what you've heard, seen, read, or imagined. You use these ideas to make judgements about people and situations. Since each person is unique, and everyone has had different experiences, so we have all developed quite different personal constructs. Every time you do something you are testing some hypothesis that has supported some personal construct. If your outcome is successful the personal construct is confirmed, otherwise it may be modified.

Some personal constructs are broad and general. They organize our normal approaches to things. Perhaps people who know you judge that you are optimistic, happy, friendly, and extravert. You fit in with their personal constructs for what optimistic, happy, friendly, and extravert people are like.

Personal constructs may be fairly permanent. As we said earlier with impression formation, if your first impression of someone is unfavourable, you may treat the person with suspicion. You will not change your mind easily either and your attitude may become part of your personality. So if you believe that football fans are all aggressive hooligans then you will avoid them as much as possible. Any contact you do have is likely to confirm your suspicion. You develop a personal construct that becomes part of your view of certain classes of people. Even if you find that several people that you know and like turn out to be football fans, you will still be unwilling to change your personal construct straight away. If they persuade you to go with them to a match and you don't see any trouble then your constructs can change.

▷ In science a hypothesis is a statement that researchers test in order to support or reject. A psychological hypothesis might be that as we grow tired our ability to attend to complicated material selectively decreases. We could test it by having some tired people and some alert people concentrate on the material then test them to see how well they have understood it.

▷ A personal construct is the general name given for each of the ways in which individuals try to perceive, understand, predict, and control their situation.

Exercise on personal constructs

1 What features do you regard as likeable and unlikeable or attractive and unattractive in:
   (a) another person of your own sex and age?
   (b) same age, opposite sex?
   (c) someone twice your age?
   (d) someone over seventy years old?
2 How would your personal constructs dispose you to behave towards someone in these groups?

Scripts

▷

In the theatre the script is the list of instructions of what each actor is to do and say in each scene of the play. Social scripts are the same kinds of thing for social situations, except that we have long since learned most of the instructions.

A script is the knowledge that each of us has of what kind of things should happen in different situations. For example in class you simply know who does what to whom, when, where, and why. This knowledge about the social situation called a lesson is a part of your cognition. You learned it many years ago and now you just seem to know it. In a shop you know what the various people are for. Shoppers buy things and assistants advise and take the money. Customers don't go behind the counter and mess with the till and the assistants don't spend hours in the changing rooms trying on the clothes while the shop is open. It's a script that you have about what goes on in shops. The script has become automatic. You don't need to think about it You just do it. The only time you do think about it is when you find someone who doesn't follow the script.

The idea for scripts was proposed by **Roger Schank and Robert Abelson** in 1977. Here is an example of what they mean, quoted in Michael Eysenck and Mark Keane's *Cognitive Psychology – A Student's Handbook*:

'Ruth and Mark had lunch at a restaurant today. They really enjoyed the meal but were worried about the eventual cost of it. However, after the ice cream, when the bill arrived, they were pleasantly surprised to find that it was very reasonable.'

In order to make sense of it we have to make certain assumptions. For example, that the meal referred to was at the restaurant mentioned. That they ate the ice cream as part of the meal, and that a waiter brought the bill. In order to make sense of this simple story Schank and Abelson argue that we must have some idea of the sequence of events involved here. We assume that the people entered the restaurant, sat at a table, read the menu, chose and ordered their food, it was prepared and delivered to their table by a waiter, they ate it, the waiter wrote out and brought their bill, they paid it and left! This knowledge is a script.

▷

Scripts are ideas that people develop for appropriate behaviour in particular circumstances. They are learned through direct experience (e.g. eating in restaurants), or through indirect experiences (e.g. reading about what goes on).

Scripts usually involve people. For example the waiter and the customers in a restaurant. As a customer a part of your restaurant script includes the role of waiter. If you are a waiter a part of your script includes how to deal with customers. Having scripts usually acts as a filter for how we will regard and respond to people in our scripts. Occasionally you come across someone who isn't familiar with the script. They talk loudly in the library, they don't realize that they are supposed to pay on the bus, they don't offer anyone their sweets whilst always taking one when others offer. Knowing the script is a personal filter that affects how we will behave towards others.

Exercise on scripts

1 What is a script?
2 What would be the first part of the script for Ruth and Mark? What would be the last part?
3 If you were told that you were to take part in a traditional native

wedding ceremony amongst the Indians in the tropical rain forest in deepest Amazon country, why might you have some possible cause for concern?

4 Do you have a script for the following situations?

Situation	YES	NO
A meal in an expensive restaurant?		
Attending a professional football match?		
A traditional Jewish wedding ceremony?		
Using a canteen or cafeteria?		
Trading in stocks and shares?		

5 Explain why having scripts about many familiar situations is helpful to us.

6 How does knowing the script help us to deal with:
(a) a police officer in the line of her duty?
(b) a traffic warden,
(c) a cashier at the building society?

Summary of personal filters

Personal filters include paying attention to some features of a person or situation more than others, applying our own personal constructs about what such people are like, and applying a script for the situation that they are in.

Social filters

So far we have seen that each of us develops our own personal filters of information which affect our views or the ways that we behave. There are social filters too. Social filters are the ways that other people or institutions control the kinds of information we can have. Here we will suggest how our social roles influence our perceptions, and how aspects of the media do too.

Social roles

A **social role** is the behaviour that is expected of certain people in certain situations. Social roles are closely related to social scripts which we discussed in Chapter 1 (see page 20). For example, what behaviour is expected of a student in a classroom lesson? These expectations form part of our scripts for students in lessons. The role is that of being a student. The script is the behaviour and events associated with people playing certain roles. The script that someone has in the role of student is different from the script which is expected of the same person who works as an assistant in a shoe shop at the weekend. It often involves their having certain rights and responsibilities. The situation is different and so are the social roles and social scripts.

 Activity

	Rights	Responsibilities
Students		
Shop assistant		

Construct a small table like this:

Working in groups ask your friends:

1   *What rights do students have?*

2   *What rights do shop assistants have?*

3   *What responsibilities do students have?*

4   *What responsibilities do assistants have?*

Agree the best answers and complete the table. Compare yours to the answers suggested by the other groups.

When you are playing your role you are a role-holder. Role-holders may be trained, encouraged, or expected to perform the appropriate behaviour to that role. Nurses are trained to nurse, young children are encouraged to find out, students are expected to behave in student-like ways. Or role-holders may simply have learned that certain behaviour is appropriate or inappropriate by observing others. A social role may be temporary (e.g. the winner of a raffle prize), it may last for quite a while (e.g. being an adult or a child), or it may be fixed for life (e.g. being a male or a female).

Each of us plays several social roles each day. Someone may be a daughter, a parent, a cook, a driver, a customer, a student, and work as a surgeon all in one day. (Can you explain how?) We come into contact with other people playing their roles every day too. The roles we are playing are likely to affect how we respond to them in their roles too. Our social roles become a part of our personal constructs and our scripts. We become so used to people in their roles that we expect them to behave in the specific ways that we associate with those roles, so we only really take much notice when they don't!

 Activity
The following table lists some social roles. For each role identify some of the behaviour that goes with it and say whether the role-holder has been trained, encouraged, or is expected to perform the behaviour.

Role	Behaviour	Where acquired?
Teacher		
Parent		
Student		
Shop customer		

Our roles are extremely important to us. They help us to define who we are. One of the first questions that people ask when they meet someone new is 'what do you do?'. We define other people largely by what roles they play. Our roles become absorbed into our self-concept. Sometimes the role becomes so important to us that it changes how we think about ourselves. A teacher who is so used to the discipline she uses at school might start to expect obedience at home. Several studies have been made of how people can become so absorbed into their roles so that their real personalities seem to disappear. The first such study was by **Erving Goffman** who spent a year studying staff and patients in an American mental hospital in the late 1950s. Goffman thinks that similar principles apply to all people who are in what he calls total institutions. A total institution is one which dominates most aspects of your life for a lengthy period of time. Army and prisoner-of-war camps, prisons and boarding schools, ships at sea for a long time, monasteries and convents are examples of total institutions.

▷
A total institution is one which dominates most aspects of the lives of the people in it. Soldiers, prisoners, patients and nuns all have social roles that are determined by their role. They can't escape from them (for long). They will become a part of the individual's self-concept. Individuality may be sacrificed to group norms.

Exercise on social roles (1)

1 Name three social roles that you play.
2 Outline a few of the things you do in each role.
3 What is a role-holder?
4 What is a self-concept?
5 Where does the self-concept come from?

Goffman's research led him to conclude that patients and staff learn their roles. He found that the staff had the power to reward and punish the patients in order to make them behave in ways that the organization expected of them. The patients could respond in one (or more) of five ways. These ways also applied to people who were not mental patients (such as students, nurses, or shop assistants). They could help us to understand the way we use our social roles.
• First, individuals can withdraw into themselves and refuse to take much notice of anything unless it is directly important to them.
• Second, they can rebel and refuse to cooperate.
• Third, the participants redefine their roles as mental patients and learn the routines of the institution. They become institutionalized and would find it difficult to live outside the institution.
• Fourth, participants might take this even further. They conform

closely to what the staff seem to see as their model role. The individual's personality seems to have been submerged into the new one. The patients become unable to think of themselves in any ways other than as mental patients who must do what the staff expect.

- The last response is typical of many people. They play it cool. They use whichever of the first four responses is most likely to help them gain whatever they want at the time.

The people in Goffman's studies were either diagnosed as suffering from some mental breakdown, or were in a long-term situation from which there was no easy chance of escape. The pressures on them to conform to other people's expectations of their role were enormous. However, social roles do not need to be so permanent or involuntary in order to have a great effect on how people see themselves. In the 1960s **Philip Zimbardo** and his colleagues conducted an experiment that was to run for two weeks. Twenty-one physically and psychologically mature young men were eventually recruited after intensive screening (three more were in reserve). Of this sample, nine were chosen at random to play the part of prisoners and twelve were to be prison guards. The basement of Stanford University in California's psychology department had been converted to look like a prison with cells and guard rooms. The prisoners were informed that 'they would be under constant surveillance, some civil rights would be suspended, but there would be no physical abuse.' The guards were told to 'Maintain the reasonable degree of order within the prison for its effective functioning.' With that, the researchers left the participants to carry on and oberved what happened.

The guards soon began to behave badly towards the prisoners. They insulted them and removed most of their rights. They insisted on being treated with absolute obedience and anyone that answered back or didn't obey immediately would be locked up, refused food, even refused to be allowed to use the toilet. Some of the prisoners became very depressed, their thinking started to become confused. Some began plotting to harm the guards. Other prisoners conformed absolutely to their new roles and tried to gain favour with the guards by reporting on the other prisoners. The more they gave in to the guards, the more cruel the guards became. By the sixth day Zimbardo closed the experiment down because of 'excessive zeal' (enthusiasm and eagerness) on the part of the guards. Within just a few days these psychologically mature and normal people had absorbed their roles so completely that their own personalities were submerged.

▷
In Goffman's study (entitled 'Asylums') the social roles that participants in total institutions are expected to play influenced how they saw themselves, how they regarded the institution, and how they interacted with the staff and each other.

▷
This experiment relied on a group of people role-playing. Some people soon adopt their role, others are more resistant, insisting that 'it is just an experiment, it isn't real'. This was true in this study, but most of the participants were soon playing along.

▷
The guards wore khaki uniforms, and mirrored sunglasses, they carried truncheons and enjoyed their power to humiliate the prisoners. Four of the nine prisoners had to be removed from the experiment because they started to show symptoms of disturbed thinking and it was feared that they might suffer some psychological damage.

Exercise on social roles (2)

1 What does Goffman mean by 'a total institution'?
2 What do you think the term 'institutionalized' means?
3 Name some ways in which some students might adopt Goffman's fifth response in college?

4 Zimbardo's study shows how quickly people absorb their social roles. Can you think of some social roles that would take rather longer to acquire?

5 Here are some examples of social roles. How might holding each of them influence how the role-holder regards other people?
   (a) Police officer
   (b) Doctor
   (c) Park attendant
   (d) Shop owner
   (e) Teacher

The Media

▷
The media can be divided into sources of information that we can read, watch, or hear.

The media, or to give them their full name 'the mass media of communication', is the term which covers all the sources through which other people deliberately provide us with information. They can be printed for reading (e.g. newspapers, comics, magazines and journals), they can be static and fairly permanent (e.g. posters and notices), they can be visual for watching and listening (e.g. television, video, and film), or they can be heard (e.g. radio and tape-recordings).

▷
see Chapter 5 for a review of the relationship between television and aggression.

For more than thirty years psychologists have been studying the effects on behaviour of watching various kinds of television. Albert Bandura's social learning theory stresses the importance of models that children (and adults) can observe and imitate. Here we are more interested in the role of the media to provide information about what our society is like, and what we might think about it. Most of us learn some of our opinions and attitudes from television, the papers, films, and radio. However, not everything that happens in the world is going to be reported to us so we will never know that it has happened. For example, the official government policy in communist China has been not to tell the outside world about national disasters that happen in their country, such as earthquakes and floods. The media act as social filters, reporting some things more than others.

There are two views regarding the mass media in Britain. One is that they are a part of the democratic process. They simply reflect what people think. It is true that if people hold strong opinions about some issue, they aren't likely to change their mind just because the media stresses opposing opinions. If people don't like what they read or see they will change their reading and viewing habits. Many criticisms about unfair reporting, invasions of privacy, and making things up are levelled at the tabloid press. Yet the tabloids sell millions of copies between them every day. Somebody must like what they say! In Britain there is no government control of the Press or Broadcasting – except in National emergencies, such as war – and the media can, and do, report events that are hostile to the government and to other state institutions. This supports the view that the media merely report what is there.

▷
Inevitably more events will happen than will be reported to the media. If the media don't know, they can't tell us.

The other view is that there are rich and powerful people in any society who are described as the ruling class or dominant group. They own shares in large businesses, they chair large financial organizations, they even own the newspapers and independent television companies. The media are said

Do the media merely reflect what most people think? Or do they actively shape the way people think about society?

to reflect their views. As the most powerful groups are benefiting from the way things are as they stand, they look to the mass media to tell people that most things are okay and that radical change would be bad. This view suggests that the media do not merely report what is happening, but actively try to influence people's opinions and behaviour.

As we said earlier, the world is a very complex place and we construct our own understanding of it which we called our social reality. The media can play a major role in this. Journalists interview people who give one point of view or another. Some are published, some are not. There isn't time or space to publish everything, and it may not be in everyone's interests to have everything published or broadcast anyway. The people who decide ultimately what we can and will not be told about (by them) are the editors in news services or producers in other programmes. These people have been called **gatekeepers** because they decide what information should and should not be filtered through into the public domain.

Gatekeepers can open or close the flow of information. They make the judgement according to a number of factors such as whether it would be interesting, whether it would improve the reputation or increase the audience or advertising revenue, etc., or possibly whether the owner of the media would approve. Either way, their decision affects what we are told and what we are not. Gatekeepers are social filters of information.

Some people or institutions will usually be treated well by the media and readers, viewers, and listeners will receive a positive image of those people. Some examples would be the Queen, our democracy, the freedom of the media, cricket, some politicians or sports stars (whose reputations are still intact), and local heroes such as lifeboat men who have saved lives. Other things vary in their treatment, either reflecting or shaping their part in our social reality. These include the Church, younger members of the Royal Family, some aspects of football, and some politicians. Others are usually treated harshly. These include all 'extremists', most social workers, communists, trade-union leaders, strikers, social-security claimants, most local government, and some politicians.

▶▶▶ *Activity*
Collect a variety of daily newspapers over a few days and analyse their main stories to decide what opinion is being expressed. Is it a positive or negative opinion? How do the papers compare with one another? Compile a list of pet hates and pet loves. (You'll find rather more hates than loves!)

Exercise on the media

1 Name some examples of the mass media of communication
2 Name three that you use most.
3 What do gatekeepers do?
4 Give an example of two items that have been in the news recently.
5 What has been the public reaction to each of them?

Summary of social filters
Social filters include social roles, which contain all the expectations of appropriate behaviour for the person in the role. There is also the media that contribute to, or reflect, public opinion. People gather information about right and wrong, good and bad behaviour, from these two sources.

Ways of discovering and testing in psychology

▷
Scientific methods generally allow researchers to control and measure things. Nonscientific methods rely more on observing relationships, although observations can also be highly controlled.

As we have seen, psychologists have conducted studies into many aspects of human (and animal) behaviour. Some of them employ scientific methods and we may have some confidence in their claims. Others rely less on science and more on carefully designed and controlled observations. There is some disagreement among psychologists about which produces a better understanding, although most would probably agree that both scientific and nonscientific approaches have their uses.

Several psychologists (particularly in the past) have offered grand theories to explain some area of human functioning, such as Freud's explanation for personality or Skinner's theory of learning. Some explanations are largely untestable (e.g. Freud's) so their claim to be scientific is rather doubtful. They might be regarded more as philosophy than psychology. Others, like Skinner, see psychology as an applied science. More recent explanations have been less ambitious. Rather than try to understand the whole way in which something works, psychologists have concentrated on explaining aspects of human functioning. In this chapter we will be examining how psychologists collect and interpret their data, and the major problems associated with the various methods used.

Ways of discovering psychological knowledge

Three types of research

Psychological research can be of three broad types, although some research may well combine them. We will look at each type in turn.

Cross-sectional research

In cross-sectional research we study our participants all in one go. For instance, we could take a group of children between the ages of three and five and compare some particular feature such as how easily or confidently they mix with other children. We could find that most 3-year-olds are less likely to interact, and that many 5-year-olds have great social confidence. We might find a sex difference, or a cultural one. Earlier we saw how Piaget found that children below the age of seven couldn't conserve or decentre, while children learned these skills between then and puberty (see page 208). Kohlberg had children of ten, thirteen, and sixteen answer moral-dilemma stories to investigate moral reasoning (see page 237).

Cross-sectional research gives us a snapshot of the group we are studying. The group we are aiming our research at is called a **target population**, and the members who are actually studied are a **sample**. The main advantage of cross-sectional research is that it can be fairly fast and can be relatively easy to do. We can obtain our results quickly, so for those topics where we need a fairly speedy response it is ideal. Its main limitation is that we can never be sure that the sample studied really was representative of the target population unless we could test all of them. Sometimes this is possible, although the usual way around this problem is to have a large sample. Another problem is that some issues that are interesting for psychologists only occur gradually, such as the development of language or cognition. For this we need longitudinal research.

A cross-sectional study

Exercise on cross-sectional research

1 What is a target population?
2 Why do psychologists use samples?
3 List the main advantages and disadvantages of cross-sectional research.

Longitudinal research

In longitudinal research, we study the same group of people over several months or years. This kind of study would show us some of the effects that growing older and gaining more experience have on people's behaviour. William Goldfarb found that children adopted after a few years in an orphanage do not develop to be as emotionally secure as children adopted soon after birth (see page 43). This suggests that the routines and atmosphere of family life are more beneficial to children than those of some orphanages. Skeels and Dye found that children reared by girls who had some intellectual problems still developed a higher IQ than those who remained in an unstimulating orphanage (see page 156). This suggests that stimulation, encouragement, handling, and emotional attachment accompanies intellectual development.

A longitudinal study

▷

In some research it is necessary to divide our participants between groups so that each group contains similar people. Doing this requires us to match our participants. So, for example, for every introvert female in one group there is an introvert female in the other. Cross-sectional research may require some kind of matching.

Longitudinal research is the only type of research that can show the effects of age and experience on behaviour and thinking. This is a major advantage over the other types. You probably behave differently now from the way in which you behaved, say, five years ago. If we had studied you then and again now we could measure these differences. The other major advantage of longitudinal research is that, because the same individuals are studied they do not need to be matched in any way with any other group. On the other hand, the main drawbacks are that it may take a long time to conduct, possibly fifteen years or more. During that time some of the participants may be lost. They may be ill, or have died. They may have moved and become not easy to trace, or they may refuse to participate further.

1 Name three examples of longitudinal research that has been conducted by psychologists. Include in your answer both the topic studied and the researcher who studied it.
2 List the main advantages and disadvantages of longitudinal research.
3 Take each of the three examples named in your answer to question 1 and show how the advantages and disadvantages named in question 2 apply to it.

Cross-cultural research

If we study a particular group in one society or culture (e.g. babies less than a year old, or teenagers) then we are conducting cross-sectional research. If we then study a similar group from another culture, we are conducting another cross-sectional study. If we then compare the two groups we are conducting cross-cultural research. Mary Ainsworth studied attachment behaviour in babies and mothers in the West and among the Ganda people in Uganda (see page 39). Many studies have been made comparing child-rearing patterns in a kibbutz with more usual patterns in the West. Urie Bronfenbrenner studied attitudes to children's schooling in Russia and America (see page 18).

The major benefit of cross-cultural research is that it can show which aspects of development are the result of socialization and which are the result of genetic inheritance. For example, if babies from all cultural backgrounds start to talk after about ten months, you might sensibly conclude that this is when they are (genetically) mature enough for talking. If, on the other hand, children start talking at different ages in different cultures we might think it was because they had learned to talk at that age.

The most obvious problem with conducting cross-cultural research is that it is likely to be more expensive than the other types. It often involves researchers in travelling to, and living in, other places. It is possible to use local researchers in each of the cultures, but a team leader may still need to visit and oversee the research. If we use the same researchers in different cultures to do the observations, testing, etc., they may allow their own ideas and values to influence their interpretations. They may believe that their cultural background is superior to the others they are studying. This cultural bias could influence the conclusions of cross-cultural research.

▷
If all people develop a particular characteristic – such as the ability to use language – then the likelihood is that it has something to do with genetic inheritance. If different cultures have different characteristics, such as sex and gender roles, than social experiences are more likely to be involved.

1 Name three examples of cross-cultural research that has been conducted by psychologists, naming both the topic studied and the researcher who conducted it.
2 List the main advantages and disadvantages of cross-cultural research.
3 Take each of the three examples named in question 1 and show how the advantages and disadvantages named in question 2 apply to it.

Summary of the three main types of research

1 Cross-sectional research compares people from similar groups or backgrounds to see if changes have occurred in any psychological variable.
2 Longitudinal research shows the effects of time and age on behaviour.
3 Cross-cultural research compares people from different cultures to show the effects of environment or different cultural practices.

Quantitative and qualitative research.

Whether our research is cross-sectional, longitudinal, or cross-cultural we have a number of methods for actually gathering the data. We could conduct observations, experiments, surveys, etc., or we could use a combination of different methods. Psychologists have quite a few methods to choose from. The choice of which to use depends on exactly what issue is being studied, what the research aims to discover, what previous work has been conducted in this area, the researcher's personal preference, the type of subjects being studied, and the resources (especially money) available.

One other factor in deciding which method to choose is the use to which the results are to be put. Some methods provide **quantitative data** (i.e. in the form of numbers which can be analysed statistically). They describe the results which have been gathered, and may be presented using descriptive statistics such as percentages and averages. Or the data may be qualitative such as opinions, attitudes and ideas. These are presented as reports, presentations, articles and discussions.

Quantitative research gathers information in the form of numbers, or responses which can easily be converted into numbers. e.g. 80 per cent of thumb suckers suck their thumbs for the same reason. Karl's IQ was found to be 103. The average age at which babies say their first word in Britain is ten months. 10 per cent of all people in Britain will suffer some form of serious mental illness. 40 per cent of Bowlby's sample of thieves had been separated from their mothers. 20 per cent of all families in Britain are one parent families. 4 per cent of all crimes involve violence. All these statements are the result of quantitative research.

Qualitative research asks for opinions, feelings, attitudes, etc. It can involve observations, discussions, case studies, and interviews. It is useful for providing detailed information, often about deeply personal or sensitive issues which could not be investigated using quantitative measures. Information about wives who are deserted could be gathered by patient, caring and gentle discussions. It couldn't be gathered by experiments or questionnaires!

Qualitative research may become quantified later. After conducting a large number of discussions into a particular topic we might be able to say something like 60 per cent of wives who were deserted by their husbands expressed feelings of insecurity, 30 per cent were receiving medical attention for depression, etc.

We can divide psychological methods into non-experimental methods and experimental methods. We will discuss each.

> Government and other agencies generally prefer quantitative data because they can be used to make predictions. Knowing the rate of increase in births allows us to predict the amount of money we'll need for family allowances, the number of school places and number of teachers, books, etc.

Non-experimental methods

The observation method

Whenever you see anyone do anything, you are conducting an observation. The main difference between our observations and those of psychologists is that we are rather quick to give our opinions and judgements on a topic, based on just a few observations. Psychologists, on the other hand, try to be more careful and **objective**, describing exactly what they see, and not what they think they see. They also try to make a large number of observations so they have more data on which to base their conclusions.

There are several ways of conducting observations. We could conduct **naturalistic observations**, where the people or animals we are studying are all visited in their own, familiar environments, whether it be an airport lounge, a busy street, the subway train, a shopping centre, or a playground. Trevarthen and Richards naturalistically studied mothers and babies interacting during their longitudinal study of interactional synchrony (see page 33). Spitz and Wolf naturalistically observed 123 prison babies and their mothers (see page 43). James and Joyce Robertson naturalistically observed and filmed eight children in brief separation from their mothers (see page 45). Usually the subjects do not know that they are being watched and that their behaviour is being noted or recorded (often by hidden cameras). Alternatively, the researcher will become familiar to them so that they continue to behave normally despite being recorded. This method was used by J.B. Watson during the 1920s and became popular with ethologists, like Konrad Lorenz, from the 1930s onwards.

For psychologists, one particular advantage of naturalistic observations is that the behaviour they can observe is what the subjects normally do under certain circumstances. It is natural behaviour. Also, it is possible for the observer to record things that cannot be studied by any other method. For example, consider the studying of children who are taken into care for various reasons. It would be impossible to remove children deliberately from their parents to see what effects the separation might have. It is possible to observe those children who have been separated already. Watching children's play teaches us a great deal about their cognitive development.

One problem with naturalistic observation is that people only show a small range of their total behaviour in the shopping centre, the shops, the classroom, etc. There are probably lots of things you do that you certainly wouldn't do in such public places. Second, if people know that they are being observed, they may well behave differently. Also, observers may be influenced by their own opinions about what ought to happen. Another problem concerns ethics (the moral issues concerning the right anyone has to spy on others without their knowledge. We will come to a discussion on ethics on page 314).

Apart from naturalistic observations there are also **controlled observations**. These are conducted by researchers who have deliberately set up

Objective means based on measuring something which is real and can be tested free from any bias or preference. The boiling point of water, for instance, can be tested objectively by applying heat to it and noting the reading on the thermometer when it starts to bubble.

Naturalistic observations are used to gather qualitative information about people in their usual environments.

Naturalistic observation is used where it is possible to observe behaviour and no other method could be used. Everyone uses it, and most of us offer explanations for other people's behaviour based on our own observations.

a situation to see how someone will react. Latané and Darley had artificial smoke pour into a room in which someone was filling in a form (see page 262). Hidden cameras would record what they would do. And would it make any difference if there were two, three, or more others also waiting in the room? Zimbardo's mock prison was wired so that observers could follow what was happening between the guards and prisoners (see page 286). The same problems exist as for naturalistic observation.

Both naturalistic and controlled observations are non-participatory, i.e. the researcher doesn't become involved with his or her subjects. **Non-participant observation** allows the researcher to stay on the outside and remain detached and able to gather objective data. For example, watching the behaviour of the homeless from the security of a car will give some insights into their lifestyle. The advantage is that the observers may be able to remain objective. However, it can never have the feel for the people being studied which participant observation can have. In **participant observation** the observer becomes a part of the target group and observes from within. One valuable way in which a psychologist can find out how it feels to be homeless in a major city is to live on the streets for a few weeks.

The advantage of participant observation is that it is possible to obtain very detailed, high quality data, including quite personal information, which reveals such things as attitudes, motivations or feelings. The disadvantage is that the researcher might lose his or her objectivity and begin to sympathize with (or become hostile towards) the subjects of the observation.

▷ Controlled observations are often used by psychologists to record people's behaviour as a part of experimental research, as we shall see later.

▷ In participant observation the researcher becomes part of the group being observed. This can be very difficult, and possibly dangerous, if the group members do not know that they are being observed. It is a method more likely to be used by sociologists or anthropologists than psychologists. In non-participant observation the researcher observes the group from a distance, from outside the group.

Exercise on observational methods

1 Name three examples of psychological studies which have included observation, naming both the topic studied and the researcher who conducted it.
2 List the main advantages and disadvantages of the observational method.
3 Take each of the three examples named in question 1 and show how the advantages and disadvantages named in question 3 apply to it.
4 Name two topics that could be studied by participant observation and two that could be studied by non-participant observation.

Surveys

Surveys comprise interviews and questionnaires and involve asking questions to find out people's attitudes, opinions, habits, interests, memories, etc.

Interviews

There are many forms of interview, ranging from the informal, casual chat to the formal clinical interview. Both were used by Piaget in his studies of children's cognition (see Chapter 10). Clinical interviews were used by Freud to learn about his patients' symptoms and to develop psychoanalytic theory. These are unstructured. This means that the questions are not usually planned beforehand. The next question asked usually depends on the answer to the previous question. Clinical interviews are useful for gathering sensitive data, and confidentiality, therefore, is most important.

The main advantages to unstructured interviews is that people tend to answer more naturally, more straightforwardly, and often more truthfully than they might in a more formal setting. There are problems as well, however. The main problem concerns sampling (finding some respondents to answer). Because most people don't give interviews to psychologists, those that are willing to be interviewed must be untypical – the sample is biased. One problem is that whatever we find from the people we have used in clinical interviews, we cannot then apply to anyone else. Whatever we understand about what's going on in your mind may not help us to understand someone else's mental state. Also, interviews are expensive. One skilled interviewer may spend quite some time gathering information from just one respondent.

▷
Interviews may also be structured, where the questions must be taken in the set order. These are used for market research and public opinion surveys rather than by psychologists.

Questionnaires

Questionnaires are almost a form of written interview. Questions are usually preset. They may require multiple-choice or open-ended answers. A large sample is needed to make their conclusions useful. Questionnaires are useful for gathering factual information about people's behaviour, or for gathering opinions. If the sample is large enough then the conclusions may well be convincing. And questionnaires can be relatively cheap if many respondents answer them.

There are some disadvantages. The questions need to be worded very carefully and this is quite a difficult task. If the meaning of any word is not absolutely clear and obvious, it can make the whole question ambiguous. Constructing a reliable questionnaire can be difficult, time-consuming and, therefore, expensive, particularly if only a few people are going to be answering it. Questionnaires aren't widely used by psychologists, as people often wouldn't want to give answers to the kinds of question psychologists might want to ask! We can never be sure that respondents are telling the truth anyway. It is also very difficult to conclude from survey data that one thing causes another.

Exercise on survey methods

1 What do surveys consist of?
2 Name two topics that psychologists might be interested in which could be investigated by a survey.
3 List the main advantages and disadvantages of the survey method.

Case studies

Case studies are detailed studies of one individual, usually involving clinical interviews. They allow us to see the effects of one event on another, e.g. the effect that severe deprivation during people's early life has on their later personality, intelligence, social and emotional state, etc. Koluchova constructed a case study of the Czech twins (see page 50). Freud and Dann conducted a case study of six war orphans (see page 47). Skeels and Dye performed a case study of thirteen nineteen-month-old babies who were reared by intellectually impaired girls (see page 156).

Case studies are used in several types of therapy to try to see what factors in people's experiences are causing what consequences in their behaviour. One main advantage is that case studies allow us to study situations which we couldn't study using any other method. For instance, we cannot deliberately deprive a child of love or stimulation in order to study the effects it might have. This is what happened to the Bulldogs Bank orphans and the twins studied by Koluchova.

The disadvantages are that we cannot generalize from one individual to anyone else, so we have no way of knowing whether the same effects would follow the same events in other people. Case studies also involve people in trying to remember past events and how they felt at the time. But as we really cannot rely on people's memories at the best of times, we can do so even less if those people have suffered some personal, social, or emotional problem.

Psychometric tests

The 'psycho' part of psychometrics is to do with what psychologists study: human thinking and behaviour. The 'metric' refers to measurement. Psychologists have tried to invent tests which measure accurately such mental characteristics as your intelligence and your personality, as well as potential skills such as mechanical or musical aptitude. Alfred Binet in Paris was one of the first psychologists to try to measure intelligence, just before the First World War and others have been continuing the effort ever since. They are meant to provide quantitative measurements – such as an IQ score – which can be used to describe and compare people. Elaine has an IQ of 123 while Amanda has an IQ of 103. Therefore we may be tempted to believe that Elaine is more intelligent than Amanda. However, the scores probably only tell us that, on the day of the test, Elaine could answer more of the questions in the way the test markers agreed with than Amanda could.

If we try to construct a test to measure intelligence we are assuming that intelligence is something which can be measured. Do we all have a certain 'amount' of intelligence that can be measured? Do we all have a personality that can be investigated by answering some questions in a psychological quiz? The answer is probably not. Devising a test which is likely to be of any use at all is extremely difficult. It may be fun to do the twenty-question test in popular magazines that is supposed to show you who your ideal partner is, or whether you make a good friend or not, but such a test reveals very little scientifically acceptable psychological data at all.

1 Name two psychological topics which psychologists have attempted to measure psychometrically.
2 What is quantitative data?
3 Outline some of the problems involved in devising psychometric tests.

Correlational research

Psychologists are often interested in how one thing affects another. If we wanted to discover whether eating more sweets would make us better at solving intelligence-test questions, we could find a group of people who would eat twice as many sweets as a similar group over a period of six months. We could then present them with some intelligence-test questions to answer. Here, we are measuring two variables. A variable is just about anything which can vary. More specifically, it is an amount of something of which there can be more or less. The effects of different amounts of noise, temperature, and tiredness on aspects of human behaviour are variables that have been tested by psychologists.

▷ A variable is anything that can vary either because it can have different quantities or amounts, such as temperature or noise, or because it can come in different forms, such as age or sex.

Correlation is a statistical device for measuring the extent to which any two variables occur together. We could ask one group of students to rate some pictures of spiders for how frightening they think they are, and another group to rate them for how ugly they think the spiders are. We could then perform a correlation on the data and find if spiders which are rated as frightening are the same ones which are rated as ugly. Or we could test the nature–nurture debate over intelligence by finding a sample of parents who all have fairly high IQs and measure their children's IQ (assuming that we believe that IQ tests do measure intelligence). If we find that the children also have, on average, high IQs we may be tempted to draw a simple conclusion. What is it? Or if we find that parents who are extrovert have children who are also extrovert, might we think that extrovert parents produce extrovert children?

▷ Extrovert means outgoing and sociable. Can you think of another reason why extrovert parents might have extrovert children?

Correlation is not a method of gathering data, which all the methods discussed so far have been. Correlation is a method of analysing data (that may already have been gathered). Michael Rutter conducted a correlational study on the Isle of Wight and in London to measure the relationship between the variables of conflict between parents in the home during childhood and the amount of delinquent behaviour shown when a teenager. He found that youngsters whose parents had argued a great deal were much more likely to behave in delinquent ways than those whose parents had not argued much. The more conflict there was between the parents, the more likely the boys were to be delinquent.

Correlations can be plotted on a scattergram. This is a diagram where each score for one variable is plotted on the horizontal axis, while the score for the other variable is plotted on the vertical axis.

If one of the variables changes in the same way as the other – for example, the more there is of one, the more there is of the other – then the correlation is positive. (Rutter found a positive correlation in his studies. See Chapter 2.) On the other hand, if one variable increases while the other decreases then we have a negative correlation. There is a negative correlation between the number of hours you spend watching television when you should be studying, and achieving good marks at college. The more time you watch television, the lower your grades will be.

All statistics involve numbers. Any trend between the sets of scores for each variable shown on the scattergram can be shown as a number between –1 and +1. A correlation of +1 is a **perfect-positive correlation**. A correlation of –1 is a **perfect-negative correlation**. Such perfection would probably never occur in psychology. A correlation of 0 means there is no statistical relationship between the variables. There is probably no correlation between the number of CD players purchased in each year over the last ten years in Britain and the amount of volcanic activity recorded on the moon for the same years.

One very important point to bear in mind is that correlation *does not* and *cannot* show that changes which occur in one of the variables cause any change to occur in the other. Correlation only shows that the amounts of the variables do seem to be related, *not that one necessarily influences the other*. You may watch television a great deal and still do well in college tests. You might simply be brilliant. Here we have a third variable – intelligence – which explains the performance of one or both of the other variables. The length of your left leg might have grown at the same rate as the length of your right leg during each year since you were born. There would be a highly positive correlation between them. But the length of your left leg does not determine the length of your right leg.

One advantage to conducting correlations is that many things can be studied which couldn't be studied by other methods. How else could Rutter have established the relationships he found? Correlations can be relatively inexpensive, as computers can do much of the statistical analysis, the data are often available anyway, in the medical records, for example, and not many people need to be employed in the research. The drawback is that they cannot show cause. To do this we need the only scientific method which can give us confidence that one thing does cause another to change: the experiment.

▷ Perfect-positive and perfect-negative correlations are extremely rare in psychology. People do all kinds of things for all kinds of reasons. While most might respond in one way or another in a particular situation, there will be many who will behave in very different ways.

▷ In the past some psychologists have assumed that changes in one variable may be causing a change in another. Bowlby found that some of his sample of forty-four juvenile thieves had been separated from their mothers during childhood. He suggested that such separation increased the likelihood that someone would become delinquent.

Exercise on correlation

1 What is a variable?
2 What is correlation?
3 Name two variables that would be positively correlated.
4 Name two variables that would be negatively correlated.
5 Why do psychologists use correlational studies?

Summary of qualitative and quantitative reseach

Psychologists use various kinds of observation for gathering data that would be difficult to gather using other methods. If the data is in the form of attitudes, preferences, opinions, etc., then surveys are used. Case studies are employed to gather detailed information about an individual or a small group of people. There are thousands of psychometric tests for gathering data on everything, from personality and IQ to mechanical and musical aptitude. Correlations are statistical measures of the extent to which variables vary together.

Experiments

The main problem with all the methods described so far is that they allow us to make educated guesses about what is going on, but do not allow us to control any of the variables in the situation. We can only see what is already happening. Control is the key to scientific research. To see how one variable affects another we need to set up a situation which we control, then alter one variable and record any changes in the behaviour of the people we are studying. If their behaviour changes every time we alter the amount of our variable, we might be able to claim that it is causing the change in the other. For this we use the controlled experiment.

The controlled experiment

Let's imagine that we have noticed that we lose arcade games more quickly after nine o'clock at night than we do in the early afternoon. Our reaction times seem to grow longer as we become more tired. We will conduct an experiment to discover if there is a relationship between the variable 'speed of reaction time' and the variable 'amount of fatigue'. Let's take a sample of people, and divide them into group A and group B. We will test the reaction times of both groups by getting each participant to hit the space bar on a computer keyboard as soon as they see a light appear on the computer screen. The computer will measure the time between the light's coming on and the space bar being hit. We'll call this their reaction time. We'll wake all of our participants up at 7am. Group A can take the test at 2pm, seven hours after they were woken. Group B can take their test eight hours later, at 10pm.

This would be a controlled experiment. We've controlled what the participants have to do, and when and where they have to do it. We can make sure that they all experienced the same amount of fatigue by getting all the people up at the same time. Other variables that could affect their performance will also be controlled. If they weren't they could affect some of the participant's results. They are called **confounding variables** and the research would be described as confounded if they were allowed to influence the results. For example, people are slower when they are warm so we will have the same temperature in the laboratory at 2pm and 10pm. The amount of light in the laboratory will be controlled too. If we did not make sure that each experimental condition was so similar then the differences could influence the participants' behaviour and the research is

▷ Confounding means allowing the results to be influenced by some other variables that we had overlooked or not bothered about. Confounding is the consequence of poor design.

▷

The independent variable is controlled by the experimenter. How the participants respond to it is called the dependent variable.

confounded. Each variable which the researcher controls is called an **independent variable** (IV). The participants' response (in this case the speed of their reaction) is the **dependent variable** (DV) because (it is hoped) any change in it depends on how we've changed the IV.

One advantage of controlled experiments is that we can define and manipulate some variables and measure exactly any changes in the participants' responses. If these changes appear to vary consistently when the independent variable is altered, then we can be confident that it is the IV that is influencing the DV. Psychologists have learned a great deal about human behaviour from conducting controlled experiments on babies (Bower on perception, Carpenter on recognition), children (Hughes on decentring and McGarrigle and Donaldson on conservation), and adults (Sherif and Asch on conformity, Piliavin on bystander intervention).

▷

Even where the results of experiments look very interesting, or even convincing, they may not apply directly to the situations that they were originally intended to investigate. Does Asch's line-length experiment really test conformity in everyday situations?

There are some problems with controlled experiments, however. Even if we find that reaction time on the computer is longer we still can't be absolutely certain that this explains why we lose more arcade games at night rather than during the day. Variables could exist in the arcade which don't exist in the laboratory. For example, the kinds of people who play in the arcades later may be very different. They're noisier and they jostle and push. This distracts us. Perhaps our losses are explained more by these factors than by fatigue. Experiments are sometimes rather artificial situations which remove variables which might have been important in order to test the variables that the researcher thinks are important.

▷

Participants in psychological research often try to guess what the research is about, and their behaviour may change accordingly. In such cases the research may be confounded.

People who know that they are taking part in psychology experiments may look for any clues that the researcher or other participants are giving about what the research is about and so how they should behave. Even the researcher's tone of voice can give some idea about what's going on.

They also look for any nonverbal signals such as facial expressions, body posture, hand movements, etc., which give clues as to what to expect. A participant may have heard something about the research, or will try to guess anyway. Experimenters should tape-record instructions so that the participants can't detect anything in their voice, they should appear to be neutral so they don't influence the participant to say anything, and they must guard against giving any nonverbal body language clues.

Controlled experiments are useful to psychologists, although many aspects of human behaviour could not be tested in a laboratory study. For example, in controlled laboratory research we couldn't learn much about mental disorders, gender development, the use of social scripts, or the consequences of broken attachment bonds. There are two other types of experiment briefly worth mentioning.

Exercise on controlled experiments

1 What is a controlled experiment?
2 Explain how a controlled experiment differs from a correlational study.
3 What are confounding variables?
4 Explain the sentence in the text: 'Experiments are sometimes rather artificial situations.'

Field experiments

Field experiments are conducted in the participants' own natural environment, rather than in the psychologist's laboratory. Stein and Friedrich used a playground for studying the effects of television viewing on children's pro- or anti-social behaviour. Klaus and Kennel used a maternity ward for studying the effects of timing in early experiences between new-born babies and their mothers. Berscheid and Walster used a students' dance for investigating attractiveness in dating choices. In each of these the independent variables were manipulated by the researcher.

The advantage of field experiments is that they are natural. Because the participants do not know that they are being studied as part of an experiment, or that a psychologist is watching them, their behaviour should be entirely normal. It is possible to generalize our findings from field experiments to other people in similar situations because field experiments test people's natural behaviour. A drawback is that they can be expensive – compared to laboratory research – and it is quite possible that other variables which we aren't controlling could explain some of our participants' behaviour.

Natural experiments

Natural experiments involve studying naturally occurring variables such as gender, age, or ethnicity. In natural experiments these independent variables already exist and do not need to be controlled. Their effects are observed and recorded. Michael Lamb observed three- to five-year-old boys and girls playing. He noted what happened when a member of either sex picked up a toy that was more usually played with by a child of the other sex. For example, when a boy picked up a doll he was criticized by the other boys and he soon dropped the toy. The benefit of this method is that there are no experimenter effects, but the problem is that there is very little control, and only a relatively small number of variables that psychologists are interested in could be researched in this way.

Exercise on field and natural experiments

1 What is the difference between a field experiment and a natural experiment?
2 Name one advantage and one drawback that psychologists might face in using field experiments.
3 Name two examples of topics that could be researched using field or natural experiments that could not easily be investigated using controlled experiments?
4 Take the hypothesis that females are more likely than males to be computer-phobic (afraid of computers). Outline how you would investigate this using
(a) a controlled experiment,
(b) a field experiment,
(c) a natural experiment.

Summary of experimental methods
Controlled experiments are used by psychologists where the main variables are known and can be controlled. The effects of the independent variable on the dependent one can be measured. In field experiments the data is gathered in the subjects' own environment if the main independent variables can be introduced there. In natural experiments the independent variables already exist.

Carrying out practical research

Aims and hypotheses

Before beginning any research project, the most important thing to establish is exactly what it is that we are going to investigate. We must first state our aim. The aim can be fairly general. Our aim could be to investigate the development of empathy in children aged between two and six years. Or to investigate altruism in pre-school children. As we discover what research has already been conducted in this area our aim will need to be refined and made more specific. Investigating the role of high-status models in moral development amongst five-year-olds is fairly specific. At some point we will have to operationalize our variables such as high-status models and moral development. To operationalize means to define exactly what we are going to mean by a particular term for the purposes of our research. For example, in a correlational study of intelligence and speed of decision making, I might operationalize intelligence as being the IQ score obtained on the particular intelligence test that I used. Speed of decision making could be operationally defined as how quickly participants responded to questions about moral dilemmas.

▷
A hypothesis may state that a change in one variable causes a change in another. Hypotheses are stated as though they were the explanation for how the two variables go together. They are never stated as a question.

If our research is to be thought of as scientific we will state our aim as a hypothesis. A hypothesis states or assumes that one thing causes another. It is written down in a way that could be the starting point for some research. Having found out as much as we can about some topic in which we are interested we work out exactly what else we would like to know. Jean Piaget thought that children had difficulties in imagining what the world looked like from where other people were standing. He called it being egocentric. His aim was to investigate egocentrism in young children. His hypothesis was that children below seven years of age could not identify a picture representing a view other than their own. He investigated this hypothesis using a model of some papier-mâché mountains.

In order to find support for our hypotheses, or to reject them if we can't find enough support, scientists have to test them, and perform some statistical analysis of their results. We can never be 100 per cent certain that one variable will always cause the change predicted in the other. Reaction time will not always increase as someone grows more tired. Not all peoples' reaction times slow with fatigue anyway. Instead, scientists have to accept that as long as one of their variables causes the predicted change in the other at least 95 per cent of the time, then they can claim to have supported their hypothesis. The way they do this is to state their hypothesis the other way around. So we might say that either fatigue doesn't lead to any increase in reaction time, or that any increase in reaction time occurs by chance. This is called a **null hypothesis**. If we then find that reaction time does increase when people are tired on 95 per cent of occasions, then we can reject the null hypothesis and support the experimental hypothesis.

Having stated our aim or hypothesis we must find some people to study.

▷
A null hypothesis states that one variable does not cause the change suggested by the hypothesis in the other variable. Moreover, any change that does appear must have occurred by chance.

Exercise on aims and hypotheses

1 What is the difference between an aim and a hypothesis?
2 What are the names of the two types of variable that are studied in experiments?
3 Make up a hypothesis for Bandura's Bobo doll experiment. (See page 106 if you need to refresh your memory.)
4 State your Bobo-doll experiment's hypothesis in its null form.

●●● **Summary of hypotheses**
All research needs an aim. More scientific research needs its aim stated as a hypothesis. A hypothesis states that altering the amount of the independent variable will cause a change in the amount of the dependent variable. A null hypothesis states the opposite and claims that any change that does occur happens by chance.

Sampling

Most research is conducted on specific groups of people such as students, pre-school children, adolescents, mothers of infants, fathers of older children, etc. Each of these groups has been the target of some research as the **target population**. It wouldn't be possible to study all members of a target population unless it were quite small so we draw a sample of people from it. With luck, the sample we choose will be fairly typical or representative of all the other members of the target population. Otherwise any conclusions we draw from the sample may not apply to the rest of the target population.

▷
A target population comprises all the people who possess the characteristics that we are studying so could be a part of our research. The sample comprises the ones we actually study.

There are several ways of choosing a sample. Which sample we use will depend on factors such as our own preferences, how much time and resources we have – as some take longer and are more complicated than others, – what the data is to be used for, etc. We will look here at three of the main samples.

Random samples

In a random sample every member of the target population has the same chance of being chosen as everyone else. For this reason these samples are very rarely used. If we are studying college students in your area we could decide that all the people who attend your local college would be a satisfactory target population. Because the college office has all their names and addresses on their enrolment cards, we could randomly draw 200 names out of the file, or instruct the computer to choose 200 names at random. No student has any greater or lesser chance of being chosen than any other. Unfortunately, psychologists usually require rather larger populations than students at one college.

▷
In a random sample everyone in the target population has the same opportunity to be chosen to be in the sample.

Opportunity samples

An opportunity sample is that group of people that the researcher can most easily find. The research may proceed much more quickly if we do not need to hunt for our sample. It will probably be cheaper too. One estimate says that 90 per cent of American psychology experiments have been conducted using American college students as their subjects. This would be because most psychological research is conducted in colleges and universities by professors who have access to lots of students. The obvious problem is that American college students are not necessarily going to be representative of all people. Students are generally younger, probably brighter, and may have different socially constructed realities than non-students.

Quota sample

▷
Quota samples are rather more difficult to find than others, but should be as representative. They may need fewer participants compared to the others.

Where a target population is large and has lots of different characteristics it may not be possible to take a sample which is likely to be truly representative. A psychologist investigating the possible effects of living near high-power overhead electricity cables on emotional stability has a very large target population of about 20,000 people in Britain, comprising males and females of all ages. Just under half could live in cities or towns, about the same in villages, and about 10 per cent are isolated dwellers. It may be necessary to take a part of the sample from each group. So 45 per cent of the sample includes both sexes and all ages who live in towns and cities, the same from villages, and 10 per cent from isolated farmhouses. We are taking a quota of representatives from each of the main groups within our target population.

Although we can never be certain that our sample is truly representative of the target population, the larger the sample is, the more representative it is likely to be. A sample of twenty people who live near overhead electricity cables couldn't have enough city dwellers, village dwellers, or isolated dwellers to be representative of all people in those groups. A sample of a thousand is much more likely to be representative. The problem that researchers face, however, is that the more participants they study, the more testers, recordings, computer time, etc., they will need, and the more expensive it becomes to conduct the research. On the other hand, the fewer (and therefore cheaper) participants there are, the less representative they are likely to be, and the less useful the results may be. The size of the sample will often be a compromise between what we want and what we can afford.

Exercise on sampling

1 What is a target population?
2 What is a sample?
3 Why should a sample be representative of a target population?
4 Copy this table and fill in the gaps

Summary of sampling

We could not study everyone who has some of the variables that we are interested in, so we choose a sample of them to study. The members could be selected randomly, so that everyone has an equal chance of being selected, or by taking a particular quota of people with the various variables that we are interested in. The simplest sample is the one that we can obtain most easily, an opportunity sample.

Research design

Imagine that we were repeating Asch's research into social conformity (see page 61). We would be wanting to measure whether people will agree with others who say something that they can see is untrue. We would show them cards with three vertical lines of different lengths, and ask them to say which one of the lines is the same length as a another, separate line. Some will be in groups with two other confederates, some will be with six others, and some with ten others. The confederates all know when to start to lie. Research design refers to how we place our sample into the various conditions. There are three possibilities here.

	Advantages	Disadvantages
Random		
Opportunity		
Quota		

Independent measures or independent groups

In **independent-measures** or **independent-groups** design, the participants are randomly distributed between the experimental conditions. If we have a sample of thirty participants, and three experimental conditions, there will be ten participants in each experimental condition. We could write A, B and C each on a separate piece of paper, and write the thirty names, each on a separate piece of paper. We could then draw out of a hat, first the letter of the experimental condition, and then ten names that would be the first group. We could then repeat this process for the other two experimental conditions.

Unfortunately, with only ten people in each group there is a possibility that one group will contain more nonconformers, or more keen

$\triangleright$
An experimental condition is a procedure where participants will be exposed to the independent variables. The same IVs could be used with different subjects, or the same subjects under different conditions. Or different variations on the IVs could be used. Experimental groups are the participants who are placed in experimental conditions.

▷
A random error is one that occurs simply by chance. Some participants in any research will be more or less experienced, alert, interested, willing, motivated, nonconformist, etc. Random errors usually cancel themselves out when we have fairly large groups, as there are likely to be equal numbers of similar participants in the other groups.

▷
Counterbalancing is an experimental procedure where some participants take part in each of the conditions first. So, if there are two conditions, half participate in A and then in B, while the others participate in B and then A.

▷
If participants start to change their behaviour according to what they think the experiment is about, then the results will become confounded.

conformers, than another. This is an example of **random error**. If we have a large sample, any random errors will cancel themselves out. There will be as many keen conformers as nonconformers in each group. The main drawback of independent groups is that they require us to use a large sample. The main advantage is that it is easy to place our participants into the groups.

Repeated measures

In a **repeated-measures** design all the participants are placed in each of the experimental groups on separate occasions. So they would each be tested with ten others, six others, and two others. The problem here is that some of their conformity – or lack of it – is caused by what they have learned in the previous conditions, or because they are tired (a fatigue effect), or bored (a boredom effect). Or it could be a result of their being used to what happens in an experiment (a practice effect). Any changes in the participants' behaviour caused by the order in which they went through the conditions is called an **order effect**. One way to minimize order effects is called **counterbalancing**. Those participants who were in group A then make up group B, and then group C. Those in B go on to be in C, then A. Those who began in C go through A and B. Alternatively, you might randomize the order in which participants go through each condition, or randomize the types of thing you want them to judge. You might use size of objects rather than length of lines, for instance. Another possibility is to leave a few days between each test so that any effects may have worn off. If these suggestions don't help, and there are still likely to be some effects, use a different research design.

There are a couple of advantages to using this design. First, we have far more data to analyse for the same number of participants. In an independent-measures design, if we had thirty participants, ten in each of three groups, we would have thirty scores altogether. If we had thirty participants in each of three groups in repeated-measures design we would have ninety scores in total. Second, we can't have random errors occurring between members of groups because the members of each group are the same participants. There is a major problem though. By the time someone has been through one condition they can sometimes guess the aim of the research and change their behaviour to fit in with what they think the researcher wants. This is an example of a **subject expectation.** Also, participants may not always be available to be in each experimental condition. Other commitments might mean they will be absent when the test is conducted.

Obviously we can't use repeated-measures design when we have to use new participants in each condition. Sometimes research will involve representatives from particular groups within society, such as students, the middle class, housewives, etc. If we compare students to non students on certain tests, then we can't use the same people in each condition! We can't use the same participants when comparing housewives to women who live alone, or middle class to working class people.

Matched subjects

It may be possible to match the subjects in the different groups so that the groups are very similar. For example, we could investigate whether intelligent, extrovert men perform simple tasks worse when they are bored than when they are interested. We need a large sample of intelligent, extrovert men. Put half in one group and half in another. Give one group boring tasks and the other more interesting things to do, and measure how well they perform. This is a very simple version of **matched-subjects** design.

The advantage of this design is that it allows us to investigate the effects of subject variables such as intelligence and personality. The problems, on the other hand, are enormous. Where would we find a sample which would contain enough participants to make up identical groups? We would need to test hundreds of men to find enough who are extrovert, intelligent, and willing to take part in our research. We would have spent most of our research budget trying to find the sample! We don't even always know what the key variables are.

Exercise on research design

1 What is meant by random error?
2 In independent-groups design we divide our sample randomly between the experimental conditions. What does randomly mean? Suggest one way in which we could divide the sample randomly between the conditions.
3 What is the main advantage of repeated-measures design over independent-groups design?
4 What are order effects? How might they be reduced?
5 Give one example of a hypothesis that could not be tested using repeated measures. (NB Remember how to state a hypothesis – it mustn't be a question.)
6 Why are matched-subjects designs rarely used in psychology?

●●● **Summary of research design**
We could randomly divide our subjects between the various research conditions (an independent-measures design), or use all of them in each condition (a repeated-measures design). Or we could match the various groups. Which design we use will depend on factors such as the resources we have available, the topic we are studying, and the purpose to which our results are to be put.

Gathering the data

Here is a summary of what we have accomplished so far. We have made some observations that have tempted us to conduct some research. We have stated the aims of our research, and formulated one of those aims into a hypothesis. This has meant deciding the main variables involved and deciding to control one and measure the other. We have chosen a relevant sample, using an appropriate method. We have decided how to divide the sample between our various experimental or other conditions. We are now ready to test our hypothesis. This will mean we have to conduct the experiment, make the observations, conduct the survey, or compile the case study.

If the data we gather supports our hypothesis, and other researchers find more support, then the hypothesis may be regarded as a theory. Theories are hypotheses which have been supported by the data that has been collected and analysed. They are usually published in psychology journals where they are read and reviewed by other psychologists who will criticize or accept the arguments and ideas. Other researchers might conduct research that challenges the original conclusions. Their own theories are published and will be criticized, supported, and so on. The procedure starts all over again. This is how all scientific knowledge is gained.

▷ Note that we say that our data 'supports' our hypothesis rather than 'proves' it. This is an important distinction.

Displaying data

We can display our data in numbers or in pictures. We can use simple statistics to give us the mean average or the most typical or middle-ranking score. Or we can use tables and graphs to show us how often something occurs, or if any trend can be detected. There are several ways in which we can analyse our data to describe what we have found. One is to find the middle or average score, which is called the **mean**. To find the mean, we add all the scores together, and divide this by how many scores there were in total. The number of scores is usually abbreviated to N. The **mode** is the name of the score that occurs most often. The **median** is the exact mid-point between the highest and the lowest scores when they have all been ranked in order from lowest to highest.

So, if we wanted to find the mean score from a set of test marks out of ten for a class of thirteen GCSE-psychology students, we would calculate it as follows:

marks = 3, 3, 4, 5, 5, 5, 6, 6, 7, 8, 8, 9, 9

total (of the thirteen scores) = 78

number of scores (N) = 13

so, $\dfrac{78}{13} = 6$

The mean score, therefore, is six.

Some of the students had the same score. The score that appeared most was five. There are three fives. Five is, therefore, the mode score.

The exact middle point is the seventh score in from either end, as there are thirteen scores. This is six. Six is, therefore, the median score. If there were an even number of scores the median would be half-way between the middle pair of scores. For instance, in the series of scores 2, 4, 6 and 8, the two middle scores are four and six, so the median is five.

The mean, median and mode all give some idea of how the average student is performing. We might also like to know about the rest. Are all the students performing similarly in their marks? To calculate this we use the **range**. To find the range, we subtract the lowest score from the highest score. Taking again the series of scores above, the highest is nine and the lowest is three. so the range is $9 - 3 = 6$.

The results of psychological research are often displayed in tables and graphs. Tables allow data to be displayed very accurately, often to several decimal places. If the data is fairly simple or straightforward then tables are very useful. However, if the data is more detailed you can need to study a table quite hard in order to take in what it is showing. Also, tables are best used to show how much or how often something has occurred. They are less useful for showing trends in data. For this we use graphs. There are several forms of graph which we will look at here.

Frequency polygons

The frequency polygon has a vertical line (the vertical axis) and a horizontal line (the horizontal axis). Each score is plotted by a dot placed above the horizontal line, marking the score on the vertical one. The dots are connected by a line passing through them. It's very easy to understand a frequency polygon once you have looked at the title and the labels for the axes. They are especially useful for overlaying more than one set of scores so that direct comparisons can be seen at a glance. They are also good for displaying trends.

▷ The mean, median, and mode are called three measures of central tendency because they show what the middle, or typical, score is. The range shows how far the group of scores is spread around that middle score.

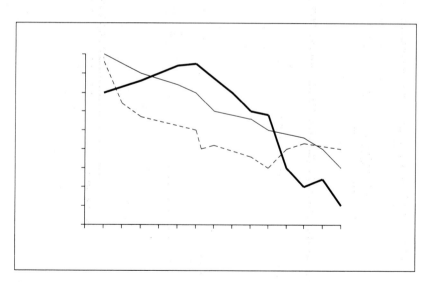

A frequency polygon

Bar charts

Bar charts are even more visually dramatic. They are used to show simple frequency data, i.e. how often something has occurred. As the bars are showing data not directly related to each other, there is usually a space between them. Bar charts are not meant to show very high quality data.

311

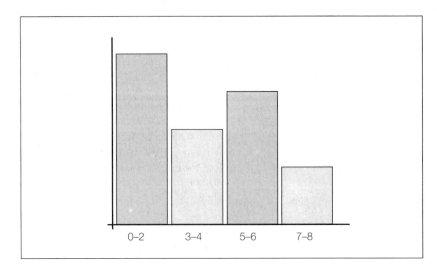

A bar chart

Histograms

Histograms look a bit like bar charts but are much more precise. They are drawn to an exact scale so that the area (height × width) of each column shows the proportion of scores that fall in each class, category, or interval on the horizontal axis. All categories are shown, even where no scores occurred. Unlike bar charts, histograms show no spaces between the bars.

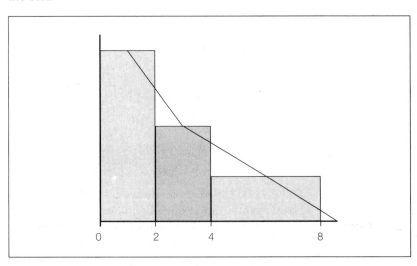

A histogram

The curve of normal distribution

There is a rather special graph which has several very useful features in statistics, allowing us to make certain predictions from it. It is called **the curve of normal distribution** or the bell-shaped curve. If an enormous number of measurements of, for example, people's height, could be taken, and plotted on a frequency polygon, the resulting curve would be symmetrical and look a bit like a bell (see the example on page 144). Some psychologists believe that psychological dimensions such as intelligence, aggression, personality disorders, introversion, schizophrenia, etc., are also normally distributed, although this is an assumption (or possibly a hope!) rather than a fact. The reason why the curve of normal distribution is rather special is that it obeys rules which let us work out the exact percentage of cases between any two points on the curve. So, if I know the number of children who are entering secondary school this year and I assume that IQ is normally distributed, I can tell you exactly how many children will have any particular IQ score, and the number of children whose IQ lies between any two scores. This could help the government ensure that there are enough school places and specialist teachers available.

See Chapter 7 for a discussion of the assumptions made about IQ.

Exercise on displaying the data

1 Name the three measures of central tendency.

2 Here is a set of scores: 2, 3, 5, 7, 8.
   (a) What does N equal?
   (b) What is the mean score?
   (c) What is the range?

3 What is the main advantage of tables for displaying data?

●●● **Summary of displaying data**
Psychologists can display data in tables very accurately. Unfortunately, tables often require quite detailed reading and interpretation. Bar charts are useful for showing the frequency with which some event occurs. Histograms show data in accurate proportion to its actual appearance. Frequency polygons are useful for displaying trends in our data, or for comparing the progress of two groups.

Interpreting psychological research

Many of us do believe a great deal of what psychologists have discovered in their research, but we must not accept their results unquestioningly. We need to be a little more interested in how those results were discovered, and whether we feel confident enough to trust them.

If people always told the truth when asked questions by psychologists, always behaved normally when observed by them, and always performed in the psychologist's experiments as they usually do, then we would have far fewer problems understanding human behaviour. However, we all construct our own social reality. We have self-awareness, the ability to think, and we often try to understand and manipulate our situations, perhaps by being a subject in psychological research. Whenever we read about psychological research, including all the studies mentioned in this book, we must remember that human adults both conduct research and are often the subjects of research. Both the participants and the researchers can influence many features of the research, and its conclusions have to be treated with care.

Ethical concerns

▷

Ethics is concerned with those aspects of human behaviour which are regarded as acceptable or unacceptable in a particular society at a particular time.

Ethics is concerned with judgements about whether human behaviour is acceptable or unacceptable. For example, is it right for psychologists to use people as subjects in their research without the people knowing it, as in many field experiments? There are two possible areas of ethical concern in psychological research.

First there are the methods themselves. Some psychological methods are more likely to cause concern than others. For example, controlled experiments may involve lying to people – for example, in the conformity experiments (see pages 60–1), – or setting them up to behave in certain ways – for example, in the bystander-intervention experiments (see page 261). Methods which are least likely to give rise to ethical problems are correlational studies, surveys, and naturalistic observations. The more control the researcher has over the subjects' behaviour the greater the possibilities of ethical problems.

Second, the ways in which psychologists use these methods may give cause for concern. Particular problems are whether psychologists should become involved in other people's lives, whether they should cause their participants a great deal of stress, and whether they should deliberately lie to them. In addition there are several special issues. For example, to what extent should researchers explain to their participants after the research what has been happening? Also, the need for confidentiality, and whether it is acceptable to use animals in psychological research, are serious concerns.

Intervention

Skeels and Dye found that the development of children who were moved from an unstimulating orphanage and reared by adolescent girls made very rapid advances. No doubt they would have liked to have removed all children from unstimulating environments into more stimulating ones, but this simply was not possible. The children temporarily fostered by the Robertsons suffered the distress of disruption from their normal routines much less than children in less caring placements. The Robertsons could not make it possible for all children to suffer less disruption. Countless children continued to suffer. Ethical questions could be raised about who chooses those people who are to benefit from those who will continue to suffer?

▷

Is it acceptable for psychologists to intervene in people's normal routines? People have been studied, without their knowledge or consent. Some psychologists do not find that this kind of research is acceptable.

Very many studies have been conducted where participants' behaviour has been deliberately manipulated. We might become particularly worried when children are involved. Yet children at school have been told that blue-eyed children are more favoured than brown-eyed children, and then told the opposite to see how the information affected their behaviour (see page 81). Sherif manipulated many aspects of some youngsters behaviour in The Robber's Cave experiment on prejudiced attitudes (see pages 88–9).

Dehumanization

> People may be tricked into doubting their own perceptions, and this could make them anxious. Dehumanization refers to the possibility that people come to feel robbed of their ability to make judgements.

Dehumanization refers to the way in which some research has put people in positions where their normal personality, attitudes, and behaviour are suspended and they respond in quite uncharacteristic ways. Zimbardo had participants play out their prisoner and guard roles in the Stanford University obedience experiment (see page 286). Although he stopped the experiment after six days, many of the participants still found it difficult to believe that they could have behaved as they did. Some of the people who had conformed to the majority view over the length of a line in Asch's research later felt that they had to give all kinds of explanations for their behaviour (see page 61).

If researchers suspect that their studies might cause stress they must tell their participants before their research starts, and remind them that they can withdraw at any point during the research. If the researchers have reason to believe that the participants are suffering mental or physical discomfort, they should cancel the research.

Deception

> Deception may sometimes be necessary in order to conduct research. If it is, the participants must be informed afterwards.

Psychologists are often interested in what people would do in various circumstances. If we asked them, they might not tell the truth. So research is set up to find out the truth. This can very often involve deception. Latané and Darley deceived participants into believing that they were hearing someone have an epileptic fit, or that smoke from a genuine fire was filling their room (see page 262). Piliavin misled subway passengers into thinking that a disabled person, or someone with an ugly facial disfigurement, had slipped and fallen (see page 264). Berscheid and Walster lied to students that their personalities, preferences, etc., had been matched with their blind date by computer (see page 72).

Debriefing

> Debriefing means explaining to our subjects after the research exactly what the purpose of it was. They should be encouraged to ask questions, either immediately after the research or at any point in the future.

Whenever psychologists use people in their research they have a duty to explain to them afterwards what has been happening. They must outline the true purpose of the study, and how the participants have contributed to the research. Ideally, people should not leave the research feeling any different about themselves from how they felt when they arrived. Some of Asch's conformers had realized something about themselves. They may have learned something of benefit, or may have felt foolish for being so easily deceived.

If possible, participants should always be informed that they are taking part in some research before it begins. Where children are involved their parents must be fully informed about the nature of the research, what exactly the researchers want to do with the children, and what they anticipate might be any possible effects on the child.

Confidentiality

Participants in research have the same rights to privacy as anyone else. Psychologists must not plant hidden microphones or cameras in participants' homes, workplaces, etc. It is essential that the identity of all participants and their contributions must be kept absolutely secret. If any records, such as photographs, films or tapes, are made, then the participants must be asked for their permission for these records to be kept and shown to others, and the participants must be told that they are entitled to ask for all such material to be destroyed.

If it is possible, all participants should be sent a copy of the final report of the research. This should include a detailed explanation of why the research was necessary, what exactly happened, what results were found, and how the study has contributed to scientific knowledge.

Animals as participants.

Animals have been used in psychological research ever since Pavlov first measured salivation in association with bells, buzzers, and metronomes. Some of the studies have caused discomfort to the animals, such as Harlow's privation of rhesus monkeys. Reisen kept kittens in the dark, Blakemore and Cooper reared them in striped drums. Sperry rotated the eyes of salamanders. Young injected hormones into monkeys. Other research has had no harmful effects. For instance, Skinner demonstrated behaviour modification by training pigeons to turn in circles, peck at particular objects, and play a version of table tennis.

Supporters of animal research claim that we can use animals when we cannot use humans. For example, we can control all the variables such as when things will happen. We can breed several generations of animals to observe the effects of genes or experience. Although we cannot compare animal behaviour and human behaviour directly, we might gain some insights about human experiences from studying animals.

Opponents of animal research, on the other hand, claim that some animal responses are so determined by instinct that they have no relevance to human behaviour. Humans take many years to mature and gain experiences that enable them to understand their world and construct their own social reality. Other animals rely more on their genetically inherited instincts and respond directly to their own experiences as and when they happen. Opponents claim that most animal research is simply unnecessary. Why remove monkeys from their mothers when there are, sadly, many children in orphanages who have no mothers? Why rear animals in all sorts of conditions, when children somewhere in the world have probably already suffered similar conditions? Finally some people argue that it is simply wrong to use animals in experiments, as humans are exploiting animals who cannot defend themselves.

In Britain the British Psychological Association has issued guidelines on conducting animal research. Here is a summary: It may only be allowed if considerable knowledge would be gained, the smallest numbers of subjects must be used (and never any from endangered species), if any kind of deprivation or distress could occur its effects must be considered carefully, if possible the research should be naturalistic and not based in a laboratory.

Exercise on special issues in ethics

1 What are ethical concerns?
2 Why are they important in psychology?
3 Think of an example of something which could be naturalistically observed and something else that could be experimented on. Which of the two methods is likely to have the more serious ethical implications? Compare your answer with other people's.
4 Explain in your own words why intervention and dehumanization are ethical issues in psychological research.
5 Give one example of a research project that would need to involve deception. Try to think of one for yourself rather than one from this book.
6 Name three psychological studies which used animals as subjects. Then answer the following questions for each:
(a) Did the animals suffer in any way?
(b) If yes, would the suffering have long-term or short-term effects?
(c) What did we learn from this research?
(d) Is this of benefit to understanding humans?

●●● Summary of ethical concerns

Ethics is concerned with the acceptability of the methods and procedures used in gathering the data. To what extent should researchers interfere in other people's lives? Should people ever be put in positions that could cause them some distress or anxiety? To what extent should psychologists lie and manipulate people just to see what they would do? What guarantees about confidentiality should be made? What special safeguards should be built in when animals and children are used in psychological research?

Index